THE EXTRATERRITORIAL APPLICATION OF THE HUMAN RIGHT TO WATER IN AFRICA

International human rights law has only recently concerned itself with water. Instead, international water law has regulated the use of shared rivers, and only states *qua* states could claim rights and bear duties towards each other. International human rights law has focused on its principal mission of taming the powers of a state acting territorially.

Takele Soboka Bulto challenges the established analytic boundaries of international water law and international human rights law. By demonstrating the potential complementarity between the two legal regimes and the ensuing utility of regime coordination for the establishment of the human right to water and its extraterritorial application, he also shows that human rights law and the international law of watercourses can apply in tandem with the purpose of protecting non-national non-residents in Africa and beyond.

TAKELE SOBOKA BULTO is Assistant Professor of Law at the University of Canberra, where he teaches international human rights law and international law. He is also a Visiting Fellow of the Centre for International Governance and Justice at the Australian National University.

THE EXTRATERRITORIAL APPLICATION OF THE HUMAN RIGHT TO WATER IN AFRICA

TAKELE SOBOKA BULTO

CAMBRIDGE
UNIVERSITY PRESS

CAMBRIDGE
UNIVERSITY PRESS

University Printing House, Cambridge CB2 8BS, United Kingdom

Published in the United States of America by Cambridge University Press, New York

Cambridge University Press is part of the University of Cambridge.

It furthers the University's mission by disseminating knowledge in the pursuit of education, learning, and research at the highest international levels of excellence.

www.cambridge.org
Information on this title: www.cambridge.org/9781107031081

First published 2014

A catalogue record for this publication is available from the British Library

ISBN 978-1-107-03108-1 Hardback

To my late father, Soboka Bulto Dori
To my mother, Disso Itissa Kelbessa
I can never thank you enough for your endless love, selfless support and relentless encouragement. Thank you for keeping the faith when I needed it most.

CONTENTS

PREFACE AND ACKNOWLEDGMENTS

Since it was declared as a human right in the General Comment of the Committee on Economic, Social and Cultural Rights (CESCR) in 2002, the human right to water has been a favourite subject of academic controversy. Much of the debate has been about whether the right exists as such, and, if so, whether it exists as an auxiliary right or as an autonomous, self-standing entitlement. This debate arises from the absence of an explicit reference in the texts of the main human rights treaties to the right to water. The CESCR found the right in the implicit terms of related rights. This purposive approach to 'reading-in' the right has been endorsed by the African human rights monitoring and adjudicatory body, the African Commission on Human and Peoples' Rights, a conclusion that is supported in the present study.

This book joins the debate (albeit mainly from the perspective of the African human rights system) but, more importantly, goes ahead of the current controversy and analyses the immediate implementation problems triggered by the declaration of the right, given the shared nature of scarce water resources in regions such as Africa. Unlike or beyond the necessities of implementing other socio-economic rights, the human right to water often depends primarily on a uniquely international resource for its realisation. Of the fifty-four African states, fifty-one are dependent for drinking and sanitation water on international rivers that are shared between two to ten co-riparian states. An action or omission relating to a shared river in one state thus has a direct impact on the fate of the human right to water in co-riparian states. Unless riparian states are held to account for their (in)actions that produce extraterritorial effects, some co-riparian states would be unable to realise the human right to water within their territories. Thus, the declaration of the human right to water would be an empty gesture for the right-holders unless the relevant legal regime provides for ways to hold foreign states accountable for their acts or omissions that cause the violation of the human right to water abroad.

The book thus analyses the extraterritorial scope of the right to water, relevant state duties and attendant remedies. The central question of the book is whether states owe extraterritorial obligations directly to individual and group right-holders in a co-riparian state's territory for the realisation of their human right to water. After analysing the corpus of relevant international and regional human rights treaties, the rules and principles of international water law and related case law (which may be relied upon as 'inspirational sources' of the African Charter on Human and Peoples' Rights), the book answers this question in the affirmative.

It is argued that, while the extraterritorial duties to respect and protect the human right to water have firm legal bases in the international human rights regime, the duty to fulfil – a crucial guarantee in water-scarce regions such as Africa – needs to be sought in international water law. The book therefore calls for 'humanising' international water law, and pinpoints textual bases in the 1997 Convention on International Watercourses and related customary rules for such an approach.

The book is a revised version of my doctoral thesis, undertaken at the Melbourne Law School, University of Melbourne, under the supervision of Professor Carolyn Evans and Associate Professor Jacqueline Peel. My principal debt of gratitude therefore goes to Professors Evans and Peel for their invaluable guidance, tireless advice, insightful, incisive and very timely comments and frank and constructive criticisms on the various drafts of the then Ph.D thesis. I am especially grateful to Professor Carolyn for the considerable kindness she has shown to me and for treating me as family during my Ph.D years at Melbourne and beyond.

This study would have been impossible without the generous financial assistance of the University of Melbourne and the Melbourne Law School, whose joint scholarship helped cover the cost of my studies and my living expenses.

I have also been very lucky to have been surrounded by an extremely supportive Faculty during my Ph.D years. I especially owe a word of gratitude to Associate Professors Michelle Foster and John Tobin, and Professors Lee Godden and Gerry Simpson who have always shown interest in this study and have been willing to discuss aspects thereof, shared advice, materials or comments related thereto.

Chapter 5 of this book largely draws on material previously published by this author, entitled; 'Patching the "Legal Black Hole": The Extraterritorial Reach of States' Human Rights Duties in the African Human Rights System', 27 *South African Journal on Human Rights* (2011) and 'Towards Rights–Duties Congruence: Extraterritorial

Application of the Human Right to Water in the African Human Rights System', 29(4) *Netherlands Quarterly of Human Rights* (2011). I am grateful to the two journals for readily and kindly granting permission that allowed me to reproduce, albeit updated versions of, the relevant materials here.

Last, but by no means least, I have been greatly supported by the love and encouragement of my family. Emebet Tura took the family responsibility off my shoulders so I could focus on my research. My sons, Lubebas and Sena, have been pleasant distractions. Thank you for learning to sleep early to ensure my sanity; and for waking up early with hearty smiles as if you knew just how much I needed them. All three were ready to suffer quietly along with me as I scribbled these pages. A million thanks.

Takele Soboka Bulto
Canberra
April 2013

TABLE OF CASES

African cases

European cases

Inter-American cases

International courts and tribunals

United Nations treaty bodies

National cases

Botswana

India

Namibia

South Africa

United Kingdom

United States

1

Introduction

> Watersheds come in families; nested levels of intimacy. On the grandest scale the hydrologic web is like all humanity – Serbs, Russians, Koyukon, Indians, Amish, the billion lives in the People's Republic of China – it's broadly troubled, but it's hard to know how to help. As you work upstream toward home, you're more closely related. The big river is like your nation, a little out of hand. The lake is your cousin. The creek is your sister. The pond is her child. And, for better or worse, in sickness and in health, you are married to your sink.[1]

1.1 Introduction

Water is the lifeblood of every living being. With no equivalent or substitute, it is an indispensable constituent of all life. Given its quality as a bearer of life and universal necessity, it is axiomatic that individuals' and groups' access to water for drinking and sanitation be legally guaranteed. However, international human rights law did not explicitly recognise access to drinking and sanitation water as an autonomous human right until after the turn of the new millennium.[2] Currently defined as an entitlement to 'sufficient, safe, acceptable, physically accessible and affordable water for personal and domestic uses',[3] a fully fledged human right to water has found no explicit mention in the

[1] Michael Parfit, quoted in Maude Barlow and Tony Clarke, *Blue Gold: The Battle against Corporate Theft of the World's Water* (The New Press, 2002) xi.

[2] There has, however, been a qualified recognition of (aspects of) the right as a constituent element of other rights such as the right to health. Such an approach narrows down the scope of the right such that it can only be invoked in specifically limited circumstances and benefits only a defined group of people protected under some human rights treaty regimes. Detailed analysis of this topic is presented in Chapter 2.

[3] CESCR, 'General Comment No. 15: Substantive Issues Arising in the Implementation of the International Covenant on Economic, Social and Cultural Rights (Adopted 11–29 November 2002)' (UN Committee on Economic, Social and Cultural Rights, 11–29 November 2002), para. 2.

major United Nations (UN) treaties.[4] Similarly, it has not been mentioned in the main African human rights instrument, the African Charter on Human and Peoples' Rights ('Charter' or 'African Charter').[5] Fresh attempts to establish the human right to water have therefore been plagued by legal paucity.[6] However, due to the increasing scarcity of fresh water resources, and the growing number of people without basic access to the same,[7] the right has recently received growing recognition as a free-standing human right, albeit mainly in the form of soft laws.[8]

Alongside the problem of recognition and the difficulty associated with establishing its legal basis, the implementation of the human right to water faces particularly intractable challenges due to water scarcity and the internationally shared nature of water resources on which its realisation often depends. This book explores the legal basis of the human right to water and the immediate implementation problems triggered by the declaration of the human right to water in Africa. It analyses the extraterritorial application of the human right to water and correlative states' obligations in international human rights law

[4] Amanda Cahill, 'The Human Right to Water – A Right of Unique Status: The Legal Status and Normative Content of the Right to Water', 9(3) *International Journal of Human Rights* 390 (2005) 389–410; Stephen C. McCaffrey, 'The Human Right to Water' in Edith Brown Weiss, Laurence Boisson de Chazournes and Nathale Bernasconi-Osterwalder (eds.), *Fresh Water and International Economic Law* (Oxford University Press, 2005) 93, 93.

[5] Adopted by the eighteenth Assembly of Heads of State and Government, June 1981, Nairobi, Kenya; entered into force 21 October 1986. It is now binding on all the fifty-four member states of the African Union.

[6] United Nations Office of the High Commissioner for Human Rights, 'The Right to Water: Fact Sheet No. 35' (United Nations Office of the High Commissioner for Human Rights, UN-Habitat, and WHO, 2010) 3. See also Ling-Yee Huang, 'Not Just Another Drop in the Human Rights Bucket: The Legal Significance of a Codified Human Right to Water', 20 *Florida Journal of International Law* (2008) 353–70, 353; Vrinda Narain, 'Water as a Fundamental Right: A Perspective from India', 34 *Vermont Law Review* (2010) 917–25.

[7] Currently, some 884 million people do not have access to improved sources of drinking water, while 2.5 billion lack access to improved sanitation facilities. Worse, these figures do not tell the whole truth, as millions of poor people living in informal settlements are simply missing from the statistics. See OHCHR (note 6 above) 1.

[8] For instance, the UN General Assembly Resolution recognises water as a human right. It was passed with 122 states (including African countries) voting in favour and 41 states abstaining. See 'General Assembly Adopts Resolution Recognizing Access to Clean Water, Sanitation' (Sixty-Fourth General Assembly Plenary 108th Meeting (AM) (General Assembly GA/10967), 28 July 2010). See also Huang (note 6 above) 319; Narain (note 6 above) 917.

generally and in the African human rights system specifically in relation to the manner and scope of states' uses of waters of shared international river basins, with a special focus on the African situation.[9] In addition, it examines the role and capacity of international human rights law in addressing possible transboundary violations of the human right to water that arise from the constraints brought to bear on states' capacities by water scarcity and the shared nature of water resources. This analysis is critical for countries in regions such as Africa where water for vital human needs cannot be met solely from domestic water sources.

Unless transboundary water resources are shared among states in a manner sensitive to the requirements of the human right to water for the benefit of the entire riparian populations inhabiting the river basins, some states would be unable to realise the right in their respective jurisdictions. It may simply prove impossible for many states to fulfil the right. This is due to the distributional pattern of water resources and the possible 'dispossession' by some states and 'deprivation' of others of the water hitherto at their sovereign disposal. Of the fifty-four African countries, for instance, fifty-one states depend on water resources of shared rivers for the realisation of the human right to water within their jurisdictions.[10] Moreover, these rivers are very unevenly distributed. Most fresh water resources are concentrated in western and central Africa, whereas northern, southern and eastern Africa are experiencing acute water scarcity.[11] Ninety-five per cent of total fresh water emerges

[9] According to the 'Maastricht Principles on Extraterritorial Obligations of States in the Area of Economic, Social and Cultural Rights', extraterritorial obligations encompass: (a) obligations relating to the acts and omissions of a state, within or beyond its territory, that have effects on the enjoyment of human rights outside of that state's territory; and (b) obligations of a global character that are set out in the Charter of the United Nations and human rights instruments to take action, separately, and jointly through international cooperation, to realise human rights universally. See 'Maastricht Principles on Extraterritorial Obligations of States in the Area of Economic, Social and Cultural Rights', adopted on 28 September 2011 at a gathering convened by Maastricht University and the International Commission of Jurists (a group of experts in international law and human rights). The document is available at http://hrbaportal.org/archives/noticeboard/launch-of-maastricht-principles-on-the-extraterritorial-obligations-of-states-in-the-area-of-economic-social-and-cultural-rights (accessed 7 November 2012).

[10] The only exceptions are the few island states such as Madagascar and Cape Verde. See the African Transboundary Water Law page at www.africanwaterlaw.org/html (accessed 23 February 2011).

[11] Elli Louka, *Water Law and Policy: Governance without Frontiers* (Oxford University Press, 2008) 14–15.

from central and western Africa, while the arid and semi-arid parts of the continent produce a mere 5 per cent.[12] Some transboundary waters such as the Nile are already fully used,[13] and need to be redistributed among the co-riparian states in a manner that caters for the human right to water.

In water-scarce regions such as the African continent, this requires the apportionment of shared water resources in a manner that ensures access to drinking and sanitation water for the entire population of a given river basin that is dependent on the waters of a shared river. This in turn entails that co-riparian states guarantee that their domestic actions, inactions, legislation, policies and decisions do not jeopardise the water rights of third states' populations who are dependent on shared rivers for the realisation of their own water rights.

The book contends that human rights norms require a state to utilise shared water resources in a way that ensures the continued flow of that minimum amount and quality of water needed to realise the human right to drinking and sanitation water in other co-riparian states extraterritorially. Therefore, it is argued that the realisation of the right to water calls for the need to expand relevant states' duties to cover those rights-holders situated beyond its own territorial jurisdiction who could be affected by states' domestic actions related to the use of the shared river. Without such, the right may remain an empty signifier and its declaration may flatter to deceive. Unless the relevant legal regime devises a means of ensuring right-holders' access to the necessary resource base, the right to water may promise what it cannot deliver, a scenario that is at times referred to as 'rights inflation'.[14]

Despite the contentious legal basis of the human right to water, the book argues that the existing corpus of international human rights law, including the African Charter, supplemented by other principles of

[12] *Ibid.*, 15.

[13] Lucius Caflisch, 'Regulation of Uses of International Watercourses' in Salman M. A. Salman and L. Boisson de Chazournes (eds.), *International Watercourses: Enhancing Cooperation and Managing Conflict: Proceedings of a World Bank Seminar* (World Bank, 1998) 3, 13; Ashok Swain, 'Managing the Nile River: The Role of Sub-Basin Co-operation' in Manas Chatterji, Saul Arlosoroff and Gauri Guha (eds.), *Conflict Management of Water Resources* (Ashgate, 2002) 145, 146–52. See generally Patrick Parenteau, 'Come Hell and High Water: Coping with the Unavoidable Consequences of Climate Disruption', 34 *Vermont Law Review* (2010) 957–73.

[14] I owe this expression to Katharine G. Young, 'The Minimum Core of Economic and Social Rights: A Concept in Search of Content', 33 *Yale Journal of International Law* (2008) 113–75, 114.

international law – particularly international water law – provides a firm legal basis for the right and its extraterritorial application. The book is written from the perspective of the right-holders. From this angle, the recognition of the human right to water would only be meaningful if the relevant legal regime devises ways of ensuring the availability of the necessary resource base for the right's realisation. The central concern of the book is therefore how to enable the right-holders to prevent violations of their right to access drinking and sanitation water and to have their right to water remedied when they occur. In this vein, the book demonstrates that, properly analysed and used by human rights advocates and relevant human rights tribunals, the provisions of international treaties, including the African Charter and the Charter's 'inspirational sources',[15] provide adequate support to found a free-standing human right to water in Africa that is capable of extraterritorial application against other states.

1.2 The normative status of the human right to water

The birth of the human right to water was both slow and controversial. Not until after the UN Committee on Economic, Social and Cultural Rights (CESCR)[16] issued its General Comment[17] No. 15 on the human right to water in 2002 has access to drinking and sanitation water been authoritatively defined as a human right.[18] Saving some narrow exceptions,[19] the major UN treaties or the African human rights instruments do not make an explicit mention of a fully fledged human right to

[15] Under Article 60 of the Charter, the African Commission on Human and Peoples' Rights, the Charter's monitoring and enforcement mechanism, has been tasked to 'draw inspiration from international law on human and peoples' rights', including African and UN instruments. As shown in Chapter 2, below, the Commission frequently refers to UN, European and Inter-American treaties and emerging case law to aid its interpretation and application of the provisions of the Charter.

[16] The Committee on Economic, Social and Cultural Rights (CESCR) is a body of independent experts that monitors implementation of the International Covenant on Economic, Social and Cultural Rights by its states parties. The CESCR was established under ECOSOC Resolution 1985/17 of 28 May 1985 to carry out the monitoring functions previously assigned to the United Nations Economic and Social Council (ECOSOC) in Part IV of the Covenant.

[17] General Comments are expert human rights monitoring bodies' interpretation of the content of human rights treaty provisions they are established to monitor. While highly persuasive, they are not binding in the strict sense of the term.

[18] Narain (note 6 above) 919; McCaffrey (note 4 above) 101.

[19] See note 2 above.

water.[20] The CESCR found the right in the implicit terms of the twin provisions of the International Covenant on Economic, Social and Cultural Rights (ICESCR)[21] on the right to an adequate standard of living (Article 11) and on the right to the enjoyment of the highest attainable standard of physical and mental health (Article 12). Consequently, it broke new ground by unequivocally affirming that the ICESCR contains provisions that implicitly contain an autonomous human right to water.[22]

For its part, the African Charter's monitoring and enforcement body, the African Commission on Human and Peoples' Rights ('Commission' or 'African Commission'),[23] has recognised the existence of the human right to water in the Charter and found states responsible for violating the same and ordered remedies to rectify the violations of the right.[24] As stated above, the human right to water does not feature in the Charter in explicit terms, and the Commission has yet to define comprehensively the scope of the human right to water.[25] It has, however, ruled that 'the right to water [is] implicitly guaranteed under Articles 4, 16 and 22 of the Charter as informed by standards and principles of international human rights law'.[26] The implicit sources relied on by the Commission to found the human right to water, namely, Articles 4, 16 and 22 of the Charter, respectively provide for the right to respect for life and the integrity of a person, the right to enjoy the best attainable state of physical and mental health and the right to economic, social and cultural development.

[20] See generally Stephen C. McCaffrey, 'A Human Right to Water: Domestic and International Implications', 5(1) *Georgetown International Environmental Law Review* (1992) 1–24; Stephen Tully, 'A Human Right to Access Water? A Critique of General Comment No. 15', 23 *Netherlands Quarterly of Human Rights* (2005) 35–63; Peter H. Gleick, 'The Human Right to Water', 1(5) *Water Policy* (1998) 487–503; Cahill (note 4 above).

[21] Adopted and opened for signature, ratification and accession by General Assembly Resolution 2200A (XXI) of 16 December 1966; entered into force 3 January 1976.

[22] CESCR, General Comment No. 15 (note 3 above), para. 2. For an in-depth discussion of the normative content of the human right to water, see Chapter 2.

[23] The Commission is established under Article 30 of the Charter to perform promotional and protective mandates assigned to it under Article 45 of the regional instrument.

[24] See Chapter 3.

[25] See Chapter 3. As the African Commission stated, 'the African Charter does not directly protect the human right to water and sanitation'. See (Draft) Principles and Guidelines on Economic, Social and Cultural Rights in the African Charter on Human and Peoples' Rights (2011), para. 71.

[26] (Joined) Communication 279/03, *Sudan Human Rights Organization* v. *The Sudan* and Communication 296/05, *Centre on Housing Rights and Evictions* v. *The Sudan, 28th Annual Activity Report* (2010), para. 124.

Regardless of these authoritative statements by the CESCR and the African Commission, due to the lack of an explicit and comprehensive recognition of the right, the legal basis and the existence of a free-standing human right to water have continually been called into question.[27]

However, the increasing recognition in recent years of the human right to water by the CESCR, other UN bodies and regional human rights tribunals such as the African Commission has far-reaching legal consequences for the discourse about the right to water. The declaration of the human right to water and its incorporation in the human rights discourse takes the analysis of water rights beyond its traditionally statist framework. Traditionally water rights have been regulated by the rules and principles of international water law, whose ambit has been limited to the regulation of how much of shared water resources a riparian state must forfeit in favour of other co-riparian states, or is entitled to receive from such resources, or both.[28] International water law treats water rights as an inter-state issue rather than as an entitlement pertaining to individuals and groups residing in those states. Within the statist framework, only states are rights-holders and duty-bearers reciprocally as against co-riparian states *qua* states. Only they may claim remedies when a right protected under international water law is violated, as the damage caused by the infringement is deemed to have been suffered by the state *qua* state.

The acceptance of individuals' and groups' access to drinking and sanitation water as a human right therefore expands the focus of analysis regarding the right-holders and the duty-bearers in relation to shared water resources. As a human right, individuals and groups are now entitled to claim access to a minimum amount and quality of water for drinking and sanitation purposes.[29] This right pertains to human right-holders independently and alongside inter-state water rights claims.

[27] Amanda Cahill, 'Protecting Rights in the Face of Scarcity: The Right to Water' in Mark Gibney and Sigrun Skogly (eds.), *Universal Human Rights and Extraterritorial Obligations* (University of Pennsylvania Press, 2010) 194, 214; Huang (note 6 above) 353–4; Narain (note 6 above) 919.

[28] Ellen Hey, 'Sustainable Use of Shared Water Resources: The Need for a Paradigm Shift in International Watercourses Law' in Gerald H. Blake, William Hilldesley, Martin Pratt, Rebecca Ridley and Clive Schofield (eds.), *The Peaceful Management of Transboundary Resources* (Graham & Trotman, 1995) 127, 129.

[29] See Chapter 2.

Despite the emerging trend of progressive development of the human right to water, the establishment of its legal basis and normative content has been hampered by the apparent lack of explicit and comprehensive provisions for the right in the relevant international treaties. The right's very existence and legal status has continued to be challenged,[30] with consequent implications for the states' duty to implement the right domestically. In a situation where the very existence of the right continues to be contentious, raising the possibility even for the domestic state to deny that it owes any duty to realise the same, thornier problems await the analysis of its extraterritorial application in favour of the supposed right-holders. As Cahill has observed, 'compliance with extraterritorial obligations regarding water is even more difficult than that of other economic and social rights due to its relatively new and debated status as an independent right'.[31] The obscurity surrounding the legal status of the right must therefore be clarified before its extraterritorial application is considered. This is the task of Chapter 2 of the book, which provides a detailed analysis of the legal basis and the normative content of the human right to water.

1.3 The imperatives of extraterritorial application of the human right to water in Africa

The need for the extraterritorial application of human rights and of related states' duties is generally justified with reference to the forces of globalisation.[32] The increasingly globalising world has seen the shrinking role of states' borders, fewer trade barriers and the development of new weapons that enabled some states to cause harm to individuals and groups situated in third states with little or no difficulty. The invention of new technologies such as unmanned drones has meant that states could cause violations of human rights abroad with relative ease. As outlined in Chapter 5, states have so far been held responsible for human rights violations they caused abroad mainly when they exercised control over

30 See generally Tully (note 20 above); McCaffrey (note 4 above); Cahill (note 4 above).
31 *Ibid.*
32 See Michal Gondek, *The Reach of Human Rights in a Globalising World: Extraterritorial Application of Human Rights Treaties* (Intersentia, 2009) 1; Sigrun Skogly and Mark Gibney, 'Introduction' in Mark Gibney and Sigrun Skogly (eds.), *Universal Human Rights and Extraterritorial Obligations* (University of Pennsylvania Press, 2010) 1, 2.

foreign territory[33] or on individuals situated in another state's jurisdiction.[34]

In contrast, the human right to water can be violated without any need for the foreign state to control the territory of the victim's home state or the person of the victim. All that is needed for a state to violate the human right to water in third states is, in the language of the *Trail Smelter* decision, 'to use or permit the use of its territory in such a manner as to cause injury . . . in or to the territory of another or the properties or persons therein'.[35] Suffice for a state to reduce the water volume or quality within its own borders to cause the violation of the human right to water in a co-riparian state without necessarily occupying another state's territory or controlling individuals therein. This is especially so when such reductions and pollution occur in relation to fully used rivers, and where there is an existing water scarcity in the basin. It is mainly through local (in)action, decisions, policies and legislation that co-riparian states cause harm to the holders of the human right to water abroad.

Africa has already been 'globalised' through its international rivers. States' residents have long been potentially susceptible to extraterritorial harm with respect to their human right to water. Each non-island state depends on water originating in shared waters: in Africa, '[r]ivers have a perverse habit of wandering across national borders'.[36] At least thirty-four rivers are shared by two countries, and twenty-eight are shared by three or more states.[37] Put differently, ten river basins – Congo, Limpopo, Niger, Nile, Ogooue, Okavango, Orange, Senegal, Volta and Zambezi – are shared by four or more African states.[38] Every country in continental Africa has at least one international river within its territory,

[33] In the case of *Loizidou* v. *Turkey*, the applicant complained to the European Court of Human Rights that she was prevented from accessing her own plots of land in northern Cyprus by the occupying Turkish authorities. See *Loizidou* v. *Turkey* (Preliminary Objections), Application No. 40/1993/435/514, ECtHR, 23 March 1995.

[34] In the *Lopez Burgos* case, the complaint concerned the abduction and torture of Lopez Burgos by Uruguayan security forces in Argentina, on foreign soil, without having control of the Argentinean territory. See *Sergio Euben Lopez Burgos* v. *Uruguay*, Communication No. R.12/52 (UN Human Rights Committee), adopted by the UN Human Rights Committee on 29 July 1981.

[35] *Trail Smelter* case (*US* v. *Canada*), 3 RIAA (1941), para. 49.

[36] John Waterbury, *Hydropolitics of the Nile Valley* (Syracuse University Press, 1979) 2.

[37] Claudia W. Sadoff, Dale Whittington and David Grey, *Africa's International Rivers: An Economic Perspective* (World Bank, 2002) 7.

[38] *Ibid.*

forty-one of the fifty-four states of the continent have two or more and fifteen states have five or more.[39] Guinea has fourteen international rivers, while both Côte d'Ivoire and Mozambique have nine such rivers each in their territories.[40] An (over-)utilisation or pollution of the shared waters in one state therefore inevitably influences the capacity of other co-riparian states along the continuum of the river's flow to control and use the shared water resources for the realisation of the human right to water in their respective domestic spheres.

As Waterbury noted, states have 'a perverse habit of treating whatever portion of the flows within their borders as a national resource at their sovereign disposal'.[41] Such an approach allows unilateral actions and inactions that would impact on the rights of foreign residents in relation to their right to water. Some states may tend to over-utilise shared water resources for the exclusive benefit of their own residents and to the detriment of those in co-riparian states.[42] Their (in)actions could therefore directly jeopardise the right of access to drinking and sanitation water in other co-riparian states. In such situations, a domestic state's abstention from violating the human right to water in its jurisdiction is little consolation for the right-holders situated within its territory if the right is already threatened or violated due to scarcity or pollution of water resources caused by an (in)action of a foreign co-riparian state.

This is without mentioning the increasingly debilitating effects of climate change which is a text-book example of a state's use of its territory in a manner that causes harm to territories of and persons in third states. States' contribution to climate change would influence the quality and amount of water available abroad.[43] While a state's contribution to climate change at home may contribute to the violations of a

[39] *Ibid.* [40] *Ibid.* [41] Waterbury (note 36 above) 2.

[42] For a similar scenario in the Nile basin, see A. Dan Tarlock, 'Four Challenges of International Water Law', 23 *Tulane Environmental Law Journal* (2010) 369–408, 375. For the political debate surrounding the sharing of the Nile waters amongst Ethiopia, Egypt and Sudan, see generally Ashock Swain, 'Ethiopia, the Sudan and Egypt: The Nile River Dispute', 35(4) *Journal of Modern African Studies* (1997) 675–94; Yacob Arsano, *Ethiopia and the Nile: Dilemmas of National and Regional Hydropolitics* (Centre for Security Studies, Swiss Federal Institute of Technology, 2007); Simon A. Mason, *From Conflict to Cooperation in the Nile Basin: Interaction Between Water Availability, Water Management in Egypt and Sudan, and International Relations in the Eastern Nile Basin* (ETH Zurich, 2004).

[43] John H. Knox, 'Climate Change and Human Rights', 50(1) *Virginia Journal of International Law* (2009) 164, 178–80.

wide catalogue of human rights abroad,[44] it has direct and far-reaching effects on the enjoyment of the human right to water. According to the UN Independent Expert on the Human Right to Water and Sanitation:

> [c]limate change presents a serious obstacle to the realisation of the rights to water and sanitation. Water is a key medium through which climate change impacts upon human populations and ecosystems, particularly due to predicted changes in water quality and quantity. The impacts of climate change need to be seen in light of its direct effects on water resources as well as its indirect influence on other external drivers of change, in particular increasing population pressures and changing consumption patterns.[45]

There have been warnings of severe consequences of the effect of climate change on the availability of water in Africa. By 2020, an estimated 75 million to 250 million people in Africa will be under situations of water stress due to climate change.[46] In the Nile basin, for instance, it has been projected that global climatic changes will reduce the Nile's flow by as much as 25 per cent in the not too distant future by substantially altering the established pattern of precipitation and evaporation in the basin.[47]

The impacts of climate change on access to water, and hence on the realisation of the human right to water, are not limited to its consequences on water quantity. It also contributes to or exacerbates water scarcity through its drastic effects on water quality, thereby making it difficult for states to make effective use of the often meagre quantity of water that is available to them for the purposes of realising their residents' human right to water. It leads to an increased intensity and frequency of heavy

[44] Jacqueline Peel, 'Climate Change Law: The Emergence of a New Legal Discipline', 32 *Melbourne University Law Review* (2009) 922–79, 931. See also generally Malcolm Langford, 'A Sort of Homecoming: The Right to Housing' in Mark Gibney and Sigrun Skogly (eds.), *Universal Human Rights and Extraterritorial Obligations* (University of Pennsylvania Press, 2010) 166; John H. Knox, 'Diagonal Environmental Rights' in Mark Gibney and Sigrun Skogly (eds.), *Universal Human Rights and Extraterritorial Obligations* (University of Pennsylvania Press, 2010) 82; Amy Sinden, 'Climate Change and Human Rights' (Legal Studies Research Paper Series, Research Paper No. 2008-49, Beasley School of Law, Temple University, 2008).

[45] Catarina de Albuquerque, 'Climate Change and the Human Rights to Water and Sanitation' (Position Paper of the Independent Expert on the Issue of Human Rights Obligations Related to Access to Safe Drinking Water and Sanitation, 2010), para. 2.

[46] Report of the Intergovernmental Panel on Climate Change (IPCC), Assessment Report 4, Working Group II, Summary for Policy Makers (2007) 13–15 and 59–63.

[47] Abu-Zeid, as quoted in Arun P. Elhance, *Hydropolitics in the Third World: Conflict and Cooperation in International River Basins* (United States Institute of Peace Press, 1999) 58.

rainfall events, causing, among other things, more polluted runoff, more flooding, more water quality impairment and more waterborne diseases.

Therefore, there is a pressing need to hold states extraterritorially responsible for their part in violations of the human right to water abroad through their domestic (in)actions, including through their contribution to climate change.[48] Whether it is through pollution, over-utilisation or contribution to water shortage through climate change, a state could use or allow the use of its territory in a manner that facilitates the violation of the human right to water in other states. The ensuing harm could materialise without the author of the violation occupying a foreign state's territory or a person located therein. The effects of (in)actions by one state could easily spill beyond its national borders or be exported to another state's territory where they cause violations of the human right to water.

1.4 Extraterritoriality as a new legal problem

The violation of the right to water in one state by a co-riparian state raises different sets of issues for international human rights law than those attributable to the right-holder's home state. In cases where the cause of the non-realisation of the human right to water is attributable to the home state, individual and group right-holders would have recourse against the same, which would be held responsible for any failure to meet its duties to realise the right. A state's recognition of the human right to water gives rise to individuals' and groups' right to complain against its violation by and to seek and obtain remedies therefor from the home state.[49] But such a course of action may prove to be of little avail when the relevant home state is willing but demonstrably unable to realise the right due to resource constraints caused by an (in)action of a co-riparian state. The home state may plead supervening impossibility to evade responsibility.[50] Jennings argues that impossibility of performance of

[48] See Stephen Humphreys, 'Competing Claims: Human Rights and Climate Changes' in Stephen Humphreys and Mary Robinson (eds.), *Human Rights and Climate Change* (Cambridge University Press, 2010) 37, 38–9.

[49] Knut Bourquain, *Freshwater Access from a Human Rights Perspective: A Challenge to International Water Law and Human Rights Law* (Martinus Nijhoff Publishers, 2008) 192.

[50] See *Case Concerning the Gabčíkovo-Nagymaros Project* (*Hungary* v. *Slovakia*), Judgment of 25 September 1997, *ICJ Reports* 1997, para. 94 (quoting Article 61 of the Vienna Convention on the Law of Treaties, 1969).

an obligation that involves, *inter alia*, the disappearance or destruction of an object that is essential for the fulfilment of the obligation is a justifiable ground for absolving states of responsibilities under international treaties.[51] Such grounds include the drying up of a river or the destruction of a dam that is indispensable for the execution of a treaty obligation.[52] Thus, legal recourse against the right-holders' home state may produce no or little results when the home state is not responsible for the violations complained of. Unless mechanisms are devised whereby foreign states are held to account for their (in)actions that cause violation of the human right to water, right-holders in co-riparian states constantly remain faced by the 'incapacity of their national governments, and hence [will] only ever be able to represent themselves as potential claimants or aspirational rights-holders'.[53]

An entirely different question emerges when such violations are caused by a co-riparian state or non-state actors situated across international borders for which the co-riparian state is answerable. Defences based on, among other things, jurisdiction, *locus standi* and sovereignty may curtail individuals' and groups' right to have a legal recourse against a foreign state. In the end, the right-holders' claims for redress may remain without a remedy, and the duty-bearers, if any, may evade responsibility for the breaches of the rights and freedoms they caused abroad. The possibility of redressing victims' rights therefore heavily depends upon the degree of states' extraterritorial duties to aid the realisation of the human right to water and abstain from contributing to its non-realisation in other co-riparian states' territories. Thus, the analysis of the extraterritorial reach of the human right to water and attendant state's obligations in Africa is not merely one of academic interest but is also part of the search for the means of ensuring immediate survival needs.

However, the African Charter is silent on the extraterritorial reach of the rights and freedoms it enshrines or correlative states' obligations. There is no mention of the territorial or jurisdictional reach or limitation of any categories of the Charter's rights and freedoms or attendant states' duties. Similarly, academic analysis of human rights and their

[51] R. Y. Jennings, 'Treaties' in Mohammed Bedjaoui (ed.), *International Law: Achievements and Prospects* (UNESCO, 1991) 135, 160.

[52] *Ibid.*

[53] Matthew Craven, 'The Violence of Dispossession: Extra-Territoriality and Economic, Social and Cultural Rights' in A. Mashood and Robert McCorquodale Baderin (eds.), *Economic, Social and Cultural Rights in Action* (Oxford University Press, 2007) 71, 85.

extraterritorial application in the context of the African human rights system is almost non-existent.[54] This book therefore responds to the urgent need for an examination of the normative possibility of accessing water rights through the extraterritorial application of the right and related state obligations in the water-scarce African continent.

1.5 State of the art and the claim

Judicial and quasi-judicial scrutiny of the extraterritorial reach of human rights and correlative states' obligations leapfrogged related academic debate. Questions of whether a state owes a duty not to cause or contribute to violations of the human rights of non-national non-residents, on the one hand, and to help insure the rights' realisation in third states, on the other, have become a subject of rumbling academic debate only in the past decade.[55] The prospect of linking a state and people of third states through extraterritorial (diagonal) human rights obligations has marked such a radical development as to represent a 'quantum leap' in the norms of human rights law whose normal operation had been vertically territorial.[56] Where it exists, scholarship on the extraterritorial application of human rights and attendant state obligations is still in its infancy,[57] and is described as 'the least developed in the theory and practice of international human rights law'.[58] Even so, keeping with the familiar trend of the marginalisation of socio-economic rights discourse and enforcement,[59] the analysis of their extraterritorial application has been ignored relative to that concerning their civil and political counterparts.[60]

[54] Only rare passing remarks have been made by a few authors about the extraterritorial application of human rights in the African human rights system. The existing literature is in agreement that a state cannot be held responsible for not realising the human rights of non-national non-residents. See Carlson Anyangwe, 'Obligations of State Parties to the African Charter on Human and Peoples' Rights', 10(4) *African Journal of International and Comparative Law* (1998) 625–59, 627; Frans Viljoen, 'Admissibility under the African Charter' in Malcolm Evans and Rachel Murray (eds.), *The African Charter on Human and Peoples' Rights: The System in Practice, 1986–2000* (Cambridge University Press, 2002) 61, 78.

[55] See Gondek (note 32 above) 4. [56] Skogly and Gibney (note 32 above) 3.

[57] Cahill (note 27 above) 216.

[58] Sigrun I. Skogly, 'The Obligation of International Assistance and Co-operation in the International Covenant on Economic, Social and Cultural Rights' in Morten Bergsmo (ed.), *Human Rights and Criminal Justice for the Downtrodden: Essays in Honour of Asbjørn Eide* (Martinus Nijhoff Publishers, 2003) 403, 404.

[59] See Chapter 2. [60] Gondek (note 32 above) 292–3.

Moreover, the newly emerging analysis and related jurisprudence in the area of extraterritorial human rights and states' obligations has focused on what a state cannot (and should not) do against persons in third states.[61] In other words, the existing literature has been limited in scope to the analysis of states' negative extraterritorial duty, i.e. the states' duty to abstain from infringing human rights abroad (or, more appropriately, the *duty to respect* human rights). The analysis of states' extraterritorial positive duties, namely, a state's duty to realise human rights in third states, and what it should do to meet that duty, has been neglected. Moreover, to the extent that it has been examined, the analysis has been general, and the scrutiny has been as to whether a given human rights treaty[62] or the overall human rights regime engenders extraterritorial obligations of states at all.[63] Saving rare exceptions,[64] the existing literature has yet to begin the examination of the extraterritorial application of each human right in its own right in the context of possible special regimes applicable to it.

[61] For instance, see Rick Lawson, 'Life after Bankovic: On the Extraterritorial Application of the European Convention on Human Rights' in Fons Coomans and Menno T. Kamminga (eds.), *Extraterritorial Application of Human Rights Treaties* (Intersentia, 2004) 83.

[62] See, for instance, Christina M. Cerna, 'Extraterritorial Application of the Human Rights Instruments of the Inter-American System' in Fons Coomans and Menno T. Kamminga (eds.), *Extraterritorial Application of Human Rights Treaties* (Intersentia, 2004) 141; Michal Gondek, 'Extraterritorial Application of the European Convention on Human Rights: Territorial Focus in the Age of Globalisation?', 52(3) *Netherlands International Law Review* (2005) 349–87; Martin Scheinin, 'Extraterritorial Effect of the International Covenant on Civil and Political Rights' in Fons Coomans and Menno T. Kamminga (eds.), *Extraterritorial Application of Human Rights Treaties* (Intersentia, 2004) 7; Dominic McGoldrick, 'Extraterritorial Application of the International Covenant on Civil and Political Rights' in Fons Coomans and Menno T. Kamminga (eds.), *Extraterritorial Application of Human Rights Treaties* (Intersentia, 2004) 4; Rolf Kunnemann, 'Extraterritorial Application of the International Covenant on Economic, Social and Cultural Rights' in Fons Coomans and Menno T. Kamminga (eds.), *Extraterritorial Application of Human Rights Treaties* (Intersentia, 2004) 201.

[63] See Theodor Meron, 'Extraterritoriality of Human Rights Treaties', 89 *American Journal of International Law* (1995) 78–82; Ralph Wilde, 'Triggering State Obligations Extraterritorially: The Spatial Test in Certain Human Rights Treaties', 40(2) *Israel Law Review* (2007) 503–26; Damira Kamchibekova, 'State Responsibility for Extraterritorial Human Rights Violations', 13 *Buffalo Human Rights Law Review* (2007) 87; Rolf Kunnemann and Sandra Ratjen, 'Extraterritorial Obligations: A Response to Globalization' in George Kent (ed.), *Global Obligations for the Right to Food* (Rowman and Littlefield Publishers Inc., 2008) 33.

[64] There are new beginnings towards the examination of extraterritorial application of specific rights. See, for instance, Langford (note 44 above); Knox (note 44 above); Cahill (note 27 above).

As this book demonstrates, in the area of socio-economic rights, rather than or as much as the negative state's duties, the challenge has been to reach beyond traditional concepts of state sovereignty in order to ensure global justice in the process of redistribution of resources upon which the fulfilment of the rights depends.[65] In the context of the human right to water, a state's use or pollution of the waters originating in or traversing its territory diminishes the quantity and quality of water available to a co-riparian state for the latter's use to meet its domestic duties of realising the human right to water. In some cases, a state's utilisation or pollution of a shared water resource may jeopardise the realisation of the core minimum absolutely needed for bare survival in other co-riparian states. This book demonstrates that the current approach to the analysis of extraterritorial human rights and obligations is too narrow an approach that overlooks much of the socio-economic rights issues of inter-state resource sharing, especially water resources.

1.6 Analytical framework and methodology

The dearth of scholarship on the human right to water and problems of its extraterritorial application in the context of the African human rights system has already been stated. This work examines the rules of the regional (African) and international human rights treaties and the case law of the mechanisms established thereby. The approach used is predominantly doctrinal and comparative. The study is therefore primarily about the examination of the *current status* and *future potential* of *the law as it is.* The book seeks to establish a free-standing human right to water in Africa and related state obligations from the combined use of the rules of African human rights treaties, UN human rights instruments, international water law and other relevant regimes.

The study mainly employs a comparative methodological approach to treaty (legal) interpretation. This is an approach that is almost routinely used by the African Commission.[66] Indeed, a comparative approach to the interpretation and application of the African human rights treaties is explicitly mandated in the text of the African Charter, which instructs

[65] Fons Coomans, 'Some Remarks on the Extraterritorial Application of the International Covenant on Economic, Social and Cultural Rights' in Fons Coomans and Menno T. Kamminga (eds.), *Extraterritorial Application of Human Rights Treaties* (Intersentia, 2004) 183, 183–4.

[66] See Chapter 3.

the Commission to 'draw inspiration' from non-African human rights instruments to aid the promotion and protection of the rights recognised in the African treaties.[67] As demonstrated in subsequent chapters, the Commission regularly borrows, where relevant, from UN and regional (European and Inter-American) instruments and related case law. A comparative approach to the study of the legal basis of the human right to water and its extraterritorial application is therefore in line with the terms of the regional Charter and relevant jurisprudence.

Particular attention will, however, be devoted throughout the book to the ICESCR, General Comment No. 15 of the CESCR, the African Charter and the African Commission's case law. These are the main sources of the human right to water and its possible extraterritorial application in Africa. Regional and global treaties, including those of international water law and environmental law, where relevant, are used in the analysis of the human right to water and its extraterritorial application. Additionally, decisions and jurisprudence of the Inter-American, European as well as relevant UN bodies' and other arbitral awards are analysed. This is complemented by related academic writings.

Many illustrative examples have been taken from the Nile basin situation. The main reason for this focus is the fact that some of the Nile riparian states – notably Egypt and Sudan – can only meet their duties to realise the human right to water domestically if nine other upstream riparian states are held extraterritorially responsible for the realisation of the human right to water for the benefit of residents of the other co-riparian states. The prevailing situation in the Nile basin illustrates the salient features of water scarcity, heightened inter-state dependence and a state's incapacity to meet its domestic obligations in the realisation of the human right to water. Another reason is the fact that, to date, all the major decisions of the African Commission on the extraterritorial application of states' human rights duties have involved all the Nile basin states. Indeed, there appears to be a trend of uniform acquiescence by the Nile co-riparian states to their extraterritorial human rights responsibilities. This trend needs to be analysed in the broader context of the regional human rights regime. Thus the Nile basin represents an ideal test case for the analysis of extraterritorial states' obligations associated with the human right to water in Africa.

[67] See Article 60 of the African Charter.

1.7 Significance of the study

Until recently, water has not been the subject of international human rights law. Instead, the regulation of the use of shared rivers has been a proper subject of international water law. Under international water law, only states *qua* states can claim rights and bear duties towards each other. The proper role of the rules and principles of international water law has therefore been confined to the delineation of the rights and duties of co-riparian states without regard to ensuring access to such water resources by human beings inhabiting them. It has been a regime of *horizontal* application.

On the other hand, the regime of human rights law applies *vertically* as between a state and its residents. The norms of regional and global human rights law have been understood as prescribing what a state must do for and cannot do to individuals and groups within its territorial jurisdiction.[68] International human rights law has focused on its principal mission of taming the powers of a state acting territorially.[69] Consequently, states' human rights obligations have generally been applied almost exclusively to the effects of their domestic actions or omissions, and human rights norms and claims have so far operated between right-holders and their home state.[70]

The significance of the contribution made by this book lies in the challenge it poses to the established analytic boundaries of international water law and international human rights law. The book demonstrates the *potential* complementarity between the two legal regimes and the ensuing utility of regime coordination for the establishment of the human right to water and guarantee its enjoyment. It illustrates that there are crucial human rights dimensions in the texts and case law of the normally statist regime of international water law. Accordingly, international human rights law and relevant tribunals can draw on the rules and principles of international water law in order to establish the human right to water and states' extraterritorial duties for the realisation of the human right to water. From this perspective, the book establishes that

[68] Sandra Fredman, *Human Rights Transformed: Positive Rights and Positive Duties* (Oxford University Press, 2008) 1.

[69] Malcolm D. Evans, 'State Responsibility and the European Convention on Human Rights: Role and Realm' in Malgosia Fitzmaurice and Dan Sarooshi (eds.), *Issues of State Responsibility before International Judicial Institutions* (Hart Publishing, 2004) 139.

[70] Knox (note 44 above) 82.

one source of the legal basis of the human right to water and its extraterritorial application can be found in international water law. To locate human rights in the normally statist regime of international water law has so far been an odd proposition. Conversely, the book depicts that the extraterritorial application of the human right to water contributes to the regulation of the extent and manner of permissible utilisations of waters of shared rivers by co-riparian states, playing the role traditionally assigned to international water law.

Secondly, the book further demonstrates that the human rights regime provides a robust avenue for the application of the rules and principles of international water law and environmental law by human beneficiaries. The latter regimes have lacked effective monitoring and adjudicatory bodies for their promotion and protection. They do, however, provide for rules and principles that could be directly used by human beings to enforce their rights in human rights tribunals. The human rights regime, not least the African Charter, would therefore provide relevant procedures and tribunals wherein the rules of relevant international water law and environmental law can be adjudicated and applied in conjunction with human rights treaty texts relating to the right to water.

Thirdly, the book extends the focus of the current debate on the human right to water that has thus far been almost exclusively focused on 'finding the law' underlying the right. It takes related discussion to the implementation stage, and highlights problems of enforcement and enjoyment of the right posed by water scarcity and the shared nature of water resources.

Fourthly, the book goes beyond the current literature that predominantly analyses the states' duty to abstain from violating human rights abroad. Besides such negative duties of states, the book explores states' duties to prevent, punish and provide remedies for domestic acts that are capable of violating the human right to water abroad, on the one hand, and to provide water resources needed for the realisation of the right in third states, on the other.

Finally, the book fills the gap in the literature on the subject of the legal basis of the human right to water, and its extraterritorial application. This study is among the first few on the subject of the human right to water and its extraterritorial application of states' duties generally and in the African human rights system specifically. As such, it promises to start the search for the solution to problems of implementation of the emerging human right to water but does not, and indeed cannot, purport to provide a final answer.

1.8 Scope of the research

This book examines a subject that is otherwise a broader problem of the international human rights regime through the prism of the human right to water. The scope of the book is limited by three parameters: it examines a specific right (the human right to water); it examines a particular resource (water from shared rivers); and it focuses mainly on a specific geographical area (Africa). Within this framework, the book analyses the extraterritorial application of the human right to water in relation to co-riparian states of a river basin, to the exclusion of others. Moreover, the duties of non-riparian states or of non-state actors, to the extent they exist, are not covered. Furthermore, the study focuses on the uses of 'blue water' as opposed to virtual water.[71]

The question of extraterritorial rights and relevant states' duties can be analysed in the context of almost all rights in the catalogue of international human rights law. The focus on the human right to water was dictated by the near impossibility of realising the human right to water in many of the African states unless its extraterritorial application is ensured. African states are too interdependent on each other for water resources to be able to realise the right in their respective territories without their co-riparian states being held accountable to use shared waters in a certain way for the benefit of non-national, non-resident right-holders.[72]

This study is confined to the analysis of the duties of states in relation to the use of shared rivers in the realisation of the human right to water. First, as stated above, fresh water from rivers is the principal source of water used for drinking and sanitation purposes in Africa.[73] Secondly, unlike other types of water-related extraterritorial impacts of states'

[71] For an analysis of the extraterritorial harms to individuals through import-export of virtual water, see generally Ashok K. Chapagaina and Arjen Y. Hoekstrab, 'The Global Component of Freshwater Demand and Supply: An Assessment of Virtual Water Flows between Nations as a Result of Trade in Agricultural and Industrial Products', 33(1) *Water International* (2008) 19–32.

[72] In the Nile basin, for instance, the ten co-riparian states do not have any significant alternatives to the sharing of the bounty of the waters of the shared river. See Takele Soboka Bulto, 'Between Ambivalence and Necessity: Occlusions on the Path Towards a Basin-Wide Treaty in the Nile Basin', 20(1) *Colorado Journal of International Environmental Law and Policy* (2009) 291–320, 320.

[73] This similarly holds true elsewhere in the world. Overall, rivers provide human beings with about 80 per cent of their fresh water needs across the globe. See Elhance (note 47 above) 8.

(in)actions that may require difficult scientific evidence to prove,[74] the injury caused to human rights beneficiaries through over-utilisation or pollution of rivers is clearer and more immediate. In the context of the newly emerging study of states' extraterritorial duties that is already overly complex and unsettled, the study of shared rivers provides a simpler test case to explain the imperatives of regulating extraterritorial harms that states cause beyond their own borders. Thus, the emerging discussion of important issues of possible water rights violations through a state's over-utilisation of cloud waters,[75] or its contribution to climate change that leads to regional water shortage,[76] and questions of equitable utilisation of the atmosphere,[77] are beyond the scope of the current research, and deserve major studies in their own right.

While the analysis in this book is relevant to or even applicable in the context of other river basins beyond Africa, the scope of the present study is geographically limited to the examination of problems associated with the realisation of the right in Africa. This choice was based on three interrelated considerations. For one, Africa, next to Australia, is the driest inhabited continent and is facing a major water shortage crisis, meaning studies such as the present one are of immediate practical relevance. For another, Africa is the only continent where all states depend on shared waters and the analysis of extraterritorial state obligations is of immediate relevance. Thirdly, for all the numerous attempts by individuals at holding states extraterritorially responsible for violating their human rights under African human rights treaties, relevant literature has been scarce. This book seeks to bridge that literary gap. The combination of

[74] Blake R. Bertagna, '"Standing" up for the Environment: The Ability of Plaintiffs to Establish Legal Standing to Redress Injuries Caused by Global Warming', *Brigham Young University Law Review* (2006) 415–71; see generally Arne Vandenbogaerde and Wouter Vandenhole, 'The Optional Protocol to the International Covenant on Economic, Social and Cultural Rights: An Ex Ante Assessment of Its Effectiveness in Light of the Drafting Process', 10(2) *Human Rights Law Review* (2010) 207–37.

[75] See, for example, Tarek Majzoub *et al.*, '"Cloud Busters": Reflections on the Right to Water in Clouds and a Search for International Law Rules', 20(3) *Colorado Journal of International Environmental Law and Policy* (2009) 321–66.

[76] See, for example, Paul Hunt and Rajat Khosla, 'Climate Change and the Right to the Highest Attainable Standard of Health' in Stephen Humphreys and Mary Robinson (eds.), *Human Rights and Climate Change* (Cambridge University Press, 2010) 238; Knox (note 43 above); Knox (note 44 above).

[77] See, for example, Dinah Shelton, 'Equitable Utilization of the Atmosphere: A Rights-Based Approach to Climate Change' in Stephen Humphreys and Mary Robinson (eds.), *Human Rights and Climate Change* (Cambridge University Press, 2010) 91.

these factors would render the analysis of extraterritorial state obligations a matter of necessity and immediate relevance in Africa.

1.9 Structure of the study

A complete analysis of the degree of protection accorded the human right to water necessitates an examination of the right from three interrelated dimensions: the legal basis and normative content of *the right*, and the consequent states' *duties* and *remedies* available to the right-holders in the event of the infringement of their right to water.

The analysis of the human right to water is beleaguered by the absence of an explicit and comprehensive legal basis, and there are rumbling debates about the very existence of the right in the first place. Unless the legal basis of the right is established, the discussion of its extraterritorial application would be irrelevant. Seeking to establish the legal basis of the right to water, Chapter 2 examines the rules of international environmental law, international water law, global human rights treaties and related jurisprudence. It pays particular attention to the CESCR's General Comment No. 15 (the African Charter's inspirational source) and the propriety of the manner whereby the human right to water was derived from the other more explicit provisions of the ICESCR. It also analyses the normative basis and content of the right in the global human rights instruments and other treaties and the role of its increasing inclusion in the CESCR's recent work through purposive interpretation. It concludes that there is indeed a free-standing human right to water under the ICESCR. Chapter 3 approaches the analysis of the normative bases of the human right to water from the perspective of African treaties and state practice. It brings together the norms of the African Charter and other human rights norms, the African Commission's case law, regional environmental rights treaties and extra-African experiences to 'discover' the human right to water.

Once the human right to water is established as an independent right, questions of implementation and the consequent states' duties towards that end arise immediately. Chapter 4 analyses states' duties to realise the human right to water in the domestic sphere. It explains states' human rights obligations in terms of the four layers now almost universally accepted as useful tools for the analysis of states' human rights duties: the duties to respect, protect, promote and fulfil. By juxtaposing the willing state's human rights duties and its capacity to discharge the same, this chapter shows that some states would find it perennially impossible to discharge their duties due mainly to lack of territorial water resources as they may be severely dependent on shared resources originating in third states. Through the analysis of the various layers of states' human rights obligations, it demonstrates that the realisation of the human right to water necessitates, at least for some states, accessing resources originating in co-riparian states.

Chapter 5 takes up the other side of the question: do co-riparian states of shared rivers owe human rights duties *diagonally* towards residents of co-riparian states extraterritorially? This chapter examines the possibility of extraterritorial application of the provisions of the African Charter and other regional and universal sources of international law from which the African Commission draws inspiration while interpreting and applying the Charter. Thus, Chapter 5 employs the four layers of states' obligations for the purpose of gauging states' extraterritorial human rights duties. It concludes that states' duties to respect and protect the rights of residents of co-riparian states have clearer and stronger normative bases while the duty to fulfil and the degree and incidents of its application still remain controversial, necessitating progressive norm development and clarification.

Chapter 6 argues that the relatively controversial layers of co-riparian states' positive duties in the international human rights regime (Chapter 5) have been firmly rooted in international water law although principles from this source have yet to be used before human rights tribunals. The chapter examines the rules, principles and case law of international water law in an attempt to establish relevant legal bases for riparian states' extraterritorial duties to 'respect, protect, promote and fulfil' the human right to water. The underlying premise is that there is room for potential complementarity between the regimes of international human rights law and international water law in the realisation of the human right to water and its extraterritorial application.

Accordingly, Chapter 6 argues that states' extraterritorial obligations have long been part of rules of international water law, albeit in inter-state relations. Questioning the almost exclusively statist interpretation of the rules and principles of international water law, this chapter demonstrates that the principles of equitable utilisation and no significant harm entail the duty that all co-riparian states' populations must be taken into consideration by each co-riparian state in ensuring access to drinking and sanitation water for all. By elevating 'vital human needs' above others, international water law has attached a heightened priority to the human right to water, and the duty to achieve such is apportioned amongst all co-riparian states of a river basin. To the extent of a co-riparian state's omission or commission in causing harm to vital human needs (water needed for drinking and sanitation), each state is deemed to have caused significant harm irrespective of the nationality of the victim or place of the injury. The causation of such harm entails state responsibility. The culprit state must allow extraterritorial right-holders to access its domestic judicial and administrative bodies and must provide them with such remedies as would have been provided to its own nationals, hence the prohibition of extraterritorial discrimination. In the final analysis, Chapters 5 and 6 show the complementarity of the rules and principles of international human rights law and international water law in the establishment of each state's extraterritorial duties to abstain from violating, and also to contribute to the realisation of, the human right to water for the benefit of residents of all co-riparian states.

As the old maxim has it, there is no right without a remedy. Chapter 7 discusses the remedial aspect of the right and the states' duties. It focuses on the legal basis and practical application of the right to national and extra-territorial remedies in cases of violations of the human right to water by commissions or omissions attributable to third states. This chapter demonstrates that international law in general and international human rights law in particular accord primacy to domestic remedies over international ones. The victim should therefore exhaust those remedies that are available within the legal system of the implicated foreign riparian state before resorting to international procedures and remedies. However, Chapter 7 also demonstrates that proof of the unavailability, inadequacy or ineffectiveness of such remedies within the domestic jurisdiction of the culprit state would engender a situation where the victims are exempt from exhausting local remedies in such a state and are allowed to access international remedies immediately. It shows that the lack of such remedies or their effectiveness or inadequacy in Africa is more the norm than the exception as regards the human right to water, and that the African Commission could be forced to act as a court of first instance for complaints involving extra-territorial violations of the human right to water. Accordingly, Chapter 7 completes the substantive study taken up in the book.

A summary of the overall findings of the book is presented in Chapter 8, which pulls the threads together to conclude the study. This chapter points to salient outstanding problems pertaining to the extra-territorial application of the human right to water. Thus, it highlights the limitations of the scope of the current study and suggests directions for further research.

2

The human right to water at the global level

> [I]n the present state of national rivalries and political jealousies, it is not to be hoped that there could be a sort of declaration of a Human Right to the present benefit of water.[1]

2.1 Introduction

The birth of the human right to water has been both slow and controversial. Indeed, perhaps no other right in the catalogue of international socio-economic rights has had its status and normative basis as contested as has the human right to water. Not until after the UN Committee on Economic, Social and Cultural Rights (CESCR) issued General Comment No. 15[2] on the human right to water[3] in 2002 has the right to drinking and sanitation water been authoritatively defined as a human right.[4] Save for some narrow

[1] See Report of Professor Arnold W. Knauth to the meeting of the International Law Association (ILA) at its 48th Conference (New York, 1958) in Arnold W. Knauth, 'Uses of the Waters of International Rivers Report' (1959) 48 *International Law Association Reports of Conferences* (1959) 19–102, 96.

[2] General Comments are authoritative interpretations by expert human rights monitoring bodies of the content of human rights treaty provisions they are established to monitor. While highly persuasive, they are not legally binding.

[3] CESCR, 'General Comment No. 15: Substantive Issues Arising in the Implementation of the International Covenant on Economic, Social and Cultural Rights (Adopted 11–29 November 2002)' (UN Committee on Economic, Social and Cultural Rights, 11–29 November 2002) ('General Comment No. 15'). According to Para. 2 of General Comment No. 15, the human right to water 'entitles everyone to sufficient, safe, acceptable, physically accessible and affordable water for personal and domestic uses'.

[4] Vrinda Narain, 'Water as a Fundamental Right: A Perspective from India', 34 *Vermont Law Review* (2010) 917–25, 919; Stephen C. McCaffrey, 'The Human Right to Water' in Edith Brown Weiss, Laurence Boisson de Chazournes and Nathalie Bernasconi-Osterwalder (eds.), *Fresh Water and International Economic Law* (Oxford University Press, 2005) 93, 101.

exceptions,[5] the major UN human rights instruments do not make explicit mention of a fully fledged human right to water.[6] Lacking comprehensive legal recognition in the major UN human rights instruments, the human right to water creates a hierarchy within a hierarchy, as it sits on the lowest rung of the already marginalised category of socio-economic rights. The absence of a comprehensive guarantee for the human right to water in the universal human rights treaties has variously been dubbed 'odd, at best'[7] and 'startling'.[8] Humans can survive more than a month without food, but only about a week without water, as their bodies are between 60 and 80 per cent water by weight, depending upon the individual.[9] It is disquieting that a right so basic and fundamental for bare human survival has not been given explicit expression in the major UN human rights treaties.

Fresh attempts to establish the human right to water have been plagued by legal paucity.[10] The CESCR has had to 'read in'[11] the right from the implicit terms of Articles 11 and 12 of the International

[5] There has been a qualified recognition of aspects of the right to water as constituent elements of other rights. Such an approach narrows the scope of the right to water such that it can only be invoked in specifically limited circumstances and to benefit only a defined group of people protected under the relevant human rights treaty regimes: see section 2.2 below.

[6] See generally Stephen C. McCaffrey, 'A Human Right to Water: Domestic and International Implications', 5 *Georgetown International Environmental Law Review* (1992) 1–24; Stephen Tully, 'A Human Right to Access Water? A Critique of General Comment No. 15', 23 *Netherlands Quarterly of Human Rights* (2005) 35–63; Peter H. Gleick, 'The Human Right to Water', 1 *Water Policy* (1998) 487–503; Amanda Cahill, '"The Human Right to Water – A Right of Unique Status": The Legal Status and Normative Content of the Right to Water', 9 *International Journal of Human Rights* (2005) 389–410; Anton Kok, 'Privatisation and the Right to Access to Water' in Koen de Feyter and Felipe Gómez Isa (eds.), *Privatisation and Human Rights in the Age of Globalisation* (Intersentia, 2005) 259, 259; Narain (note 4 above) 919.

[7] McCaffrey (note 4 above) 94.

[8] Matthew Craven, 'Some Thoughts on the Emergent Right to Water' in Eibe Ridel and Peter Rothen (eds.), *The Human Right to Water* (Berliner Wissenschafts-Verlag, 2006) 37, 39.

[9] Stephen C. McCaffrey, *The Law of International Watercourses: Non-Navigational Uses* (Oxford University Press, 2001) 3–4.

[10] See generally the United Nations Office of the High Commissioner for Human Rights, 'The Right to Water: Fact Sheet No. 35' (the United Nations Office of the Commissioner for Human Rights, UN-Habitat, and WHO, 2010) 3; see also Ling-Yee Huang, 'Not Just Another Drop in the Human Rights Bucket: The Legal Significance of a Codified Human Right to Water', 20 *Florida Journal of International Law* (2008) 353–4, 353; Narain (note 4 above) 917.

[11] 'Reading-in' is an act of interpretation whereby a judicial or quasi-judicial body, following the object and purpose of a legal instrument, includes in its reading of a legislative instrument words or phrases that are not explicitly stated in the document. The effect is to read the instrument '*as if* certain words appeared in the statute. The

Covenant on Economic, Social and Cultural Rights (ICESCR),[12] which respectively provide for the right to an adequate standard of living and the right to the enjoyment of the highest attainable standard of physical and mental health. Consequently, the CESCR broke new ground by unequivocally affirming that the ICESCR contains provisions that implicitly contain an autonomous human right to water.[13]

However, for all its innovative approaches to carving the human right to water out of other more explicit rights of the ICESCR, the CESCR and its General Comment No. 15 have been criticised as 'revisionist',[14] and the CESCR's approach to the interpretation of Articles 11 and 12 of the ICESCR has been criticised as 'unreflective'.[15] The CESCR has been admonished for inventing a novel right to water,[16] which has been referred to as a 'new-born thing',[17] in a way that – to these commentators – is at odds with or ahead of state practice or what states parties envisaged upon their ratification of or accession to the ICESCR.[18] The human right to water thus continues to be a favourite subject of academic controversy.

Arguments against the legal recognition of the right to water have taken two related approaches. To some, the right lacks an explicit and comprehensive expression in international human rights law, and it does

words are notionally "included" to reflect in express, and therefore more readily observable form, the true construction of the words actually used, by way of a strained construction': James Spigelman, *Statutory Interpretation and Human Rights* (University of Queensland Press, 2008) 133–4 (emphasis in original).

12 International Covenant on Economic, Social and Cultural Rights, opened for signature 16 December 1966, 993 UNTS 3 (entered into force 3 November 1976) ('ICESCR').

13 As Malcolm Langford has observed, 'General Comment [No. 15] may be of some surprise. The word "water" does not appear in the Covenant. Recent international declarations ... do not mention the right to water.' Malcolm Langford, 'The United Nations Concept of Water as a Human Right: A New Paradigm for Old Problems?', 21 *Water Resources Development* (2005) 273–82, 275 (emphasis omitted).

14 Tully (note 6 above) 37, quoting Michael J. Dennis and David P. Stewart, 'Justiciability of Economic, Social and Cultural Rights: Should There Be an International Complaints Mechanism to Adjudicate the Rights to Food, Water, Housing and Health?', 98 *American Journal of International Law* (2004) 493–515, 462.

15 Stephen Tully, 'Flighty Purposes and Deeds: A Rejoinder to Malcolm Langford', 24 *Netherlands Quarterly of Human Rights* (2006) 461–72, 461.

16 See Tully (note 6 above). 17 McCaffrey (note 4 above) 115.

18 McCaffrey argues thus: 'While thus far State Parties to the Covenant have not objected to the interpretation contained in the General Comment [No. 15], State practice occurs more through accretion than avulsion. Thus it may take some time for countries to react, one way or the other.' See McCaffrey (note 4 above) 115.

not exist as such.[19] To others, it can be derived from such rights as the right to health and the right to life, but its scope is limited. For example, it cannot be claimed except when the rights of which it is a component are threatened because of a lack of an adequate quantity or quality of water.[20] This is meant to imply that the right to water is a derivative or ancillary right, available only in the context of the other more explicit rights of the ICESCR. In this sense, the right to water is an auxiliary entitlement that is subservient to other explicitly protected rights, and is dependent on the main right in the interest of which access to water is guaranteed.[21] The right to water thus lacks an independent or free-standing status in its own right, and its realisation *per se* cannot be demanded. On this argument, access to drinking and sanitation water should be 'enveloped' with other rights and claimed as such.

Consequently, the normative terrain underlying the human right to water remains muddied. Academic literature on the human right to water has added to the prevailing confusion, and has given some credence to the reticence of many states to recognise and implement the right domestically. For instance, the UN General Assembly resolution that recognised water as a human right was passed with a positive vote of 122 states, but saw as many as 41 states abstaining in the belief that they did not owe a legal obligation to ensure the right for their respective residents.[22] This is a doubly dangerous trend. For one, it allows states wide wriggle room to evade responsibility for realising the right. Indeed, General Comment No. 15 came about because the CESCR was alarmed by the fact that it was 'confronted continually with the widespread denial of the right to water in developing as well as developed countries'.[23] In the absence of formal recognition of the right, the correlative obligations of states to *respect*, *protect* and *fulfil* the right do not

[19] See generally Amanda Cahill, 'Protecting Rights in the Face of Scarcity: The Right to Water' in Mark Gibney and Sigrun Skogly (eds.), *Universal Human Rights and Extraterritorial Obligations* (University of Pennsylvania Press, 2010) 194; McCaffrey (note 4 above).

[20] See generally Cahill (note 6 above). [21] Cahill (note 19 above) 194.

[22] 'The Human Right to Water and Sanitation', General Assembly Resolution 64/292, UN GAOR, 64th Session, 108th Plenary Meeting, Agenda Item 48, UN Doc. A/RES/64/292 (3 August 2010). According to Paula Gerber and Bruce Chen, the adoption of this declaration 'suggests that the tide has turned, and the right to water is now a legitimate part of international human rights law'. Paula Gerber and Bruce Chen, 'Recognition of the Human Right to Water: Has the Tide Turned?', 36 *Alternative Law Journal* (2011) 21–6, 26. However, since this resolution is merely a declaration, its nature as a soft law instrument might render it too soft to command compliance as a matter of legal duty.

[23] General Comment No. 15, UN Doc. E/C.12/2002/11, para. 1.

apply.[24] For another, right-holders would not be able to have their rights addressed or violations thereof remedied. Unless the right is firmly established, lack of access to basic drinking and sanitation water would give rise to a scenario where 'there is no breach of obligation, nobody at fault, nobody who can be held to account, nobody to blame and nobody who owes redress'.[25] In a situation of worsening scarcity of fresh water resources, and the increasing number of people without basic access to the same,[26] the analysis of the uncertainty surrounding the legal basis and status of the human right to water is not merely of academic interest. It is also part of addressing the practical problems of ensuring right-holders' access to water for survival needs through its contribution to the clarification of the legal basis of the right and related state obligations. It may help relevant right-holders, activists and litigants, policy-makers and duty-bearers in the interpretation, application or remedying of the right in question.[27]

This chapter argues that a free-standing human right to water has been an implied and latent component of other, more explicitly guaranteed, socio-economic rights of the ICESCR and other water-related treaties. It demonstrates that General Comment No. 15 of the CESCR has simply articulated a pre-existing right that had a prior autonomous existence and a firm legal basis in the ICESCR, supported by state practice and international environmental law and international water law. It also suggests that the CESCR approach to the analysis of the human right to water has grounded the right on a narrowly defined legal

[24] The whole international human rights regime is tailored towards establishing a binary right–duty relationship, hence between right-holders and duty-bearers: see Margot E. Salomon, *Global Responsibility for Human Rights: World Poverty and the Development of International Law* (Oxford University Press, 2007) 132; Frédéric Mégret, 'Nature of Obligations' in Daniel Moeckli *et al.* (eds.), *International Human Rights Law* (Oxford University Press, 2010) 130–2.

[25] Onora O'Neill, 'The Dark Side of Human Rights', 81 *International Affairs* (2005) 427–39, 430.

[26] Currently, some 884 million people do not have access to improved sources of drinking water, while 2.5 billion lack access to improved sanitation facilities. Worse, these figures do not tell the whole truth as millions of poor people living in informal settlements are simply missing from the statistics: see United Nations Office of the High Commissioner for Human Rights (note 10 above) 1; 'The Human Right to Water and Sanitation', UN Doc. A/RES/64/292, 2.

[27] In this sense, academic commentators are sometimes referred to as an 'open community of constitutional interpreters' and as a group of 'free and rational society receptive to a pluralist interplay of forces and ideas' shaping the destiny of a certain legal instrument: Lourens Du Plessis, 'Legal Academics and the Open Community of Constitutional Interpreters', 12 *South African Journal on Human Rights* (1996) 214–29, 215.

basis, as the scope of the CESCR's analysis in General Comment No. 15 was limited to the human rights regime. The chapter contends that a comprehensive analysis of the normative basis of the human right to water requires reading the ICESCR in conjunction with the rules and principles of international water law and environmental law. The combined use of these three legal regimes reveals that the right has been latently, as well as patently, recognised in the relevant rules of international treaties and that it has been supported by an ever increasing body of state practice.

Section 2.2 charts the normative basis of the human right to water in the texts of relevant human rights treaties. Sections 2.3 to 2.5 analyse three approaches to the 'discovery' of the human right to water, through which the CESCR grounded the human right to water in the latent corpus of international human rights law in general and the ICESCR in particular. Section 2.6 analyses parallel developments beyond the human rights regime. It highlights that there has been a growing recognition of the human right to water as part of debates on principles of international environmental law and international water law. Section 2.7 draws the threads together and concludes that the human right to water is an independent entitlement, with its legal basis scattered in the ICESCR, international water law and environmental law regimes.

2.2 The human right to water in the texts of human rights treaties

Notwithstanding the relative marginalisation that has characterised their implementation compared to their civil and political counterparts,[28] international socio-economic rights have gone past the stage in their normative development where questions are asked as to whether they are rights *per se* or are mere aspirations of moral character devoid of legal

[28] See Joseph Oloka-Onyango, 'Reinforcing Marginalized Rights in an Age of Globalization: International Mechanisms, Non-State Actors, and the Struggle for Peoples' Rights in Africa', 18 *American University International Law Review* (2003) 851–914; Christof Heyns, 'Civil and Political Rights in the African Charter' in Malcolm Evans and Rachel Murray (eds.), *The African Charter on Human and Peoples' Rights: The System in Practice, 1986–2000* (Cambridge University Press, 2002) 137, 137; Asbjørn Eide and Allan Rosas, 'Economic, Social and Cultural Rights: A Universal Challenge' in Asbjørn Eide, Catarina Krause and Allan Rosas (eds.), *Economic, Social and Cultural Rights: A Textbook* (Martinus Nijhoff Publishers, 2nd edn, 2001) 3, 3; David Beetham, 'What Future for Economic and Social Rights?', 43(4) *Political Studies* (1995) 41–60, 41.

bite.[29] Legal protections of socio-economic rights emerged much later than those afforded civil and political rights whose standards had gone through long processes of progressive development, norm clarification and judicial scrutiny.[30] Indeed, socio-economic rights came into full prominence only in the late twentieth century.[31] As a consequence, the ambit, core content and attendant state duties relative to socio-economic rights are still evolving.[32] Nevertheless, since these rights have been formally consecrated in international human rights treaties, the identification of a specific legal basis for the majority of socio-economic rights guarantees has generally become an easier matter of locating a specific provision in the relevant human rights treaties. Even staunch critics of the international legal protection or justiciability of socio-economic rights agree that this group of rights has now attained universal recognition.[33] The principal questions that arise in relation to these rights now pertain instead to how to enhance their justiciability and enforceability as well as the examination of the normative content of the entitlements and the corresponding state duties that their international recognition entails. As Martin Scheinin noted, '[t]he problem relating to the legal nature of social and economic rights does not relate to their validity but

[29] Foremost among the early sceptics was E. W. Vierdag, who argued that 'only enforceable rights will be considered as "real", legal rights' and that the lack of a complaints procedure under the ICESCR would reduce the rights enshrined therein to nothing more than hortatory. According to Vierdag, the word 'rights' should be reserved 'for those rights that are capable of being enforced by their bearers in courts of law, or in a comparable manner': E. W. Vierdag, 'The Legal Nature of the Rights Granted by the International Covenant on Economic, Social and Cultural Rights', 9 *Netherlands Yearbook of International Law* (1978) 69–105, 73; cf. G. J. H. van Hoof, 'The Legal Nature of Economic, Social and Cultural Rights: A Rebuttal of Some Traditional Views' in P. Alston and K. Tomaševski (eds.), *The Right to Food* (Martinus Nijhoff Publishers, 1984) 97.

[30] See Robert E. Robertson, 'Measuring State Compliance with the Obligations to Devote the "Maximum Available Resources" to Realizing Economic, Social, and Cultural Rights', 16 *Human Rights Quarterly* (1994) 693–714, 693–4; Philip Alston, 'Putting Economic, Social and Cultural Rights Back on the Agenda of the United States' (Working Paper No. 22, Center for Human Rights and Global Justice, New York University School of Law, 2009) 2.

[31] O'Neill (note 25 above) 427.

[32] Scott Leckie and Anne Gallagher (eds.), *Economic, Social, and Cultural Rights: A Legal Resource Guide* (University of Pennsylvania Press, 2006) xiii, xiii.

[33] O'Neill (note 25 above) 428; Michael J. Dennis and David P. Stewart, 'Justiciability of Economic, Social and Cultural Rights: Should There Be an International Complaints Mechanism to Adjudicate the Rights to Food, Water, Housing, and Health?', 98 *American Journal of International Law* (2004) 462–515, 463.

rather to their applicability'.[34] But, as they are set out in explicit provisions in human rights treaties, questions about the very existence of the rights seldom arise.[35]

The same cannot be said of the human right to water. As noted above, the human right to water is still vying for a status similar to the other explicitly recognised socio-economic rights. A human rights treaty that mentions the right to water by name is more of an exception rather than the norm. This temporarily stopped the UN Sub-Commission on the Protection and Promotion of Human Rights from appointing its Special Rapporteur on the right to water. The Commission, observing that the human right to water was undefined, had to temporarily postpone the appointment of its first Special Rapporteur on the human right to water.[36] It requested a Senegalese jurist, Mr El Hadji Guissé, to investigate the status of the right to water for drinking and sanitation purposes.[37] Mr Guissé submitted his report on the right to water,[38] and was subsequently entrusted with the promotion and protection of the right as a Special Rapporteur on the same.[39]

The right to water has been such a 'great unknown' in the human rights catalogue, that some have even asked 'if it is proper to name it so [as a human right]'.[40] This has meant that questions are raised about the propriety of the use of a definite article before the right as 'the' right to water as opposed to 'a' right to water.[41] The argument is that the human right to water cannot be accorded the same legal status and recognition

[34] Martin Scheinin, 'Economic, Social and Cultural Rights' in Asbjørn Eide, Catarina Krause and Allan Rosas (eds.), *Economic, Social and Cultural Rights: A Textbook* (Martinus Nijhoff Publishers, 2nd edn, 2001) 29, 29.

[35] See generally Sage Russell, 'Minimum State Obligations: International Dimensions' in Danie Brand and Sage Russell (eds.), *Exploring the Core Content of Socio-Economic Rights: South African and International Perspectives* (Protea Book House, 2002) 11.

[36] Tully (note 6 above) 36. [37] *Ibid.*

[38] See El Hadji Guissé, 'The Right of Access of Everyone to Drinking Water Supply and Sanitation Services (Working Paper)', UN ESCOR, 50th Session, Agenda Item 4, UN Doc. E/CN.4/Sub.2/1998/7 (10 June 1998).

[39] Tully (note 6 above) 36.

[40] Richard P. Hiskes, 'Missing the Green: Golf Course Ecology, Environmental Justice, and Local "Fulfillment" of the Human Right to Water', 32 *Human Rights Quarterly* (2010) 326–41, 327.

[41] McCaffrey (note 4 above) 93–4; Stephen C. McCaffrey and Kate J. Neville, 'Small Capacity and Big Responsibilities: Financial and Legal Implications of a Human Right to Water for Developing Countries', 21 *Georgetown International Environmental Law Review* (2009) 679–704, 681 (intentionally referring to the right as 'a' right instead of 'the' right).

as the other more explicitly guaranteed socio-economic rights within the existing corpus of the international human rights regime. Some have even called for the adoption of a global convention that accords the right to water the status of a right *per se*.[42] Thus, any meaningful analysis of the problems of implementation of the right and associated states' obligations must examine the normative basis of the right as a starting point.

The implementation of a given human right depends upon the extent of its legal recognition in a binding instrument. It is difficult for monitoring and adjudicatory bodies to respond to violations of a right that is imprecise about the individual freedoms and entitlements or the state obligations it entails.[43] After all, the existence of a human right is contingent upon its formal approbation in a given legal regime. This applies to the human right to water. Moreover, the obscurity of the normative basis of a right (and hence its content) makes it significantly more difficult for rights-holders or activists and litigants acting on their behalf to 'spot' breaches with ease and specificity, thereby negatively impacting upon their implementation and enforcement.[44] Accordingly, the former Special Rapporteur on the Right to Water, Mr El Hadji Guissé, found it essential to identify and clarify the legal basis of the human right to water 'since it would be impossible for individuals to call for this right without a legal text to support them'.[45]

The explicit provisions of the ICESCR and the Universal Declaration of Human Rights[46] are silent about the right to water. At the universal level, there are only two human rights instruments that make explicit, if brief, mention of water. In the Convention on the Elimination of All

[42] See, for example, Kerry Tetzlaff, 'Towards a Global Convention on the Right to Water?', 2 *New Zealand Postgraduate Law E-Journal* (2005) 2–33, 31.

[43] See Takele Soboka Bulto, 'The Utility of Cross-Cutting Rights in Enhancing Justiciability of Socio-Economic Rights in the African Charter on Human and Peoples' Rights', 29 *University of Tasmania Law Review* (2010) 142–76, 151–2.

[44] Takele Soboka Bulto, 'The Indirect Approach to Promote Justiciability of Socio-Economic Rights of the African Charter on Human and Peoples' Rights' in Rachel H. Murray (ed.), *Human Rights Litigation and the Domestication of International Human Rights in Sub-Saharan Africa* (International Commission of Jurists, Kenya, 2009) 135.

[45] Sub-Commission on the Promotion and Protection of Human Rights, 'Sub-Commission Begins Consideration of Economic, Social and Cultural Rights' (Press Release, 7 August 2003) www.unhchr.ch/huricane/huricane.nsf/0/9E2A907D8C9AB866C1256D7C0026017B?opendocument.

[46] Universal Declaration of Human Rights, GA Res. 217A (III), UN GAOR, 3rd Session, 183rd Plenary Meeting, UN Doc. A/810 (10 December 1948).

Forms of Discrimination Against Women (CEDAW),[47] state parties are duty bound to ensure that women have the right to 'enjoy adequate living conditions, particularly in relation to . . . water supply'.[48] Under the Convention on the Rights of the Child (CRC),[49] states parties undertake to combat disease and malnutrition 'through the provision of adequate nutritious food and clean drinking water'.[50]

While these provisions are the only two global instruments that explicitly provide for the human right to water,[51] they are far from comprehensive. In the CEDAW, the right to water is recognised only in the context of ensuring adequate living conditions for women, and arguably does not apply to any other group of people. In the CRC, it is a means of prevention of disease and malnutrition of children. The scope of the provisions also excludes adults, as they apply only to children. Moreover, even in relation to the beneficiaries of the instrument – children – the provision in the CRC only relates to a certain aspect, namely, quality of water, and is silent about the quantity of water which the beneficiaries are entitled to claim.[52] Furthermore, the CRC and the CEDAW only place a duty on governments to ensure that the human right to water is provided to persons, without providing for corresponding subjective entitlements for human beings in human rights terms.[53]

2.3 Evolution through interpretation: the CESCR General Comment No. 15 and beyond

The most comprehensive and authoritative interpretation of the human right to water to date is General Comment No. 15 of the CESCR, adopted in November 2002.[54] Its adoption has drawn increased attention from scholars and practitioners to the examination of theoretical and practical

[47] Convention on the Elimination of All Forms of Discrimination against Women, opened for signature 18 December 1979, 1249 UNTS 13 (entered into force 3 September 1981) (CEDAW).

[48] CEDAW, Article 14(2)(h).

[49] Convention on the Rights of the Child, opened for signature 20 November 1989, 1577 UNTS 3 (entered into force 2 September 1990) (CRC).

[50] *Ibid.*, Article 24(2).

[51] See Cahill (note 6 above) 391.

[52] *Ibid.*; Melvin Woodhouse, 'Threshold, Reporting, and Accountability for a Right to Water under International Law', 8 *University of Denver Water Law Review* (2004) 171–99, 173.

[53] McCaffrey (note 4 above) 98.

[54] McCaffrey and Neville (note 41 above) 681–2.

dimensions of the emergent human right to water.[55] Indeed, the contribution of General Comment No. 15 to the debate surrounding the development and explication of the human right to water cannot be overstated. First, it clearly stated for the first time that there is an autonomous (free-standing) human right to water under existing human rights instruments, notably the ICESCR.[56] Secondly, it elaborated the normative content of the right under the ICESCR.[57] In addition, the CESCR addressed the typologies and extent of discrete obligations of states in the realisation of the human right to water.[58]

2.3.1 The teleological interpretation approach

The lack of an explicit protection of the human right to water in the ICESCR meant that the CESCR was forced to find innovative ways to ground the right in the elastic and inclusionary terms of the ICESCR through the use of teleological (purposive) interpretation. This approach to interpretation dictates that primary importance should be given to the object and purpose of a legal provision, rather than giving the instrument a narrow and restricted meaning. The overall effect is that a court or quasi-judicial body is to prefer a construction that would promote the purpose of legislation in all stages of the process of interpretation.[59] An interpretation method that is at the heart of the jurisprudence of the European Court of Human Rights,[60] the African Commission[61] and

55 See Eibe Riedel, 'The Human Right to Water and the General Comment No. 15 of the CESCR' in Eibe Riedel and Peter Rothen (eds.), *The Human Right to Water* (Berliner Wissenschafts-Verlag, 2006) 19, 19; Narain (note 4 above) 919.

56 General Comment No. 15, UN Doc. E/C.12/2002/11, para. 2.

57 *Ibid.*, paras. 10–15. 58 *Ibid.*, paras. 17–38.

59 Kath Hall and Claire Macken, *Legislation and Statutory Interpretation* (LexisNexis Butterworths, 2nd edn, 2009) 74; Donald Gifford, *Statutory Interpretation* (Law Book Company, 1990) 49–51.

60 Mireille Delmas-Marty (ed.), *The European Convention for the Protection of Human Rights: International Protection versus National Restrictions* (Christine Chodkiewicz trans., Martinus Nijhoff Publishers, 1992) 292; Henry G. Schermers and Denis F. Waelbroeck, *Judicial Protection in the European Union* (Kluwer Law International, 6th edn, 2001) 21–2.

61 See Danwood Mzikenge Chirwa, 'African Regional Human Rights System: The Promise of Recent Jurisprudence on Social Rights' in Malcolm Langford (ed.), *Social Rights Jurisprudence: Emerging Trends in International and Comparative Law* (Cambridge University Press, 2008) 323, 338. This is also in line with the rule of interpretation under Article 31(1) of the Vienna Convention on the Law of Treaties, opened for signature 23 May 1969, 1115 UNTS 331 (entered into force 27 January 1980) (VCLT): see note 87 below and the accompanying text.

domestic courts,[62] the teleological approach to treaty interpretation – also called the purposive interpretation approach[63] – dictates that ambiguities and lacunae in treaty provisions should be interpreted in such a way that best serves the object and purpose of the treaty.[64]

Teleological interpretation is used, *inter alia*, to promote the objectives for which the rule of law was designed, and to fill legal gaps in a given legal order.[65] The CESCR's approach in its General Comment No. 15 serves these two purposes. By defining the right-holders' entitlements and duty-bearers' obligations in the realisation of the human right to water, it expanded and promoted the human rights guaranteed under the ICESCR. More importantly, by explicating the latent content of the ICESCR in relation to the human right to water, it attempted to fill the gap in the protective regime relating to the human right to water that had been missing from the explicit terms of the ICESCR.

The CESCR carved out a free-standing right to water from, *inter alia*, the provisions of Article 11 (the right to an adequate standard of living) of the ICESCR. Article 11(1) provides that:

> The States Parties to the present Covenant recognize the right of everyone to an adequate standard of living for himself and his family, including adequate food, clothing and housing, and to the continuous improvement of living conditions. The States Parties will take appropriate steps to ensure the realization of this right, recognizing to this effect the essential importance of international co-operation based on free consent.

The CESCR put special emphasis on the usage of the word 'including' in the phrase 'including adequate food, clothing and housing'. Undeterred by the lack of any mention of the right to water in the list, the CESCR viewed the manner in which the word 'including' is put in front of the list (food, clothing and housing) as indicative of the fact that the catalogue of rights guaranteed under Article 11(1) of the ICESCR is not exhaustive. Since Article 11 seeks to guarantee the right to an adequate standard of living to right-holders, the prerequisites of which comprise food, housing and clothing, the inclusion of the right to water in the list is in consonance with the object and purpose of Article 11(1). Access to an adequate quantity and quality of water is as crucial as – or, arguably, even more crucial than – the more explicitly guaranteed elements of the right to an adequate standard of living listed under Article 11(1).

[62] Gifford (note 59 above) 49. [63] See Schermers and Waelbroeck (note 60 above) 21.
[64] *Ibid.*; Delmas-Marty (note 60 above) 292–3.
[65] Schermers and Waelbroeck (note 60 above) 21.

The approach of the CESCR has therefore taken care not to overstretch the ambit of Article 11, as it only added a similarly essential component of the rights guaranteed under the provision. The CESCR stated that '[t]he right to water clearly falls within the category of guarantees essential for securing an adequate standard of living, particularly since it is one of the most fundamental conditions of survival'.[66]

2.3.2 *General Comment No. 15 and its discontents*

Despite its utility in the explication of the right to water in an authoritative form, General Comment No. 15 has not been without its critics. Foremost among these is Stephen Tully, who severely criticises the manner in which the CESCR used the term 'including' for the purpose of locating the human right to water within Article 11.[67] Pointing to the imprecision of the term 'including', he argues that it leaves one 'to speculate on the number and nature of other characteristics essential to an adequate standard of living but not explicitly guaranteed by the Covenant'.[68] Tully enumerates a seemingly endless list of possible candidates for inclusion in the 'including' word of Article 11, and argues that, if one were to follow the approach of the CESCR, the list would include such things as access to the Internet and postal delivery services.[69] Tully essentially calls for a restrictive interpretation of treaty provisions when the language used in the treaty is vague and capable of bearing diverging interpretations. He thus criticises the CESCR for adopting a 'revisionist' approach in General Comment No. 15 in an attempt to remedy a gap that, according to him, states parties should have filled through treaty amendment.[70]

However, Tully's argument falters on numerous counts. The use of the word 'including' is not novel to legal drafting, as any law-making body – be it domestic or international – cannot be always completely exhaustive in the list of rights and behaviours it seeks to regulate. In the human rights treaty-making processes, ambiguities such as the instant one are constructive, as they allow the incorporation of emerging fundamental rights that eluded the explicit list of the law-making body at a particular time, the best example of which is the right to water itself.[71] In instances

[66] General Comment No. 15, UN Doc. E/C.12/2002/11, para. 3.

[67] See Tully (note 6 above) 37–8. [68] *Ibid.*, 37. [69] *Ibid.* [70] *Ibid.*

[71] This is also true of the interpretation of domestic statutes. See Kent Greenawalt, *Legislation: Statutory Interpretation – 20 Questions* (Foundation Press, 1999) 128.

where a treaty is fluid along its margins, the clarification of the normative content is the proper task of treaty-interpreting bodies such as the CESCR. Such ambiguities allow room for updating and elaborating treaty norms in keeping with emergent international problems without the need to resort to the rigorous treaty amendment procedures. Additionally, Tully's warning against the pursuit of the CESCR's purposive approach to treaty interpretation represents a misunderstanding of General Comment No. 15, as well as of the basic rules of legal interpretation.[72] As for the first, Tully's approach equates the human right to water with postal services and access to the Internet. A reading of General Comment No. 15 reveals that the CESCR's selection of words is crafted carefully, so as to incorporate only such rights that are fundamental and that can clearly fit within the list of rights essential for the 'adequate standard of living' guaranteed under Article 11. As the CESCR commented in General Comment No. 15, the right to water was included in the list 'particularly since it is one of the most fundamental conditions of survival'.[73] This CESCR approach obviates the possibility of including an endless list of relatively less essential categories under the guise of the imprecision built into Article 11(1) through the word 'including'. Jenny Grönwall observes that the approach of the CESCR means '[t]here will hardly be any flood of new rights only because the special status of water is recognised'.[74]

Admittedly, Tully's argument that the word 'including' is imprecise is doubtlessly correct. But it is equally clear that the imprecise word was designed from the outset to include some unnamed rights, and is not an empty signifier. And, if the imprecise word 'including' implies any latent rights, surely the human right to water which seeks to guarantee the bare necessities of life falls into that category. An approach that excludes the human right to water from those entitlements implied by the word 'including' under Article 11(1) renders the latent content of the provision practically meaningless and inapplicable. One is left to wonder whether there is a right that is more essential for bare human survival to merit inclusion under Article 11(1) of the ICESCR ahead of the human right to water.

72 For a critical appraisal of Tully's arguments, see generally Malcolm Langford, 'Ambition That Overleaps Itself? A Response to Stephen Tully's Critique of the General Comment on the Right to Water', 24 *Netherlands Quarterly of Human Rights* (2006) 433–59.

73 General Comment No. 15, UN Doc. E/C.12/2002/11, para. 3.

74 Jenny T. Grönwall, *Access to Water: Rights, Obligations and the Bangalore Situation* (Ph.D. Thesis, Linköping University, 2008) 215.

Indeed, the CESCR approach of deriving latent human rights from other related and more explicit human rights guarantees has been accepted by other tribunals. In the European human rights system, environmental human rights have been derived from other rights such as the right to respect for private life and family life.[75] Similarly, the approach has been used in the African human rights system, where there is no explicit protection of the human right to water.[76] The regional human rights tribunal, the African Commission on Human and Peoples' Rights, used the same approach applied by the CESCR of locating an implicit human right to water in explicit provisions of the regional human rights treaty. In *Free Legal Assistance Group and Others* v. *Zaire*, the Commission held that the 'failure of the government to provide basic services such as safe drinking water and electricity . . . and the shortage of medicine . . . constitutes a violation of Article 16 [right to health]'.[77] Similarly, in the *SERAC* case, the Commission decided that contamination of sources of drinking water by state or non-state actors was a violation of Article 16 (the right to health) and Article 24 (the right to a satisfactory environment).[78] In a case against Sudan, the Commission ruled that 'the right to water [is] implicitly guaranteed under Articles 4, 16 and 22 of the Charter as informed by standards and principles of international human rights law'.[79] These decisions exemplify the Commission's acceptance and application of the same logic (as that of the CESCR) of reading the human right to water into or from other explicit rights.

While the human right to water had been recognised in some domestic jurisdictions such as India and Argentina long before the CESCR

[75] For an excellent analysis and summary of these cases, see generally Ole W. Pedersen, 'European Environmental Human Rights and Environmental Rights: A Long Time Coming?', 21 *Georgetown International Environmental Law Review* (2009) 73–111.

[76] See Chapter 3.

[77] African Commission on Human and Peoples' Rights, Communications 25/89, 47/90, 56/91, 100/93, *World Organization against Torture, Lawyers' Committee for Human Rights, Jehovah Witnesses, Inter-African Union for Human Rights* v. *Zaire*, 19th Session (March 1996) [4], [47].

[78] See African Commission on Human and Peoples' Rights, Communication No. 155/96, *Social and Economic Rights Action Centre and the Centre for Economic and Social Rights* v. *Nigeria*, 30th Session (13–27 October 2001) 8–9.

[79] African Commission on Human and Peoples' Rights, Communication 279/03, *Sudan Human Rights Organization* v. *The Sudan*; and Communication 296/05, *Centre on Housing Rights and Evictions* v. *The Sudan*, 45th Session (13–27 May 2009) 125.

adopted its General Comment No. 15,[80] the General Comment has also been accepted in and begun to influence domestic judicial decisions involving the human right to water. This has been seen in decisions in Argentina, where the courts have directly quoted General Comment No. 15 in the course of rendering decisions.[81] Similarly, in South Africa, a country that was not even a party to the ICESCR at the time, both the High Court[82] and the Supreme Court of Appeal[83] have directly referred to and quoted General Comment No. 15.

The approach of the CESCR and General Comment No. 15 whereby the latent human right to water has been explicated is thus not new and has been part of national or international human rights jurisprudence for some time. In any case, to exclude the human right to water from the unnamed rights envisaged by the word 'including' under Article 11(1) of the ICESCR would have deviated from the rules of treaty interpretation generally. Restrictive interpretation of treaties is not an interpretative method generally accepted under international law.[84] Treaties should be interpreted in light of the overall 'object and purpose' of the treaty in question.[85] The object and purpose of a human rights treaty is the effective protection of human rights,[86] and the exclusion of some of the basic guarantees (such as the human right to water) from the ambit of the ICESCR does not have the effect of promoting human rights protection. As the Inter-American Court of Human Rights emphasised:

80 The Supreme Court of India, for instance, had derived the human right to water from the right to life. It ruled that the right to life 'includes the right of enjoyment of pollution free water and air for full enjoyment of life': see *Subhash Kumar* v. *State of Bihar* [1991] All India Reporter 420, 424 (Supreme Court of India, 1991). See Christian Courtis, 'Argentina: Some Promising Signs' in Malcolm Langford (ed.), *Social Rights Jurisprudence: Emerging Trends in International and Comparative Law* (Cambridge University Press, 2008) 163, 179.

81 See Courtis (note 80 above) 179.

82 See, for example, *S.* v. *Mazibuko* [2008] ZAGPHC 106, [36], [124], [128].

83 See, for example, *The City of Johannesburg and Others* v. *L. Mazibuko and Others* [2009] 3 SA 592, [17], [28], [34].

84 See Alexander Orakhelashvili, 'Restrictive Interpretation of Human Rights Treaties in the Recent Jurisprudence of the European Court of Human Rights', 14 *European Journal of International Law* (2003) 529, 530; Ian Brownlie, *Principles of Public International Law* (Oxford University Press, 1998) 636; see generally Rudolf Bernhardt, 'Evolutive Treaty Interpretation, Especially of the European Convention on Human Rights', 42 *German Yearbook of International Law* (1999) 11–25.

85 See VCLT, Article 31(1).

86 Ulf Linderfalk, 'On the Meaning of the "Object and Purpose" Criterion, in the Context of the Vienna Convention on the Law of Treaties, Article 19', 72 *Nordic Journal of International Law* (2003) 429–48, 433–5.

> the interpretation [of a human rights treaty] to be adopted may not lead to a result that weakens the system of protection established [by the treaty], bearing in mind the fact that the purpose and aim of that instrument is the protection of the basic rights of individual human beings.[87]

It has been argued that the lack of an explicit and comprehensive provision for the human right to water in the UN human rights treaties does not imply that there was an intention to exclude the human right to water. According to Matthew Craven, the right is 'neither here nor there' in that there was not an intentional omission or a deliberate exclusion of the right to water from the list under Article 11(1) of the ICESCR.[88] Keen analyses of the *travaux préparatoires* of the ICESCR revealed that the right to water was neither discussed[89] nor rejected[90] in the course of the drafting and adoption of the ICESCR. Some argued that its inclusion was either assumed, just like air, as a precondition for enjoying all other human rights, or that the drafters of the ICESCR did not realise that water was to become such a scarce resource.[91] The situation surrounding the omission of the human right to water from the list under Article 11(1) thus represents a neutrality of the drafters towards the right, the type that was 'neither desired nor opposed'.[92] The absence of the human right to water from the list is therefore neither an inclusionary nor an exclusionary absence 'but results simply from a lack of cognition/recognition'.[93]

In conclusion, the absence of an explicit provision on the human right to water does not mean that the right to water is not guaranteed under the ICESCR. Instead, it can be seen as a member of the illustrative list of Article 11 of the ICESCR. Put differently, the human right to water can be treated as an independent right, deserving of equal protection just like the other more explicit rights listed under Article 11 of the ICESCR. The right to water is thus not dependent upon the finding of violations of other related rights but is an autonomous right that can be violated when its constituent elements are infringed. In this sense, the human right to water is no more 'novel' or 'newborn' than the more explicit rights such as the right to food and health, of which it is an unnamed sibling under Article 11 of the ICESCR. Therefore, the CESCR's discovery – and not an

[87] *Proposed Amendments to the Naturalisation Provisions of the Constitution of Costa Rica* [1984] 4 Inter-American Court of Human Rights, Ser. A, No. 4, [24].

[88] Craven (note 8 above) 41. [89] *Ibid.* 40. [90] Langford (note 72 above) 439.

[91] See McCaffrey (note 4 above) 94; McCaffrey and Neville (note 41 above) 681.

[92] Craven (note 8 above) 38. [93] *Ibid.*

invention – of a free-standing right to water under Article 11 is in consonance with the rules of treaty interpretation which emphasise the need to promote the object and purpose of the particular instrument.

2.4 The derivation approach

In addition to the teleological (purposive) approach to interpretation it applied to Article 11 of the ICESCR, the CESCR also employed an approach of deriving the human right to water from the other explicitly guaranteed rights. In General Comment No. 15, it made use of Article 12 of the ICESCR which guarantees the right to the enjoyment of the highest attainable standard of physical and mental health. Article 12(1) stipulates: 'The States Parties to the present Covenant recognize the right of everyone to the enjoyment of the highest attainable standard of physical and mental health.'

The CESCR has taken into account the inextricable relationship of the human right to water with other more explicit rights of the ICESCR, which for their realisation depend on the concomitant fulfilment of the right to water.[94] The CESCR stated that the human right to water should be seen in conjunction with the guarantees of Article 12(1), namely, 'the right to the highest attainable standard of health', the rights to 'adequate housing and adequate food', and 'other rights enshrined in the International Bill of Human Rights, foremost amongst them the right to life and human dignity'.[95]

This line of thought is a double-edged sword, as it carries potentially contradictory implications about the legal basis of the human right to water. On the positive side, the right to water is a necessary and inherent element of the rights to health and housing. Since the more explicit rights cannot be realised without access to an adequate quality and quantity of water, the human right to water would be treated as part and parcel of such rights as the right to health, life, housing and dignity.[96] Thus, the right to water springs from its necessity for the realisation of other explicitly guaranteed rights.

[94] For an elaborate discussion of the sources from which the human right to water can be derived, see Inga T. Winkler, *The Human Right to Water: Significance, Legal Status and Implications for Water Allocation* (Hart Publishing, 2012) 41–55.

[95] General Comment No. 15, UN Doc. E/C.12/2002/11, para. 3.

[96] Cahill (note 6 above) 394.

The negative implication of the approach arises from the positive implication. Because the human right to water is protected on account of its utility to other rights, the human right to water would take the form of a derivative or subordinate right the violation of which can only be complained of when the parent rights – for instance, the right to food, health or life – are violated. But it would not have an independent existence or protection. In the derivative sense, the relationship between the human right to water and its derivative source (parent right) is such that the former is a small subset of the latter. Its violation thus arises only when the parent right is violated in situations that involve the victim's access to adequate quantity and quality of water. Consequently, the right to water in its derivative sense can only be guaranteed to the extent of its utility to and overlapping with the derivative source from which it springs. The implication of the derivative human right to water for the duty of the states is equally problematic: the obligation it creates varies depending upon whether the right is subsumed under other human rights or is recognised as a standalone right.[97] As Amanda Cahill observes, in its derivative sense, 'surely only certain aspects of the right to water will be protected and implemented'.[98]

This leaves the right on a shaky ground where it is neither fully recognised nor fully excluded from the ambit of the protection of Article 12 of the ICESCR and related provisions. Violations of the human right to water can take place independently of the right to health, life or of dignity or housing. For instance, a state's provision of water may fall below the amount or quality needed to realise right-holders' basic access to drinking and sanitation water, thereby violating the human right to water. However, the impact of such a scenario on the right to health or food of the right-holders might not be visible in the short term. Therefore, the derivative approach to the human right to water, taken on its own, gives a truncated and abbreviated picture of the right of its beneficiaries.

Used alongside the teleological approach of the CESCR (which leads to an independent human right to water), however, the derivative approach to the human right to water offers more benefits than harm to the normative development of the right. Locating the right to water in related rights that have been accorded explicit recognition in the international human rights

[97] See generally Amy Hardberger, 'Whose Job Is It Anyway? Governmental Obligations Created by the Human Rights to Water', 41 *Texas International Law Journal* (2006) 533–68, 535.

[98] Cahill (note 6 above) 394.

treaties, it provides another legal basis to argue for the protection of the human right to water. It also helps emphasise the utility of the indivisibility, interdependence and interrelatedness of human rights that was proclaimed in the Vienna Declaration and Program of Action.[99]

2.5 Recognition through the state reporting procedure: the CESCR Concluding Observations and states' acquiescence

Besides the teleological and derivative approaches to the discovery of the human right to water, the CESCR also relied on and made reference to its own 'consistent' practice that has addressed the right to water in the course of consideration of states parties' reports.[100] The CESCR had criticised states, long before the adoption of General Comment No. 15, for their various shortcomings in the national implementation of the human right to water. It raised the issue of domestic implementation of the right with states parties in the context of examination of state reports. According to Eibe Riedel, the CESCR addressed the human right to water in 33 of the 114 Concluding Observations it adopted between 1993 and the adoption of General Comment No. 15 in 2002.[101] For instance, the CESCR expressed its dismay regarding the violations of the right to water in Cameroon in its 1995 concluding observations, where it stated:

> The Committee regrets the lack of access to potable water for large sectors of society, especially in rural areas where only 27 per cent of the population have access to safe water (within reasonable reach), while 47 per cent of the urban population have such access ... The Committee calls upon the State party to make safe drinking water accessible to the entire population.[102]

The CESCR on another occasion raised the problem of water pollution that had negative impacts on the related rights of health and food in the

[99] It was declared that: 'All human rights are universal, indivisible and interdependent and interrelated. The international community must treat human rights globally in a fair and equal manner, on the same footing, and with the same emphasis': see Vienna Declaration and Program of Action, UN Doc. A/Conf.157/23 (12 June 1993), para. 5.

[100] General Comment No. 15, UN Doc. E/C.12/2002/11, para. 5.

[101] Riedel (note 55 above) 25.

[102] Committee on Economic, Social and Cultural Rights, *Concluding Observations of the Committee on Economic, Social and Cultural Rights: Cameroon*, UN ESCOR, 21st Session, 54th Meeting, UN Doc. E/C.12/1/Add.40 (8 December 1999), paras. 27, 40.

Russian Federation.[103] In its 1998 Concluding Observations on the State Report of Israel, the CESCR stated:

> excessive emphasis upon the State as a 'Jewish State' encourages discrimination and accords a second-class status to its non-Jewish citizens ... This discriminatory attitude is apparent in the lower standard of living of Israeli Arabs as a result, *inter alia*, of lack of access to housing, [and] water ... while the Government annually diverts millions of cubic meters of water from the West Bank's Eastern Aquifer Basin, the annual per capita consumption allocation for Palestinians is only 125 cubic metres per capita while settlers are allocated 1,000 cubic metres per capita ... [T]hat a significant proportion of Palestinian Arab citizens of Israel continue to live in unrecognised villages without access to water, electricity, sanitation and roads ... Bedouin Palestinians settled in Israel ... have no access to water, electricity and sanitation.[104]

In spite of the fact that the human right to water is not an explicit component of the ICESCR, none of the state parties criticised by the CESCR for violating the right has denied that the right inheres in the provisions of the ICESCR.[105] It is clear that the CESCR has taken the silence on the part of ICESCR state parties in the face of the CESCR's criticisms of their domestic implementation (or violation) of the human right to water as indicative of tacit assent by states to the fact that the ICESCR contains the human right to water and consequent state obligations.

However, the reporting procedure is a non-adversarial process which is heavily reliant on 'constructive dialogue' between the reporting state and the monitoring body.[106] The Concluding Observations of the CESCR lack the threat of enforcement, meaning states might listen to the CESCR without feeling the need to tender arguments about their domestic obligations relating to the human right to water.[107] The

[103] Committee on Economic, Social and Cultural Rights, *Concluding Observations of the Committee on Economic, Social and Cultural Rights: Russian Federation*, UN ESCOR, 16th Session, 25th Meeting, UN Doc. E/C.12/1/Add.13 (20 May 1997), paras. 25, 38.

[104] Committee on Economic, Social and Cultural Rights, *Concluding Observations of the Committee on Economic Social and Cultural Rights: Israel*, UN ESCOR, 19th Session, 53rd Meeting, UN Doc. E/C.12/1/Add.27 (4 December 1998), paras. 10, 24, 26, 28.

[105] Malcolm Langford and Jeff A. King, 'Committee on Economic, Social and Cultural Rights' in Malcolm Langford (ed.), *Social Rights Jurisprudence: Emerging Trends in International and Comparative Law* (2008) 477, 509–14.

[106] Takele Soboka Bulto, 'Beyond the Promises: Resuscitating the State Reporting Procedure under the African Charter on Human and Peoples' Rights', 12 *Buffalo Human Rights Law Review* (2006) 57–92, 58.

[107] Generally, the 'main teeth [of the reporting procedure] – the mobilisation of shame – have been too weak a threat to ensure compliance'. See Bulto (note 43 above) 151–2.

argument that states' silence in the face of the CESCR's Concluding Observations that are critical of the degree of their domestic enforcement of the human right to water constitutes a source of binding state practice may be too slender a reed to lean on. On its own, it might prove too weak an indicator of states' acceptance of the human right to water, especially given the fact that such a 'state acquiescence' is not a result of an adversarial and evidence-based process where a real case is litigated at the international level.[108]

Thus, the conclusion of the CESCR that its own consistent practice in its dialogue with ICESCR member states is strong enough on its own to give rise to state practice is questionable. However, through the use of the three outlined approaches (analytical devices) – teleological interpretation, derivative approaches to the right, and the acquiescence of states in the reporting procedure – the CESCR has established a firm legal basis for the human right to water. The combined effect of the three approaches leads to the conclusion that there is a strong normative basis for the human right to water and attendant state obligations in the ICESCR.

2.6 The human right to water outside the human rights regime

The CESCR made only a passing reference to the role of rules and principles of international law that lie beyond the mainstream human rights regime. It stated that '[t]he right to water has been recognised in a wide range of international documents, including treaties, declarations and other standards'.[109] While it took note of the incorporation of the right in a multiplicity of soft laws and binding treaties in General Comment No. 15,[110] it failed to analyse the rules and principles of related legal regimes where the human right to water is provided for in more explicit terms. Its narrow focus on the ICESCR has been followed by subsequent scholarship. As a result, the search for the legal basis of the right has hitherto been confined to the corpus of human rights treaties,

[108] Until and unless the Optional Protocol to the ICESCR, which provides for a complaints procedure, comes into force, the CESCR's main tool of supervision will continue to be entirely dependent upon the non-adversarial state reporting procedure: see Optional Protocol to the International Covenant on Economic, Social and Cultural Rights, opened for signature 10 December 2008, UN Doc. A/RES/63/117 (not yet in force).

[109] General Comment No. 15, UN Doc. E/C.12/2002/11, para. 4.

[110] For an excellent description of the body of soft laws for the protection of the human rights to water, see generally Tetzlaff (note 42 above); Desheng Hu, *Water Rights: An International and Comparative Study* (IWA Publishing, 2006) 97–104.

with a special focus on the ICESCR. This section seeks to locate the human right to water in the related international legal regimes of environmental law and international water law, from which the human rights regime and related tribunals may borrow in order to enrich the analysis, and possible adjudication, of the human right to water.

2.6.1 *Acceptance and recognition in international environmental (soft) law*

The right to water has long been debated and recognised in other areas of international law, notably in international environmental law. Indeed, attempts to clarify the legal basis of a human right to water came to light a few decades ago in the context of debates on international environmental concerns. The evolution of the right to water is traced back to developments of the early 1970s.[111] The United Nations Conference on the Human Environment, held in Stockholm in 1972, identified water as one of the natural resources that needed protection. Principle 2 of the Declaration of the United Nations Conference on the Human Environment ('*Stockholm Declaration*') stipulated that 'the natural resources of the earth, including the air, water, land, flora and fauna ... must be safeguarded for the benefit of the present and future generations through careful planning and management, as appropriate'.[112]

The Stockholm Conference was followed by the United Nations Water Conference, held in Mar del Plata, Argentina, in 1977. This conference, exclusively devoted to discussion of emerging water resource problems, issued the Mar del Plata Action Plan, which addressed issues such as water use efficiency, environmental health and pollution control, and regional and international cooperation.[113] As the direct outcome of the Conference and as part of the Action Plan, an agreement was reached to

[111] Salman M. A. Salman and Siobhán McInerney-Lankford, *The Human Right to Water: Legal and Policy Dimensions* (World Bank, 2004) 7. Amanda Cahill also points out that the question of whether a human right to water exists had been the subject of little attention prior to the past two decades: see Cahill (note 6 above) 389.

[112] See *Report of the United Nations Conference on the Human Environment*, UN Doc. A/CONF.48/14/Rev.1 (1 January 1973), Chapter I ('Declaration of the United Nations Conference on the Human Environment'), Principle 2.

[113] See *Report of the United Nations Water Conference, Mar del Plata*, UN Doc. E/CONF.70/29 (25 March 1977), Chapter 1 ('Mar del Plata Action Plan'). The United Nations General Assembly adopted the Report of the United Nations Water Conference on 19 December 1977: see GA Res. 32/158, 32nd Session, 107th Plenary Meeting, Agenda Item 12, UN Doc. A/RES/32/158 (19 December 1977).

proclaim the period 1981 to 1990 as the 'International Drinking Water Supply and Sanitation Decade', during which governments would assume a commitment to bring about substantial improvements in drinking water supply and sanitation.[114] Resolution II on '[c]ommunity water supply' declared that '[a]ll peoples, whatever their stage of development and their social and economic conditions, have the right to have access to drinking water in quantities and of a quality equal to their basic needs'.[115] Cognisant that the scarcity of water may hamper the implementation of the right at the national level, Resolution II called for full international cooperation among states 'so that water is attainable and is justly and equitably distributed among the people within the respective countries'.[116] The debate on the human right to water can be traced back to this conference and the resultant resolution which, for the first time, explicitly and unequivocally recognised individuals' and groups' right to water.[117]

Since that time, water problems have been a subject of numerous international conferences. The International Conference on Water and the Environment, held in January 1992 in Dublin, reiterated the need to recognise the right to water, but *at an affordable price.*[118] The Dublin conference was a preparatory meeting for the United Nations Conference on Environment and Development (UNCED) that was held in Rio de Janeiro, Brazil, in June 1992 (the 'Rio Summit').[119] Agenda 21 of the Rio Summit, referred to as the 'Programme of Action for Sustainable Development', included a separate chapter – Chapter 18 – on fresh water resources.[120] Chapter 18 not only endorsed the resolution of the Mar del Plata Water Conference that all peoples have the right to drinking water but it also called this principle 'the commonly agreed premise'.[121]

114 International Drinking Water Supply and Sanitation Decade, GA Res. 40/171, UN GAOR, 40th Session, 119th Plenary Meeting, Agenda Item 12, UN Doc. A/RES/40/171 (17 December 1985); Mar del Plata Action Plan, UN Doc. E/CONF.70/29, 14.

115 Mar del Plata Action Plan, UN Doc. E/CONF.70/29, 66. 116 *Ibid.*, 67.

117 See Salman and McInerney-Lankford (note 111 above) 8.

118 The statement declared that 'it is vital to recognise first the basic right of all human beings to have access to clean water and sanitation *at an affordable price*': 'Dublin Statement on Water and Sustainable Development' (International Conference on Water and the Environment, Dublin, Ireland, 31 January 1992), Principle 4 (emphasis added). However, the Dublin Principles do not define the concept of affordability.

119 See Report of the United Nations Conference on Environment and Development, UN Doc. A/CONF.151/26/Rev.1 (Vol. 1) (1 January 1993).

120 *Ibid.*, Annex II, Chapter 18.

121 See Salman and McInerney-Lankford (note 111 above) 10, quoting the Report of the United Nations Conference on Environment and Development, UN Doc. A/CONF.151/26/Rev.1 (Vol. 1) (1 January 1993), Annex II, para. 18.47.

The debates in the conferences and the emerging declarations and principles were endorsed by the United Nations General Assembly in 2000, in a resolution on the right to development.[122] This resolution reaffirmed that, in the realisation of the right to development, 'the rights to food and clean water are fundamental human rights and their promotion constitutes a moral imperative both for national governments and for the international community'.[123] This statement was considered at the time to be 'the strongest and most unambiguous' of its type in declaring a human right to water.[124]

This trend of recognising the human right to water in soft laws continued unabated after the adoption of General Comment No. 15. Numerous fora have explicitly recognised that the human right to water is a fundamental right, the enjoyment of which states are obliged to ensure. The Abuja Declaration, adopted by forty-five African and twelve South American states at the First Africa–South America Summit in 2006, contained a commitment by participating states to 'promote the right of our citizens to have access to clean and safe water and sanitation within our respective jurisdictions'.[125] Similarly, the Message from Beppu, adopted by thirty-seven states from the wider Asia–Pacific region at the First Asia–Pacific Water Summit held in Beppu, Japan, in December 2007, clearly recognised 'the people's right to safe drinking water and basic sanitation as a basic human right and a fundamental aspect of human security'.[126] Moreover, eight South Asian states adopted the Delhi Declaration, in which they recognised 'that access to sanitation and safe drinking water is a basic right, and according national priority to sanitation is imperative'.[127] More recently, the right has been recognised by the UN General Assembly, acknowledging that access to drinking and sanitation water is a fundamental human right.[128]

[122] See The Right to Development, GA Res. 54/175, UN GAOR, 54th Session, Agenda Item 116(b), UN Doc. A/Res/54/175 (15 February 2000).

[123] *Ibid.*, para. 12(a).

[124] See Salman and McInerney-Lankford (note 111 above) 11–12.

[125] 'Abuja Declaration' (First Africa–South America Summit, Abuja, Nigeria, 30 November 2006), para. 22.

[126] 'Message from Beppu' (First Asia–Pacific Water Summit, Beppu, Japan, 4 December 2007), para. 2.

[127] 'Delhi Declaration' (Third South Asian Conference on Sanitation, Vighan Bawan, Delhi, 21 November 2008), para. 1.

[128] See The Human Right to Water and Sanitation, UN Doc. A/RES/64/292. For an analysis of this resolution, see Gerber and Chen (note 22 above).

The biggest handicap of these declarations, principles, resolutions and action plans is the fact that they remain statements of policy that do not possess the quality of legal enforceability. While they indicate a gradually emerging trend of international opinion and state practice, and could also lead to the incremental evolution of these rules into binding treaties,[129] they do not immediately lead to binding entitlements for the beneficiaries nor to justiciable duties of the states.

However, with the passage of time, they could possibly undergo a process of hardening and evolve into binding rules,[130] and even play a catalytic role for the development of international custom,[131] which is binding *erga omnes*. René-Jean Dupuy has long made the argument that the Stockholm Declaration, for instance, has already achieved customary status, as it commands the near-consensus of the international community, and as its rules are responses to the state of hydrologic necessity.[132] Contentious as such conclusions might be, there are indeed traces of judicial reference to the principles of the Stockholm Declaration.[133]

Soft laws have also been considered to be 'experimental response[s]' to new challenges such as the realisation of the human right to water.[134] As Martin Köppel observes, soft laws facilitate 'learning processes or

[129] Dinah Shelton, 'Editor's Concluding Note: The Role of Non-Binding Norms in the International Legal System' in Dinah Shelton (ed.), *Commitment and Compliance: The Role of Non-Binding Norms in the International Legal System* (Oxford University Press, 2003) 554, 555; see generally Edith Brown Weiss, 'Conclusions: understanding Compliance with Soft Law' in Dinah Shelton (ed.), *Commitment and Compliance: The Role of Non-Binding Norms in the International Legal System* (Oxford University Press, 2003) 535.

[130] Douglass Cassel, 'Inter-American Human Rights Law, Soft and Hard' in Dinah Shelton (ed.), *Commitment and Compliance: The Role of Non-Binding Norms in the International Legal System* (Oxford University Press, 2003) 393, 395.

[131] Christine Chinkin, 'Normative Development in the International Legal System' in Dinah Shelton (ed.), *Commitment and Compliance: The Role of Non-Binding Norms in the International Legal System* (Oxford University Press, 2003) 21, 32.

[132] René-Jean Dupuy, 'Humanity and the Environment', 2 *Colorado Journal of International Environmental Law and Policy* (1991) 201–4, 203.

[133] For instance, the Supreme Court of India quoted at length from the Stockholm Declaration to support its decisions on citizens' rights and state duties. In that case, the Court ordered the closure of twenty-nine tanneries operating on the banks of the Ganga river for failure to treat industrial effluence: see *M. C. Mehta* v. *Union of India and Others* [1988] All India Reporter 1037, 1038–9 (Supreme Court of India).

[134] Mary Ellen O'Connell, 'The Role of Soft Law in a Global Order' in Dinah Shelton (ed.), *Commitment and Compliance: The Role of Non-Binding Norms in the International Legal System* (Oxford University Press, 2003) 100, 110.

learning by doing'.[135] Accordingly, they offer states the opportunity to see the practical impacts of those rules, while maintaining the flexibility to avoid 'unpleasant surprises' those soft law commitments might hold.[136] In this sense, soft laws could still have legal relevance and are located 'in the twilight zone between law and politics'.[137] As such, they may prove very effective and command more compliance as norms of international hard law.[138]

Nevertheless, at least for immediate purposes, the soft laws and action plans are devoid of enforceable claims or binding state obligations.[139] Yet the debates about, and the discussions on, the right to water at these various conferences and in their resultant action plans have led to an increased recognition of the human right to water and a fresh appraisal of the right within the framework of the corpus of international human rights law.[140] It also gives more credence to General Comment No. 15, wherein the CESCR stated that the human right to water has been part of existing rules of international soft law and other treaties. Besides, recognition of the human right to water in international soft laws shows that the right is not entirely novel and that it has been accepted in the context of international environmental law.

More importantly, such norms may be precursors of international customary law with regard to *opinio juris*, if not practice.[141] Such an outcome was envisaged by the International Court of Justice in the

[135] Martin Köppel, 'The Effectiveness of Soft Law: First Insights from Comparing Legally Binding Agreements with Flexible Action Programs', 21 *Georgetown International Environmental Law Review* (2009) 821–35, 825.

[136] Kenneth W. Abbott and Duncan Snidal, 'Hard and Soft Law in International Governance', 54 *International Organization* (2000) 421–56, 442.

[137] Jon Birger Skjærseth, Olav Schram Stokke and Jøgen Wettestad, 'Soft Law, Hard Law, and Effective Implementation of International Environmental Norms', 6(3) *Global Environmental Politics* (2006) 104–20, 104.

[138] László Blutman, 'In the Trap of a Legal Metaphor: International Soft Law', 59 *International and Comparative Law Quarterly* (2010) 605–24, 612; Köppel (note 135 above) 822; Abbott and Snidal (note 136 above) 423.

[139] See generally Alan Boyle, 'Some Reflections on the Relationship of Treaties and Soft Law' in Vera Gowlland-Debbas (ed.), *Multilateral Treaty-Making: The Current Status of Challenges to and Reforms Needed in the International Legislative Process* (Martinus Nijhoff Publishers, 2000) 25.

[140] Jacob Gersen and Eric Posner argue that soft laws, although not binding *per se*, are indicative of the future intentions of states, and point to the probable trend of norm emergence in relation to a particular legal topic to which it relates: see generally Jacob E. Gersen and Eric A. Posner, 'Soft Law: Lessons from Congressional Practice', 61 *Stanford Law Review* (2008) 573–628.

[141] Blutman (note 138 above) 617.

Nuclear Weapons Advisory Opinion.[142] It stated that 'a series of [UN General Assembly] resolutions may show the gradual evolution of the *opinio juris* required for the establishment of a new rule'.[143] According to the Court, soft laws such as UN resolutions 'can, in certain circumstances, provide evidence important for establishing the existence of a rule or the emergence of an *opinio juris*'.[144] There is thus a burgeoning trend (and hence state practice) towards recognising the human right to water at national and international levels in consonance with the line of interpretation taken by the CESCR in General Comment No. 15.

2.6.2 *The human right to water in international water law*

International water law is a regime that regulates consumptive and non-consumptive use of transboundary water resources. The rules of consumptive uses of international rivers have now been compiled in the 1997 Convention on the Law of the Non-Navigational Uses of International Watercourses ('Watercourses Convention').[145] The Watercourses Convention, from its inception, was not intended to be an instrument that primarily seeks to regulate human rights of individuals and peoples living in member states' territories. The approach to the development of international water law for consumptive uses has generally been state-centric, restricting its focus to issues of inter-state rights and duties,[146] as opposed to individuals' and groups' rights and freedoms relative to international water resources.[147] The Watercourses Convention was thus primarily devised to 'address obligations of governments rather than being

142 *Legality of the Threat or Use of Nuclear Weapons* (Advisory Opinion), *ICJ Reports* 1996, 226.

143 *Ibid.*, 255, [70]. 144 *Ibid.*, 254–5, [70].

145 Opened for signature 21 May 1997, 36 ILM 700 (1997) (not yet in force).

146 The situation was apparent during the drafting process of the Watercourses Convention, where some members of the International Law Commission felt that it was unacceptable for the Convention to refer to persons other than states. They perceived the impending treaty 'to deal with relations between states and should not extend into the field of actions by natural or legal persons under domestic law': International Law Commission, Report of the International Law Commission on the Work of Its Forty-Sixth Session, UN GAOR, 49th Session, Supplement No. 10, UN Doc. A/49/10 (1994), Chapter III(D) ('Draft Articles on the Law of the Non-Navigational Uses of International Watercourses and Commentaries Thereto and Resolution on Transboundary Confined Groundwater') 133 ('ILC Draft Articles').

147 See Neil A. F. Popović, 'In Pursuit of Environmental Human Rights: Commentary on the Draft Declaration of Principles on Human Rights and the Environment', 27 *Columbia Human Rights Law Review* (1996) 487–603, 494.

cast in terms of individual rights'.[148] It is indeed claimed that such a state-centrism entailed deadlocks such that 'no provision regarding the right could be agreed upon' in the Convention.[149] Ellen Hey has asserted that '[t]he Watercourses Convention is not about ensuring that individuals and groups, both of present and future generations, have access to sufficient clean water'.[150]

However, as adopted, the Watercourses Convention contains a provision that has a special normative utility in establishing the human right to water. Article 10(2) of the Convention, entitled 'Relationship between Different Kinds of Uses', states that a resolution of conflicts among different uses of an international watercourse should be resolved in a way that gives 'special regard ... to the requirements of vital human needs'. It is widely agreed that the 'vital human needs' provision refers to water that is required to 'sustain human life, including both drinking water and water required for the production of food in order to prevent starvation'.[151] Accordingly, the Watercourses Convention's provision on vital human needs 'is consistent with the human right to water'[152] and the requirement for catering for such vital needs 'should be informed by the human right to water'.[153]

Indeed, the phrase 'vital human needs' is a shorthand expression of the minimum core of the human right to water. As Dinah Shelton has noted, the 'vital human needs' provision is aimed at ensuring 'a guaranteed minimum amount to be provided to every person'.[154] This minimum

148 McCaffrey (note 4 above) 100. 149 Cahill (note 6 above) 389.

150 Ellen Hey, 'The Watercourses Convention: To What Extent Does It Provide a Basis for Regulating Uses of International Watercourses?', 7 *Review of European Community and International Environmental Law* (1998) 291–300, 292.

151 ILC Draft Articles (note 146 above) 110; International Law Commission Working Group, Report on the Convention on the Law of the Non-Navigational Uses of International Watercourses, UN GAOR, 51st Session, 6th Comm., Agenda Item 144, UN Doc. A/51/869 (11 April 1997) 5, [8]. See also McCaffrey (note 9 above); Peter Beaumont, 'The 1997 UN Convention on the Law of Non-Navigational Uses of International Watercourses: Its Strengths and Weaknesses from a Water Management Perspective and the Need for New Workable Guidelines', 16 *International Journal of Water Resources Development* (2000) 475–95, 483.

152 McCaffrey (note 9 above) 369. Cahill-Ripley similarly observes that the provision of Article 10(2) 'can be seen as harmonious with the human right to water'. See Amanda Cahill-Ripley, *The Human Right to Water and Its Application in the Occupied Palestinian Territories* (Routledge, 2011) 9.

153 *Ibid.*

154 Dinah Shelton, 'Equity' in Daniel Bodansky, Jutta Brunneé and Ellen Hey (eds.), *The Oxford Handbook of International Environmental Law* (Oxford University Press, 2007) 639, 648–9.

supply should be calculated on a per capita basis for the population of the riparian states who are dependent for their immediate consumption, also called 'natural wants' or 'ordinary uses' as opposed to 'artificial uses' or 'extraordinary uses'.[155] As noted by Peter Beaumont, such a calculation would 'provide a basic minimum figure of water usage that would permit a society to survive without major health threats to its population'.[156] In a recent report of the International Law Association (ILA),[157] 'vital human needs', a concept borrowed from the Convention,[158] is defined as 'waters used for immediate human survival, including drinking, cooking, and sanitary needs, as well as water needed for the immediate sustenance of a household'.[159] As Beaumont observed, '[p]resumably drinking water is the most vital human need. It almost certainly implies water for cooking and washing to maintain public health standards, but does it go beyond this?'[160] According to the ILA, '[l]egal institutions have long recognized a preference in municipal law for "domestic uses" of water, or as the Convention describes it, "vital human needs"'.[161] The accompanying ILA commentary states that the phrase 'vital human needs' refers to 'water needed for immediate human consumption'.[162] Thus, a closer scrutiny of the provision on the 'vital human needs' under Article 10(2) of the Watercourses Convention can be considered as a legal basis of the human right to water.

Unlike international environmental instruments relating to the human right to water that have so far taken the form of soft law, the provisions of the Watercourses Convention are binding on ratifying states. They will thus give rise to definite state obligations and enforceable individual and group rights to water. Coupled with the emerging trends of environmental law norms, international water law can

[155] International Law Association, 'Water Resources Law: Fourth Report' (Paper presented at the Berlin Conference, Berlin, Germany, 2004) 12.

[156] Beaumont (note 151 above) 484.

[157] The International Law Association (ILA) was founded in Brussels in 1873. Its duties are the study, clarification and development of international law, both public and private, and the furtherance of international understanding and respect for international law. The ILA has consultative status, as an international non-governmental organisation, with a number of the United Nations specialised agencies: see International Law Association, 'About Us', at www.ila-hq.org/en/about_us/index.cfm. It is an organisation that contributed greatly to the development of international water law, through its studies, debates at its conferences and publications.

[158] International Law Association (note 155 above), Article 14.

[159] *Ibid.*, Article 3.

[160] Beaumont (note 151 above) 483.

[161] International Law Association (note 155 above), Article 14.

[162] *Ibid.*, 12.

therefore be used directly as a normative source of the human right to water and attendant state obligations, hence providing supportive legal authority for General Comment No. 15.

2.7 The normative content of the human right to water

While the preceding analysis has led to the conclusion that there is a free-standing right in the universal human rights treaties, it does not answer the question of what concrete claims would accrue from the free-standing right to the right-holders. Needless to state, water is the life-blood of every living being. It is used for drinking, cooking, bathing, washing, waste disposal, irrigation (food production), industry, power production, transportation, recreation and in cultural and religious[163] practices. Without it, life is virtually impossible.

In terms of human uses to which water is put, agriculture (food production) accounts for 65 per cent and industry for 25 per cent of global water use, while water deliveries to households, schools, businesses and other municipal activities account for less than one-tenth of global water use.[164] According to Riedel, 74 per cent of the municipal uses are used for bathroom consumption, 21 per cent for washing clothes and cleaning, and only 5 per cent is used in the kitchen.[165] It is estimated that the absolute daily minimum per capita water need for a bare human survival is 2–5 litres, depending on individual and climatic conditions.[166]

As a point of departure, formulating the human right as the right of every individual and group to an adequate amount and quality of water

[163] In the Hindu and Buddhist traditions, the rivers of the earth, including the Indus, the Ganges and the Brahmaputra, originate from the mythical Mount Meru – the dwelling place of the gods – at the centre of the universe. In Early Christian tradition, the waters of the earth originate in the fountains of the Garden of Eden, which divide into the world's great streams such as the Nile, the Tigris, the Euphrates, the Indus and the Ganges. Similarly, in the holy book *Koran*, every living thing is made from water and, next to humankind, it is the most precious creation. See Peter H. Gleick, 'An Introduction to Global Fresh Water Issues' in Peter H. Gleick (ed.), *Water in Crisis: A Guide to the World's Fresh Water Resources* (1993) 3, 3; M. Falkenmark, quoted in Ashok Swain, *Managing Water Conflict: Asia, Africa and the Middle East* (Routledge, 2004) 1.

[164] Sandra Postel, *The Last Oasis: Facing Water Scarcity* (Earthscan Publications Ltd, 1st edn, 1992) 21–2.

[165] Riedel (note 55 above) 19–20. See also Arun P. Elhance, *Hydropolitics in the Third World: Conflict and Cooperation in International River Basins* (United States Institute of Peace Press, 1999) 8.

[166] Riedel (note 55 above) 20.

for all the conceivable uses would be tantamount to promising what all states cannot deliver. Put otherwise, the human right to water does not seek to entitle individuals and groups to as much water of acceptable quality as they would like, but 'merely to the bare necessities of life, no more'.[167] The approach taken by General Comment No. 15 is to identify selected types of uses and a minimum quality and quantity of water that should be immediately and continuously made available to satisfy the right-holders' basic needs.[168] Understood as such, the General Comment's main aim is to interpret the human right to water as a guarantee to every right-holder of a continuous supply of the bare minimum amount of water of adequate quality that an individual and group can reasonably expect and all states are obliged to supply.

2.7.1 *The concept of minimum core in human rights discourse*

The concept of 'minimum core' is of crucial relevance in the analysis of socio-economic rights as it refers to the very nucleus and irreducible minimum of a given right. It signifies 'the absolute minimum entitlements without which a state party would be considered to be in violation of the right concerned'.[169] According to Örücü, a minimum core of a right is that bare element which serves as the *raison d'être* of the right, and a minimum threshold the violation of which renders the whole idea of the right meaningless.[170]

167 *Ibid.*, 26.

168 It is argued that such a minimalist approach, wherein the minimum core is explicated as an immediate guarantee as a starting point of the journey towards progressive and (eventually) full realisation of a given right, implies that maximum human rights gains can be achieved through temporarily minimising goals. Accordingly, argues Young, the minimum core approach 'trades rights-inflation for rights-ambition, channelling the attention of advocates towards the severest cases of material deprivation and treating these as violations by states towards their own citizens or even to those outside their territorial reach'. See Katharine G. Young, 'The Minimum Core of Economic and Social Rights: A Concept in Search of Content', 33 *Yale Journal of International Law* (2008) 113–75, 114.

169 Bard-Anders Andreassen, Alan G. Smith and Hugo Stoke, 'Compliance with Economic and Social Rights: Realistic Evaluations and Monitoring in the Light of Immediate Obligations' in Asbjørn Eide and Bernt Hagtvet (eds.), *Human Rights in Perspective: A Global Assessment* (Blackwell Publishers, 1992) 252, 258.

170 Esin Örücü, 'The Core of Rights and Freedoms: The Limit of Limits' in Tom Campbell *et al.* (eds.), *Human Rights: From Rhetoric to Reality* (Basil Blackwell, 1986) 37, 37–46. See also Kitty Arambulo, *Strengthening the Supervision of the International Covenant on Economic, Social and Cultural Rights: Theoretical and Procedural Aspects* (Intersentia, 1999) 130–2.

The CESCR is of the view that defining the minimum core of a right helps 'ensure the satisfaction of, at the very least, minimum essential levels of each of the rights [that] is incumbent upon every State party'.[171] According to the CESCR, reading the ICESCR in such a way that does not establish a minimum core of any given right enshrined therein makes the right illusory and defeats the purposes of the ICESCR. It has stated that, '[i]f the Covenant [ICESCR] were to be read in such a way as not to establish such a minimum core obligation, it would be largely deprived of its *raison d'être*'.[172]

The limitations brought to bear on human rights implementations due to resource constraints means that states should prioritise certain aspects of each right and progressively move towards the full realisation of the same. On the other hand, in order that the very idea of rights protection does not lose its meaning, a certain minimum level of rights protection must be guaranteed at all times. The minimum core is thus 'a concept trimmed, honed, and shorn of deontological excess'.[173] Scholars have long pointed to the importance of prioritising the immediate implementation of the minimum core of each right that is essential for a life worth living. According to Örücü, there is 'a core, circumjacence and an outer edge' to each human right, while the core represents the most basic, non-derogable epicentre of the right in question.[174] If the core is limited, derogated from or violated, then the right loses its normative essence, and becomes an empty signifier for the right-holders.

This implies that each right can be presented as a concentric circle, wherein its most central, or minimum core, elements represent the aspect of a right that can be claimed by the right-holders at all times, and should be available on demand (thus commanding immediacy) without being subjected to the 'progressive realisation' catchphrase often associated with socio-economic rights. Put differently, there are different levels of implementation of a right, some of which are more immediate and essential than others whenever there are resource constraints to fully realise the right in question.[175] The minimum core of a right protects the right-holders' most urgent interest in being free from a general threat to one's survival.[176] The concept is thus designed to

[171] CESCR, 'General Comment No. 3: The Nature of States Parties' Obligations (Art. 2, Para. 1, of the Covenant)' (UN Committee on Economic, Social and Cultural Rights, 1990), para. 10.

[172] *Ibid.* [173] Young (note 168 above) 113. [174] Örücü (note 170 above) 38.

[175] David Bilchitz, *Poverty and Fundamental Rights: The Justification and Enforcement of Socio-Economic Rights* (Oxford University Press, 2007) 186.

[176] *Ibid.*, 187.

protect right-holders against a condition and state of life where bare necessities are unmet, one that Ignatieff calls 'insufferably, unarguably wrong'.[177] As such, the concept of minimum core has the interest of the most vulnerable at heart.[178] It seeks to address aspects in which people are most vulnerable and most needy. Unless this bare minimum level of each right is ensured at all times and with utmost urgency even at times of resource constraints, survival of the right-holders will immediately be threatened and the 'inability to survive wipes out all possibility for realising the sources of the value in the life of a being'.[179] While the full realisation of the non-core aspects of the right can be subjected to the 'progressive realisation' principle, and may become a subject of medium to long-term goals, the urgency of the core minimum level of a right forces immediacy of implementation.[180]

Without joining the ongoing debate[181] about the merits and demerits of the concept of minimum core, which is beyond the scope and aspirations of the current study, one can conclude that the concept of the minimum core is essential for the implementation of the human right to water which is becoming more and more scarce, leaving millions of lives on the brink of death.[182] The remainder of this section thus explores the minimum core of the human right to water (the rights aspect) as developed by the CESCR while the state obligations (duty aspect) entailed thereby are deferred to the analysis in Chapter 3.

2.7.2 *The core minimum of the human right to water*

The CESCR in General Comment No. 15 identified minimum core entitlements in relation to the human right to water. Notwithstanding the 'progressive realisation' clause which underpins fundamental rights and freedoms enshrined in the ICESCR,[183] the minimum core of any human right, including the right to water, is of an immediate nature and

[177] Michael Ignatieff, 'Human Rights as Idolatry' in Amy Gutmann (ed.), *Human Rights as Politics and Idolatry* (Princeton University Press, 2001) 53, 56.

[178] Bilchitz (note 175 above) 189. [179] *Ibid.*, 187.

[180] *Ibid.*, 189; Nsonurua Johnson Udombana, 'Shifting Institutional Paradigms to Advance Socio-Economic Rights in Africa' (Unpublished Thesis, University of South Africa, 2007) 99–102.

[181] See, for instance, Young (note 168 above). Cf. Bilchitz (note 175 above).

[182] On the scarcity of water across the globe and in Africa, see Chapter 4.

[183] Under Article 2(1) of the ICESCR, each state party undertakes the obligation to take steps 'to the maximum of its available resources, with a view to achieving progressively the full realization of the rights recognized in the present Covenant'.

should be accessible at all times. The minimum core of the human right to water has been defined in terms of the *types* of uses involved, the adequacy of the *quantity* of water available to the right-holders and its *quality* while the right to *equality* of the right-holders to such an access to the selected uses must be ensured.

2.7.2.1 The types of uses As is the case with many of the other socio-economic rights guaranteed under the ICESCR, the realisation of the human right to water depends on the availability of resources to the implementing state and does not necessarily entail the fullest and immediate implementation of all aspects of the right. However, as noted above, the implementation of the minimum core entails a state's obligation to implement it immediately. Put differently, as regards the minimum core, individuals and groups are entitled to claim the immediate fulfilment of the identified minimum threshold of a right in issue.

The implication is that the selection of the minimum core of a given right must be made very carefully for it to be capable of immediate translation into reality by all states irrespective of their degree of access to resources (the means at their disposal) and level of development. In relation to the human right to water, this means that not all types of uses are part of the minimum core of the right. Only two types of uses qualify as a minimum core of the human right to water, namely, personal use and domestic use.[184] The two types of uses comprise the use of water for drinking, washing, cooking, bathing and other sanitation purposes.[185] In selecting these uses as the minimum core of the human right to water, the CESCR has been mindful of the variety of essential uses to which water can be put but made a deliberate choice to single out the two uses

[184] General Comment No. 15, UN Doc. E/C.12/2002/11, paras. 2, 6 and 12.

[185] This is in line with other global and regional treaties as well as expert opinions. See the Protocol on Shared Watercourse Systems in the Southern African Development Community (SADC) Region, adopted on 23 August 1995 (entered into force on 29 September 1998); ILC, 'Draft Articles on the Law of the Non-Navigational Uses of International Watercourses and Commentaries Thereto and Resolution on Transboundary Confined Ground Water', 2(2) *Yearbook of the International Law Commission* (1994) 89, 110; ILA, 'The Berlin (Revised Helsinki) Rules' (adopted at the Berlin Conference, 2004) 12. See also Dinah Shelton, 'Equity' in Daniel Bodansky, Jutta Brunneé and Ellen Hey (eds.), *The Oxford Handbook of International Environmental Law* (Oxford University Press, 2007) 639, 648–9; McCaffrey (note 9 above) 371; Beaumont (note 151 above) 483–4.

as forming the minimum core of the right.[186] It thus excluded such uses of water as is necessary to produce food (the right to adequate food), religious and cultural practices (the right to take part in cultural life) and environmental hygiene (the right to health).

The approach has been criticised for being too restrictive in defining the human right as an entitlement merely to water required for personal and domestic uses.[187] Biswas, for instance, argues that the approach to the elaboration of the human right to water should have cast the net wider in a manner that includes within its ambit such entitlements as the right required for environmental requirements, agriculture, energy production, industrial and regional development, environmental conservation and tourism.[188]

This is, apparently, a result of a misunderstanding of the ramifications of General Comment No. 15. The approach of the General Comment does not preclude the possibility of claiming the waters needed for other purposes in the context of the realisation of other closely related rights. For instance, some amount of water could be claimed for production of food as part of the right to food, or for cultural practices under the right to take part in cultural life. The General Comment has the main purpose of identifying that amount of a non-derogable bare minimum amount of water that should always sit at the heart of claims of the human right to water *per se* and the related implementation duties of states. Accordingly, the General Comment stated:

> Water is required for a range of different purposes, besides personal and domestic uses, to realize many of the Covenant rights. For instance, water is necessary to produce food (right to adequate food) and ensure environmental hygiene (right to health). Water is essential for securing livelihoods (right to gain a living by work) and enjoying certain cultural practices (right to take part in cultural life). *Nevertheless, priority in the allocation of water must be given to the right to water for personal and domestic uses. Priority should also be given to the water resources required to prevent starvation and disease, as well as water required to meet the core obligations of each of the Covenant rights.*[189]

186 See General Comment No. 15, UN Doc. E/C.12/2002/11, para. 6.

187 Asit K. Biswas, 'Water as a Human Right in the MENA Region: Challenges and Opportunities', 23(2) *International Journal of Water Resources Development* (2007) 209–25, 219–21.

188 *Ibid.*, 219–20.

189 General Comment No. 15, UN Doc. E/C.12/2002/11, para. 6 (emphasis added).

In effect, the quantity and quality of water required for the purpose of realising claims other than the human right to water should be analysed in the context of those particular rights. The UN Special Rapporteur on the Right to Food, Jean Ziegler, for instance, has shown in at least two of his reports[190] that the water needed for the realisation of the right to food should be analysed separately from the human right to water.[191]

The preferential treatment of water allocation for personal and domestic uses had already been enshrined in the 1997 Watercourses Convention.[192] Under its Article 10(2), the Watercourses Convention provides that, in the event of conflicts between different uses of water, the conflict 'shall be resolved with special regard being given to the requirements of vital human needs'. The International Law Commission (ILC), the UN body that was responsible for drafting and elaborating the provisions of the Watercourses Convention, explained that the 'vital human needs' proviso is designed to protect and prioritise the water needed 'to sustain human life, including both drinking water and water required for the production of food in order to prevent starvation'.[193] Similarly, the International Law Association (ILA), a highly influential body composed of experts in the field of international law, whose earlier works provided a model draft for and influenced the final content of the Watercourses Convention,[194] also stated that 'the vital human needs' phrase under Article 10(2) of the Watercourses Convention underscores the need to prioritise water uses for 'natural wants'.[195] It stressed:

190 CESCR, 'Preliminary Report of the Special Rapporteur of the Commission on Human Rights on the Right to Food, Jean Ziegler' (United Nations General Assembly (A/56/210), 2001), paras. 58–71; CESCR, 'Report submitted by the Special Rapporteur on the Right to Food, Jean Ziegler, in Accordance with Commission on Human Rights Resolution 2002/25' (United Nations Economic and Social Council (E/CN.4/2003/54, 10 January 2003)), paras. 44–51.

191 On the necessity of treating the human right to water differently from the right to food, see Popović (note 147 above) 526–7.

192 The United Nations Convention on the Law of the Non-Navigational Uses of International Watercourses, adopted by the General Assembly of the United Nations on 21 May 1997 (not yet in force). See GA Res. 51/229, Annex, GAOR, 51st Session, Supplement No. 49 (A/51/49).

193 ILC, 'Draft Articles on the Law of the Non-Navigational Uses of International Watercourses and Commentaries Thereto and Resolution on Transboundary Confined Ground Water', 2(2) *Yearbook of the International Law Commission* (1994) 89, 110.

194 See Chapter 6.

195 ILA, 'The Berlin (Revised Helsinki) Rules' (adopted at the Berlin Conference, 2004) 12.

> Whatever one terms the preferred uses, they include water needed for immediate human consumption such as drinking, cooking, and washing, and for other uses necessary for the immediate sustenance of a household, such as watering livestock for household use and keeping a kitchen garden. Any other use, including using water for commercial irrigation, in mining, in manufacturing, to generate power, or for recreation, is not included within the concept of 'vital human needs'.[196]

It also showed that the preferential treatment of water for vital human needs, otherwise referred to as personal and domestic uses, is in line with long-standing state practice. It stated that '[c]ourts and other legal institutions have long recognized a preference in municipal law for "domestic uses" of water relative to competing uses of water, or as the UN Convention, Article 10(2), describes it, "vital human needs"'.[197] Thus, the priority attached to the water required for personal and domestic uses by the CESCR in its General Comment No. 15 is neither novel nor objectionable. It has already been applied in international water-related conventions, and accepted by expert bodies including the ILC.

2.7.2.2 Adequacy of water for the selected uses

The minimum core of the right to water required for personal and domestic uses involves access to a quantitative and qualitative minimum. According to the CESCR,

> [t]he human right to water entitles everyone to sufficient, safe, acceptable, physically accessible and affordable water for personal and domestic uses. An adequate amount of safe water is necessary to prevent death from dehydration, to reduce the risk of water-related disease and to provide for consumption, cooking, personal and domestic hygienic requirements.[198]

The human right to water therefore implies access to water of adequate quantity and quality that would satisfy the personal and domestic uses of an individual and groups. According to the CESCR, this can be further broken down into the availability, quality and accessibility aspects of the water resource.

(1) *Availability*: According to the CESCR, the minimum core of the human right to water comprises the availability of a sufficient and continuous supply of water for personal and domestic uses.[199] The

[196] *Ibid.* [197] *Ibid.* See also Chapter 6.
[198] General Comment No. 15, UN Doc. E/C.12/2002/11, para. 2. [199] *Ibid.*, para. 12(a).

sufficiency of the available water is gauged in terms of each person's need for uses such as drinking, personal sanitation, washing of clothes, food preparation and other personal uses. However, General Comment No. 15 states that the 'quantity of water available for each person should correspond to the World Health Organization (WHO) guidelines'.[200] General Comment No. 15, however, accommodates a differential treatment of individuals and groups that may need additional water due to health, climate and work conditions.[201] Apart from a soft guideline, the CESCR has found it unnecessary to lay down fixed per capita water availability.[202]

(2) *Quality*: The quality of water must not be of a type that poses a threat to a person's health. As such, it must be safe, i.e. safe from micro-organisms, chemical substances and radiological hazards.[203] According to the CESCR, the water should be of an acceptable colour, odour and taste for each personal and domestic use.[204] The requirement of colour, odour and taste may not be necessary for health purposes but it has been considered to be consistent with the dignity of the individual beneficiary.[205]

(3) *Accessibility*: The human right to water entitles everyone to the right to access water and water facilities and services without discrimination. According to the CESCR, accessibility of water and water facilities and services has four aspects.[206] *Physical accessibility* implies the right to have sufficient and clean water and water facilities 'within, or in the immediate vicinity of each household, educational institution and workplace'.[207] *Economic accessibility* ensures affordability of clean and sufficient water delivery for all.[208] Affordability does not entitle individuals and groups to free water for personal and domestic uses but provides for the right to access the water at a price that everyone can afford. As will be discussed in Chapter 3, General Comment No. 15 does not rule

[200] *Ibid.* [201] *Ibid.*

[202] The CESCR stated that '[t]he adequacy of water should not be interpreted narrowly, by mere reference to volumetric quantities and technologies'. See *ibid.*, para. 11.

[203] *Ibid.*, para. 12(b). [204] *Ibid.*

[205] Anton Kok and Malcolm Langford, 'The Right to Water' in Danie Brand and Christof Heyns (eds.), *Socio-Economic Rights in South Africa* (Pretoria University Law Press, 2005) 191, 199.

[206] General Comment No. 15, UN Doc. E/C.12/2002/11, para. 12(c).

[207] *Ibid.*, para. 12(c)(i). [208] *Ibid.*, para. 12(c)(ii).

out the possibility that the state be required to provide free water for those who could not afford to pay for water for personal and domestic uses. It is the state's obligation to fulfil individuals' and groups' access to the minimum core of the right to water. According to the CESCR: 'States parties are also obliged to fulfil (provide) the right when individuals or a group are unable, for reasons beyond their control, to realize that right themselves by the means at their disposal.'[209]

Accessibility of water should be in line with the requirements of the right to *equality*, and discriminatory policies and practices are prohibited. This layer of the human right to water has wide-ranging benefits for rural communities, poorer sections of society and communal and traditional groups. Access to water implies not only the right to availability of the water resources as a physical object but also to individuals' and people's right to access information (*information accessibility*) related thereto: it incorporates 'the right to seek, receive, and impart information concerning water issues'.[210]

2.8 Conclusion

The foregoing analysis has shown that the right to water as a legal entitlement is nothing novel or newborn. The ambiguity surrounding its legal basis is in part characteristic of the remainder of all the socio-economic rights of the ICESCR, albeit aggravated in the case of the right to water by the conspicuous absence of an explicit reference to the right in the ICESCR. The CESCR has thus appropriately read in the right to water into the rights that are explicitly guaranteed in the ICESCR.

A close examination of the legal basis of the human right to water in international environmental law norms and international water law, read in conjunction with the provisions of the ICESCR, suggests that the right has been embodied in the provisions of the various treaties for a long time. That is to say – to borrow the terms of intellectual property law – the human right to water is more a discovery than an invention. It was a latent entitlement that has been waiting to be uncovered. As the analysis of the approach of General Comment No. 15 revealed, the human right to water has been an unnamed sibling of those entitlements that have been latent in the provisions on the right to an adequate

[209] *Ibid.*, para. 25. [210] *Ibid.*, para. 12(c)(iv).

standard of living in Article 11 of the ICESCR. This has been explicated by the CESCR's purposive reading of the provision in General Comment No. 15. The propriety of this approach has been affirmed by precedent and subsequent states' acquiescence in their dialogue with the CESCR in the context of the state reporting procedure, as well as through inter-state multilateral soft laws, not least in the regime of environmental law. The provision on the 'vital human needs' under Article 10 of the Watercourses Convention affirms that states have indeed been willing to recognise the human right to water, a stance that has been reiterated in the General Assembly's 2010 declaration on the human right to water.

What is more, academic debate needs to move beyond the prevailing controversy surrounding the existence or absence of the human rights to water. The right to water has always existed since the adoption of the ICESCR over half a century ago. It is incumbent upon states, therefore, to translate the right into reality. Effort must now shift to the analysis of the normative content of the human right to water, its implications for states' duties and the particularities associated with its domestic implementation and enjoyment.

In terms of its normative status, as affirmed in General Comment No. 15, the human right to water is a legal entitlement properly so called, that is, a free-standing right. It is not – as usually portrayed – merely a derivative right that should be protected only because of its utility as a precondition or element of related rights such as the right to health and an adequate standard of living.

3

The human right to water in the African human rights system

3.1 Introduction

> [M]ay you live, and all your people. I too will live with all my people. But life alone is not enough. May we have the things with which to live it well. For there is a kind of slow and weary life which is worse than death.[1]

A great deal of scholarship on socio-economic rights in the African human rights system has focused on the analysis of problems of enforcement and justiciability of this group of rights. Consensus has emerged that the justiciability and enforcement of socio-economic rights guarantees of the African Charter on Human and Peoples' Rights ('Charter' or 'African Charter')[2] have for the most part played second fiddle to their civil and political counterparts enshrined in the Charter.[3] However, the marginalisation of the socio-economic rights of the Charter is also characterised by the brevity of the catalogue of this group of rights that have found an explicit expression in the Charter. The Charter has given recognition only to a selected list of socio-economic rights.[4] It has also

[1] Prayer of Ezeulu (Ulu's chief priest) in Chinua Achebe, *Arrow of God* (Heinemann Ltd, 1989) 95.

[2] African [Banjul] Charter on Human and Peoples' Rights, adopted 27 June 1981, OAU Doc. CAB/LEG/67/3 Rev.5, 21 ILM 58 (1982) (entered into force 21 October 1986).

[3] Takele Soboka Bulto, 'The Utility of Cross-Cutting Rights in Enhancing Justiciability of Socio-Economic Rights in the African Charter on Human and Peoples' Rights', 29(2) *University of Tasmania Law Review* (2010) 142; Christof Heyns, 'Civil and Political Rights in the African Charter' in Malcolm Evans and Rachel Murray (eds.), *The African Charter on Human and Peoples' Rights: The System in Practice, 1986–2000* (Cambridge University Press, 2002) 137; Chidi Anselm Odinkalu, 'Analysis of Paralysis or Paralysis by Analysis? Implementing Economic, Social, and Cultural Rights under the African Charter on Human and Peoples' Rights', 23 *Human Rights Quarterly* (2001) 327–69.

[4] See, for instance, 'the right to work under equitable and satisfactory conditions' (Article 15), 'the right to enjoy the best attainable state of physical and mental health' (Article 16) and 'the right to education' (Article 17).

omitted to explicitly provide for a few crucial socio-economic guarantees.[5] In short, its catalogue of socio-economic rights is modest.[6]

One of the crucial guarantees that have eluded the list of the Charter's socio-economic rights is the right to drinking and sanitation water. In keeping with the trend of the global treaties, the human right to water lacks a comprehensive legal protection in the Charter, thus creating a hierarchy within a hierarchy, as it sits on the lowest rung of the already marginalised socio-economic rights. The right has found its way into regional jurisprudence mainly by dint of innovative interpretation of the Charter by its monitoring and enforcement mechanism, the African Commission on Human and Peoples' Rights ('Commission' or 'African Commission'). While this is a step in the right direction, the Commission approached the right from an overly narrow normative basis and failed to elaborate its normative content. Even so, the Commission has yet to define comprehensively the legal basis and scope of the human right to water and attendant state obligations under the Charter.[7]

This chapter explores the case law of the Commission on the human right to water, and analyses the same in light of parallel developments elsewhere. It seeks to demonstrate that, for all its innovative approach to locating the human right to water in the Charter's corpus, the Commission has conspicuously failed to elaborate its normative basis and content and lent a deaf ear when victims of the right's violations sought remedies before it. The chapter also suggests that the Commission grounded the human right to water on a narrowly defined and usually shifting legal basis, ignoring the fertile normative sources of the right in related African Union (AU) treaties. This chapter argues that the human right to water in Africa should be grounded not only in the implicit terms of the Charter, but also in the more explicit provisions of

[5] See Bulto (note 3 above) 143.

[6] Christof Heyns, 'The African Regional Human Rights System: The African Charter', 108 *Penn State Law Review* (2004) 679–702, 690.

[7] In 2009, the Commission had drafted and circulated for comments the 'Draft Principles and Guidelines on the Implementation of Economic, Social and Cultural Rights in the African Charter on Human and Peoples' Rights', which contained a specific section on the 'right to water and sanitation'. The draft Guidelines were adopted on 24 October 2011. The draft Guidelines devoted paras. 71–5 to an analysis of the legal bases and normative content of the right to water and sanitation. However, at the date of writing, its final version has not been made public. Thus, the analysis of a draft document would not add much value to the debate, and is not discussed here. The draft Guidelines is available at www.achpr.org/instruments/economic-social-cultural (accessed 7 November 2012).

the usually neglected African Nature Convention.[8] It seeks to examine the right and its normative content through an analysis of the broader African regional instruments and their 'inspirational sources' in the universal treaties.

Section 3.2 discusses the textual basis of the right to water in the mainstream regional human rights treaties, and analyses the case law of the Commission and the potential utility of other continental treaties the primary focus of which is not on human rights. In section 3.3, the analysis focuses on the inspirational value of the approach of the global human rights bodies in carving the right to water from similarly obscure normative sources. Section 3.3 relies on these non-African approaches to the normative scope of the human right to water, and concludes that a similar approach may be adopted by the African Commission.

3.2 The normative basis of the human right to water in the Charter

The absence of a comprehensive guarantee for the human right to water in the universal human rights treaties has variously been dubbed 'odd, at best'[9] and 'startling'.[10] Its analogous absence in the African Charter[11] is equally disquieting given the degree of water scarcity in the continent. In the Millennium Development Goals, countries of the world could promise merely to halve the number of people without access to drinking and sanitation water.[12] Indeed, Africa faces 'steep challenges' just to meet this minimalist yet seemingly ambitious undertaking,[13] a fact that renders

[8] African Convention on the Conservation of Nature and Natural Resources, adopted in Algiers on 15 September 1968 (entered into force on 16 June 1969). According to the publicly available data on the website of the AU, as at 31 May 2013, the African Nature Convention was ratified or acceded to by thirty of the fifty-three states of the member states of the African Union. See status of ratifications at www.africa-union.org/root/au/Documents/Treaties/List/African%20Convention%20on%20nature%20and%20natural%20resources.pdf (accessed 12 June 2013).

[9] Stephen C. McCaffrey, 'The Human Right to Water' in Edith Brown Weiss, Laurence Boisson de Chazournes and Nathale Bernasconi-Osterwalder (eds.), *Fresh Water and International Economic Law* (Oxford University Press, 2005) 93, 94.

[10] Matthew Craven, 'Some Thoughts on the Emergent Right to Water' in Eibe Riedel and Peter Rothen (eds.), *The Human Right to Water* (Berliner Wissenschafts-Verlag, 2006) 37, 39.

[11] A qualified recognition of the human right to water has been made in other regional treaties, but the normative status of the right remains auxiliary to other related but more explicit rights. See Chapter 2.

[12] See the UN Millennium Development Goals Report (2009) 46.

[13] *Ibid.*, 45–6.

the examination of the legal basis of the human right to water in the continent a matter of urgency.

3.2.1 The right in the mainstream African human rights instruments

In contrast to the total absence of any mention of the right to water under the African Charter, the Charter on the Rights and Welfare of the Child (ACRWC)[14] provides that state parties are required to take measures to 'ensure the provision of adequate nutrition and safe drinking water'.[15] The ambit of the provision of the ACRWC is limited such that it merely regulates quality (safety) of available water and it applies only to children.

It is silent on the (adequacy of the) amount of water that states have to provide their children. Similarly, the Protocol to the African Charter on Human and Peoples' Rights on the Rights of Women in Africa ('Women's Protocol')[16] provides that state parties shall take 'appropriate measures to . . . provide women with access to clean drinking water'.[17] This instrument also says nothing about the quantity of water that is to be provided by the states to the beneficiaries of the right.

Accordingly, the normative content and legal basis of a free-standing and comprehensive right to water is only ambiguously situated in the mainstream regional human rights instruments. However, there is adequate legal basis upon which the Commission can rely to 'discover' the human right to water. There is room for interpreting the Charter's provisions in a way that allows the 'reading-in' of an independent human right to water. Besides, there is a potential to use other African treaties that are not specifically human rights instruments but have relevance thereto in order to give legal protection to the right. But the potential of explicating the human right to water from the relevant regional treaties heavily depends upon how the Commission approaches claims and complaints related to the human right to water. As discussed below,

[14] African Charter on the Rights and Welfare of the Child, OAU Doc. CAB/LEG/24.9/49 (1990) (entered into force 29 November 1999).

[15] *Ibid.*, Article 14(2)(c).

[16] Adopted by the 2nd Ordinary Session of the Assembly of the Union, Maputo, Mozambique, OAU Doc. CAB/LEG/66.6 (13 September 2000) (entered into force 25 November 2005).

[17] Women's Protocol, Article 15(a).

the human right to water in the case law of the Commission has had a troubled normative status.

3.2.2 The approach of the African Commission

The recognition of the human right to water in the African human rights system – to the extent of its existence – owes its roots to quasi-judicial innovation of the African Commission, whose case law facilitated its appearance in the regional human rights system. The Commission read the right to water into or from other rights that have been clearly provided for in the regional instruments. The promotional mandate of the Commission enunciated under Article 45 of the Charter empowers the regional body to set standards and formulate principles and rules aimed at solving legal problems relating to human and peoples' rights and fundamental freedoms. This has enabled the Commission to read aspects of the right to water into other guarantees of the Charter.

So far, the Commission mainly interpreted the right to water as a subset of the right to dignity (Article 5), the right to health (Article 16) and the right to a healthy environment (Article 24) of the Charter. In the *Free Legal Assistance Group and Others* v. *Zaire*, the Commission held that the 'failure of the government to provide basic services such as safe drinking water and electricity and the shortage of medicine . . . constitutes a violation of Article 16 [right to health]'.[18] Similarly, in the landmark case against Nigeria, the Commission decided that contamination of sources of drinking water by state or non-state actors is a violation of Article 16 (the right to health) and Article 24 (the right to a satisfactory environment).[19] In a case against Sudan, there was a complaint that Sudan was complicit in poisoning wells and denying access to water sources in the Darfur region.[20] Here too, the Commission ruled that 'the poisoning of water sources, such as wells, exposed the victims to serious health risks and amounts to a violation of Article 16 of the Charter'.[21]

18 (Joined) Communications 25/89, 47/90, 56/91, 100/93, *Free Legal Assistance Group and 2 Others* v. *Zaire*, 9th Annual Activity Report (1995–6), para. 47.

19 See Communication 155/96, *Social and Economic Rights Action Centre and the Centre for Economic and Social Rights* v. *Nigeria*, 15th Annual Activity Report (2001–2), paras. 49, 57 and 66 ('the *SERAC* case'), paras. 50–4.

20 (Joined) Communication 279/03, *Sudan Human Rights Organization* v. *The Sudan* and Communication 296/05, *Centre on Housing Rights and Evictions* v. *The Sudan*, 28th Annual Activity Report (2010), para. 207.

21 *Ibid.*, para. 212.

Despite a clear and emphatic request from the complainants to declare the existence of an independent right to water under the Charter (and the violations thereof in the instant case), the Commission evaded the request without any reasoning whatsoever. Indeed, the Commission itself stated that '[t]he Complainant invites the Commission to develop further its reasoning in the *SERAC* case by holding that the right to water is also guaranteed by reading together Articles 4, 16, and 22, of the African Charter'.[22] For a quasi-judicial body such as the African Commission to bypass a clear prayer of the complainants without an apparent reason in a case involving such massive and serious violations of vital human rights including the human right to water is anomalous, to say the least. Given a golden opportunity to rule on the status and legal basis of the human right to water, the Commission threw the baby away with the bathwater.

Similarly, in a case against Angola in which the present author was one of the legal counsel for the complainants, it was proven that Angola carried out a massive series of arrests of foreign nationals (in which over 126,247 individuals were arbitrarily arrested *en masse*) and put them in detention centres before deporting them. In these detention camps – some of which were initially used to house animals and contained a plethora of animal waste, hence far from suitable for human habitation – the complainants proved that bathroom facilities consisted solely of two buckets of water per day for over 500 detainees, and the bathroom was located in the same one room where all detainees were compelled to eat and sleep. The Commission could only find the respondent state in violation of the right to dignity and the protection against inhuman and degrading treatment. It ruled that the situation is 'clearly a violation of Article 5 of the African Charter since such a treatment cannot be called anything but degrading and inhuman'.[23] There was no attempt by the Commission at explicating the right to water and no mention of the manifestly clear violations of the right that were committed by the respondent state.

The Commission's consistent approach to the human right to water is therefore to treat the right as an auxiliary right that attracts protection as a component of other more explicit rights. This has been the case not only in the Commission's jurisprudence, but also in the 'Pretoria

[22] *Ibid.*, para. 126.

[23] Communication 292/2004, *Institute for Human Rights and Development in Africa* v. *Republic of Angola*, 24th Annual Activity Report (2008), para. 51.

Statement' on the socio-economic rights of the Charter, where the right to health (Article 16) was taken to entail 'access to basic . . . sanitation and adequate supply of safe and potable water'.[24] While this approach is not entirely wrong, it represents a mixed blessing for the progressive development of the human right to water under the Charter. The derivative approach to explicating the right is a double-edged sword, as it carries potentially contradictory implications about the legal basis of the right.

On the positive side, the Commission stated the obvious stance that the right to water is a necessary and inherent element, *inter alia*, of the rights to health, life, dignity and housing. Since the more explicit (parent) rights cannot be realised without access to adequate quality and quantity of water, the human right to water would be treated as part and parcel of such rights.[25] Thus, the right to water springs out of its necessity for the realisation of other explicitly guaranteed rights.

The negative repercussions of the approach spring out of the positive implication. Critics of the derivative approach argue that the right to water, as derived from such rights as the right to health and the right to life, lacks an autonomous existence and is limited in scope. For example – it is argued – it cannot be claimed except when the parent rights of which it is a subset are jeopardised due to lack of an adequate quantity or quality of water.[26] That is meant to imply that the right to water is a derivative or ancillary right, available only in the context of the other more explicit rights of the African Charter and other regional instruments. In this sense, the right to water is an auxiliary entitlement that is subservient to other explicitly protected guarantees, and is dependent on the main right in the interest of which the right to water is protected.[27] It thus lacks an independent or free-standing status in its own right, and its realisation *per se* cannot be demanded by right-holders.

On this argument, the right to drinking and sanitation water remains under the 'shadows' of such rights as the right to health and the right to

[24] See 'Statement from Seminar on Social, Economic and Cultural Rights in the African Charter' (adopted in Pretoria, 13–17 September 2004; published in 5 *African Human Rights Law Journal* (2005) 182, 186 (para. 7).

[25] Amanda Cahill, '"The Human Right to Water – A Right of Unique Status": The Legal Status and Normative Content of the Right to Water', 9(3) *International Journal of Human Rights* (2005) 389–410, 394.

[26] See generally *ibid.*

[27] Amanda Cahill, 'Protecting Rights in the Face of Scarcity: The Right to Water' in Mark Gibney and Sigrun Skogly (eds.), *Universal Human Rights and Extraterritorial Obligations* (University of Pennsylvania Press, 2010) 194, 194.

dignity. Claims of the right to water should thus be 'enveloped' therewith and claimed as such. Because the human right to water is protected due to its utility to other rights, the human right to water would take the form of a derivative or subordinate right the violation of which can only be complained of when the parent rights are violated. In the derivative sense, the relationship between the human right to water and its derivative source (parent right) is such that the former is a small subset of the latter.[28] Its violation thus arises only when the parent right is violated in situations that involve the victim's access to an adequate quantity and quality of water. Consequently, the right to water in its derivative sense can only be guaranteed to the extent of its utility to and overlapping with the derivative source from which it springs.

The implication of the derivative human right to water for the duty of the states is equally problematic: the obligation it creates varies depending upon whether the right is subsumed under other human rights or is recognised as a stand-alone right.[29] As Cahill observed, in its derivative sense, 'surely only certain aspects of the right to water will be protected and implemented'.[30]

This leaves the status of the right on shaky ground where it is neither fully recognised nor fully excluded from the ambit of the protection of the Charter's guarantees. Unlike its jurisprudence on the right to housing and the right to food, in which it unambiguously affirmed the existence of free-standing rights, the Commission left the normative status of the right to water in a penumbra of doubt.

Needless to say, the parent rights can be protected or violated without necessarily involving the violations of the right to water, and the right to water can be realised or violated independently of the parent rights. For instance, a state's provision of water may fall below the amount or quality needed to realise right-holders' basic access to drinking and sanitation water, thereby violating the human right to water. However, the impact of such a scenario on the right to dignity, health or food of the right-holders might not be visible in the short term.

Moreover, under the derivative approach, the scope of the right to water varies depending upon which right it is assumed to be part of, and its legal basis remains diffuse. This obscures the normative content of the

[28] *Ibid.*

[29] See Amy Hardberger, 'Whose Job Is It Anyway? Governmental Obligations Created by the Human Rights to Water', 41 *Texas International Law Journal* (2006) 533–68, 535.

[30] Cahill (note 25 above) 394.

right and bedevils its standardisation and progressive development as an independent entitlement. Therefore, the derivative approach to the human right to water, taken on its own, gives a truncated and abbreviated picture of the right.

Normally, the African Commission has been far less hesitant to read latent rights into the more explicit guarantees of the Charter. And the Commission has explicitly stated that it would consistently follow its own jurisprudence in its approach to the interpretation and application of Charter-based rights.[31] However, the Commission has fallen behind its own jurisprudence in the explication of the human right to water. Its case law on the right to water is in stark contrast to its usually purposive interpretation of the Charter that enabled the discovery of latent rights. In its decision in the *SERAC* case, the Commission took a very innovative approach of reading-in fundamental rights and freedoms that were not explicit in the Charter.[32] Following a teleological approach to the interpretation of the provisions of the regional treaty, the Commission read in and inferred the rights to food and housing from other more explicit rights of the African Charter. The Commission stated:

> [t]he Communication argues that the right to food is implicit in the African Charter, in such provisions as the right to life (Art. 4), the right to health (Art. 16) and the right to economic, social and cultural development (Art. 22). By its violation of these rights, the Nigerian Government trampled upon not only the explicitly protected rights but also upon the right to food implicitly guaranteed.[33]

In the same vein, the Commission ruled that the human right to housing, one of those rights that are not explicit in the African human rights treaties, is implicit in other rights that are more explicitly guaranteed. It acknowledged the lack of an explicit guarantee for the right to shelter in the African Charter, but read in the same from related guarantees of the regional treaty. It ruled:

> [a]lthough the right to housing or shelter is not explicitly provided for under the African Charter, the corollary of the combination of the provisions protecting the right to enjoy the best attainable state of mental and physical health, cited under Article 16 above, the right to property,

[31] See note 58 below and the accompanying text.

[32] Dinah Shelton, 'Decision Regarding Communication 155/96 (Social and Economic Rights Action Centre/Centre for Economic and Social Rights v. Nigeria)', 96 *American Journal of International Law* (2002) 937–42, 941.

[33] *SERAC* case, paras. 64–5.

> and the protection accorded to the family forbids the wanton destruction of shelter because when housing is destroyed, property, health, and family life are adversely affected. It is thus noted that the combined effect of Articles 14, 16 and 18(1) reads into the Charter a right to shelter or housing which the Nigerian Government has apparently violated.[34]

In effect, the Commission has shown a willingness to explicate some of the implicit human rights from other explicitly recognised guarantees. The analysis of the somewhat limited jurisprudence of the African Commission has shown that socio-economic rights that are not explicitly recognised in the Charter should be regarded as implicitly included. Commenting on the emerging jurisprudence of the Commission, authors have concluded that, 'where content falls short of international standards, the Commission is ... interpreting the provisions of the Charter in ways that generally conform to such standards'.[35]

But, having been presented with numerous opportunities to elaborate the normative basis and content of the human right to water, the Commission consistently side-stepped the question. Considered against the backdrop of the emerging trend of the African Commission's case law in which the Commission read implicit rights into those which are explicitly guaranteed, it may be expected that the Commission would follow the same route in future cases to declare the existence of a free-standing human right to water under the African Charter.

This is a sensible approach on many scores. First, it serves the purpose and object of the Charter, in which member states undertook the 'duty to promote and protect human and peoples' rights and freedoms'.[36] Secondly, it is also in line with the Commission's duty 'to formulate and lay down principles and rules aimed at solving legal problems relating to human and peoples' rights and fundamental freedoms upon which African Governments may base their legislation'.[37] Thirdly, in discovering and explicating what is only a latent right of the Charter, the Commission would only affirm what numerous African states have already accepted elsewhere at the international level. For instance, in the Abuja Declaration, adopted by forty-five African and twelve South American states at the First Africa–South America Summit in 2006,

[34] *Ibid.*, para. 60.

[35] Heyns (note 6 above) 69; Gino J. Naldi, 'Limitation of Rights under the African Charter on Human and Peoples' Rights: The Contribution of the African Commission on Human and Peoples' Rights', 17 *South African Journal on Human Rights* (2001) 109–18, 117.

[36] African Charter, Preamble, para. 11.

[37] African Charter, Article 45(1)(b).

states undertook to 'promote the right of our citizens to have access to clean and safe water and sanitation within our respective jurisdictions'.[38] This trend was repeated at the global level, particularly when a resolution unambiguously recognising the human right to water was put to the vote of the member states at the UN General Assembly.[39] This resolution was passed with 122 votes in favour, including the positive votes of at least thirty-two African states, none voting against it.

Granted, the Commission would not create a totally new right or obligation that states have not undertaken or envisaged. As noted above, elements of the human right to water have already been provided for at the African level in the ACWRC, the Women's Protocol and the Nature Convention. Finally, member states of the African Charter have already enshrined the right to water in their domestic legislation[40] or judicial decisions.[41] The Commission, in addition to Charter-based grounds of the right to water, may rely on African domestic legislative and judicial practices recognising the right to water as inspirational sources in order to ground the right in the African Charter. While Article 45 of the Charter normally envisages the situation where the Commission's case law inspires domestic legal principles and judicial practices, there is nothing in the Charter that prevents the reverse scenario, wherein the Commission borrows from domestic laws and judicial practices. After all, the monitoring and promotional mandate of the Commission is designed to enable the Commission to obtain the whole picture of the human rights situation in the continent and then 'distil the wisdom of that collective experience into advice which is made available to all interested parties'.[42] In this sense, the rights and freedoms enshrined in the Charter are in a constant dialogue with domestic legal

[38] Abuja Declaration, adopted at First Africa–South America Summit, 26–30 November 2006 (Abuja, Nigeria), para. 18, available at www.asasummit-abuja2006.org (accessed 23 June 2011).

[39] See General Assembly Adopts Resolution Recognizing Access to Clean Water, Sanitation, 64th General Assembly Plenary, 108th Meeting (AM)) (General Assembly GA/10967), 28 July 2010.

[40] For a South African example, see Anton Kok and Malcolm Langford, 'The Right to Water' in Danie Brand and Christof Heyns (eds.), *Socio-Economic Rights in South Africa* (Pretoria University Law Press, 2005) 191, 197–8.

[41] This has been the case in South Africa and Botswana. See *Lindiwe Mazibuko and Others* v. *City of Johannesburg and Others*, Case CCT 39/09, [2009] ZACC 28. See also *Matsipane Mosetlhanyane and Others* v. *Attorney-General of Botswana*, Court of Appeal, CALB-074-10 (unreported).

[42] 'The African Commission on Human and Peoples' Rights Information Sheet No. 4', www.achpr.org/ACHPR_inf._sheet_No.4.doc (accessed 30 August 2011).

systems and practices, influencing and at the same time being influenced by positive legislative and judicial developments at the domestic plane in the member states. This is not confined to the practice of the Commission or Africa as judicial and quasi-judicial bodies elsewhere have long heeded the approach.[43]

3.2.3 *Other regional treaties: the African Nature Convention*

The African region is the foremost continent to have adopted binding treaties, albeit not human rights norms *per se*, that provide for direct and indirect legal grounds for the normative development, protection and promotion of the human right to water. Predating the adoption of any of the African human rights treaties, the African Nature Convention was described, as at 1985, as 'the most comprehensive multilateral treaty for the conservation of nature yet negotiated'.[44] Its adoption was necessitated, among other things, by the level of environmental disasters on the continent such as drought, desertification and deterioration of water resources.[45] In terms of the impact of the Nature Convention on legislative reforms, as early as two decades ago, studies have revealed that the Nature Convention 'has stimulated useful conservation measures in some countries and remains the framework on which a substantial body of legislation is based'.[46]

The Nature Convention contains substantive provisions that are pertinent to the promotion and protection of the human right to water. Under its Article II (fundamental principle), state parties thereto undertook 'to adopt the measures necessary to ensure conservation, utilization and development of soil, water ... in accordance with scientific

[43] See generally Anthea Roberts, 'Comparative International Law? The Role of National Courts in Creating and Enforcing International Law', 60(1) *International and Comparative Law Quarterly* (2011) 57–92.

[44] Simon Lyster, *International Wildlife Law: An Analysis of International Treaties Concerned with the Conservation of Wildlife* (Grotius Publications, 1985) 115. See also Michel Prieur, 'Protection of the Environment' in Mohammed Bedjaoui (ed.), *International Law: Achievements and Prospects* (UNESCO, 1991) 1017, 1035.

[45] Morne van der Linde, 'A Review of the African Convention on Nature and Natural Resources', 2 *African Human Rights Law Journal* (2002) 33–59.

[46] Lyster (note 44 above) 115. A study revealed that no less than thirty constitutions of the then fifty-four states of the continent enshrine the right to environment, and it is within the framework of this right that the human right to water is usually mentioned in Africa. See Christof Heyns and Waruguru Kaguongo, 'Constitutional Human Rights Law in Africa', 22(4) *South African Journal on Human Rights* (2006) 673–717, 707.

principles and with due regard to the best interests of the people'. The Nature Convention enunciates both the quantity and quality components of water provisions. The most pertinent provision, however, is found under Article V(1).[47] It relates to the provision of water quantity, and stipulates:

> The contracting States shall establish policies for conservation, utilization and development of underground and surface water, and *shall endeavour to guarantee for their populations a sufficient and continuous supply of suitable water.*[48]

On the other hand, Article V(1)(d) addresses the issue of water quality, and provides for states' duty of 'prevention and control of water pollution'. Although the provisions are stated in the language of state duties (as opposed to subjective rights), these duties are meant to accrue to the human beneficiaries and, by implication, may be claimed by individuals and groups. The cumulative reading of Article II and Article V of the Nature Convention leads to the conclusion that states parties are obliged to provide a sufficient and continuous supply of unpolluted water to their respective populations (hence, individuals and groups in those states are entitled to claim the same). The African Commission can also ground its analysis and interpretation of the human right to water on this Convention. Under Article 61, the Commission 'shall also take into consideration … general or special international conventions, laying down rules expressly recognised by Member States of the Organization of African Unity'. Conversely, the member states of the Charter have affirmed from the outset 'their adherence to the principles of human and peoples' rights and freedoms contained in the declarations, conventions and *other instruments adopted by the Organization of African Unity*'.[49]

The Nature Convention was revised[50] in order to bring it into line with the principles and guidelines developed at various conferences,

[47] See Desheng Hu, *Water Rights: An International and Comparative Study* (IWA Publishing, 2006) 97.

[48] Article V(1), emphasis added.

[49] See African Charter, Preamble, para. 10 (emphasis added).

[50] African Convention on the Conservation of Nature and Natural Resources, adopted in Maputo, Mozambique, on 11 July 2003. It will enter into force thirty days after the deposit of the fifteenth instrument of ratification in accordance with its Article 38. As at 16 May 2013, the Convention had been ratified or acceded to by nine states and will need a further six in order to come into force. See Status of Ratifications at: http://au.int/en/treaties (accessed 28 June 2013).

including the Rio Declaration.[51] In its preamble,[52] it clearly states that the revised Nature Convention was adopted so as to respond to the 'need to continue furthering the principles of the Stockholm Declaration, to contribute to the implementation of the Rio Declaration and of Agenda 21, and to work closely together towards the implementation of global and regional instruments supporting their goals'.[53]

As discussed below, the right of individuals and groups to be provided with a 'sufficient' and 'continuous' supply of 'suitable' water, which is provided for under Article V(1) of the Nature Convention, corresponds to the minimum core of the human right to water. Arguably, therefore, the Nature Convention enshrines a concrete and firm normative source for the states' duty to ensure the enjoyment of the human right to water in Africa. The African Commission could avail itself of the provisions of the Nature Convention in the determination and/or elaboration of relevant cases related to the human right to water.[54]

3.3 The use of extraneous rules and the relevance of developments at the universal level

A special feature of the African Charter is a wide latitude of sources from which the African Commission is to draw inspiration in its promotional and protective mandates.[55] The promotional mandate of the Commission includes setting standards and formulating principles related to human and people's rights entrusted to it under Article 45 of the Charter. The African Commission:

> shall draw inspiration from international law on human and peoples' rights, particularly from the provisions of various African instruments on Human and Peoples' Rights, the Charter of the United Nations, the Charter of the Organization of African Unity, the Universal Declaration of Human Rights, other instruments adopted by the United Nations and by African countries in the field of Human and

[51] As regards the human right to water, the content of relevant provisions remains intact in the revised Nature Convention. For a detailed discussion of the revised version of the Convention and the changes introduced thereby, see, Linde (note 45 above) 49–56.

[52] See para. 12.

[53] As Linde commented, the substantive provisions of the 1968 Nature Convention are not exactly in line with the Rio instruments and other contemporary multilateral treaties and subsequent developments on the subject. See Linde (note 45 above) 43.

[54] See note 49 above and the accompanying text.

[55] Under Article 30 of the African Charter, the Commission is entrusted with the duty 'to promote human and peoples' rights and ensure their protection in Africa'.

> Peoples' Rights, as well as from the provisions of various instruments adopted within the Specialised Agencies of the United Nations of which the Parties to the present Charter are members.[56]

The Charter has thus provided a broad reference to sources on which the African Commission may rely in interpreting the rights and freedoms implicitly and explicitly guaranteed under the Charter. The use of the phrase 'shall draw inspiration' implies that the Commission is enjoined to have recourse to international law, principles, jurisprudence and precedents of the universal and regional human rights systems and mechanisms.

The interpretive latitude provided by Article 60 of the Charter is of crucial relevance in constructing ambiguities involving such cases as the human right to water which clearly falls within the visions of the Charter but lacks express protection. The Charter sought to instruct and empower the Commission to give due consideration to the wisdom, experience and emerging jurisprudence of the other regional systems and UN bodies to enrich its own promotional and protective roles. It has been noted that Article 60 of the Charter bears testimony to the fact that the Charter's provisions were inspired by universal human rights norms embedded in the UN Charter, the Universal Declaration of Human Rights and other global human rights instruments.[57] The Commission has stated its compliance with this provision: '[i]n interpreting the African Charter, the African Commission relies on its own jurisprudence, and as provided by Articles 60 and 61 of the African Charter, on appropriate and relevant international and regional human rights instruments, principles and standards'.[58] Developments in the area of human and peoples' rights in the other regional human rights system as well as within the UN system of human rights have thus influenced the interpretation and application of the African Charter.

Accordingly, global and regional developments in the area of human and peoples' rights will continue to have more than knock-on effects on the African regional human rights jurisprudence.[59] Indeed, the

[56] African Charter, Article 60.

[57] George William Mugwanya, *Human Rights in Africa: Enhancing Human Rights through the African Regional Human Rights System* (Transnational Publishers, 2003) 190.

[58] Communication 292/2004, *Institute for Human Rights and Development in Africa* v. *Republic of Angola*, 24th Annual Activity Report (2008), para. 78.

[59] It has been rightly asserted that the Commission would use only those practices and precedents which are in line with the letter and the spirit of the Charter, and the duty to

Commission has used the provisions of Article 60 very liberally in order to bring the Charter into line with international practices.[60]

More specifically, the Commission has repeatedly referred to the General Comments of the United Nations Committee on Economic, Social and Cultural Rights (CESCR) in the interpretation of some of the controversial provisions of the African Charter. In the *SERAC* case, the Commission clearly stated that it sought to draw inspiration from General Comment No. 7 of the CESCR on the definition of forced evictions, the meaning of which was lacking under the African Charter.[61] Likewise, the Commission relied on General Comment No. 4 of the CESCR for an analysis of the right to adequate housing.[62]

This approach would certainly prove helpful as regards clarification of the legal basis of the human right to water under the African Charter. In this context, General Comment No. 15 of the CESCR is currently the single most pertinent, comprehensive, elaborate and firmly persuasive source of inspiration for the determination of issues relating to the legal basis, implementation and redress of violations of the human right to water in the African human rights system.

As discussed in Chapter 2, General Comment No. 15 of the CESCR relied on three overlapping approaches to the discovery of the latent human right to water: teleological interpretation, the derivative approach and state practice. All three approaches are relevant for the progressive development of the fledgling case law of the African Commission, some of which has already been employed by the regional human rights body.

Given the object and purpose of the African Charter, which include securing individuals' and groups' right to the necessities of livelihood, it is appropriate for the African Commission to read the right to water into other rights that are explicitly guaranteed in the African Charter (such as the right to life, dignity, health, healthy environment) in a way that helps establish a free-standing entitlement which the beneficiaries can claim in

draw inspiration from non-African legal sources does not necessarily imply, perhaps obviously, a wholesale grafting of the latter in the interpretation of the Charter. However, when the Charter is silent on certain aspects or all of a right deserving of protection, the Commission would borrow the principles applied at the level of other regional human rights jurisdictions and the UN bodies. See Odinkalu (note 3 above) 352–4.

60 See Heyns (note 6 above) 688–9; Fatsah Ouguergouz, *The African Charter on Human and Peoples' Rights: A Comprehensive Agenda for Human Dignity and Sustainable Democracy in Africa* (Kluwer Law International, 2003) 567–8.

61 *SERAC* case, para. 63.

62 *Ibid.*

its own right. This is in line with the regional jurisprudence, where the Commission allowed the 'reading-in' of implicit rights to food and shelter into other rights and freedoms of the African Charter. The Commission has indeed ruled that 'the Charter must be interpreted holistically and all clauses must reinforce each other'.[63] What is more, the Commission should follow the example of the CESCR to affirm the existence of a fully fledged, free-standing human right to water within the regional human rights instruments.

3.4 Conclusion

The human right to water has been a Cinderella of the Charter's socio-economic rights guarantees. The ambiguity surrounding the legal basis and normative content of the right to water is in part characteristic of the remainder of all the socio-economic rights of the Charter, albeit aggravated in the case of the right to water by the absence of an explicit mention of the right in the regional instrument. However, the effects of the absence of an explicit and comprehensive protection of the human right to water in the African Charter have been somewhat mitigated by the African Commission's purposive approach to the interpretation of other guarantees of the Charter in a manner that envelops the right to water. The Commission grounded the legal basis of the right in provisions guaranteeing the right to health, the right to a healthy environment and the right to dignity. Yet, the Commission has failed to explicate the normative status and content of the right. There also remains abundant doubt as to whether the right is an autonomous entitlement *per se* or is an auxiliary guarantee that is used to ensure the realisation of other rights of the Charter. In addition, the legal basis of the right is rendered diffuse as the Commission has located it in differing rights on a case-by-case basis. This has left the right to water on shifting and amorphous legal bases and has entailed normative problems for the right-holders as well as duty-bearers. In short, the Commission has grounded the right on narrowly defined legal bases. The Commission should follow the approach of General Comment No. 15 which declared an autonomous right to water, and defined its normative content and related states' obligations. In short, the right only needs discovery instead of invention.

[63] Communication 211/98, *Legal Resources Foundation* v. *Zambia*, 14th Annual Activity Report (2000), para. 17.

The Commission needs to revisit its stance on the right to water, and clearly state that the Charter does indeed protect the right, albeit in implicit terms. It has to return to its usual stance of reading-in implicit rights in such a way that facilitates the right's explication. The analogous practice of the CESCR where the right to water is not explicit in the ICESCR also suggests that the Commission would be within its right to have recourse to such a purposive approach to treaty interpretation in order to bring out the latent content of the treaty.

4

The human right to water and states' domestic obligations

> Human rights come to institutional existence in their performative declaration, which declares what it creates and creates the ground upon which it stands.[1]

4.1 Introduction

Human rights guarantees are promises whose realisation depends upon the fulfilment of the correlative duties[2] by state and, to a lesser degree, non-state actors. The human right to water is no exception. Traditionally, international human rights law has seen state actors as the primary duty-bearers,[3] and this is still mainly[4] the case to

1 Costas Douzinas, *The End of Human Rights: Critical Legal Thought at the Turn of the Century* (Hart Publishing, 2007) 343.

2 The whole international human rights regime is tailored towards establishing 'a binary relationship between right-holders and duty bearers'. See Margot E. Salomon, *Global Responsibility for Human Rights: World Poverty and the Development of International Law* (Oxford University Press, 2007) 132.

3 Ronald Tinnevelt and Gert Verschraegen, 'Global Justice between Cosmopolitan Ideals and State Sovereignty: An Introduction' in Ronald Tinnevelt and Gert Verschraegen (eds.), *Between Cosmopolitan Ideals and State Sovereignty: Studies in Global Justice* (Palgrave Macmillan, 2006) 1, 7–8; Hadewych Hazelzet *et al.*, 'Conclusions – New Human Rights Duty-Bearers: A Conversation on Policy Implications' in Margot E. Salomon, Arne Tostensen and Wouter Vandenhole (eds.), *Casting the Net Wider: Human Rights, Development and New Duty-Bearers* (Intersentia, 2007) 395, 396.

4 There is now an emerging realisation of the significance of the increasingly proliferating and powerful non-state actors whose acts or omissions could promote or jeopardise the realisation of human rights across the globe. Accordingly, there has been a growing discussion and normative development towards the direct attribution of human rights duties to non-state entities such as United Nations (UN) bodies, multinational corporations, non-governmental organisations and others. See, for example, CESCR, 'General Comment No. 15: Substantive Issues Arising in the Implementation of the International Covenant on Economic, Social and Cultural Rights (Adopted 11–29 November 2002)' (UN Committee on Economic, Social and Cultural Rights, 11–29 November 2002),

date.[5] A complete account of a human rights regime therefore necessitates an analysis of the right in question and the correlative duties[6] of the agents charged with the responsibility of carrying the human rights promises into reality.[7] A right is fulfilled when the correlative duty is performed by the relevant agent. The performance of the duty could involve the carrying out of a required action (positive duty) or the abstention from the commission of a prohibited action (negative duty).[8] A right is infringed when the relevant agent fails to perform a positive duty, or when it fails to refrain from the commission of a negative obligation, or both.[9] In other words, the implementation of human rights, including the human right to water, necessitates 'a

para. 60 (referring to 'obligations of actors other than states'); Andrew Clapham, *Human Rights Obligations of Non-State Actors* (Oxford University Press, 2006); Celia Wells and Juanita Elias, 'Catching the Conscience of the King: Corporate Players on the International Stage' in Philip Alston (ed.), *Non-State Actors and Human Rights* (Oxford University Press, 2005) 141; Francesco Francioni, 'Alternative Perspectives on International Responsibility for Human Rights Violations by Multinational Corporations' in Wolfgang Benedek, Koen de Feyter and Fabrizio Marrella (eds.), *Economic Globalisation and Human Rights* (Cambridge University Press, 2007) 245; Shadrack Agbakwa, 'A Line in the Sand: International (Dis)order and the Impunity of Non-State Corporate Actors in the Developing World' in Antony Anghie *et al.* (eds.), *The Third World and International Disorder: Law, Politics and Globalization* (Martinus Nijhoff Publishers, 2003).

5 As has been affirmed by the World Conference on Human Rights in Vienna in 1993, states continue to bear the primary responsibility for human rights enforcement. See Vienna Declaration and Program of Action, United Nations, A/CONF.157/23, Preamble (5th paragraph) and Part I, para. 1 (para. 3).

6 The analysis of the normative structure of rights through rights–duties correlatives was developed by Hohfeld. In Hohfeld's scheme of *fundamental legal conceptions*, *jural correlatives* refer to the two parties in an elementary juridical relationship. A's right in relation to B corresponds to B's duty towards A. See Wesley Newcomb Hohfeld, *Fundamental Legal Conceptions as Applied in Judicial Reasoning and Other Legal Essays* (Yale University Press, 1923) 5. According to Scheinin, the Hohfeldian binary relationship of jural opposites 'can be reduced into each other', and to say that A has a right is the same as saying that B has a duty towards A in relation to the right in question. He thus argued, 'only one of them is actually needed for describing the normative structure'. See Martin Scheinin, 'Direct Applicability of Economic, Social and Cultural Rights: A Critique of the Doctrine of Self-Executing Treaties' in Drzewicki Krzysztof, Catarina Krause and Allan Rosas (eds.), *Social Rights as Human Rights: A European Challenge* (Institute for Human Rights, Abo Akademi University, 1994) 73, 77. For a similar argument, see generally A. K. W. Halpin, 'Hohfeld's Conceptions: From Eight to Two', 44(3) *Cambridge Law Journal* (1985) 435–57.

7 Alan Gewirth, 'Are There Any Absolute Rights?' in Jeremy Waldron (ed.), *Theories of Rights* (Oxford University Press, 1984) 91, 92.

8 *Ibid.* 9 *Ibid.*

normative direction concerning the conduct of related actors',[10] giving rise to the challenge of linking the expectations of individual and group right-holders to the obligations owed by duty-bearers.

The preceding two chapters analysed the normative content of the human right to water, with the implications that at least the minimum core of the right must be carried into effect immediately and continuously by the duty-bearers irrespective of the amount of resources available at their disposal. The present chapter examines the correlative duties of states in the implementation of the human right to water in their respective jurisdictions. The analysis explores the layers (typologies) of interrelated and interdependent state duties in the implementation of human rights in general, with an eye on its implications for the realisation of the human right to water in particular. Using the typologies of state duties, the chapter also revisits the implications of resource constraints in the implementation of states' duties in the realisation of the human right to water. The exploration of the duties of immediate implementation and progressive realisation of the human right to water leads to the reappraisal of the state's international duty of assistance and cooperation, an area where little normative progress has been made jurisprudentially. It is argued that the shared nature of the great bulk of the world's fresh water sources means that the implementation of the human rights duties of states and the fate of right-holders would be in jeopardy unless the rights and duties entailed by international assistance and cooperation are made fully operational.

4.2 The typologies of state obligations

Regardless of their normative content and sources, all international human rights standards such as the human right to water are meant for domestic implementation. The desired result of human rights treaties is the enjoyment by individual human beings and groups of the rights stipulated in those treaties. Thus an ideal human rights treaty is one under which the principal rights and entitlements are exercised and enjoyed by a wide range of individuals and groups on the domestic plane.[11]

[10] Stephen R. Tully, 'The Contribution of Human Rights to Freshwater Resource Management', 14 *Yearbook of International Environmental Law* (2003) 101–37, 103.

[11] Kevin Boyle, 'Stock-taking on Human Rights: The World Conference on Human Rights, Vienna 1993', 43(1) *Political Studies* (1995) 79–95, 82.

Consequently, the success or failure of any international human rights treaty is measured by its impact on human rights practices on the domestic level.[12] While ratification of international human rights treaties is a crucial first step towards the promotion and protection of human rights on the ground, 'ratification in itself is largely formal and in some cases an empty gesture'[13] unless the promises of the treaties are implemented by the ratifying states.

The human rights treaties almost invariably provide for specific human rights and mechanisms of monitoring and/or enforcement for their provisions in the form of, among others, courts, commissions and expert bodies. This has sometimes tended to impart the impression that the international mechanisms set up under the treaties are the prime actors (agents) for the realization of the rights and enforcement of states' duties under the relevant instrument.[14] Yet, it is the state – with its various laws, institutions and domestic procedures – that bears the primary brunt of responsibility for the translation of the treaty-based rights within the domestic sphere into reality. This has been reaffirmed by the World Conference on Human Rights in 1993, which stressed that '[the] protection and promotion [of human rights] is the *first responsibility* of governments'.[15]

In addition, the principle of subsidiarity dictates that international human rights standards supplement and complement the domestic human rights standards and that the primary agent for the implementation of international human rights remains the state party to a treaty.[16] As Henkin noted:

[12] C. H. Heyns and Frans Viljoen, *The Impact of the United Nations Human Rights Treaties on the Domestic Level* (Kluwer Law International, 2002) 1.

[13] *Ibid.*

[14] Jean-Bernard Marie, 'National System for the Protection of Human Rights' in Janusz Symonides (ed.), *Human Rights: International Protection, Monitoring and Enforcement* (Ashgate, 2003) 257, 275; Sigrun I. Skogly, 'The Obligation of International Assistance and Co-operation in the International Covenant on Economic, Social and Cultural Rights' in Morten Bergsmo (ed.), *Human Rights and Criminal Justice for the Downtrodden: Essays in Honour of Asbjørn Eide* (Martinus Nijhoff Publishers, 2003) 403, 403.

[15] See Vienna Declaration (note 5 above), Preamble (5th paragraph) and Part I, para. 1 (para. 3) (emphasis added). In the words of Lauterpacht, '[t]he preoccupations with the enforcement of the [international] Bill of Rights ought not to conceal the fact that the most effective way of giving reality to it is through the normal activity of national courts and other organs'. See H. Lauterpacht, *International Law and Human Rights* (Archon Books, 1968) 356; see also generally Boyle (note 11 above).

[16] Paolo G. Carozza, 'Subsidiarity as a Structural Principle of International Human Rights Law', 97 *American Journal of International Law* (2003) 38, 38; Marie (note 14) 257–8;

> [t]he international law of human rights parallels and supplements national law, superseding and supplying the deficiencies of national constitutions and laws, but it does not replace and indeed depends on national institutions.[17]

The need to move towards domestic implementation of international treaty provisions imposes essential obligations on the ratifying/acceding states. As Nickel observed:

> an emphasis on duties connected with rights has a number of practical advantages. One advantage of the emphasis on duties connected with rights is that it moves the debate in the direction of implementation, towards the question of who has to do what if these rights are to be realized.[18]

In contradistinction to the nature and content of specific human rights whose ambit may vary depending on the normative content of the right and the recognition of the same by states through ratification or accession to the relevant treaty,[19] a state's obligations engendered by the ratification of international human rights treaties enshrining the rights are more or less uniform and can comfortably fall into distinct categories. In other words, compared to (and independently of) the differing contents of the specific human rights, the framework within which a state's obligations are analysed shows elements of durability and universality. In the words of Leckie, 'the methodology of outlining state duties has proven a durable means of establishing accountability on economic, social and cultural rights, and has assisted greatly in work towards more clearly identifying, deconstructing and redressing violations of these rights'.[20] As the African Commission emphasised in its landmark decision of the *SERAC* case:

Mattias Kumm, 'The Legitimacy of International Law: A Constitutionalist Framework of Analysis', 15(5) *European Journal of International Law* (2004) 907–31, 920–1.

17 Louis Henkin, *The Rights of Man Today* (Stevens, 1979) 95.

18 James W. Nickel, 'How Human Rights Generate Duties to Protect and Provide', 15 *Human Rights Quarterly* (1993) 77–86, 85.

19 Young, for instance, argues that the right to health calls for priorities, duties and methods of supervision that are different to those necessitated by other rights such as the right to water or food. See Katharine G. Young, 'The Minimum Core of Economic and Social Rights: A Concept in Search of Content', 33 *Yale Journal of International Law* (2008) 113–75, 156. See also Lavanya Rajamani, *Differential Treatment in International Environmental Law* (Oxford University Press, 2006) 20. Cf. Upendra Baxi, *Human Rights in a Posthuman World: Critical Essays* (Oxford University Press, 2007) 40.

20 Scott Leckie, 'Another Step towards Indivisibility: Identifying the Key Features of Violations of Economic, Social and Cultural Rights', 20 *Human Rights Quarterly* (1998) 81–124, 91.

> [i]nternationally accepted ideas of the various obligations engendered by human rights indicate that all rights – both civil and political rights and social and economic – generate at least four levels of duties for a State that undertakes to adhere to a rights regime, namely the duty to respect, protect, promote, and fulfil these rights. These obligations *universally apply to all rights and entail a combination of negative and positive duties.* As a human rights instrument, the African Charter is not alien to these concepts and the order in which they are dealt with here is chosen as a matter of convenience and in no way should it imply the priority accorded to them. Each layer of obligation is equally relevant to the rights in question.[21]

A similar approach has been adopted by the other regional human rights mechanisms.[22] Indeed, it has been broadly acknowledged both in doctrine and in jurisprudence on human rights that states incur both positive and negative obligations in the realisation of all categories of human rights.[23] There is an emerging consensus that the realisation of any human right – including the human right to water – entails obligations on the part of the state parties to respect, protect, promote and fulfil.[24] This stratification of a state's human rights duties at four levels has consistently been used by the African Commission. This is explicit in its more recent decisions. For instance, in a case against Cameroon, it ruled that the four layers of obligations are analytic tools for gauging whether and to what extent a state has been implementing (or violating) a given human right,[25] while they also reflect the manner in which the

[21] Communication 155/96, *Social and Economic Rights Action Centre and the Centre for Economic and Social Rights* v. *Nigeria*, 15th Annual Activity Report (2001–2), para. 44 (emphasis added) ('the *SERAC* case').

[22] See, for instance, *X and Y* v. *The Netherlands*, 91 ECHR (1985), Ser. A; Inter-American Court of Human Rights, *Velàsquez Rodríguez Case*, Judgment of 19 July 1988, Ser. C, No. 4.

[23] Walter Kalin and Jorg Kunzli, *The Law of International Human Rights Protection* (Oxford University Press, 2009) 96.

[24] For the application and use of the four layers of state obligations in the analysis of specific human rights, see, for instance, the following General Comments of the CESCR: General Comment No. 19 (2008) on Right to Social Security, paras. 40–1; General Comment No. 18 (2005) on the Right to Work, paras. 23–8; General Comment No. 15 (2002) on the Right to Water, paras. 20–9; General Comment No. 14 (2000) on the Right to Health, paras. 30–7. See also CESCR, 'The Right to Food: Report of the Special Rapporteur on the Right to Food, Jean Ziegler' (UN Economic and Social Council (E/CN.4/2006/44, 16 March 2006)), paras. 21–7.

[25] See Communication 272/2003, *Association of Victims of Post Electoral Violence and Interights* v. *Cameroon*, 27th Annual Activity Report (2009), paras. 86–92.

state must behave in order to discharge its human rights obligations.[26] The CESCR has used a slightly different approach and treats the state's human rights obligations as three layers: respect, protect and fulfil. What the African Commission considers as a stand-alone *duty to promote* is subsumed under the *duty to fulfil* in the General Comments of the CESCR. According to the CESCR, therefore, the duty to 'fulfil' comprises the state's obligations to facilitate, promote and provide.[27] The African Charter[28] and the African Commission[29] treat the duty to promote as a separate, stand-alone duty of states.[30] Nevertheless, the essence of the duty to fulfil remains the same, both at the CESCR and at the African Commission levels, as it imposes the state's duty to facilitate the realisation of the right in question. For purposes of convenience and consistency with the African regional human rights system which is also the more proximate forum for victims of the human right to water in Africa, this book uses the four layers of duties as a framework of analysis.

4.2.1 The duty to respect

This layer of the state's obligation implies that the state should refrain from disturbing individuals' and groups' enjoyment of the right in question. In other words, it would be a violation of its human rights duties for a state to encroach upon the rights being exercised by the beneficiaries. The state should not do anything that has the direct or indirect effect of worsening the existing level of enjoyment of the human right concerned. The obligation to *respect* a human right therefore 'constitutes what is essentially a negative duty on the part of the state to neither impede nor restrict the exercise of these rights'.[31] In the *SERAC* case, the African Commission ruled that the duty to respect the Charter's rights and freedoms 'entails largely non-interventionist conduct from the State for example, not [*sic*] from carrying out, sponsoring

[26] Magdalena Sepúlveda, *The Nature of the Obligations under the International Covenant on Economic, Social, and Cultural Rights* (Intersentia, 2003) 172.

[27] See, for instance, CESCR, General Comment No. 15 (note 4 above), para. 25.

[28] See Articles 30 and 45 of the African [Banjul] Charter on Human and Peoples' Rights, adopted 27 June 1981, OAU Doc. CAB/LEG/67/3 Rev.5, 21 ILM 58 (1982) (entered into force 21 October 1986) ('African Charter').

[29] See *SERAC* (note 21 above), para. 44.

[30] See *ibid*., paras. 44 and 46.

[31] Scott Leckie and Anne Gallagher, 'Introduction: Why a Legal Resource Guide for Economic, Social and Cultural Rights?' in Scott Leckie and Anne Gallagher (eds.), *Economic, Social, and Cultural Rights: A Legal Resource Guide* (University of Pennsylvania Press, 2006) xiii, xx.

or tolerating any practice, policy or legal measures violating the integrity of the individual'.[32]

The duty to 'respect' human rights thus entails the injunction that the state should not encroach upon the existing enjoyment of human rights through, *inter alia*, the arbitrary revocation of law, principle or practice.[33] For instance, in a situation where a privatisation contract reassigns the water resources hitherto available to individuals and groups to a private company, the act of re-assignment might lead to the violation of the state's duty to respect the human right to water. This is particularly the case where the privatisation results in the curtailment of the individuals' and groups' access to adequate quantity and quality of water or makes the conditions of such access more onerous for the right-holders.[34] According to the African Commission, 'the obligation to respect entails that the State should refrain from interfering in the enjoyment of all fundamental rights; it should respect right-holders, their freedoms, autonomy, resources, and liberty of their action.'[35]

In the final analysis, the obligation to *respect* is primarily, if not exclusively, about those right-holders who have enjoyed the right in question. It basically requires inaction from the state concerned without necessarily requiring a state's positive action to improve the situation of those who are currently not accessing/enjoying the benefits of a given right. As the African Commission noted:

> [w]ith respect to socio-economic rights [including the human right to water], this means that the State is obliged to respect the free use of resources owned or at the disposal of the individual alone or in any form of association with others, including the household or the family, for the purpose of rights-related needs. And with regard to a collective group, the resources belonging to it should be respected, as it has to use the same resources to satisfy its needs.[36]

It is thus a 'minimalist undertaking'[37] and an obligation of 'primary level'[38] for states. As such, it constitutes an immediate obligation for the

[32] *SERAC* (note 21 above), para. 52. [33] *Ibid.*

[34] Melina Williams, 'Privatisation and the Human Right to Water: Challenges for the New Century', 28 *Michigan Journal of International Law* (2007) 469–506, 486.

[35] *SERAC* (note 21 above), para. 45 (footnote omitted). [36] *Ibid.*

[37] Philip Alston and Gerard Quinn, 'The Nature and Scope of States Parties' Obligations under the International Covenant on Economic, Social and Cultural Rights', 9 *Human Rights Quarterly* (1987) 156–229, 185.

[38] *SERAC* (note 21 above), para. 45.

state party to the African Charter or to the ICESCR.[39] The notion of states' duty to respect human rights as only encapsulating inaction and non-interference on the part of the state is reminiscent of the liberal political philosophy that advocates for a minimalist state, one which interferes as little as possible in individuals' autonomy and freedom.[40] This view considers the role of the state to be one of oversight (as opposed to interference), that sees to it that right-holders enjoy their rights and freedoms – the type referred to by Skogly as 'the night-watchman state', whose role is to protect its citizens from danger.[41] Although the duty to respect human rights is more closely related to rights traditionally categorised as civil and political, it has now equally come to be intimately associated with socio-economic rights, such as the human right to water.[42]

As a result, the implementation of this level of obligation generally does not involve resource redistribution or reallocation and, as such, it does not help improve the situation of those who do not have the preconditions necessary for the enjoyment of the right in question. In other words, the *respect* layer of a state's duty generally does not necessitate the allocation of safe and adequate quantity and quality of water to those who have not been able to enjoy their human right to water. It creates a situation where those who have enjoyed their human right to water continue to benefit from their prevailing advantageous position while the situation of those who have not had access to the enjoyment of the right remains the same at best.

4.2.2 The duty to protect

It is true that the human right to water can be violated unnecessarily and arbitrarily by commissions or omissions attributable to state interferences in the water resources, among others, through pollution, diversions and inequitable allocations. However, even when the duty to *respect* the

39 Manisuli Ssenyonjo, 'Reflections on State Obligations with Respect to Economic, Social and Cultural Rights in International Human Rights Law', 15(6) *International Journal of Human Rights* (2011) 969–1012, 975.

40 Sigrun I. Skogly, *Beyond National Borders: States Human Rights Obligations in International Cooperation* (Intersentia, 2006) 57.

41 *Ibid.*

42 Victor Dankwa, Cees Flinterman and Scott Leckie, 'Commentary to the Maastricht Guidelines on Violations of Economic, Social and Cultural Rights', 20 *Human Rights Quarterly* (1998) 705, 714.

human right to water is fully implemented by the state, it may be violated by third party actors (third states and non-state actors) in a manner that does not directly implicate the home state's responsibility. While the duty to respect is essentially about the imposition of limitations on the state's freedom of action, requiring it to refrain from deprivation of rights already in place, the duty to protect requires the state to act positively to regulate, prevent and remedy similar interferences by non-state actors.[43] As the African Commission stated, the protection of human rights requires legislation and the provision of effective remedies to ensure that right-holders are protected against other subjects and political, economic and social interferences.[44]

The duty to protect therefore requires the state to prevent and/or remedy the violations of human rights by third party interferences.[45] According to General Comment No. 15 of the CESCR, third parties include individuals, groups, corporations and other entities as well as agents acting under their authority.[46]

The obligation involves a heightened (positive) responsibility of the state in contrast to the duty to respect, due to the ensuing requirement that the state must issue laws and procedures and provide legal and institutional remedial avenues to enforce the horizontal duty of non-state and third-state actors. The duty to protect thus 'introduces a three-way relationship between the State, the right-holder . . . and the perpetrator of the breach'.[47] According to the CESCR, the state's duty to protect the human right to water entails:

> *inter alia*, adopting the necessary and effective legislative and other measures to restrain, for example, third parties from denying equal access to adequate water; and polluting and inequitably extracting from water resources, including natural sources, wells and other water distribution systems.[48]

[43] See Daphne Barak-Erez and Aeyal M. Gross, 'Introduction: Do We Need Social Rights? Questions in the Era of Globalisation, Privatisation, and the Diminished Welfare State' in Daphne Barak-Erez and Aeyal M. Gross (eds.), *Exploring Social Rights: Between Theory and Practice* (Hart Publishing, 2007) 3, 7–8; Aeyal M. Gross, 'The Right to Health in an Era of Privatisation and Globalisation: National and International Perspectives' in Daphne Barak-Erez and Aeyal M. Gross (eds.), *Exploring Social Rights: Between Theory and Practice* (Hart Publishing, 2007) 289, 303.

[44] *SERAC* (note 21 above), para. 46. [45] *Ibid.*

[46] CESCR, General Comment No. 15 (note 4 above), para. 23.

[47] Sandra Fredman, *Human Rights Transformed: Positive Rights and Positive Duties* (Oxford University Press, 2008) 73.

[48] CESCR, General Comment No. 15 (note 4 above), para. 23.

In the *SERAC* case, the African Commission found Nigeria in violation of its duty to protect the victims' (the Ogoni ethnic group) rights to life, food, water, shelter etc., which were blatantly violated through spoliation of the environment and water resources by the consortium of the Dutch Shell Company and the Nigerian National Petroleum Company.[49] Similarly, in the *Union des Jeunes Avocats* v. *Chad*, the African Commission decided that the state has the duty to protect its citizens through legislative and enforcement measures from the damaging acts that may be perpetrated by third parties in violation of the fundamental rights and freedoms guaranteed under the African Charter.[50] Chad was consequently found to be in violation of its duties under the African Charter because 'the state failed to protect the rights in the Charter from violation by other parties'.[51] The state's duty to protect remains intact in all circumstances and 'even a civil war in Chad cannot be used as an excuse by the State violating or permitting violations of rights in the African Charter'.[52] According to the African Commission, it is immaterial for the purposes of a state's duty to protect whether the state agents are actively involved in human rights violations:

> [t]he Charter specifies in Article 1 that the States Parties shall not only recognize the rights, duties and freedoms adopted by the Charter, but they should also 'undertake . . . measures to give effect to them'. In other words, if a state neglects to ensure the rights in the African Charter, this can constitute a violation, even if the State or its agents are not the immediate cause of the violation.[53]

In the area of the human right to water, the state's duty to protect assumes an enhanced significance due to the increasing tendency of privatisation of water services delivery in many countries. As Williams noted, in a privatisation of water services delivery the state must ensure that the service provider meets the requirements of the human right to water and, as such, the state's duty to protect individuals and groups remains intact despite privatisation of the delivery of the relevant services.[54] As Craven observed, 'even if the State may wish to leave the provision of public goods in the hands of private individuals or corporations, it remains ultimately responsible for the realisation of the

[49] *SERAC* (note 21 above), para. 46.

[50] See Communication 74/92, *Commission Nationale des Droits de l'Homme et des Libertes* v. *Chad*, 9th Annual Activity Report (1995–6).

[51] *Ibid.*, para. 18. [52] *Ibid.*, para. 21. [53] *Ibid.*, para. 20.

[54] See Williams (note 34 above) 486.

right'.[55] This duty requires the state to ensure that 'the operation of the market is fair and equitable and that marginalised and disadvantaged sectors of the population are guaranteed at least minimum levels of enjoyment'.[56]

According to the CESCR, while such privatisation arrangements *per se* do not constitute a violation of the state's duty to protect and can co-exist with the human right to water, a privatisation agreement does not entail a reassignment of the state's duty. In its General Comment No. 15, the CESCR observed that '[w]here water services (such as piped water networks, water tankers, access to rivers and wells) are operated or controlled by third parties, States parties must prevent them from compromising equal, affordable, and physical access to sufficient, safe and acceptable water'.[57] In order to prevent or remedy third parties' violations of the human right to water, 'an effective regulatory system must be established, in conformity with the Covenant and this General Comment [No. 15], which includes independent monitoring, genuine public participation and imposition of penalties for non-compliance'.[58]

4.2.3 *The duty to promote*

Another positive state obligation in the enforcement of human rights is the duty to *promote* human rights. This layer of state duties involves the facilitation of the enjoyment of the rights in question through the removal of obstacles that stand in the way of rights implementation and through the provisions of legal protections and procedures that pave the way for the enforcement of the rights. This implies that a comprehensive review of legislation takes place with a view to identifying laws and policies that negatively impact on the exercise of the rights.[59] In terms of the CESCR's General Comment No. 4, the duty to promote entails two separate state obligations.[60] On the one hand, it places emphasis on the necessity of preventing the designing and

[55] Matthew Craven, 'The International Covenant on Economic, Social and Cultural Rights' in Raija Hanski and Markku Suksi (eds.), *An Introduction to the International Protection of Human Rights: A Textbook* (Institute for Human Rights, Abo Akademi University, 2nd reprint edn, 2002) 101, 110.

[56] *Ibid.* [57] CESCR, General Comment No. 15 (note 4 above), para. 24. [58] *Ibid.*

[59] Leckie and Gallagher (note 31 above) xxi.

[60] See CESCR, 'General Comment No. 4: The Right to Adequate Housing (Art. 11(1) of the Covenant)' (UN Committee on Economic, Social and Cultural Rights, 13 December 1991), para. 11.

implementation of policies and legislation that have the tendency or effect of benefiting the already advantaged social groups at the expense of others. On the other hand, it requires the state to give due priority to those social groups living in unfavourable conditions by giving them particular consideration.

According to the African Commission, the state parties' commitment to 'give effect' to the rights and guarantees of the African Charter[61] entails the duty to ensure that individuals and groups are able to exercise the rights and freedoms enshrined in the Charter. This is achieved 'for example, by promoting tolerance, raising awareness, and even building infrastructures'.[62] In the context of the human right to water, the obligation to promote requires that states take steps to ensure, among other things, that there is 'appropriate education concerning the hygienic use of water, protection of water sources and methods to minimize water wastage'.[63] It also includes the provision of relevant environmental and hygienic information.

4.2.4 *The duty to fulfil*

This layer of state duties entails a 'direct provision of basic needs such as food or resources' in the event that the individuals and groups lack the means to access these resources.[64] The CESCR, referring to it as the *duty to provide* as part of the duty to fulfil, stated that the duty requires that the state supplies to individuals and groups water or the means to access it in the event that the right-holders are unable to access the water resources themselves due to causes beyond their control.[65]

The most important common denominator underpinning the approach of the African Commission and that of the CESCR is that the duty to fulfil is owed to those who, for one reason or another, could not access the resources necessary for the enjoyment of their rights. In relation to the human right to water, it means that, where, for instance, there is a lack of physical access to water resources within reasonable

[61] Article 1 of the African Charter stipulates: 'The Member States of the Organization of African Unity, parties to the present Charter shall recognise the rights, duties and freedoms enshrined in the Charter and shall undertake to adopt legislative or other measures to *give effect to them*' (emphasis added).

[62] *SERAC* (note 21 above), para. 46.

[63] CESCR, General Comment No. 15 (note 4 above), para. 25.

[64] *SERAC* (note 21 above), para. 47.

[65] CESCR, General Comment No. 15 (note 4 above) 25.

distances, the state is required to ensure water delivery at the local level. This is to ensure the establishment of water delivery facilities to provide water services within reachable distances.

Yet, this might benefit only those who could pay for the service thus provided, leaving out those without the capacity to pay for the services from their own means. Such a situation puts in jeopardy not only the human right to water, but also the related rights including the right to life, health and the right to equality. The duty to fulfil is therefore understood as entailing the state's duty to provide a minimum amount of free water for those who lack the resources to pay for the water they need for their personal and domestic uses.[66] Put otherwise, a state's duty to fulfil entails the state's obligation to provide the minimum amount of free water supplies to poorer and/or marginalised sections of the society whose very survival would be in peril without such assistance.

4.3 Interdependence of states' obligations

As outlined above, the four typologies of state obligations in the implementation of human rights are analytical tools for measuring the extent of the realisation (or the breach) of a given right. They are useful instruments for the translation of the complexities of human rights duties into simpler categories.[67] As Shue succinctly described them:

> [t]ypologies are at best abstract instruments for temporarily fending off the complexities of concrete reality that threaten to overwhelm our circuits ... [They] are ladders to be climbed and left behind, not monuments to be caressed and polished.[68]

Thus the full realisation of a human right depends on the performance by a state of all layers of its duties. There is no *a priori* order attached to the importance of the typologies of state obligations. Just in the same manner that human rights are interrelated and interdependent, so are the states' duties.[69] An attempt at the full implementation of a given

[66] *Ibid.*; Stephen McCaffrey, 'The Coming Fresh Water Crisis: International Legal and Institutional Responses', 21 *Vermont Law Review* (1997) 803–21, 817.

[67] Sepúlveda (note 26 above) 171. Writing a decade ago, Leckie similarly noted that '[w]ork on the right to housing, the right to health, the right to food, the right to education, and other [rights] has disaggregated the constituent elements of these rights based upon this now widely accepted interpretive tool'. See Leckie (note 20 above) 91.

[68] Henry Shue, *Basic Rights: Subsistence, Affluence, and US Foreign Policy* (Princeton University Press, 2nd edn, 1996) 160.

[69] Sepúlveda (note 26 above) 170.

human right necessitates the performance by the state of all layers of its duties.[70] According to the African Commission:

> [d]epending on the type of rights under consideration, the level of emphasis in the application of these duties varies. But sometimes, the need to meaningfully enjoy some of the rights demands *a concerted action from the State in terms of more than one of the said duties.*[71]

Craven observed that even the state's duty to respect human rights which would normally necessitate abstention requires the provision by the state of judicial remedies (duty to promote) in cases where the rights are breached.[72] The interdependence of states' duties has long been endorsed by the European Court of Human Rights in the *Marckx* case, where it was stated that:

> [a]s the Court stated in the 'Belgian Linguistic' case, the object of the Article is 'essentially' that of protecting the individual against arbitrary interference by the public authorities ... *Nevertheless it does not merely compel the State to abstain from such interference: in addition to this primarily negative undertaking, there may be positive obligations inherent in an effective 'respect' for family life.*[73]

Similarly, the duty to respect cannot be dissociated from the duty to protect as the non-interference by the state in the enjoyment of the rights would prove inadequate in the face of the possibilities of human rights violations by non-state actors.[74] In the same vein, if the state focuses merely on the implementation of its duty to respect and fails to protect individuals from third party encroachments, there is a real chance that right-holders will be deprived of the enjoyment of their rights by acts or omissions of non-state actors which would make it more cumbersome for the state to fulfil the duty relative to the right in issue.[75] In as much as human rights are indivisible, interrelated and interdependent irrespective of their traditional categorisations, the ensuing duties of states must be understood to operate in a state of systematic interdependence among them.[76] The typologies of state obligations are, therefore, of 'heuristic, mnemonic, pedagogical, and rhetorical value'.[77] They are convenient tools 'mixed together in various proportions in the implementation of

[70] *Ibid.* [71] *SERAC* (note 21 above), para. 48 (emphasis added).
[72] Craven (note 55 above) 109; Alston and Quinn (note 37 above) 184.
[73] *Marckx* v. *Belgium* (Merits and Just Satisfaction), Application No. 00006833/74 (Judgment of 13 June 1979), para. 31.
[74] Shue (note 68 above) 55. [75] Sepúlveda (note 26 above) 170–1.
[76] See Shue (note 68 above) 83–6; Leckie (note 20 above) 92. [77] Shue (note 68 above) 84.

just about every right'.[78] Each type of obligation is potentially a subject of violation and hence leads to state responsibility.[79] As Liebenberg observed:

> [t]hese duties cannot be surgically separated from each other and are often entwined in practice. For example, the duty to refrain from unfair discrimination (duty to respect) can frequently only be fulfilled by the taking of positive measures (e.g. to provide facilities for people with disabilities to participate equally in employment and society). Similarly, forced arbitrary evictions are a violation of the duty to respect the right to adequate housing, but also impose positive duties to take steps to provide appropriate alternative accommodation.[80]

The implementation of the four layers of obligations, therefore, involves the imposition of limitations on the state's freedom of action or requires the state's action as a protector and provider or both.[81] It must be noted that the real question is how to ensure that the state obligations are made operative in a manner that maintains the balance between the constraints the state human rights duties impose and the actions that they require in order that all layers of duties are translated into practice.[82]

4.4 Implementation of states' obligations: temporal dimensions

4.4.1 Introduction

Variations in the quantity and quality of resources at a state's disposal may make it more onerous for some states to ensure the full and immediate realisation of the specific human rights enshrined in the international human rights treaties. This invariably applies to the human right to water. However, each of the rights enshrined in the relevant treaties (including the human right to water) requires immediate and uninterrupted implementation by the state of the minimum core of the specific rights, while the full realisation of these rights may only entail the

[78] Henry Shue, 'The Independence of Duties' in P. Alston and K. Tomaseviski (eds.), *The Right to Food* (Martinus Nijhoff Publishers, 1984) 83, 84.
[79] Leckie (note 20 above) 92.
[80] Sandra Liebenberg, 'Adjudicating the Positive Duties Imposed by Economic, Social and Cultural Rights', 15(3) *Interights Bulletin* (2006) 109–13, 109.
[81] Asbjørn Eide, 'Realization of Social and Economic Rights and the Minimum Threshold Approach', 10(1–2) *Human Rights Law Journal* (1989) 35–51, 37–8.
[82] *Ibid.*, 38.

obligation to move towards a 'progressive' realisation. Under the obligations clause (Article 2(1)) of the ICESCR:

> [e]ach State Party to the present Covenant undertakes to take steps, individually and through international assistance and co-operation, especially economic and technical, to the maximum of its available resources, with a view to achieving progressively the full realization of the rights recognized in the present Covenant by all appropriate means, including particularly the adoption of legislative measures.

Accordingly, it is clearly open to states to implement some aspects of the rights in a progressive manner,[83] but they must nevertheless take steps immediately to that end, and must do so to the 'maximum of available resources' – in this case, principally water resources. The 'progressive realisation' clause cannot be used by states to delay indefinitely the implementation of the rights in question. The resource constraints cannot be used as an excuse for doing nothing.[84] According to the CESCR, Article 2(1) of the ICESCR entails 'an obligation to move as expeditiously and effectively as possible towards that goal [of full realisation of the rights recognised under the ICESCR]'.[85] If states possess the necessary resources, there would not be any justification for their failure to implement the rights fully and immediately.[86] It is necessary therefore to analyse the interplay of the immediate versus progressive dichotomy of states' obligations in light of the relevant treaty provisions.

[83] Notably, the socio-economic rights of the African Charter (and other regional instruments) are unencumbered by the incremental clauses of 'progressive realisation' associated with most ICESCR provisions. Coupled with the fact that socio-economic rights are put on an equal footing in the African instruments with civil and political rights, the absence of a language of incremental implementation has given rise to the argument that socio-economic rights – hence, by necessary implication, the right to water – are of immediate application. See Chidi Anselm Odinkalu, 'Implementing Economic, Social and Cultural Rights under the African Charter on Human and Peoples' Rights' in Malcolm Evans and Rachel Murray (eds.), *The African Charter on Human and Peoples' Rights: The System in Practice, 1986–2000* (Cambridge University Press, 2002) 178, 196.

[84] Craven (note 55 above) 108.

[85] CESCR, 'General Comment No. 3: The Nature of States Parties' Obligations (Art. 2, Para. 1, of the Covenant)' (UN Committee on Economic, Social and Cultural Rights, 1990), para. 9.

[86] Writing about the implementation of ICESCR rights in Australia, Otto and Wiseman observed that, in a developed state like Australia, 'the resources available should enable the government to come very close to fully realising the rights in the ICESCR'. Dianne Otto and David Wiseman, 'In Search of "Effective Remedies": Applying the International Covenant on Economic, Social and Cultural Rights to Australia', 7 *Australian Journal of Human Rights* (2001) 5–46, 18.

4.4.2 *Obligations of conduct and obligations of result*

The implementation of the four layers of state obligations necessitates an assessment of not only *whether* the state has achieved what is required of it under its human rights treaties, but also *how* it has conducted its affairs in the process of performing its obligations. In order to gauge the performance of a state in discharging these duties, the states' actions, inactions and achievements must be assessed in terms of the human rights standards.

For present purposes, the analysis of a state's performance in relation to the four obligations can further be broken down, depending upon whether the specific obligation prescribes or prohibits a certain type of *conduct* or necessitates the achievement of a certain *result*. Distinction is thus made between 'obligations of result' and 'obligations of conduct', a dichotomy that is 'considered essential for determining the existence of a breach of an international obligation [the four layers of duties] and when that breach has occurred'.[87]

An obligation of conduct can be active or passive,[88] but it points to behaviour which the duty-holder should follow or abstain from[89] without guaranteeing the achievement of the desired result. It requires states to take or refrain from taking a combination of certain legislative, executive and judicial measures in the implementation of human rights obligations.[90] The obligations of conduct raise the legal expectation on the part of the right-holders that the state must strive towards the realisation of a certain result.[91] In essence, it is an obligation to demonstrate due diligence in the discharge of the relevant duties.[92] In the *SERAC* case, the African Commission ruled that the duty to respect the Charter's rights and freedoms 'entails largely non-interventionist conduct from the State for example, not [*sic*] from carrying out, sponsoring or tolerating any practice, policy or legal measures violating the integrity of the individual'.[93] In finding Nigeria in violation of numerous rights and freedoms of its own citizens, the Commission decided that, not only its failure to promote and fulfil the rights at issue, but the way the government failed to respect and protect the victims was equally

[87] Sepúlveda (note 26 above) 186. [88] *Ibid.*, 185; Eide (note 81 above) 38.
[89] Eide (note 81 above) 38. [90] Sepúlveda (note 26 above) 186.
[91] Pierre-Marie Dupuy, 'Reviewing the Difficulties of Codification: On Ago's Classification of Obligations of Means and Obligations of Result in Relation to State Responsibility', 10(2) *European Journal of International Law* (1999) 371–85, 375.
[92] *Ibid.*, 378. [93] *SERAC* (note 21 above), para. 52.

prejudicial: '[b]y any measure of standards, its [Nigeria's] practice falls short of the minimum conduct expected of governments.'[94]

In contrast, the obligation of result is less concerned with (but without ignoring) the means used, and focuses on the achievement or avoidance of the results depending upon the type of the requisite result.[95] A state's failure to bring about the desired result implicates the state's responsibility for violation of the duty in question. The duty-bearer thus owes a precise result.[96] According to Sepúlveda, the key element of the obligation of result is that it allows the state the discretion as to the choice of means but requires that the results be achieved.[97] Consequently, whether the state provides the water necessary for the fulfilment of the human right to the same through state agencies, private companies or a combination of both is immaterial as long as the required quality and quantity of water is made accessible to the right-holders in a manner required by the human right to water.

The dividing line between obligations of result and obligations of conduct lies in the fact that, in the former, the mere fact of non-materialisation of the result constitutes a violation of the obligation, while the latter entails an obligation to make a *bona fide* effort with a view to achieving the result, but without guaranteeing its materialisation.[98] As a result, the obligation of result is considered as a 'perfect' obligation as opposed to obligations of conduct which are dubbed 'imperfect'.[99] Failure of a state either in relation to the required conduct or result constitutes a violation of its duties under the human rights treaties. State obligations to respect, protect, promote and fulfil consist simultaneously of dimensions of obligations of conduct and obligations of result.[100]

94 *Ibid.*, para. 58. 95 Eide (note 81 above) 38. 96 Dupuy (note 91 above) 375.

97 Sepúlveda (note 26 above) 186.

98 Georges Abi-Saab, 'The Legal Formulation of the Right to Development' in Rene-Jean Dupuy (ed.), *The Right to Development at the International Level, Workshop of the Hague Academy of International Law 1979* (Sijthoff and Noordhoff, 1980) 159, 173–4.

99 See generally George Rainbolt, 'Perfect and Imperfect Obligations', 98(3) *Philosophical Studies* (2000) 233–56; Baxi (note 19 above) 40; Eide (note 81 above) 38.

100 See Justice N. Nwobike, 'The African Commission on Human and Peoples' Rights and the Demystification of Second and Third Generation Rights under the African Charter: Social and Economic Rights Action Centre (SERAC) and the Centre for Economic and Social Rights (CESCR) v. Nigeria', 1 *African Journal of Legal Studies* (2005) 129–46, 130; Leckie (note 20 above) 92; 'The Maastricht Guidelines on Violations of Economic, Social and Cultural Rights' (Faculty of Law, University of Maastricht, 22–26 January 1997), para. 7 ('Maastricht Guidelines'). For an explanatory note on the Maastricht Guidelines, see note 135 below.

Making an explicit reference to the dichotomy introduced into international law by earlier works of the International Law Commission's (ILC) work on state responsibility,[101] the CESCR has used the obligations of conduct and obligations of result analysis as a tool of evaluating a state's performance in discharging their obligations entailed by the ICESCR.[102] Conversely, at least in one of its early reports on state responsibility, the ILC itself specifically recognised the relevance of the conduct–result dichotomy in the analysis of the degree of a state's implementation of human rights, and stated: '[a]n instance of a case where the distinction was of value ... was provided by Article 2, Paragraph 1 [addressing the nature of state obligations] of the International Covenant on Economic, Social and Cultural Rights, which contained a delicate mix of obligations of conduct and obligations of result.'[103] With its origin in the civil law tradition,[104] the dichotomy 'remains crucial in assessing a State's human rights performance under its treaties'.[105]

Yet, the interplay between the obligations of conduct and obligations of result and their respective relationship to the 'respect, protect, promote and fulfil' layers of state duties is a complex one. The state's duty to respect individuals' enjoyment of the right available is an obligation of result; all the state needs to do is to refrain from interfering in the existing enjoyment of rights.[106] It may well be that, for instance, the state can avoid violation of the human right to water by remaining passive, i.e. by abstention from interferences in the continued enjoyment of the right. As Eide noted, the obligation of result may not necessarily require that a state act as a provider of material goods such as water, and the fulfilment of the right in question may be ensured simply if the state remains passive.[107] Thus the state's performance of its obligation to 'respect' human rights (hence obligation of result) may lead to the

[101] CESCR, General Comment No. 3 (note 85 above), para. 1. [102] See *ibid.*

[103] See Report of the International Law Commission (51st Session, 1999), UN Doc. A/54/10 (1999), para. 132. Similarly, scholars have long used the obligations of conduct and the obligations of result dichotomy as means of gauging the state's human rights performances *vis-à-vis* its human rights obligations. See Matthew C. R. Craven, *The International Covenant on Economic, Social, and Cultural Rights: A Perspective on Its Development* (Clarendon Press, 1995), 107–9; Eide (note 81 above) 37–8; Guy S. Goodwin-Gill, 'Obligations of Conduct and Result' in P. Alston and K. Tomaseviski (eds.), *The Right to Food* (Martinus Nijhoff Publishers, 1984) 111, 111–18; Dupuy (note 96 above); Leckie (note 20 above) 92.

[104] Dupuy (note 91 above) 375. [105] Goodwin-Gill (note 103 above) 111.

[106] Eide (note 81 above) 38. [107] *Ibid.*

fulfilment of individuals' and groups' rights. Whether it is a conduct or a result that is required of a state thus depends upon circumstances and context, and this makes an answer in the abstract impossible.[108]

4.4.3 *The notion and implications of core obligations*

Due to the differential resource capacity of states, the timeline for the full implementation of socio-economic rights under the relevant treaties varies with each state party. As stated above, this does not imply that the state can lawfully postpone the realisation of the rights at the domestic level indefinitely. Some degree of each of the duties owed by states must be carried out immediately and continuously upon the coming into force of the treaty in the state under consideration. The question is as to which aspects of state duties are for immediate implementation regardless of the resource base, and which of these can be subjected to progressive realisation.

The CESCR in General Comment No. 15 identified 'a number of core obligations in relation to the right to water'.[109] Notwithstanding the 'progressive realisation' clause which underpins fundamental rights and freedoms enshrined in the ICESCR, the core obligations 'are of immediate effect'.[110] These core obligations correspond to the minimum core of the human right to water. As demonstrated in Chapters 2 and 3, the minimum core of the human right to water has been defined in terms of the types of uses involved, the adequacy of the quantity of water available to the right-holders and its quality as well as respect for equality of such access for the purposes of the selected uses.

Just in the same way that there must be non-negotiable levels of realisation of each human right (Chapters 2 and 3), there is also a minimum degree of performance required of states in the implementation of their human rights obligations. The effective implementation of states' obligations is, to varying degrees, dependent upon the resources available to the state. But the (un)availability of resources may not be used to absolve the state of its duties altogether at any one point. There is

[108] *Ibid.*

[109] CESCR, 'General Comment No. 15: Substantive Issues Arising in the Implementation of the International Covenant on Economic, Social and Cultural Rights (Adopted 11–29 November 2002)' (Committee on Economic, Social and Cultural Rights, 11–29 November 2002), para. 37.

[110] *Ibid.*, paras. 37 and 17.

a continuing, non-negotiable, and resource-independent minimum obligation that states should discharge at all times.[111] Any other approach to a state's human rights obligations makes the consequent enjoyment of human rights illusory.[112]

The concept of 'core minimum content' of state obligations was developed to curb the possible abuse by states of the 'wriggle room'[113] opened by the twin clauses of 'progressive realisation' and 'maximum available resources' under Article 2(1) of the ICESCR. It is rightly argued that '[t]he standard of progressive realisation also provides a loophole large enough in practical terms to nullify the Covenant's guarantees: the possibility that States will claim lack of resources as a reason they have not met their obligations'.[114] Despite the progressive normative clarification that Article 2(1) of the ICESCR has undergone, the definition and content of the concept of 'resources', or the 'maximum of available resources' more specifically, still remains vague at best.[115] The concept of 'minimum core obligation' therefore disentangles certain thresholds of state obligations from availability of resources and the caveat of progressivity and offers a 'non-derogable obligation, and an obligation of strict liability'.[116] This way, the minimum core of the right in question will continue to be guaranteed immediately and at all times.[117]

111 It has been argued that, 'notwithstanding the relative wealth of a given country, minimum core obligations are incumbent upon all states to secure minimum essential levels of each right found in the ICESCR'. See Dankwa, Flinterman and Leckie (note 42 above) 717.

112 The African Commission has proscribed resort to an interpretational approach that would have the effect of rending rights illusory. See African Commission, Communications 105/93, 128/94, 130/94 and 152/96, *Media Rights Agenda and Others* v. *Nigeria*, 12th Annual Activity Report (1998–9), para. 70. For the position of the CESCR on the concept of minimum core state obligations, see note 119 below and the accompanying text.

113 Robert E. Robertson, 'Measuring State Compliance with the Obligations to Devote the "Maximum Available Resources" to Realizing Economic, Social, and Cultural Rights', 16 *Human Rights Quarterly* (1994) 693–714, 694.

114 Audrey R. Chapman and Sage Russell, 'Introduction' in Sage Russell and Audrey R. Chapman (eds.), *Core Obligations: Building a Framework for Economic, Social and Cultural Rights* (Intersentia, 2002) 3, 5.

115 Sigrun Skogly, 'The Requirement of Using the "Maximum of Available Resources" for Human Rights Realisation: A Question of Quality as Well as Quantity?', 12(3) *Human Rights Law Review* (2012) 393–420, 396.

116 Young (note 19 above) 115.

117 Michelle Foster, *International Refugee Law and Socio-Economic Rights: Refuge from Deprivation* (Cambridge University Press, 2007), 172.

The 'most authoritative source'[118] of the minimum core content of socio-economic rights is to be found in the CESCR's General Comment No. 3:

> [o]n the basis of the extensive experience gained by the Committee, as well as by the body that preceded it, over a period of more than a decade of examining States parties' reports the Committee is of the view that a minimum core obligation to ensure the satisfaction of, at the very least, minimum essential levels of each of the rights is incumbent upon every State party. Thus, for example, a State party in which any significant number of individuals is deprived of essential foodstuffs, of essential primary health care, of basic shelter and housing, or of the most basic forms of education is, *prima facie*, failing to discharge its obligations under the Covenant. If the Covenant were to be read in such a way as not to establish such a minimum core obligation, it would be largely deprived of its *raison d'être*.[119]

The CESCR has since consistently used the 'core minimum obligation' yardstick in its subsequent General Comments issued in relation to various rights. Drawing inspiration from the work of the CESCR, the African Commission has also applied the 'minimum core' approach to states' duties in its decisions.[120] Consistent with its *SERAC* jurisprudence, the Commission reiterated states' duty to meet the bare minimum obligations in a relatively recent case against Kenya. It stated that the state has the 'inescapable' obligation 'of generating minimum living conditions that are compatible with the dignity of the human person and of not creating conditions that hinder or impede it'.[121] It thus held Kenya responsible for not providing the complainants with 'access to appropriate housing with the basic minimum services, such as clean water and toilets'.[122]

The minimum core obligations require a certain form of conduct or of result from the state, which should be implemented immediately regardless of the (un)availability of resources in a country or any other factors and difficulties.[123] According to the CESCR, the provision of 'sufficient, safe and regular' water for personal and domestic uses, the prohibition

[118] Chapman and Russell (note 114 above) 8.

[119] See CESCR, General Comment No. 3 (note 85 above), para. 10.

[120] See *SERAC* (note 21 above), paras. 61 and 66.

[121] Communication 276/2003, *Centre for Minority Rights Development (Kenya) and Minority Rights Group International on behalf of Endorois Welfare Council* v. *Kenya*, 27th Annual Activity Report (2009), para. 217.

[122] *Ibid.*, para. 285.

[123] CESCR, General Comment No. 3 (note 85 above), para. 9.

and prevention of discrimination in access to such uses and related facilities, the equitable distribution of available water facilities and services, and ensuring personal security of beneficiaries in accessing the water are among minimum core obligations that emerge from the recognition by a state of the human right to water.[124] Similarly, the adoption and implementation of a national water strategy that pays due attention to disadvantaged and marginalised groups, monitoring the extent of the realisation, or the non-realisation, of the right to water, adopting relatively low-cost targeted water programmes to protect vulnerable and marginalised groups and taking measures to prevent, treat and control diseases linked to water, in particular ensuring access to adequate sanitation, are the minimum core obligations entailed by the human right to water.[125]

Thus the minimum core of the provision of adequate, safe and regular water for personal and domestic uses forms an obligation of result, the non-achievement of which gives rise to the state's responsibility for the violation of the human right to water. The failure to monitor the realisation or otherwise of the right, the failure to prevent and prohibit discrimination and to adopt policies and strategies for ensuring equitable access to water by all right-holders implicates a state's responsibility for the violation of its core minimum obligation.

4.5 States' immediate obligation: obligations of result

4.5.1 The duty to take steps

As outlined above, the provisions of Article 2(1) of the ICESCR impose (at least some) specific obligations of an immediate nature. A state must show due diligence in the performance of its treaty obligations, meaning that only the duty of full realisation of the rights is progressive, while the obligation to take steps towards this end is of an immediate nature. While the full realisation of the rights guaranteed by the ICESCR may take some time, the state's duties to take measures that are 'deliberate, concrete and targeted as clearly as possible towards meeting the obligations'[126] is immediate and cannot be postponed.[127] While taking note of the resource scarcity that may hamper immediate realisation of the rights recognised under the African Charter, the Commission

124 CESCR, General Comment No. 15 (note 4 above), para. 37. 125 *Ibid.*, para. 37.
126 CESCR, General Comment No. 3 (note 85 above), para. 2.
127 Foster (note 117 above) 172.

emphasised the state's duty 'to take concrete and targeted steps, while taking full advantage of its available resources, to ensure that the right to health is fully realised in all its aspects without discrimination of any kind'.[128] This is in line with the Limburg Principles, which state that:[129]

> [t]he obligation 'to achieve progressively the full realization of the rights' requires States parties to move as expeditiously as possible towards the realization of the rights. Under no circumstances shall this be interpreted as implying for States the right to defer indefinitely efforts to ensure full realization. *On the contrary all States parties have the obligation to begin immediately to take steps to fulfil their obligations under the Covenant.*[130]

While the full realisation of the human right to water may be achieved progressively over a period of time, the duty to take measures aimed at achieving this end is immediate, constant and continuous.[131] It must be implemented either before or within a reasonably short time after ratification of the relevant human rights instrument.[132] The resulting obligation may be less demanding than a guarantee, but it clearly represents a legal undertaking. Thus the duty to take steps is a positive undertaking with both immediate and continuing effects, and the government cannot be inactive or just refrain from taking any steps that would otherwise result in a violation of the right in question.[133]

[128] Communication 241/2001, *Purohit and Moore* v. *The Gambia*, 16th Annual Activity Report (2003), para. 84.

[129] The Limburg Principles are expert explanations of the rights enshrined in and the state duties envisaged by the ICESCR. They were unanimously adopted by a group of distinguished experts in international law, at a meeting convened at Limburg, the Netherlands, 2–6 June 1986, to consider the nature and scope of the obligations of states parties to the ICESCR, the consideration of states parties reports, and international cooperation under Part IV of the Covenant. See 'The Limburg Principles on the Implementation of the International Covenant on Economic Social and Cultural Rights' (Faculty of Law, University of Limburg, 2–6 June 1986) ('Limburg Principles'). The Principles have been so influential since their adoption that they have achieved a '*de facto* official status within the [CESCR] ... as demonstrated by their incorporation into the recent general comments'. See Sage Russell, 'Minimum State Obligations: International Dimensions' in Danie Brand and Sage Russell (eds.), *Exploring the Core Content of Socio-Economic Rights: South African and International Perspectives* (Protea Book House, 2002) 11, 12.

[130] Limburg Principles, para. 21 (emphasis added).

[131] CESCR, General Comment No. 15 (note 4 above), paras. 17 and 18; Ssenyonjo (note 39 above) 975.

[132] CESCR, General Comment No. 3 (note 85 above), para. 2; Alston and Quinn (note 37 above) 166.

[133] See Otto and Wiseman (note 86 above).

Failure on the part of the state to establish carefully planned policies, laws and administrative avenues with a view to the full realisation of the right to water may even violate the prevailing enjoyment, and hence constitute a retrogressive measure which automatically implicates state responsibility. According to the CESCR, deliberately retrogressive measures can be resorted to only exceptionally 'after the most careful consideration of all alternatives and that they are duly justified by reference to the totality of the rights provided for in the Covenant in the context of the full use of the State party's maximum available resources'.[134]

4.5.2 *'[B]y all appropriate means'*

Some steps are highlighted by the ICESCR in relation to selected rights enshrined therein, while some of its provisions are silent on the steps to be taken, leaving the choice to the states' 'margin of discretion' to determine the most appropriate steps to ensure realisation and enjoyment of the particular right.[135] The CESCR has redefined and elaborated the appropriateness of the measures employed by the states in the realisation of rights and freedoms guaranteed in the ICESCR. Accordingly, measures are appropriate if they are 'deliberate, concrete and targeted as clearly as possible towards meeting the obligations recognized in the Covenant'.[136] Thus there must be not only an intention but also a causal link between the steps taken and the (potential and/or actual) progress in the realisation of the rights in question. As the African Commission ruled, '[i]t is not enough to make do with taking measures, these measures should also be accompanied with institutions that produce tangible results.'[137]

In the context of the human right to water, the CESCR pointed to an illustrative list of steps that should be taken on the road to full realisation. From the point of ensuring the quality of water, states bear the duty of ensuring that natural water resources are protected from contamination

[134] CESCR, General Comment No. 15 (note 4 above), para. 19.

[135] See Maastricht Guidelines (note 100 above), para. 8. The Maastricht Guidelines were adopted on the tenth anniversary of the Limburg Principles by a group of experts who met in Maastricht, the Netherlands, 22–26 January 1997 to 'elaborate on the Limburg Principles as regards the nature and scope of violations of economic, social and cultural rights and appropriate responses and remedies'. See 'Introduction' to the Maastricht Guidelines (note 100 above). See also Otto and Wiseman (note 133 above) 17.

[136] CESCR, General Comment No. 3 (note 85 above), para. 2.

[137] Communication 272/2003, *Association of Victims of Post Electoral Violence and Interights* v. *Cameroon*, 27th Annual Activity Report (2009), para. 108.

by harmful substances and pathogenic microbes.[138] Additionally, states are required to monitor and combat situations where aquatic ecosystems serve as a habitat for vectors of diseases wherever they pose a risk to human living environments.[139]

On the other hand, a state's duty to strive to improve the amount of water available to individuals and groups remains intact, depending upon the resources available to the state. Among others, states must take 'administrative, budgetary, [and] judicial measures as part of implementing the right'.[140] The state's margin of discretion is not limitless and is measured against the state's treaty undertakings. As the appropriateness of steps taken by states is not always self-evident, the ultimate determination as to whether appropriate measures have been taken is for the international monitoring body to make.[141] The CESCR thus stressed that the phrase 'by all appropriate means' must be construed carefully in such a manner that it is given its 'full and natural meaning'.[142]

4.5.3 *'[I]ncluding legislative measures'*

Despite the margin of discretion regarding the choice of means of implementing the human right to water (and any other right), legislative measures are indispensable among the 'appropriate measures' a state is required to take.[143] The use of the word 'including' preceding 'legislative measures' obviously implies that the list of measures envisaged is not exhaustive, implying that laws are necessary, even indispensable, but at the same time it can be read as stressing that such are insufficient.

The state's duty to provide legislative measures thus forms part of the state's duty to protect as well as the duty to promote the human right to water. As regards the former, legislative measures must restrain third parties from denying equal access to adequate water, and polluting and inequitably extracting from water resources, including natural sources, wells and other water distribution systems.[144] In the event of violations of the human right to water, there must be a remedy that is readily available, effective and sufficient to redress the violations.[145] Legislative

138 CESCR, General Comment No. 15 (note 4 above), para. 8. 139 *Ibid.*
140 Maastricht Guidelines (note 100 above), para. 6.
141 CESCR, General Comment No. 3 (note 85 above), para. 4. 142 *Ibid.*
143 *Ibid.*, para. 5. 144 CESCR, General Comment No. 15 (note 4 above), para. 23.
145 *Ibid.*, para. 55; CESCR, General Comment No. 3 (note 85 above), para. 5.

measures also form part of the duty to 'promote' the right, as such legislation must be passed in order to accord sufficient recognition of the right to water within the national political and legal systems.[146] In order to ensure domestic implementation of the human right to water, states should bring their domestic laws, strategies and policies into conformity with their treaty-based obligations that impact on the realisation of the human right to water.[147] Existing legislation, strategies and policies should be reviewed to ensure that they are compatible with the requirements of and obligations arising from the recognition of the right to water, and should be repealed or amended if they are inconsistent with treaty requirements. Legislative implementation of treaty-based rights including the human right to water is an obligation of an immediate nature.[148]

Lack of legislative measures enabling domestic implementation of the human right to water or the existence of legislative obstacles constitutes a violation of the right. According to the CESCR, '[v]iolations through *acts of omission* include the failure to take appropriate steps towards the full realization of everyone's right to water, the failure to have a national policy on water, and the failure to enforce relevant laws'.[149] Thus, not only failure to enact the necessary legislative measures but also failure to implement the said measures is a violation of the right to water.

4.5.4 *'[W]ithout discrimination of any kind'*

States are under an immediate obligation to ensure that state agents and third parties within their jurisdictions treat individuals and groups in a manner that is in line with the right to equality. Under Article 2(2) of the ICESCR:

> [t]he States Parties to the present Covenant undertake to guarantee that the rights enunciated in the present Covenant will be exercised without discrimination of any kind as to race, colour, sex, language, religion, political or other opinion, national or social origin, property, birth or other status.

146 CESCR, General Comment No. 15 (note 4 above), paras. 26 and 44(c).

147 *Ibid.*, para. 46. See also Chapter 6.

148 Yuval Shany, 'How Supreme Is the Supreme Law of the Land? Comparative Analysis of the Influence of International Human Rights Treaties upon the Interpretation of Constitutional Texts by Domestic Courts', 31(2) *Brooklyn Journal of International Law* (2006) 341–404, 348.

149 CESCR, General Comment No. 15 (note 4 above), para. 43.

The prohibited grounds of discrimination under the above provision are not exhaustive and any other unfair differentiation that jeopardises the human right to water of the right-holders constitutes discrimination. States' duty to ensure equality in the enjoyment of the human right to water has both negative (duty to respect) and positive (protect, promote and fulfil) dimensions. There have been instances where, contrary to a state's duty to respect the right, water has been used by governments as a political weapon against oppositions and minorities. The relocation by the Sudanese government of over 400,000 squatters in Khartoum – most of whom are Christians and believers of African traditional religions and hence associated with the rebels in the southern parts of the country – to camps with inadequate water supplies was characterised as a virtual 'death sentence'.[150] In the early 1990s, Israel refused to recognise at least half of about seventy Arab communities in its central and northern territories.[151] As a result of a denial of state recognition, they could not be connected to the national drinking water network, a situation which led to serious health problems and environmental distress.[152] It was asserted that the position of the Israeli state was to use water as a means to pressure the Arab communities to evacuate their places of residence and relocate against their will.[153] A more recent report[154] revealed Israel's inequitable (and discriminatory)[155] practices relating to distribution of water in the Gaza and West Bank areas, denying Palestinians hitherto existing access to water wells in the Palestinian territory, expropriation of water resources and the consequent reduction or stoppage of Palestinians' access to water. Such and similar governmental acts that have discriminatory effects on water distribution are clearly a violation of the human right to water, and of a state's duty to respect the same.

On the positive side of the states' duties, various ways of ensuring the equality of right-holders can be employed. At the very least, legislative measures should be in place to prohibit discrimination by state and non-

[150] Stephen C. McCaffrey, 'A Human Right to Water: Domestic and International Implications', 5(1) *Georgetown International Environmental Law Review* (1992) 1–24, 6.

[151] *Ibid.* [152] *Ibid.* [153] *Ibid.*

[154] See Lara El-Jazairi, 'Policies of Denial: Lack of Access to Water in the West Bank' (Centre on Housing Rights and Evictions (COHRE), 2008).

[155] It has been revealed that Israeli citizens' consumption of water per capita in the West Bank is 4.6 times more than that of the Palestinians living in the area. There are similar discriminatory trends in other areas of the Palestinian territory and in water uses other than domestic and personal uses as well. See *ibid.*, 16.

state actors. In the event where discriminatory practices have been shown, remedies should be put in place to redress the violation. Tackling inequality will also require a commitment to financing strategies – including fiscal transfers, cross-subsidies and other measures – that bring affordable water and sanitation to the poor.[156]

Studies have indicated that the poorer sections and communities of society are more often at risk of discrimination in accessing water of adequate quality and quantity. In Dakar (Senegal), for instance, poor households using standpipes pay more than three times the price paid by households connected to the utility.[157] In Manila (Philippines), the cost of connecting to a water utility represents about three months' income for the poorest 20 per cent of households, rising to six months' in urban Kenya.[158] Location is another barrier to entry. In many cities, utilities refuse to connect households lacking formal property titles, thereby excluding some of the poorest households. The result has been a combination of under-financing and low coverage, with rural women bearing the costs by collecting water from distant sources.[159]

The CESCR emphasised the necessity on the part of the states to take steps to remove *de facto* discrimination.[160] Accordingly, it stressed the necessity of giving 'special attention to those individuals and groups who have traditionally faced difficulties in exercising this right, including women, children, minority groups, indigenous peoples, refugees, asylum-seekers, internally displaced persons, migrant workers, prisoners and detainees'.[161] Similarly, special attention must be given to those sections of society who do not have the means at their disposal to purchase water for personal and domestic use. This is a means of preventing discrimination on the ground of one's economic status, on the one hand, and part of a state's duty to fulfil the human right to water on the other.

In sum, it is not enough that states take overarching measures; it is also crucial that measures that are taken with a view to immediate implementation benefit all sections of the right-holders equally. The propriety of steps taken by the state is thus gauged, among other things, with reference to the extent to which it takes into account the right-holders'

[156] UNDP, 'Beyond Scarcity: Power, Poverty and the Global Water Crisis (Human Development Report 2006)' (United Nations Development Programme, 2006) 9.
[157] *Ibid.*, 10. [158] *Ibid.* [159] *Ibid.*
[160] CESCR, General Comment No. 15 (note 4 above), para. 14. [161] *Ibid.*, para. 16.

right to equality and prevention of discrimination in the enjoyment of the human right to water.

4.6 Progressive duties: obligations of conduct

4.6.1 '[A]chieving progressively'

In addition to the immediate obligations pertaining to the realisation of the minimum core of states' duties, a level of implementation that could be programmatic and resource-dependent is envisaged by the phrase 'achieving progressively' under Article 2(1) of the ICESCR.[162] It has been remarked that the concept of 'progressive realisation' in more ways than one is 'the linchpin of the whole Covenant . . . [as] upon its meaning turns the nature of state obligations'.[163] It reflects the usually inevitable resource-contingent nature of state obligations in relation to the realisation of socio-economic rights such as the right to water. Unless carefully construed and applied, it is capable of depriving state obligations of any normative significance.[164] It plays a dual role of monumental significance in the interpretation and eventual application of the ICESCR as a whole. On the one hand, it is 'a necessary flexibility device, reflecting the realities of the real world and the difficulties involved for any country in ensuring full realization of economic, social and cultural rights'.[165] On the other hand, it mirrors the overall *raison d'être* of the ICESCR, 'which is to establish clear obligations for States parties in respect of the full realization of the rights in question'.[166]

Consequently, the fact that the human right to water may be fully realised progressively does not imply that states can indefinitely postpone the full implementation of all aspects of the right. States must move 'as expeditiously and effectively as possible' towards the full realisation of the right in question.[167] The incremental nature of the obligation means that partial implementation of the state obligations can only be justified on the grounds of resource constraints. Conversely, the fact that the implementation of some state obligations is 'progressive' means that (at least deliberately) retrogressive measures are prohibited, as they would otherwise constitute the state's failure to ensure the minimal duty to 'respect' human rights. Accordingly, if there are resources at the disposal of the state that can be put to use for the realisation of the right to water

[162] See note 83 above. [163] Alston and Quinn (note 37 above) 172. [164] *Ibid.*
[165] CESCR, General Comment No. 3 (note 85 above), para. 9. [166] *Ibid.* [167] *Ibid.*

(or any other right), the concept of 'minimum core' becomes a less useful tool or even irrelevant, and full realisation should be ensured immediately and continuously.[168]

4.6.2 *'[T]o the maximum of its available resources'*

The implementation of the progressive aspect of a state's duties hinges upon the availability of necessary resources. While a state's inability to fully realise the human right to water can be excused if justified by reasons of resource constraints, a state's unwillingness to use the maximum of its available resources for the purpose is a violation of its obligation by omission.[169] The use of the maximum amount of available resources clearly involves state expenditure for purposes, *inter alia*, of protecting the quality of available water, water conservation, preventing pollution, drilling and transporting more water, and establishing the infrastructure necessary to deliver the water services to the right-holders. While this would almost inevitably involve cost implications which in many cases could be huge, thereby stressing the state's overall capacity, it cannot be expected that modern states devote all or even a bigger portion of their resources to fulfilling the human right to water.

It has been remarked that the word 'resources' refers to the real resources of the country and not necessarily to budgetary appropriations.[170] As states are mandated to 'take steps, individually and through international assistance and co-operation' under Article 2(1) of the ICESCR, the resources available to the state must be construed to mean those that are available within its territorial limits as well as those that are acquired through international assistance and cooperation. As such, 'available resources' should be defined broadly and a state should be aggressive in its pursuit of international avenues for assistance and cooperation to realise the human rights of its domestic beneficiaries.[171] The same logic holds in relation to the human right to water.

However, the problems associated with the provision of the water necessary for personal and domestic uses occur partly due to the low priority attached to water rights by states, with the consequent allocation

[168] Otto and Wiseman (note 133 above) 18; Maastricht Guidelines (note 100 above), para. 10.

[169] CESCR, General Comment No. 15 (note 4 above), para. 41.

[170] Alston and Quinn (note 37 above) 178.

[171] Robertson (note 113 above) 702.

of meagre resources to its realisation.[172] In Ethiopia and Pakistan, for instance, the military budget in 2006 was ten and forty-seven times the size of the water and sanitation budget respectively, which is indicative of those states' failure to allocate the recommended minimum 1 per cent of their national budget thereto.[173]

In evaluating a state's performance in the realisation of the human right to water, a line should be drawn between 'inability' entailed by lack of resources and 'unwillingness' to maximise potentially available resources. A state that blames its failure on lack of water resources should bear a weighty burden of showing that every effort has been made to avail itself of the actual resources available nationally and potential resources available through international cooperation and assistance, short of which its conduct would be adjudged a violation of the relevant duty.[174] Even in situations where there are insufficient resources to achieve the state's immediate obligations or the progressive realisation of the human right to water, states should at least acknowledge the situation and address it, *inter alia*, through the development of a relief strategy and by requesting international assistance.[175]

4.7 Between willingness and inability: availability of water resources

4.7.1 Inventory of resources and impossibility of performance

In the field of international human rights law, despite the international nature of states' human rights obligations, the national state bears the responsibility of carrying into effect its treaty obligations domestically. As the Special Rapporteur on the right to food noted, 'the primary obligation to implement the right to food rests with the home state'.[176] This invariably applies to the remainder of the rights and freedoms enshrined in the corpus of international human rights law.

There is an assumption underlying international human rights treaties that every state possesses sufficient resources at least for subsistence

[172] See UNDP (note 156 above) 8. [173] *Ibid.*, 8–9.

[174] CESCR, General Comment No. 15 (note 4 above), para. 41.

[175] Maike Gorsboth, 'Identifying and Addressing Violations of the Human Right to Water: Applying the Human Rights Approach' (Brot fur die Welt (Bread for the World), 2006) 9.

[176] CESCR, 'The Right to Food: Report of the Special Rapporteur on the Right to Food, Jean Ziegler' (Commission on Human Rights, United Nations Economic and Social Council (E/CN.4/2005/47), 24 January 2005), para. 47.

purposes (hence for the fulfilment of the minimum core of human rights).[177] Under Article 2(1) of the ICESCR, 'each state' undertakes to take steps 'individually and through international cooperation' to realise the rights and freedoms 'to the maximum of its available resources'. Clearly, a state must have primary resort to its available resources for the fulfilment of its treaty obligations.

However, the realisation of the human right to water, like other rights, could be constrained due to the inability of a state to realise the right from 'its available resources'. As Simpson noted, there is an implicitly understood level of 'tolerated inequalities'[178] among states' capacities, and this is usually reflected in terms of the resources available to them nationally for the implementation of their respective human rights undertakings. This leads to 'the dilemma [that] emerges when the credibility premising [on the ability and willingness of the state's] participation in the domestic and the international framework is not necessarily commensurate'.[179]

In relation to the human right to water, this is exacerbated by the distributional patterns of fresh water resources across the globe.[180] A great proportion of the world's fresh water resources is shared between/among two or more states and there are states that do not have *any* national water resources of their own.[181] This impinges on the reliability of water resources at a state's disposal. It makes national planning extremely difficult for some co-riparian states, leaving some states at a great disadvantage as their ability to utilise shared water resources can be constantly influenced by actions and inactions in other states that also rely on the shared waters for their own national

177 Robertson (note 113 above) 702.

178 This term is coined by Gerry Simpson, who argues that ['t]he doctrine of sovereign inequality, no matter how interpreted, is compatible with an array of tolerated social inequalities . . . However it is clear that there is no general duty or obligation to produce material parity.' Gerry J. Simpson, *Great Powers and Outlaw States: Unequal Sovereigns in the International Legal Order* (Cambridge University Press, 2003) 57.

179 Lisa Yarwood, 'Willing and Able: The Domestication of International Justice', 14 *African Yearbook of International Law* (2006) 193, 200.

180 See Chapter 1.

181 A study has shown that there are some thirty-three countries in the world that have 95 per cent or more of their available water resources coming from transboundary water sources originating in other states. Swedish International Water Institute, 'Responding to Global Changes: Accessing Water for Common Good, with Special Focus on Transboundary Waters' (Swedish International Water Institute, 2009) 8.

uses. Because not all states have equal access to the bounty of rivers in order to be able to realise the human right to water on the domestic level, a 'willing' state may find it inordinately difficult or even impossible to fulfil the rights of its inhabitants because of water resource constraints unless it is allowed to share in the water resources originating elsewhere.

This is a real possibility in Africa. As outlined in Chapter 1, every continental African state shares at least one river with another state, hence amplifying the degree of inter-state dependency for the realisation of the human right to water in their respective territories.

The problem of fresh water scarcity is caused primarily by the fact that there is not always enough water of the right quality in the right place at the right time.[182] As McCaffrey noted, '[w]ater is often found where people are scarce, and people often live where water is scarce'.[183] Thus, of the total fresh water available on the earth's surface, about 77 per cent is stored in ice caps and glaciers, 22.4 per cent is in ground water and soil moisture and only 0.35 per cent is in lakes and marshes.[184] Allowing for 0.04 per cent in the atmosphere, there is a bare 0.01 per cent of the world's fresh water supplies in streams.[185]

Yet, it is rivers, carrying a mere 0.000003 per cent of all the water on the planet, that provide human beings with about 80 per cent of their fresh water needs.[186] The realisation of the human right to water thus primarily depends on fresh water from rivers. Rivers, of course, do not respect national boundaries. The great majority of the world's rivers are "successive" rivers or "boundary" rivers,[187] and thus are shared among states. States often treat that segment of a river that flows through their

[182] David H. Getches, *Water Law* (West Publishing Co., 1997) 1.

[183] Stephen C. McCaffrey, *The Law of International Watercourses* (Oxford University Press, 2nd edn, 2007) 8.

[184] Arun P. Elhance, *Hydropolitics in the Third World: Conflict and Cooperation in International River Basins* (United States Institute of Peace Press, 1999) 8.

[185] Gilbert F. White, 'Introduction: World Trends and Needs', 16(4) *Natural Resources Journal* (1976) 737, 739.

[186] Elhance (note 184 above) 8.

[187] An international river is either a successive river, traversing the territories of two or more states, or a boundary river (also called a contiguous river) if it is one that separates the territories of two or more states. Thus, an international river can be both successive, in its segments that traverse, for instance, the territories of riparian States A and B, and a boundary river, separating for instance riparian States B and C. See Jerome Lipper, 'Equitable Utilization' in A. H. Garretson, R. D. Hayton and C. J. Olmstead (eds.), *The Law of International Drainage Basins* (Oceana Publications Inc., 1967) 1, 16.

territories as any other resource at their sovereign disposal.[188] Of the average global annual runoff of 40–47 cubic kilometres, more than half is found on the Asian and South American continents, while 40 per cent flows in Africa, Australia, Europe and North America combined.[189]

In Africa, 75 per cent of total continental water resources are concentrated in eight major river basins, i.e. the Congo, the Niger, the Ogadugne (Gabon), the Zambezi, the Nile, the Sanga, the Chari-Lagone and the Volta.[190] Put otherwise, most fresh water resources are concentrated in western and central Africa, whereas northern and southern Africa and the Horn of Africa are experiencing water scarcity.[191] Ninety-five per cent of total fresh water, most of which is shared, emerges from central and western Africa, while the arid and semi-arid parts of the continent produce a mere 5 per cent.[192]

The uneven distributional pattern of fresh water resources has a direct impact on a state's capacity to realise the human right to water in its territory. An over-utilisation or pollution by a co-riparian state of the shared waters would therefore inevitably influence the capacity of the other co-riparian states to control and use the waters for the realisation of the human right to water in their domestic spheres. Accordingly, the fact that rivers traverse international boundaries may impact upon the fate of the human right to water in co-riparian states' territories.

Granted that 60–65 per cent of Africa, Asia and South America are dependent upon shared (transboundary) rivers,[193] as is 40 per cent of the North and Central Americas,[194] recognising the human right to water and the consequent correlative state obligations to realise the same raise questions of implementation that transcend a single state's capacity. An increase in the use of shared water in one state may result in scarcity of

188 It is no surprise therefore that the major theories on international water law have state sovereignty as their starting point of enquiry. See McCaffrey (note 183 above) 111–70; Bonaya Adhi Godana, *Africa's Shared Water Resources: Legal and Institutional Aspects of the Nile, Niger, and Senegal River Systems* (Lynne Rienner Publications Inc., 1985) 32–49.

189 White (note 185 above) 739.

190 See United Nations Economic Commission for Africa, 'Transboundary River/Lake Basin Water Development in Africa: Prospects, Problems, and Achievements', available at www.uneca.org/search.htm (accessed 7 May 2011).

191 Elli Louka, *Water Law and Policy: Governance without Frontiers* (Oxford University Press, 2008) 14–15.

192 *Ibid.*, 15.

193 Elhance (note 184 above) 5.

194 Tesfaye Tafesse, *The Nile Question: Hydro Politics, Legal Wrangling, Modus Vivendi and Perspectives* (Transaction Publishers, 2001) 3.

water in a co-riparian country, leading to non-realisation of the human right to water in the latter's territory. The human right to water in one state could also be violated or threatened through pollution of the shared water resource or other injurious acts committed in other co-riparian states' territories. Some 145 countries, accounting for 90 per cent of the world's population, are at least partly in shared basins, thirty of which are *entirely* within shared basins.[195] Moreover, the number of shared rivers and countries depending on them has been rising over the past decades due to the fragmentation of old states. A report showed that there were 214 international basins in the world in 1978; this has risen to 263 as at 2006.[196]

The situation is nowhere more acute than in Africa, where, with the exception of the few island states, every single country has at least a river to share with at least one neighbour.[197] In other words, all continental African states depend on international water resources to fulfil their domestic water demands. Some 85 per cent of Africa's fresh water resources are found in shared river basins.[198] At least thirty-four rivers are shared by two states, and twenty-eight are shared by three or more states.[199] Put differently, ten river basins – Congo, Limpopo, Niger, Nile, Ogooue, Okavango, Orange, Senegal, Volta and Zambezi – are shared by four or more African states.[200] Every state in continental Africa has at least one international river within its territory, forty-one states have two or more, and fifteen states have five or more.[201] Guinea has fourteen international rivers, while both Côte d'Ivoire and Mozambique have nine such rivers each in their territories.[202]

The implication of the uneven distribution and relative scarcity of water resources in some states means that, perhaps more than any other right in the current catalogue of human rights, the fate of the human right to water is inextricably tied directly to the (in)action of foreign actors, thereby undermining the role of a state acting alone. In Egypt, for example, not only the human right to water but 'all of life and human

195 UNDP (note 156 above) 205. 196 *Ibid.*

197 The only exceptions are the few island states like Madagascar and Cape Verde. See the African Transboundary Water Law page at www.africanwaterlaw.org/html/background.asp (accessed 20 June 2011).

198 Peter J. Ashton, 'Avoiding Conflicts over Africa's Water Resources', 31(3) *Ambio* (2002) 236, 236.

199 Claudia W. Sadoff, Dale Whittington and David Grey, *Africa's International Rivers: An Economic Perspective* (World Bank, 2002) 7.

200 *Ibid.* 201 *Ibid.* 202 *Ibid.*

activities' depend on the waters of the Nile River that traverse ten states before reaching Egypt.[203] Similarly, elsewhere in Africa, not less than 94 per cent of Botswana's total river flows originate outside the country.[204] Indeed, there are some thirty-three states in the world that receive 95 per cent or more of their fresh water from sources outside their territories, and thus are heavily dependent for their survival on transboundary water resources.[205]

Egypt, for example, is 'the only country in the world where all of life and human activities depend mainly on the hydraulic resource of *a* river [the Nile]'.[206] According to Elhance, 'no other country [other than Egypt] in the world is so dependent on the waters of a single river that it shares with not two or three but eight [*sic*] other states, all located upstream from Egypt'.[207] It is a country that cannot exist as a viable state without the waters of the Nile. The situation can be summed up as *aut Nilus aut nihil* (no Nile no life) in Egypt.[208] The adage, attributed to Herodotus, runs thus: 'Egypt was a gift of the Nile.'[209]

According to a 2008 United Nations Development Programme (UNDP) report, six out of the ten countries of the Nile basin (Eritrea, Ethiopia, Uganda, Tanzania, Rwanda and Burundi) lie at the bottom of 'Low Human Development' in the ranking of 177 countries surveyed in terms of their water, sanitation and nutritional status.[210] Only four (Democratic Republic of Congo, Egypt, Kenya and Sudan) of the Nile countries made it into the bottom half of the list of 'Medium Human Development', none featuring in the 'High Human Development' list.[211]

This is the starkest reminder that domestic resource deficiencies must be compensated by maximising access to extraterritorially available resources through international assistance and cooperation, especially

[203] Habib Ayeb, 'Hydraulic Politics: The Nile and Egypt's Water Use: a Crisis for the Twenty-First Century?' in Ray Bush (ed.), *Counter-Revolution in Egypt's Countryside: Land and Farmers in the Era of Economic Reform* (Zed Books, 2002) 76.

[204] Rafik Hirji and David Grey, 'Managing International Waters in Africa: Process and Progress' in Salman M. A. Salman and Laurence Boisson de Chazournes (eds.), *International Watercourses: Enhancing Cooperation and Managing Conflict: Proceedings of a World Bank Seminar* (World Bank, 1998) 77, 87.

[205] Swedish International Water Institute (note 181 above).

[206] Ayeb (note 203 above).

[207] Elhance (note 184 above). The number of sovereign states sharing the Nile has increased from nine to ten following the emergence of the newly established state of South Sudan in 2011 in the White Nile Basin.

[208] Yacob Arsano, 'Towards Conflict Prevention in the Nile Basin' (Paper presented at the 5th Nile 2002 Conference, 1997) 489.

[209] *Ibid.* [210] See UNDP Human Development Report 2007/2008, 251–4. [211] *Ibid.*

of an economic and technical nature.[212] A state whose domestic water resources fall short of what is needed to cater for the requirements of its population's human right to water must therefore seek international assistance and cooperation from other states.

4.7.2 *The right-duty of international assistance and cooperation*

As stated above, the domestic state bears the primary responsibility for the domestic implementation of human rights standards through the use of domestically available resources. Yet, although a state is legally bound to implement a human right to water domestically, it may find it impossible to live up to its human rights undertakings due to lack of water resources within its territory. The shared nature of much of fresh water in the world means that water constraints can also be caused by increased consumption, diversion, pollution, or any other activity of a co-riparian state. The implementation of the human right to water thus poses special challenges due to the type of resource upon which its realisation depends. Unlike any other resource, water does not have other substitutes and it must be accessed if people are to survive.[213]

The operationalisation of a state's duty of international assistance and cooperation becomes extremely important because much of what is taken as national water by states is in fact shared water[214] – the bulk of fresh water being in shared rivers, lakes and aquifers.[215] The enhanced use of inter-state assistance and cooperation thus plays a crucial role if states are to be able to discharge their duties of realising the human right to water.

As well as water quantity, the maintenance and improvement of water quality requires cooperation among states for them to be able to provide

[212] ICESCR, Article 2(1).

[213] See John Waterbury, *The Nile Basin: National Determinants of Collective Action* (Yale University Press, 2002) 10; Karen Bakker, 'The "Commons" Versus the "Commodity": Alter-globalization, Anti-privatization and the Human Right to Water in the Global South', 39(3) *Antipode* (2007) 430–55, 439.

[214] This invariably holds true for the countries of Africa, Asia, Europe, Latin America and North America. Moreover, the number of shared rivers and the countries depending on them has been rising over the past decades due to the disintegration of some and the formation of other (new) states. While there were 214 international basins in the world in 1978, the figure has risen to 263 as at 2006. See UNDP (note 156 above) 205.

[215] According to the 2006 report of the UNDP, 145 countries, accounting for 90 per cent of the world's population, are in shared basins, thirty of which countries are entirely within shared basins. See UNDP (note 156 above) 205.

water of adequate quality to their respective domestic right-holders. The shared nature of the bulk of fresh water used for human consumption means pollution in one state directly threatens the right to water, food, health and lives of those beyond the state's borders besides the human right to water *per se*.[216] A recent incident in China provides a good example. In November 2005, when an industrial accident caused an 80-kilometre-long chemical slick in China's Songhua River, it threatened not only the 3 million citizens of Harbin (China) but also the residents of the Russian city of Khabarovsk across the border.[217]

Unfortunately, the topic of implementation of states' human rights duties through international cooperation and assistance has so far been neglected not just in the area of the human right to water but also in the area of socio-economic rights implementation more generally.[218] According to Salomon, '[j]urisprudentially, few advances have been made in determining specifically that which constitutes a state's maximum available resources for the purpose of meeting its obligation of international assistance and cooperation'.[219] There is a need to search legal avenues to operationalise the state's international duty of cooperation and assistance 'to delineate justiciable and feasible rights-claims and to identify and hold to account agents who can and should deliver on those rights'.[220]

4.7.3 *Normative content of the duty to seek international assistance and cooperation*

The state's duty to engage in international assistance and cooperation has been emphasised both in international instruments of global and regional scope. A state's failure to seek international assistance and cooperation (or refusal to accept these when they are forthcoming) whenever its national fresh water resources fall below what is required to guarantee its inhabitants' human right to water is a clear violation of the right in question.[221]

216 Two in every five people in the world today live in these basins, which also account for 60 per cent of global river flows and half of the earth's land surface. UNDP (note 156 above) 205.

217 *Ibid.* 218 Skogly (note 14 above) 419. 219 Salomon (note 2 above) 101.

220 Andrew Kuper, 'Introduction: The Responsibilities Approach to Human Rights' in Andrew Kuper (ed.), *Global Responsibilities: Who Must Deliver Human Rights?* (Routledge, 2005) ix, xxii.

221 A state's refusal or blockade of international assistance that is made available to it is referred to in some quarters as a crime against humanity. See generally John D. Kraemer, Dhrubajyoti Bhattacharya and Lawrence O. Gostin, 'Blocking Humanitarian Assistance: A Crime against Humanity?', 372(4) *The Lancet* (2008) 1203.

It appears that the types of cooperation and assistance that a state could seek from others depend upon the degree of geographical contiguity and whether there is a shared water resource among the states involved. The closer the states are geographically, and the more there are shared water resources, the more is the possibility that the type of assistance and cooperation between them takes the form of sharing 'wet water'. But this does not exclude the possibility of financial and technical assistance and cooperation. As will be seen in Chapter 6, international law imposes a clear and continuous obligation among co-riparian states to share water for the benefit of their respective populations equitably. However, if the states involved are geographically far apart and there are no water resources shared among them, the greater is the possibility that the form of assistance and cooperation between them takes a financial and technical form, with a view to enabling the recipient state to better use the available resources.

However, numerous vexing questions still remain unanswered. First, exactly what situations trigger a state's duty to seek international assistance and cooperation? This should be answered in relation to the amount of water needed for its population's personal and domestic uses and its nationally available water resources. The state must show that it has used nationally available fresh water resources to the maximum possible extent, and that priority has been given to personal and domestic uses of its water resources.[222] Or, there must be evidence that the total nationally available water resources are insufficient for the said purposes. If personal and domestic uses on the one hand and water for agricultural and other uses on the other are competing for priority, a state must be able to demonstrate that it has given priority to the former in order for it to be able to show that the human right to water is indeed in jeopardy in its territory due to resource constraints.

The implication is that there needs to be evidence of a lack of national water resources and that the home state has put the maximum amount of those resources to use in a manner that prioritises its population's personal and domestic uses. This necessarily involves information sharing, transparency, continued consultation and notice among the co-riparian states and other states that are likely to be involved in the framework of international assistance and cooperation.

Secondly, there is a question of how much water a state may demand from other states through international cooperation and assistance. This

222 CESCR, General Comment No. 15 (note 4 above), paras. 6 and 41.

should first be answered in relation to the minimum core of the right to water. Much also depends on the amount of the available water in the territories of co-riparian states, which would be obligated to fulfil its residents' right to water. If the (shared) water resource available in the co-riparian states is below or above this bare minimum, the principle of equitable and reasonable utilisation provides the formula for the apportionment of the available water among the riparian states involved.[223] Accordingly, equally pressing interests such as the human right to water will be given equal weight for the purpose of equitable sharing of common waters.[224] The resulting dividend of the water can exceed the amount needed for the realisation of the minimum core of the human right to water in all the states involved or it could be just that or even less.

Thirdly, it must be asked who the direct duty-bearers are. The duty of international assistance and cooperation is attached to the undefined international community, and this has made it an amorphous obligation in the sense that the agent of the duty is not clearly defined. According to Salomon, the duty of international assistance has been attached to the 'undifferentiated international community', a notion too obscure to enable victims of rights violations to initiate procedures seeking international remedies.[225] As elaborated in Chapter 6, the situation of the human right to water seems to be much clearer, at least from the perspective of international water law. A direct obligation of equitable apportionment exists between co-riparian states, and states seeking assistance and cooperation for purposes of realising the human right to water must resort to co-riparian states as a first port of call. This does not, however, preclude a state's right to seek assistance and cooperation, especially of a technical and financial nature, from the rest of the international community.

4.8 Conclusion

The chapter explored the obligations of states in the realisation of human rights in general and the human right to water in particular. The violation by states of any of the obligations (to respect, protect, promote and fulfil) triggers their international responsibility for human rights violations, including violation of the human right to water. A state's duties to realise the human right to water, like any other socio-economic right,

[223] McCaffrey (note 150 above) 23. [224] See Chapter 6.
[225] Salomon (note 2 above) 180.

comprise elements of immediacy and of 'progressive realisation'. The former primarily pertains to the minimum core of the human right to water. On the other hand, the obligation of 'progressive realisation' entails the state's duty to constantly work in as expeditious a manner as possible, depending upon the availability of relevant resources, towards the achievement of the full realisation of the right.

In many states, foremost in Africa, the mere recognition of the human right to water would hold little promise for the right-holders as the states would be unable to fulfil their duties due to water constraints. The fact that major fresh water resources of the world are shared among states means that the implementation of the duties of the states and the fate of the right-holders would be in jeopardy unless the duty of international assistance and cooperation is made fully operational.

However, as the foregoing discussion has revealed, the normative development, clarification and application of this duty has been neglected. A state in which water constraints threaten the implementation of the human right to water must seek international assistance and cooperation to supplement the nationally available resources, if any. Establishing violations of a state's human rights duties is almost straightforward if it fails to seek international assistance and cooperation and permits violations of the human right to water to occur because of a shortage of resources. But, if it sought to access water resources through international assistance and cooperation, as is expected, the duty of co-riparian states to provide the assistance and cooperation needed is called into play. Little ink has been spilt to analyse the scope of this duty. A question of vital significance has yet to be answered in relation to the exposition of the legal bases and extent of external obligations of the 'donor' states in order to meet their duty of international assistance and cooperation for the realisation of the human right to water in third (co-riparian) states' territories. Hence, it is to the analysis of states' extra-territorial obligations that we now turn.

5

The human right to water and states' extraterritorial obligations

[I]t is space, not time, that hides consequences from us.[1]

5.1 Introduction

The preceding chapter demonstrated that a state's dependence on shared fresh water resources for the realisation of the human right to water may entail its inability to meet its obligations to domestic beneficiaries due to the lack of territorial water resources. As illustrated in Chapter 1, this is the case for millions of individuals and groups living in shared river basins in Africa, where all states rely on fresh water resources shared with at least one other state. This is certainly the case in the Nile basin where eleven states share the water resources of the Nile, with downstream states such as Sudan and Egypt being entirely dependent for all vital human needs (drinking and sanitation) on the bounty of this one river that originates in and traverses as many as nine and ten co-riparian states' territories respectively before it reaches these states. Granted that 85 per cent of African fresh water comes from international rivers, the realisation of the human right to water depends on the quantity and quality of shared water resources. Thus a state has the capacity to hamper the realisation of the right in third states by reducing the volume or polluting the shared river unless they are legally prevented from jeopardising the right abroad. The right would prove an empty promise for the right-holders unless they are given legal avenues to hold third states accountable for their (in)actions that produce extraterritorial consequences.

The analysis in the preceding chapter was confined to states' duties to their domestic right-holders (*vertical* obligations). It stopped short of

[1] John Berger, *The Look of Things* (Penguin, 1972) 40.

addressing whether the four layers of state's human rights obligations – respect, protect, promote and fulfil – apply as between states (*horizontal* obligations) and between a state and residents of third states (*diagonal* obligations). Postponing the discussion of the horizontal state obligations to Chapter 6, this chapter takes up the analysis of a state's diagonal human rights obligations. It explores the legal and jurisprudential basis of the extraterritorial application of human rights against duties in the African human rights system in light of the regional case law and comparative jurisprudence against the backdrop of the human rights framework that has primarily been conceived of as implying universal human rights[2] and domestic – or territorial – state duties.[3] In contrast to the prevailing approach that tends to analyse states' extraterritorial obligations when acting outside their borders (e.g. while controlling territory or persons in third states), the present chapter additionally examines states' extraterritorial *positive* obligations to individuals and groups of third states while acting from within their own territories. This is the case when a state pollutes or over-utilises a shared river on which the human right to water depends for its realisation in co-riparian states.

It is argued that the realisation of individuals' and peoples' human right to water in co-riparian states is part of the obligations of all the riparian states sharing a common river. This approach seeks to view each co-riparian state as a duty-bearer, albeit to varying degrees, for the

[2] See, for instance, the Vienna Declaration and Program of Action, World Conference on Human Rights, UN Doc. A/CONF.157/23) (UN General Assembly, 25 June 2003), para. 5, which states that '[a]ll human rights are universal, indivisible and interdependent and interrelated'; the Universal Declaration of Human Rights, Preamble, para. 6, in which 'States have pledged themselves to achieve . . . the promotion of universal respect for and observance of human rights and fundamental freedoms'; the United Nations Charter, Article 55(c), which stipulates that 'the United Nations shall promote . . . universal respect for, and observance of, human rights and fundamental freedoms for all without distinction as to race, sex, language, or religion'.

[3] The duties of states in the implementation of (treaty-based) rights are usually circumscribed by territoriality, jurisdiction and citizenship. See Mark Gibney, Katarina Tomaseviski and Jens Vedsted-Hansen, 'Transnational State Responsibility for Violations of Human Rights', 12 *Harvard Human Rights Journal* (1999) 267–95, 267. See also Gibney, who argues that '[a]lthough human rights are declared to be "universal," the enforcement and protection of those rights – and even state responsibility for violating human rights – have remained constrained by considerations of territory or citizenship'. Mark Gibney, 'Book Review: Extraterritorial Application of Human Rights Treaties, Edited by Coomans and Kamminga', 100 *American Journal of International Law* (2006) 282–3, 282.

realisation of the human right to water for the benefit of the entire population inhabiting a given river basin.

The overall analysis aims at the appraisal of the current state of international and regional human rights law and jurisprudence on states' extraterritorial duties and its implications for states' duties to share 'their' fresh waters for the realisation of the human right to water in territories beyond their own. The analysis of states' extraterritorial obligations in this chapter proceeds from the general to the specific. This is because, once the spatial reach of states' human rights obligations is established, both the positive and negative aspects of the duties normally apply to the whole gamut of relevant human rights, including the right to water. Therefore, the underlying premise of what follows is that once states' extraterritorial human rights duties – to respect, protect, promote and fulfil – are recognised and established by the instruments and/or jurisdictions in relation to a given human right, then the same logic would also apply to relevant human rights guarantees, including the human right to water. Once established, these duties correspond to a wide-ranging catalogue of human rights with the few exceptions of those rights that are inherently related to citizenship (and hence territorial) such as the right to vote;[4] the same logic would apply to the human right to water.[5] As Kalin observed, it has been broadly acknowledged both in doctrine and jurisprudence on human rights that states incur both positive and negative obligations in the realisation of all categories of human rights.[6] The analysis therefore proceeds from an implicit assumption that, as the four layers of states' obligations correspond to the entire catalogue of human rights, the spatial reach of state obligations applies to almost all human rights, including the right to water.

[4] According to the African Commission, '[a]lthough some rights, like the right to vote and to stand for election, are reserved for citizens of the particular state, human rights are in principle to be enjoyed by all persons'. See Communication 292/2004, *Institute for Human Rights and Development in Africa/Republic of Angola*, 24th Annual Activity Report (2008), para. 80. For a similar view, see General Recommendation 30 of the UN Committee on the Elimination of Racial Discrimination (CERD), HRI/GEN/1/Rev.7/Add.1 (2004), para. 3.

[5] See Chapter 3. See also Douglass Cassel, 'Extraterritorial Application of Inter-American Human Rights Instruments' in Fons Coomans and Menno T. Kamminga (eds.), *Extraterritorial Application of Human Rights Treaties* (Intersentia, 2004) 175, 175–6.

[6] Walter Kalin and Jorg Kunzli, *The Law of International Human Rights Protection* (Oxford University Press, 2009) 96. See also Scott Leckie, 'Another Step towards Indivisibility: Identifying the Key Features of Violations of Economic, Social and Cultural Rights', 20 *Human Rights Quarterly* (1998) 81, 91. See also Chapter 4.

5.2 Setting the scene: the spatial reach of states' human rights obligations

The spatial reach of states' human rights obligations under regional and global human rights treaties has recently become a subject of rumbling academic debate. At the core of the controversy is the issue of whether a state owes the four layers of duties to 'respect, protect, promote and fulfil' human rights not only to those within its own borders[7] but also to those beyond its national territory (extraterritorially).[8] It raises the question: to whom – only to those within or also to those outside a state's territory – are the state's human rights obligations owed, and on whose behalf the obligations stemming from international human rights law are to be fulfilled?[9] In other words, this debate addresses the question of whether state parties to international human rights treaties would be allowed to commit violations in another state's territory, which violations they are prohibited from committing within their own borders.[10]

The overall structure of international human rights law has hitherto been generally understood to have been designed in such a way as to protect individuals and groups against abusive domestic state power.[11] The human rights framework has primarily been conceived of as implying universal human rights[12] and domestic – or territorial – state duties.[13] Consequently, the legal community began to focus some

[7] Salomon, for instance, argued that state human rights obligations were designed to enforce and strengthen the implementation of the rights enshrined therein by the states when they act domestically. See Margot E. Salomon, *Global Responsibility for Human Rights: World Poverty and the Development of International Law* (Oxford University Press, 2007) 190.

[8] As Craven observed, 'at least as regards a duty to "respect" or "protect" the enjoyment of ESC [economic, social and cultural] rights on the part of those living in other states – the issue has clearly remained a contentious one'. See Matthew Craven, 'The Violence of Dispossession: Extra-Territoriality and Economic, Social and Cultural Rights' in A. Mashood and Robert McCorquodale Baderin (eds.), *Economic, Social and Cultural Rights in Action* (Oxford University Press, 2007) 71, 77.

[9] Kalin and Kunzli (note 6 above) 93.

[10] As Skogly noted, the common perception is that 'whether a state can in any way be held responsible for human rights violations depends not only on the state's actions, but also on where those actions took place, and/or the nationality of the victims of the violations'. Sigrun I. Skogly, 'Extraterritoriality: Universal Human Rights without Universal Obligations?' in Sarah Joseph and Adam McBeth (eds.), *Research Handbook on International Human Rights Law* (Edward Elgar, 2010) 71, 71.

[11] Gibney, Tomaseviski and Vedsted-Hansen (note 3 above) 267.

[12] See note 2 above.

[13] The duties of states in the implementation of (treaty-based) rights are usually circumscribed by territoriality, jurisdiction and citizenship. See Gibney, Tomaseviski and Vedsted-Hansen (note 3 above) 267.

attention on the spatial reach of human rights only since the 1990s.[14] This new development has been partly driven by the need to regulate state activities undertaken or producing direct or indirect effects across borders.[15] In other words, the need was felt to make the international human rights regime relevant to contemporary forms of transboundary human rights violations. This development was also partly triggered by the need to mitigate the impacts of globalisation that brought about an increasing influence on human rights of multinational companies.[16] The prospect of linking the human rights duties of a foreign state and the human rights of people of third states through extraterritorial (diagonal) human rights obligations has thus marked a radical challenge – or a 'revolution',[17] so to speak – to the norms of general international law whose normal operation had been horizontal (state versus state) regulation of international conduct.[18] According to Skogly and Gibney, such a radical development represents a 'quantum leap' in the norms of human rights law whose normal operation had been vertically territorial.[19]

Thus, the initial stages of the development of international human rights law had to focus on the mission of taming the powers of a state acting territorially.[20] As the protections and realisation of human rights have had to grapple with the idea of limiting the harms that the state can

[14] See Salomon (note 7 above) 180–2.

[15] Michal Gondek, 'Extraterritorial Application of the European Convention on Human Rights: Territorial Focus in the Age of Globalisation?', 52(3) *Netherlands International Law Review* (2005) 349–87, 351.

[16] See Fons Coomans, 'Some Remarks on the Extraterritorial Application of the International Covenant on Economic, Social and Cultural Rights' in Fons Coomans and Menno T. Kamminga (eds.), *Extraterritorial Application of Human Rights Treaties* (Intersentia, 2004) 183, 184; Surya Deva, 'Acting Extraterritorially to Tame Multinational Corporations for Human Rights Violations: Who Should "Bell the Cat"?', 5 *Melbourne Journal of International Law* (2004) 37–65, 46–50; Danwood Mzikenge Chirwa, 'The Doctrine of State Responsibility as a Potential Means of Holding Private Actors Accountable for Human Rights', 5 *Melbourne Journal of International Law* (2004) 1–36, 2–4.

[17] Sigrun I. Skogly, *Beyond National Borders: States Human Rights Obligations in International Cooperation* (Intersentia, 2006) 5.

[18] Rosalyn Higgins, *Problems and Processes: International Law and How We Use It* (Oxford University Press, 1995) 39.

[19] Sigrun Skogly and Mark Gibney, 'Introduction' in Mark Gibney and Sigrun Skogly (eds.), *Universal Human Rights and Extraterritorial Obligations* (University of Pennsylvania Press, 2010) 1, 3.

[20] Malcolm D. Evans, 'State Responsibility and the European Convention on Human Rights: Role and Realm' in Malgosia Fitzmaurice and Dan Sarooshi (eds.), *Issues of State Responsibility before International Judicial Institutions* (Hart Publishing, 2004) 139.

do to individuals and peoples in its own territory,[21] emphasis was placed on devising ways of enhancing domestic application of international human rights.[22] The primary – indeed exclusive[23] – focus of international human rights law and related scholarship has been to develop a framework within which state actors are held to account for domestic infractions of basic human rights.[24]

Consequently, the understanding about the human rights regime that was sought to be established thereby has quite often been taken to apply within a state's territory or jurisdiction.[25] This means that the development and elaboration of the regime set up by the international human rights treaties and the obligations they engender in state–individual (vertical) relationships took much of the attention of the existing national and international efforts.[26] The development of norms and monitoring and enforcement bodies for the translation of these norms into domestic benefits in the vertical relationship have for much of the last half century overshadowed the horizontal and the diagonal implications of human rights treaties.[27]

However, the premise that the domestic state is the primary violator of human rights is only partly correct. Violations of human rights at the domestic level have increasingly come to be committed by extraterritorial actors, which may be state or non-state entities. For instance, the diversion or pollution of an international watercourse[28] by a state

[21] Skogly (note 17 above) 57.

[22] Oscar Schachter, 'The Obligation to Implement the Covenant in Domestic Law' in Louis Henkin (ed.), *The International Bill of Rights: The Covenant on Civil and Political Rights* (Columbia University Press, 1981) 311, 311; Wouter Vandenhole, 'EU and Development: Extraterritorial Obligations under the International Covenant on Economic, Social and Cultural Rights' in Margot E. Salomon, Arne Tostensen and Wouter Vandenhole (eds.), *Casting the Net Wider: Human Rights, Development and New Duty-Bearers* (Intersentia, 2007) 85, 86.

[23] Skogly (note 17 above) 1.

[24] Smita Narula, 'The Right to Food: Holding Global Actors Accountable under International Law' (Centre for Human Rights and Global Justice Working Paper, New York University School of Law, 2006) 25.

[25] Fons Coomans and Menno T. Kamminga, 'Comparative Introductory Comments on the Extraterritorial Application of Human Rights Treaties' in Fons Coomans and Menno T. Kamminga (eds.), *Extraterritorial Application of Human Rights Treaties* (Intersentia, 2004) 1, 1.

[26] Evans (note 20 above) 140. [27] Skogly (note 17 above) 4–5.

[28] According to the 1997 Convention on the Law of the Non-Navigational Uses of International Watercourses (Watercourses Convention), a 'watercourse' is defined as 'a system of surface waters and ground waters constituting by virtue of their physical relationship a unitary whole and normally flowing into a common terminus'. An

might cause little or no harm to the human rights of the state's inhabitants, but could cause scarcity of water or seriously compromise the quality of water available to inhabitants of other co-riparian states.

Of course, as illustrated in Chapter 4, affected people can have recourse against their own state, but the state's internally available water resources might be below what is necessary to cater for drinking and sanitation for its population. Or, the violation of the human right to water in a state's territory may be caused by an act or omission of a third state, without the involvement of the home state where the victims reside. Clearly, the home state's duty would not be implicated if the violations occur due to a cause exclusively attributable to a co-riparian state without the knowledge and beyond the control of the former. This means that, if persons or groups of persons who are not its agents or who are not acting on its own order or under its control violate human rights, their conduct cannot be attributed to the state concerned and it does not incur responsibility for such infringements.

Territorially bound responsibilities of states thus leave gaps in the protective regime of international human rights law. Territoriality of states' human rights duties is also at odds with the principle of universality of human rights which dissociates human rights from geography, jurisdiction or citizenship. In effect, it would tie the spatial reach of human rights to a state's jurisdiction or individuals' and groups' nationality. As a result, the universal human and peoples' rights could, in circumstances which do not neatly fall within a state's territory or jurisdiction, lose their correlative duty-bearer with the effect that rights violations in certain critical situations would be without a duty-bearer to hold accountable for the infringements. This creates a yawning gap in the protective regime of international human rights law, thereby creating a situation that is referred to as a 'legal black hole'.[29]

As the discussion on the Inter-American jurisprudence shows (below), some human rights violations may be committed on the high seas, an area of sea that is under no state's exclusive territorial jurisdiction, and as such is considered as global commons.[30] The absence or

international watercourse is one the 'parts of which are situated in different States'. See Article 2(a) and (b).

[29] Gibney (note 3 above) 282; Georg Ress, 'Problems of Extraterritorial Human Rights Violations – The Jurisdiction of the European Court of Human Rights: The Bankovic Case', 12 *Italian Yearbook of International Law* (2005) 51–67, 63.

[30] See Stuart Kaye, 'Threats from the Global Commons: Problems of Jurisdiction and Enforcement', 8(1) *Melbourne Journal of International Law* (2007) 185–97.

obscurity of a state duty-bearer and the resulting lack of redress would lead to a situation where the universal nature of rights becomes empty promises for many of the supposed beneficiaries.

In the area of the human right to water, examples of extraterritorial state and parastatal violations of human rights abound. The effect in Russia of the industrial accident that polluted a transboundary river originating in China has already been mentioned.[31] Shell Nigeria, a subsidiary of the Royal Dutch Shell oil company, contaminated drinking water in the Niger Delta.[32] The Nigerian government was held responsible for the damage caused,[33] but the foreign-based entity was not held accountable for the damaging acts – including water pollution – of which it was a primary perpetrator. The operation of Ashanti goldfields in Ghana – operated by Lonrho plc, the government of Ghana, the Bank of New York and others – has polluted the River Jimi, which turned brown from sediments washed down from mining operations.[34] The river's tributary, the Sibri, is also polluted.[35] The pollution level is so grave that, for the people of Akfoum, signboards have been erected warning: 'Don't swim, Don't fish, Don't drink.'[36] Newmont's operations in Indonesia, Peru, California, Nevada and the Philippines have destroyed fisheries, polluted water and caused widespread health problems.[37] On 30 January 2000, a massive toxic stew of cyanide and heavy metals from the Bia Mare Gold Mine, operated by the Australian company Esmeralda and a Romanian joint venture partner, flowed into the Tisza and Danube rivers. The Tisza is now considered a 'dead' river.[38]

These illustrations dramatically depict the increased vulnerability of individuals' and groups' rights generally, and the human right to water specifically, to threats caused or aggravated by transboundary (state and non-state) actors. The fact that many of the human rights violations

[31] See Chapter 4.

[32] Communication 155/96, *Social and Economic Rights Action Centre and the Centre for Economic and Social Rights* v. *Nigeria*, 15th Annual Activity Report (2002), paras. 450–4 ('the *SERAC* case').

[33] *Ibid.*, paras. 54 and 69.

[34] Douglas Korsah-Brown, 'Environment, Human Rights and Mining Conflicts in Ghana' in Lyuba Zarsky (ed.), *Human Rights and the Environment: Conflicts and Norms in a Globalizing World* (Earthscan Publications Ltd, 2002) 79, 88.

[35] *Ibid.* [36] *Ibid.*

[37] Lyuba Zarsky, 'Global Reach: Human Rights and Environment in the Framework of Corporate Accountability' in Lyuba Zarsky (ed.), *Human Rights and the Environment: Conflicts and Norms in a Globalizing World* (Earthscan Publications Ltd, 2002) 31, 43.

[38] *Ibid.*

recounted above are caused by state and parastatal actors based outside the territory or jurisdiction of the state where their actions or omissions cause human rights violations tends to deny the victims the remedies they deserve. The legal hurdles hinge on the territorial reach, perceived or real, of human rights and related states' duties.

The inadequacy, or lacuna, of the human rights corpus in the face of such and other events has only recently attracted the attention of scholars towards the examination of the extraterritorial duty of the human rights obligations of states.[39] Consequently, the study of the extraterritorial application of human rights and attendant state obligations is still in its infancy. It is described as 'the least developed in the theory and practice of international human rights law'.[40] As will be shown below, even the newly emerging analyses and related jurisprudence in the area of extraterritorial human rights and states' obligations have focused on what a state cannot (and should not) do in and against persons in third states. As outlined in Chapter 1, in the area of socio-economic rights, such as the human right to water, rather than or as much as the negative states' duties, the challenge is to reach beyond traditional concepts of state sovereignty in order to ensure global justice in the process of redistribution of resources upon which the fulfilment of the rights depends.[41] More specifically, in the context of the human right to water, the need for a riparian state to use the waters originating in or traversing its territory to *fulfil* the human right to water for individuals and groups in its own territory might diminish the amount of water flowing into a co-riparian state. The same holds true of the effects of possible pollution in the upstream state. This would make it impossible or extremely onerous for the other co-riparian states to *protect* and *fulfil* the same rights in their own territories. In some cases, a state's over-utilisation or pollution of a shared water resource may jeopardise the realisation of the core minimum amount of water absolutely needed for bare survival in other co-riparian states. Questions remain, therefore, as to whether a co-riparian state has the duty not only to *respect* but also to *protect*, *promote* and *fulfil* the rights of foreign nationals in foreign states that share the same water resource for the realisation of their human

[39] Coomans and Kamminga (note 25 above) 1.

[40] Sigrun I. Skogly, 'The Obligation of International Assistance and Co-operation in the International Covenant on Economic, Social and Cultural Rights' in Morten Bergsmo (ed.), *Human Rights and Criminal Justice for the Downtrodden: Essays in Honour of Asbjørn Eide* (Martinus Nijhoff Publishers, 2003) 403, 404.

[41] Coomans (note 16 above) 183–4.

right to water. As stated at the outset, the present analysis focuses on the examination of the reach of the African Charter, the scope of which will apply to all or most of the rights and freedoms it enshrines, including the human right to water.

5.3 Extraterritorial reach of the African Charter

The African Charter is not unequivocal about the extraterritorial reach of its rights and freedoms or correlative states' obligations. There is no mention of the territorial or jurisdictional reach or limitation of any categories of the Charter's rights and freedoms or attendant states' duties. Academic analysis of human rights and their extraterritorial application in the context of the African human rights system is almost non-existent.[42] However, the African Commission has long adjudicated issues involving the extraterritorial reach of states' human rights obligations and laid down some rules and *dicta*. As outlined in this section, there are textual bases and discernible trends in the jurisprudence of the regional system for the extraterritorial application of the Charter's guarantees and states' human rights duties.

5.3.1 *Absence of jurisdiction clause*

The general 'obligations clause' under Article 1 of the Charter states:

> The Member States of the Organization of African Unity, parties to the present Charter shall recognise the rights, duties and freedoms enshrined in the Charter and shall undertake to adopt legislative or other measures to give effect to them.

The Charter does not contain an explicit provision that limits the state parties' obligations of realising the rights and freedoms to their respective territories or jurisdictions. Indeed, there is nothing in the African

[42] Only rare passing remarks have been made by a few authors about the extraterritorial application of human rights in the African human rights system. The existing literature is in agreement that a state cannot be held responsible for not realising the human rights of non-national non-residents. See Carlson Anyangwe, 'Obligations of State Parties to the African Charter on Human and Peoples' Rights', 10(4) *African Journal of International and Comparative Law* (1998) 625–59, 627; Frans Viljoen, 'Admissibility under the African Charter' in Malcolm Evans and Rachel Murray (eds.), *The African Charter on Human and Peoples' Rights: The System in Practice, 1986–2000* (Cambridge University Press, 2002) 61, 78.

Charter which has the import of 'territoriality' of states' human rights duties.[43]

Despite the conspicuous absence of a 'jurisdiction' or 'territoriality' clause in the African Charter, some scholars have asserted that a state cannot be held responsible for the realisation of the Charter's rights and freedoms beyond their own borders. According to Anyangwe:

> each state party to a human rights treaty assumes international responsibility towards its own inhabitants. A state does not assume an obligation to assist another state to fulfil its obligations to respect and to ensure the realisation of the rights of its inhabitants.[44]

Similarly, Viljoen argued that 'State Parties to the African Charter are in principle only responsible for violations that occur within their territory'.[45] In this vein, the territoriality of states' human rights obligations derives from the fact that 'States are responsible only for actions or events under their control'.[46] Viljoen contends that territoriality is a precondition for admissibility of a case against a state party to the Charter, and maintains the view that a state's extraterritorial responsibility can only be implicated for violations of the Charter's rights by reasons of 'an extra-territorial incident or event in cases where the State has *de facto* control over that incident or event'.[47] He does not categorically deny the extraterritorial reach of states' obligations but argues that such duties hinge upon the amount of control a state exercised over the relevant incident or event.

In the case of the right to water, the concern is the regulation of a state's (in)actions over waters originating in and traversing its territory. Since such actions are usually under a riparian state's *de facto* and *de jure* control, Viljoen's argument does not necessarily exclude the possibility of holding a state responsible for violating the human right to water in third states through its territorial actions and omissions.

Nevertheless, the argument that the Charter's spatial reach in relation to the remainder of the Charter's provisions is territorially or jurisdictionally limited seems to lack a textual basis in the Charter. As noted above, there is

[43] See Fatsah Ouguergouz, *The African Charter on Human and Peoples' Rights: A Comprehensive Agenda for Human Dignity and Sustainable Democracy in Africa* (Kluwer Law International, 2003) 553.

[44] Anyangwe (note 42 above) 627. [45] Viljoen (note 42 above) 107. [46] *Ibid.*

[47] Frans Viljoen, 'Communications under the African Charter: Procedure and Admissibility' in Malcolm Evans and Rachel Murray (eds.), *The African Charter on Human and Peoples' Rights: The System in Practice, 1986–2006* (Cambridge University Press, 2nd edn, 2008) 76, 107.

nothing in the explicit wording of the Charter's 'obligations clause' to suggest that the instrument was meant to apply territorially or within a state party's jurisdiction only. Indeed, a similar absence in the ICESCR and the American Declaration on the Rights and Duties of Man ('American Declaration')[48] of a clause limiting the enjoyment of the rights recognised therein to persons within the territory or jurisdiction of a state party has led to the conclusion that both the ICESCR and the American Declaration have extraterritorial application.[49]

This line of interpretation is more in line with the object and purpose of the Charter, as it promotes the protective regime established by the regional instrument. The American Declaration and ICESCR are part of the 'inspirational sources' which could potentially influence or even guide the approach of the African Commission in relation to its interpretation of the Charter's provisions.[50] Arguably, therefore, the absence of a clause limiting the rights and freedoms enshrined in the Charter and related states' obligations to a certain 'territory' or 'jurisdiction' implies that the Charter has left room open for extraterritorial application of its guarantees and correlative state duties.

5.3.2 *Substantive provisions with extraterritorial dimensions*

The Charter provides for some substantive extraterritorial human rights guarantees that have the effect of extending a state's duties beyond its territory. Under Article 12(2), the Charter enshrines every individual's right to return to the country of origin. This right protects an individual who is outside the territory (hence the jurisdiction) of the state of origin. In this sense, the protection afforded to the individual, and the duty of the state to allow the same to return home, applies extraterritorially.

Legal protections of this type are aimed at 'insulating a state's citizens from the consequences of the state's actions abroad'.[51] Extraterritorial

48 Adopted by the Ninth International Conference of American States, Bogotá, Colombia, 1948.

49 Rolf Kunnemann, 'Extraterritorial Application of the International Covenant on Economic, Social and Cultural Rights' in Fons Coomans and Menno T. Kamminga (eds.), *Extraterritorial Application of Human Rights Treaties* (Intersentia, 2004) 201; Kerstin Mechlem, 'Treaty Bodies and the Interpretation of Human Rights', 42 *Vanderbilt Journal of Transnational Law* (2009) 905–47, 935–40; Coomans (note 16 above) 184–6; Coomans and Kamminga (note 25 above) 2.

50 See section 5.4.2.2 below.

51 Tom Farer, '"Bombing for Peace: Collateral Damage and Human Rights": Remarks by Tom Farer', 96 *American Society of International Law Proceedings* (2002) 104–7, 106.

application of human rights can therefore be seen as an instrument for the protection of individuals and groups abroad from the transboundary violations of their rights by their own state of origin. In the case of the right to water, a state's violation of the right in a co-riparian state may violate the rights of its own nationals residing in the co-riparian state's territory.

As the Charter incorporates an instance of a specific substantive rule that is designed to accrue to extraterritorial beneficiaries, arguably, it does not intend to distinguish among the rights and freedoms it enshrines in terms of their spatial reach. As stated at the outset, once they are established, states' human rights duties correspond to a wide-ranging catalogue of human rights with the few exceptions of those rights that are inherently related to citizenship (and hence territorial), such as the right to vote. The African Commission stated, '[a]lthough some rights, like the right to vote and to stand for election, are reserved for citizens of the particular state, human rights are in principle to be enjoyed by all persons'.[52] As long as the Charter incorporates the principle that enjoins states from violating human rights beyond borders in relation to some rights, the same logic applies to the rest of its human and peoples' rights catalogue.[53] This may explain the absence of a territoriality or jurisdiction clause in the Charter's 'obligations clause'. Therefore, arguably, the Charter's guarantees such as the right to water would entail the extension of a state's human rights obligations beyond its territorial jurisdiction.

5.3.3 *The jurisprudence of the African Commission*

Quasi-judicial scrutiny of the extraterritorial reach of human rights and correlative states' obligations in Africa leapfrogged related academic debate. Attempts at holding states extraterritorially responsible for

[52] See Communication 292/2004, *Institute for Human Rights and Development in Africa/ Republic of Angola*, 24th Annual Activity Report (2008), para. 80.

[53] Once established, states' human rights duties correspond to a wide-ranging catalogue of human rights with the few exceptions of those rights that are inherently related to citizenship (and hence are territorial), such as the right to vote. According to the African Commission, '[a]lthough some rights, like the right to vote and to stand for election are reserved for citizens of the particular state, human rights are in principle to be enjoyed by all persons'. See *ibid.* For a similar view, see General Recommendation 30 of the UN Committee on the Elimination of Racial Discrimination (CERD), HRI/GEN/1/Rev.7/ Add.1 (2004), para. 3. See also Kalin and Kunzli (note 6 above) 96; Cassel (note 5 above) 175–6; Leckie (note 6 above) 91.

violations of human rights and freedoms guaranteed under the African Charter started to come before the African Commission almost as soon as the Commission was inaugurated in 1987.[54] Individuals sought to avail themselves of the regional mechanism for redressing violations of their rights by non-territorial actors. This is indicative of the prevalence, if not rampancy, of extraterritorial violations of individuals' and groups' rights in Africa not only by African states but even by non-African countries. None of these early communications was considered on their merits, as the states against whom the communications were lodged were non-African states over which the Commission has no jurisdiction. The communications were thus deemed irreceivable and dismissed at their early stages.[55]

However, the Commission was given other opportunities more recently to consider complaints of human rights violations by African states in other states' territories. The case relating to the invasion of the territory of the Democratic Republic of Congo (DRC),[56] which was the first ever admissible inter-state communication to the African Commission (the *DRC Invasion* case),[57] involved four of the ten Nile co-riparian states. It was submitted by the DRC against Burundi, Rwanda and Uganda complaining about the occupation of its territory by the armed forces of the three defendant states. More importantly, the DRC complained about violations of its residents' (individuals and groups) Charter-based rights by the occupying forces in the territories they forcibly occupied. The Commission found the three states to be in violation, *inter alia*, of the right to respect for life and the integrity of person (Article 4), the right to dignity (Article 5), the right to freedom of movement (Article 12), the right to property (Article 14), the right to

[54] See, for instance, Communication 7/88, *Committee for the Defence of Political Prisoners* v. *Bahrain*, 7th Annual Activity Report (1993–4); Communication 38/90, *Wesley Parish* v. *Indonesia*, 7th Annual Activity Report (1993–4); Communication 2/88, *Iheanyichukwu A. Ihebereme* v. *USA*, 7th Annual Activity Report (1993–4); Communication 5/88, *Prince J. N. Makoge* v. *USA*, 7th Annual Activity Report (1993–4); Communication 3/88, *Centre for the Independence of Judges and Lawyers* v. *Yugoslavia*, 7th Annual Activity Report (1993–4); Communication 37/90, *Georges Eugene* v. *USA and Haiti*, 7th Annual Activity Report (1993–4).

[55] See the cases cited in the previous footnote.

[56] See Communication 227/1999, *Democratic Republic of Congo (DRC)* v. *Burundi, Rwanda and Uganda*, 20th Annual Activity Report (2006) ('*DRC Invasion* case').

[57] Under the African Charter, communications are categorised as inter-state communications (submitted by a state against another state) and 'other' communications, referring to complaints by non-state entities against state parties to the African Charter. See Articles 47–55 of the African Charter.

physical and mental health (Article 16), the right to culture (Article 17), the right to unity of a family (Article 18), peoples' right to self-determination (Articles 19–20), peoples' right to dispose of their wealth and natural resources (Article 21) and peoples' right to economic, social and cultural development (Article 22) as guaranteed under the African Charter.[58]

The acts that constituted the violations of the Charter's provisions were committed entirely within the DRC's territory, outside the boundaries of any of the defendant states. This did not hinder the Commission from attributing responsibility to the defendant states, giving rise to the assumption that states are responsible for the violations of human rights they commit abroad.[59] None of the states implicated in this case raised any objections contesting the extension by the Commission of their human rights responsibilities to territories beyond their own borders. Accordingly, the defendant states were held responsible for violations of fundamental rights and freedoms that occurred within the DRC's territory that they brought under their effective control at the material time. Non-objection by the defendant states to the extraterritorial application of a regional human rights treaty has similarly led the Inter-American Commission on Human Rights to hold that the states have acquiesced to their extraterritorial human rights obligations.[60]

Another African case that has had elements of extraterritorial state responsibility once again involved, to varying degrees,[61] seven of the ten Nile basin states as defendants, namely, Ethiopia, Kenya, Tanzania, Rwanda, Uganda, Zaire and Zambia (the *Burundi Embargo* case).[62] This case arose out of the imposition of an embargo by the defendant states on 31 July 1996 against the state of Burundi as an expression of protest against the unconstitutional change (*coup d'état*) that toppled the democratically elected government in that country. The embargo was later endorsed by the African Union and the UN Security Council. A case

[58] *DRC Invasion* case, para. 98. [59] See *ibid.*, paras. 963–6.

[60] Christina M. Cerna, 'Extraterritorial Application of the Human Rights Instruments of the Inter-American System' in Fons Coomans and Menno T. Kamminga (eds.), *Extraterritorial Application of Human Rights Treaties* (Intersentia, 2004) 141, 165–8.

[61] Ethiopia was later removed from the list as it was not a party to the Charter at the material time. Communication 157/96, *Association pour la Sauvegarde de la Paix au Burundi* v. *Tanzania, Kenya, Uganda, Rwanda, Zaire and Zambia*, 17th Annual Activity Report (2003–4), para. 52.

[62] See *ibid.*

was taken on behalf of the then new military government of Burundi to the Commission complaining that the embargo, by curtailing Burundi's access to imported goods and services, violated the right to life, the right to education and related rights of Burundians. Although the Commission absolved all the defendants of any wrongdoing,[63] it laid down an important *dictum* for future cases. It decided that:

> [t]he critical question and one which may affect the legitimacy of the action is whether such action as has been determined is excessive and disproportionate, is indiscriminate and seeks to achieve ends beyond the legitimate purpose. Sanctions therefore cannot be open-ended, the effects thereof must be carefully monitored, measures must be adopted to meet the basic needs of the most vulnerable populations or they must be targeted at the main perpetrators or authors of the nuisance complained of.[64]

This *dictum* has far-reaching implications for the jurisprudence of extraterritoriality of human rights and related duties of states in Africa. It shows that the Commission was ready to find the states responsible for violations of the rights of residents of foreign states if and when they take actions that are disproportionate to the end sought to be achieved or are indiscriminate or lack monitoring mechanisms to ensure that the basic rights of individuals and groups are not jeopardised.[65] It ruled that 'sanctions are not an end in themselves. They are not imposed for the sole purpose of causing suffering.'[66] It thus commented:

> [w]e are satisfied that the sanctions imposed were not indiscriminate, that they were targeted in that a list of affected goods was made. A monitoring committee was put in place and the situation was monitored regularly. As a result of these reports adjustments were made accordingly.[67]

Both the *DRC Invasion* case and the *Burundi Embargo* case have some important common features as well as major differences. Both cases brought into focus the negative side of states' extraterritorial duties. The violations complained of involved a breach of the extraterritorial duty to *respect* the relevant rights, which is a duty of abstention. Neither

[63] *Ibid.*, para. 79. [64] *Ibid.*, para. 75.

[65] For an analysis of procedural issues such as questions of *locus standi* and admissibility requirements, see generally Alain Didier Olinga, 'The Embargo against Burundi before the African Commission on Human and Peoples' Rights (Note on Communication 157/96)', 5 *African Human Rights Law Journal* (2005) 424–32.

[66] Communication 157/96 (note 61 above), para. 77. [67] *Ibid.*, para. 76.

of the cases has thus had clear implications for positive duties of a state to residents of third states as none was involved in the relevant litigation. The Commission was not called upon to decide on questions of inter-state obligation for resource sharing – such as water resources. Nevertheless, in both cases, none of the states objected to the fact that they were being implicated for extraterritorial duties. If silence or lack of objection to extraterritorial human rights duties is indicative of state practice (as has been the case in the Inter-American human rights system),[68] eight of the eleven Nile basin states have assented to be held extraterritorially responsible for their acts as they failed to seize more than one opportunity to raise their objections.

The 'effective control' element was not a requirement in the *Burundi Embargo* case, while it was a constitutive element of state responsibility in the *DRC Invasion* case. In the former, the defendant states were accused of violating the rights of residents of Burundi through their decision to impose an embargo upon Burundi, taken at a summit held in Arusha, Tanzania. There was no semblance of territorial control or presence of these states in Burundi (the complainant state).

Although the extraterritorial application of the African Charter was recognised by the Commission, its implications for sharing transboundary water resources have yet to be established. The Commission has only confirmed that states have extraterritorial human rights duties to respect human rights and, as such, states have to abstain from the commission or omission of actions that violate the human rights of individuals and groups in third states.

However, abstention alone would offer an inadequate means for residents of water-deficient states to access water resources that emerge from beyond the boundaries of their home state or prevent the reduction of water quantity or quality they receive therefrom. Thus, the issue of whether states owe residents of other states the duty of sharing waters originating in their territories (obligation to promote and fulfil) remains vague and unsettled but holds the key to the realisation of the human right to water in Africa in general and in the Nile basin in particular.

That said, the African Commission's human rights jurisprudence should be understood in its own context. None of the cases that came before the Commission involved positive extraterritorial state obligations, and, as such, the Commission had to limit its rulings to the concrete dispute before it, i.e. the *duty to respect*. It has shown, however,

[68] See section 5.4.2.2 below.

that states are extraterritorially liable whenever their acts have the effect of jeopardising human rights in third states.

As all continental African states share waters of international rivers, and given that individuals and groups in those states depend on transboundary fresh water for the realisation of their human right to water, a state can severely jeopardise the right in question from within its own borders without any need of directly controlling a co-riparian state's territory. Consequently, many riparian states would find it either impossible or extremely arduous to fulfil their human rights obligations to their respective inhabitants unless there are ways of sharing such resources and ensuring that co-riparian states account for the harm they cause to those in other co-riparian states' territories. In the Nile basin, for instance, the entirety of life in Egypt depends upon the waters of the Nile River,[69] 86 per cent of which flows down from the Blue Nile originating in the Ethiopian highlands,[70] with the rest flowing from the White Nile of the Great Lakes region.[71] The available Nile waters have been fully used[72] and the states no longer have viable alternatives to sharing the common resources in the spirit of cooperation.[73] Given the spatial distribution of water resources in Africa, a state's extraterritorial duty to respect the human right to water is not adequate for the realisation of the human right to water in co-riparian states. It takes active cooperation in the form of equitable sharing of transboundary waters to offer a real hope of realisation of the right in all countries of the continent.

5.4 The utility of cross-reference: 'inspirational sources'

The African Charter has granted the African Commission a wide latitude under Articles 60 and 61 under which the Commission was mandated to 'draw inspiration' from rules of international law and international human rights law. The Commission stated that, '[i]n interpreting and

[69] Arun P. Elhance, *Hydropolitics in the Third World: Conflict and Cooperation in International River Basins* (United States Institute of Peace Press, 1999) 54.

[70] Yacob Arsano and Imeru Tamrat, 'Ethiopia and the Eastern Nile Basin', 67 *Aquatic Sciences* (2005) 15–27, 16.

[71] *Ibid.*, 54–6.

[72] Ashok Swain, 'Managing the Nile River: The Role of Sub-Basin Co-operation' in Manas Chatterji, Saul Arlosoroff and Gauri Guha (eds.), *Conflict Management of Water Resources* (Ashgate, 2002) 145, 146–52.

[73] Takele Soboka Bulto, 'Between Ambivalence and Necessity: Occlusions on the Path Towards a Basin-Wide Treaty in the Nile Basin', 20(1) *Colorado Journal of International Environmental Law and Policy* (2009) 291–320, 320.

applying the African Charter, the African Commission relies on its own jurisprudence, and as provided by Articles 60 and 61 of the African Charter, on appropriate and relevant international and regional human rights instruments, principles and standards'.[74] Pursuant to these provisions, the Commission has explicitly referred to the case law and treaty provisions of the global and other regional systems in interpreting the Charter's provisions and rendering decisions on cases that come before it. The Commission ruled that:

> [t]he African Commission is, therefore, more than willing to accept legal arguments with the support of appropriate and relevant international and regional human rights instruments, principles, norms and standards taking into account the well recognised principle of universality which was established by the Vienna Declaration and Program of Action of 1993 and which declares that '*all human rights are universal, indivisible, interdependent, and interrelated*'.[75]

This is not peculiar to the African Commission, just as the cross-references to extra-African legal norms in Articles 60–61 of the African Charter are not novel. There has been an increasing trend among human rights tribunals to use legal rules, principles and case law extraneous to a tribunal's main treaty.[76] Indeed, human rights courts 'work consciously to coordinate their approaches'.[77] It is, therefore, instructive to briefly scrutinise the ICESCR, the works of the CESCR, as well as case law and treaties of the other regional human rights systems as they are among the sources from which the African human rights bodies may 'draw inspiration' in the process of interpreting and applying the regional human rights instruments.

5.4.1 *The relevance of the ICESCR*

As already stated, the global human rights treaties are among the 'inspirational' sources upon which the regional bodies are mandated to model their case law. Chapters 3 and 4 have demonstrated that the African Commission repeatedly referred to the CESCR's interpretations

[74] Communication 241/2001, *Purohit and Moore* v. *The Gambia*, 16th Annual Activity Report (2003), para. 47.

[75] *Ibid.*, para. 48 (emphasis in original).

[76] See generally Duncan French, 'Treaty Interpretation and the Incorporation of Extraneous Rules', 55 *International and Comparative Law Quarterly* (2006) 281–314.

[77] Rosalyn Higgins, 'A Babel of Judicial Voices? Ruminations from the Bench', 55 *International and Comparative Law Quarterly* (2006) 791–804, 798.

of the provisions of the ICESCR in interpreting and applying similar socio-economic rights of the African Charter.[78] Especially with the adoption of the Optional Protocol to the ICESCR[79] and the inclusion of the complaints procedure therein,[80] the ICESCR is no longer merely of inspirational value to the African human rights system. It also provides an alternative forum wherein individuals and groups from Africa directly enforce, *inter alia*, their right to water and claim remedies in respect of violations of the same against African states which ratify the Optional Protocol.[81] For these reasons, a brief overview of the potential of extraterritorial application of the ICESCR provisions is essential.

5.4.1.1 The duty of international assistance: its implications for extraterritorial obligations

The Universal Declaration of Human Rights (UDHR), of which the ICESCR is a progeny, stipulates that, '[e]veryone is entitled to a social and international order in which the rights and freedoms set forth in this Declaration can be fully realized'.[82] Such an international order that is hospitable to the universal realisation of human rights cannot be a reality without active cooperation and assistance among states. Thus:

> [t]he obligations of states to respect and observe human rights owed to people everywhere might impose negative obligations in so far as they are required to abstain from any act that would violate the human right of people anywhere in the world. However, if basic rights have already been violated in a global context, and for example, people are starving, the obligation imposed is also positive – that is, every state, to a greater or lesser degree, is under an obligation to take action to remedy that violation and to prevent its continuation.[83]

[78] For an elaborate discussion of the latitude of the mandate that the African Commission is given under Articles 60 and 61 to draw inspiration from sources other than the Charter and the actual cross-references made to the ICESCR by the Commission, see Takele Soboka Bulto, 'The Indirect Approach to Promote Justiciability of Socio-Economic Rights of the African Charter on Human and Peoples' Rights' in Rachel H. Murray (ed.), *Human Rights Litigation and the Domestication of International Human Rights in Sub-Saharan Africa* (International Commission of Jurists, 2009) 135, 146–8.

[79] See Optional Protocol to the International Covenant on Economic, Social and Cultural Rights, adopted 10 December 2008, opened for signature on 24 September 2009 (not yet in force).

[80] See *ibid*., Articles 1–2.

[81] As at February 2013, no African state had ratified the Optional protocol to the ICESCR.

[82] UDHR, Article 28. [83] Salomon (note 7 above) 192.

As Coomans observed, the provision for the creation of an international order conducive to the full realisation of universal rights 'means an international order which is based on the idea that all states have a shared responsibility and obligation for realising such an order'.[84] This provision has been considered as a normative source of extraterritorial obligations of states, according to which they should be held responsible for the facilitation and the realisation of human rights not only for those in their respective jurisdictions but also for those in third states.[85]

The ICESCR, for its part, enshrines a provision that can be considered as an 'extraterritoriality clause'. Under Article 2(1), the ICESCR provides:

> [e]ach State Party to the present Covenant undertakes to take steps, individually and through international assistance and co-operation, especially economic and technical, to the maximum of its available resources, with a view to achieving progressively the full realization of the rights recognized in the present Covenant by all appropriate means, including particularly the adoption of legislative measures.

Neither 'international assistance' nor 'international cooperation' has yet been authoritatively defined.[86] However, at the very least, as Article 2(1) juxtaposes both 'assistance' and 'cooperation', it can be presumed that the drafters considered the two terms to have distinct, if partly overlapping, meanings.[87] This is in line with the rules of legal interpretation according to which all parts of a provision should be given an effective meaning. Additionally, the word 'assistance' was absent in the early drafts of the ICESCR.[88] It was a late addition, and its eventual placement in front of the word 'cooperation' is thus indicative of the fact that it has a separate role and meaning, besides cooperation, for the realisation of

[84] Coomans (note 16 above) 191.

[85] Asbjørn Eide, 'The International Human Rights System' in Asbjørn Eide *et al.* (eds.), *Food as a Human Right* (United Nations University, 1984) 152, 159; Narula (note 24 above) 3–35; Magdalena Sepúlveda Carmona, 'The Obligation of "International Assistance and Cooperation" under the International Covenant on Economic, Social and Cultural Rights: A Possible Entry Point to a Human Rights Based Approach to Millennium Development Goal 8', 13(1) *International Journal of Human Rights* (2009) 86–109, 90–4.

[86] Salomon (note 7 above) 76–7.

[87] As Salomon noted, the CESCR has yet to formally elaborate the distinction between the terms 'cooperation' and 'assistance'. See Salomon (note 7 above) 77.

[88] *Ibid.*, 204–5.

human rights. Without this approach, the two terms would end up saying the same thing, the one rendering the other redundant.

Many authors have pointed to the difficulty of defining the precise states' duties entailed by international 'cooperation' and 'assistance'.[89] First, the wording of Article 2(1) of the ICESCR has been elusive and complex, primarily due to the diplomatic negotiations that necessitated the use of such a language.[90] In addition, the CESCR has not defined the 'international assistance and cooperation' clause of the ICESCR[91] and none of its General Comments has specifically focused on the elaboration of the obligations entailed thereby.[92] Moreover, the *travaux préparatoires* of the ICESCR shed little light on the intended original meaning of the duty and are not very helpful in elucidating the discrete obligations entailed by the provisions of Article 2(1) of the Covenant.[93] Nevertheless, the territoriality of the rights and duties of the ICESCR was not discussed or intended at the drafting stages of the Covenant.[94]

On the other hand, arguments have been advanced that the generality of the provisions of Article 2(1) of the ICESCR makes it too nebulous to imply a specific obligation for states. One of the few works on the subject of international assistance and cooperation in the realisation of the human right to water argues:

[89] See, for example, Matthew C. R. Craven, *The International Covenant on Economic, Social, and Cultural Rights: A Perspective on Its Development* (Clarendon Press, 1995) 146–7; Sepúlveda Carmona (note 85 above) 87–8; Philip Alston and Gerard Quinn, 'The Nature and Scope of States Parties' Obligations under the International Covenant on Economic, Social and Cultural Rights', 9 *Human Rights Quarterly* (1987) 156–229, 187.

[90] Sepúlveda Carmona (note 85 above) 88.

[91] See Craven (note 89 above) 147; Judith Bueno de Mesquita, Paul Hunt and Rajat Khosla, 'The Human Rights Responsibility of International Assistance and Cooperation in Health' in Mark Gibney and Sigrun Skogly (eds.), *Universal Human Rights and Extraterritorial Obligations* (University of Pennsylvania Press, 2010) 104, 111.

[92] To date, the CESCR has adopted no less than twenty-one General Comments, but most of them focus primarily on the elaboration of the substantive rights contained in the ICESCR. Only some General Comments (such as General Comment No. 3, General Comment No. 8 and General Comment No. 9) have their primary focus on state duties; yet, even these General Comments have their primary focus on the elaboration of states' domestic obligations for the realisation of Covenant rights. See 'Committee on Economic, Social and Cultural Rights – General Comments' at www2.ohchr.org/english/bodies/cescr/comments.htm.

[93] Salomon (note 7 above) 77–8; Craven (note 89 above) 146–7.

[94] Skogly (note 40 above) 411.

> [t]he rule that asks for joint action and international cooperation in order to realise the human rights in the Covenant – in particular Article 2(1) and 11(2) ICESCR – *only imposes very general and unspecified obligations upon the parties. They are therefore not appropriate for deriving concrete duties like the delivery of water.*[95]

This approach is fallible for a number of reasons. A state's duty of international assistance and cooperation is repeated and stressed no less than six times in the ICESCR.[96] Seen against such reiteration and emphasis, the argument that the duty is too general to be concrete ignores the context as well as the purpose of the provision. Indeed, other substantive rights and states' duties contained in some of the provisions of the ICESCR have given some indications of the concrete meaning of the obligations sought to be entailed thereby.[97] Moreover, experts have convincingly argued that the vagueness or lack of authoritative interpretation does not warrant the conclusion that the duty of 'international assistance and cooperation' envisaged under Article 2(1) of the ICESCR is devoid of concrete meanings. Alston and Quinn commented:

> on the basis of the preparatory work it is difficult, if not impossible, to sustain the argument that the commitment to international cooperation contained in the Covenant can accurately be characterized as a legally binding obligation upon any particular state to provide any particular form of assistance. It would, however, be unjustified to go further and suggest that the relevant commitment is meaningless. *In the context of a given right it may, according to circumstances, be possible to identify obligations to cooperate internationally that would appear mandatory on the basis of the undertaking contained in Article 2(1) of the Covenant.*[98]

The same authors foresaw the possibility of progressive development and elaboration of the concepts of international assistance and cooperation, necessitated by subsequent policy trends and events, reaching a stage where they acquire clearer or even new meanings.[99] The problem has been that the implementation of states' human rights duties through international assistance and cooperation has so far been neglected.[100]

[95] Knut Bourquain, *Freshwater Access from a Human Rights Perspective: A Challenge to International Water Law and Human Rights Law* (Martinus Nijhoff Publishers, 2008) 197 (emphasis added).

[96] See Articles 2(1), 11(1), 11(2), 15(4), 22 and 23.

[97] See notes 105–6 below and the accompanying text.

[98] Alston and Quinn (note 89 above) 191. [99] *Ibid.* [100] Skogly (note 40 above) 419.

Be that as it may, cooperation primarily implies reciprocity by way of mutual action directed towards a common goal while assistance refers to 'the transfer of some "good" from one state to another'.[101] Assistance thus involves an obligation of a non-reciprocal nature as compared to the reciprocal obligations contained in the concept of cooperation. Kunnemann similarly defines 'cooperation' as 'working together in the realisation of human rights for each person'.[102]

5.4.1.2 Article 2(1) of the ICESCR as an 'extraterritoriality clause'

A close reading of Article 2(1) points to a few features of the extraterritorial aspects of states' obligations contained therein. First, Article 2(1) does not restrict the realisation of the rights in the ICESCR (or the correlative state obligations) to a territory or jurisdiction of a state. A jurisdiction clause similar to that of the European Convention on Human Rights is conspicuously absent.[103] Arguably, this implies that a state party's duty to realise the rights and freedoms enshrined in the ICESCR is not confined to its territory or jurisdiction, and its duties to realise the rights in third states are not excluded.[104] The second special feature of the ICESCR, which is most pertinent to the extraterritorial nature of a state's obligations, is its requirement that steps shall be taken not only by states acting individually but also through international assistance and cooperation. This also indicates that Article 2(1) foresees not only abstention but international action.[105] There is agreement that the illustrative list of activities under Article 23 of the ICESCR is indicative of the types of assistance and cooperation envisaged under Article 2(1).[106] Under Article 23:

> international action for the achievement of the rights recognized in the present Covenant includes such methods as the conclusion of

[101] Craven (note 89 above) 147. [102] Kunnemann (note 49 above) 212.

[103] Manisuli Ssenyonjo, *Economic, Social and Cultural Rights in International Law* (Hart Publishing, 2009) 44.

[104] According to Coomans, the absence of any mention of territory or jurisdiction in the ICESCR 'suggests that a certain extraterritorial (in the sense of international) scope was intended by the drafters and is part of the treaty'. See Fons Coomans, 'The Extraterritorial Scope of the International Covenant on Economic, Social and Cultural Rights in the Work of the United Nations Committee on Economic, Social and Cultural Rights', 11(1) *Human Rights Law Review* (2011) 1–35, 1.

[105] Craven (note 89 above) 147.

[106] Kunnemann (note 49 above) 203; Craven (note 89 above) 147; Skogly (note 17 above) 95–6.

> conventions, the adoption of recommendations, the furnishing of technical assistance and the holding of regional meetings and technical meetings for the purpose of consultation and study organized in conjunction with the Governments concerned.

Similarly, the obligations of international assistance and cooperation have been recognised under both Articles 11 and 12 of the Covenant. As shown in Chapter 3, these very provisions provide the normative bases for the human right to water. The explicit provision for international assistance and cooperation in these two provisions means that the realisation of the human right to water, among other rights guaranteed therein, entails obligations of an international character.

Thirdly, the obligations under Article 2(1) are neutrally worded and the duties of international assistance and cooperation are attached invariably to 'recipient' and 'donee' states. The generality of the wording implies that the obligation contained therein not merely requires the recipient states to seek international assistance and cooperation but also obliges the 'donee' states to provide the same.[107]

Fourthly, there is nothing in Article 2(1) of the ICESCR to indicate that the measures taken 'individually' refer to territorial obligations and those 'through international assistance and cooperation' to extraterritorial obligations.[108] Accordingly, both territorial and extraterritorial human rights obligations can be undertaken by states acting individually and/or in cooperation with others not only for the benefit of domestic right-holders of the state owing the duties, but also for the benefit of individuals and groups in third states. For instance, as shown in Chapter 6, the obligation of a riparian state not to over-utilise transboundary water to the prejudice of the right to adequate water provision in other co-riparian states implies a state's individual domestic action (or forbearance), but the resultant benefit accrues extraterritorially.

Finally, the obligation of 'international assistance and cooperation' is a general duty corresponding to all rights in the ICESCR. As part of the general obligations clause under Article 2(1) of the ICESCR, the duties it entails correspond to each right guaranteed in the Covenant, including the human right to water. Accordingly, there are international obligations of states which require the states 'to take joint and separate action to achieve the full realisation of the right to water'.[109] The international

[107] Kunnemann (note 49 above) 204. [108] *Ibid.*

[109] CESCR, 'General Comment No. 15: Substantive Issues Arising in the Implementation of the International Covenant on Economic, Social and Cultural Rights (Adopted

obligations comprise both the positive and negative layers of states' duties.[110] It has been argued that 'the question should consequently be *what type* and *scope* of obligations extending beyond the territorial jurisdiction of states the ESC [economic, social and cultural] rights can give rise to'.[111]

5.4.1.3 Extraterritorial state obligations under General Comment No. 15 of the CESCR

General Comment No. 15 of the CESCR has stressed the need to distinguish between a state's *inability* and its *unwillingness* in relation to the realisation of the human right to water.[112] A state's unwillingness is about its wilful failure to use the maximum of its available resources to realise the right, and it clearly constitutes a violation of the right.[113] However, a state's inability to fulfil its human rights duties does not automatically implicate the state's responsibility but entails 'the burden of justifying that every effort has nevertheless been made to use all available resources at its disposal in order to satisfy, as a matter of priority . . . [its human rights] obligations'.[114] The successful justification by the state of such shortfalls, according to the CESCR, triggers third states' extraterritorial duty to realise the human rights of those in the resource-deficient state, if so requested.[115] The inability of a state to realise its human rights duties calls into play its duty to seek and/or access international assistance and cooperation, and the 'donor' state's duty to provide the same. Thus, from the donor state's perspective, the CESCR considers the duty of extraterritorial assistance and cooperation to be among the state's core human rights obligations.[116]

Accordingly, the CESCR, in General Comment No. 15, has stressed the necessity of and affirmed the legal basis for extending the state's human rights obligations to the protection and promotion of the human right to water in third states.[117] Be that as it may, General Comments of

11–29 November 2002)' (UN Committee on Economic, Social and Cultural Rights, 11–29 November 2002), para. 30 ('General Comment No. 15').

110 Salomon (note 7 above) 184.

111 Maija Mustaniemi-Laasko, 'The Right to Education: Instrumental Right Par Excellence' in Margot E. Salomon, Arne Tostensen and Wouter Vandenhole (eds.), *Casting the Net Wider: Human Rights, Development and New Duty-Bearers* (Intersentia, 2007) 331, 337.

112 CESCR, General Comment No. 15 (note 109 above) 41. 113 *Ibid.* 114 *Ibid.*

115 *Ibid.*, para. 34. 116 *Ibid.*, para. 38.

117 This position is also supported by the UN Special Rapporteurs. See, for instance, the report of Jean Ziegler, the Special Rapporteur on the Right to Food, CESCR, 'The Right to Food: Report of the Special Rapporteur on the Right to Food, Jean Ziegler'

the UN treaty Bodies – including General Comment No. 15 on the human right to water – have a major drawback in that they are persuasive instruments but are not binding *per se*.[118] They cannot create new human rights or state obligations. Their persuasive force hinges upon the degree to which the rights or duties elaborated in these instruments are grounded in explicit or implicit legal instruments.

In relation to General Comment No. 15, it has been asserted that '[w]hile no doubt a highly authoritative interpretation of the Covenant, the Committee's [i.e. the CESCR's] finding does not bind the 147 States that are parties to it, let alone other states'.[119] Some writers have argued that the CESCR's approach that seeks to obligate states to account for their roles in the realisation or hindrance of the human right to water in territories beyond their own (as does General Comment No. 15 of the CESCR) is ahead of state practice, and falls within the realm of *de lege ferenda*.[120] According to McCaffrey, while it may take some time for state parties to the ICESCR to explicitly accept or reject the interpretation of General Comment No. 15, states' current silence about it does not suffice to give rise to the acknowledgment of extraterritorial obligations through state practice.[121] He thus argues, 'state practice occurs more through accretion than avulsion'.[122]

Opinion is thus divided as to whether states owe extraterritorial obligations to third states and the latter's residents for the realisation of human rights. As outlined in Chapter 1, this divergence of opinion ranges from the totally negationist view that denies the normative existence of extraterritoriality to the view that unequivocally affirms the adequacy of the legal basis for states' extraterritorial obligations. It is thus important to examine the rules of the regional and international human rights treaties and the case law of the mechanisms established thereby alongside related scholarship in order to gauge the legal basis of extraterritorial state obligations in the realisation of international human rights generally, and the human right to water specifically.

(UN Economic and Social Council (E/CN.4/2006/44), 16 March 2006), paras. 28–38; CESCR, 'The Right to Food: Report of the Special Rapporteur on the Right to Food, Jean Ziegler' (Commission on Human Rights, United Nations Economic and Social Council (E/CN.4/2005/47), 24 January 2005), paras. 34–59.

118 See Chapter 2.

119 Stephen C. McCaffrey, 'The Human Right to Water' in Edith Brown Weiss, Laurence Boisson de Chazournes and Nathale Bernasconi-Osterwalder (eds.), *Fresh Water and International Economic Law* (Oxford University Press, 2005) 93, 94.

120 *Ibid.*, 114–15. 121 *Ibid.*, 94. 122 *Ibid.*

5.4.2 *Extraterritoriality in other regional human rights systems*

5.4.2.1 Extraterritoriality in the European human rights system

Unlike the African human rights treaties, the main regional human rights treaty in Europe – the European Convention on Human Rights (ECHR) – hangs the enjoyment of the rights and freedoms it enshrines and the correlative state duties on the hook of its jurisdiction clause. Its 'obligations clause' provides:

> [t]he High Contracting Parties shall secure to *everyone within their jurisdiction* the rights and freedoms defined in Section I of this Convention.[123]

At least on its face, this provision stipulates that victims of human rights violations must show that they were within a relevant state party's jurisdiction at the material time in order for the victim to bring a case against a state party and claim a remedy. Put otherwise, the threshold requirement for the applicability of a state's responsibility for human rights violations is the question of whether the victim or the alleged violation or the act or omission causing it falls within the jurisdiction of a state party to the ECHR. Article 1 of the ECHR makes it clear that, *prima facie*, questions of jurisdiction must first be settled before embarking on consideration of any state's responsibility for extraterritorial human rights violations.[124]

Numerous cases involving state responsibility for human rights violations occurring beyond the borders of the implicated states have been brought in Europe. The emerging jurisprudence has had to explore the meaning and implications of the 'jurisdiction' clause in Article 1 of the ECHR. An 'overly and unduly restrictive' interpretation[125] was assigned to this clause in the most criticised and most controversial[126] – yet most

[123] ECHR, Article 1 (emphasis added). [124] Gondek (note 15 above) 352.

[125] Indeed, it has been argued that, in the *Bankovic* case and other decisions, 'the Court arguably acted at the margins of its mandate'. See Alexander Orakhelashvili, 'Restrictive Interpretation of Human Rights Treaties in the Recent Jurisprudence of the European Court of Human Rights', 14(3) *European Journal of International Law* (2003) 529–68, 531.

[126] Michael O'Boyle, 'The European Convention on Human Rights and Extraterritorial Jurisdiction: A Comment on "Life after Bankovic"' in Fons Coomans and Menno T. Kamminga (eds.), *Extraterritorial Application of Human Rights Treaties* (Intersentia, 2004) 125, 125.

authoritative – judgment[127] of the Grand Chamber of the European Court of Human Rights (ECtHR) in the *Bankovic* case.[128]

This case was brought before the ECtHR by six citizens of the Federal Republic of Yugoslavia (FRY) against seventeen European countries which are members of the North Atlantic Treaty Organization (NATO).[129] Five of the six applicants were not only victims themselves but had family members who perished in the air raid carried out in the FRY by NATO air forces, while one of the applicants was a direct victim of the attacks, who survived the bombing. The applicants sought extraterritorial redress from NATO states for violation of the right to life (Article 2), freedom of expression (Article 10) and the right to effective remedy (Article 13) of the ECHR.

As expected, the case raised the question of whether the victims were in the NATO–ECHR parties' jurisdictions at the relevant time. The meaning to be assigned to the jurisdiction clause of Article 1 of the ECHR was thus determinative of the outcome of the case. Crucially, the Court upheld the preliminary plea of the respondent states that the claims of the applicants did not fall within their jurisdictions in terms of Article 1 of the ECHR as the complainants were outside the ECHR jurisdiction (legal space) at the material time. The Court noted that 'the jurisdictional competence of a State is primarily territorial',[130] and that the accused states were not in effective control of the victims or of the territory of the FRY 'as a consequence of military occupation or through the consent, invitation or acquiescence of the government of that [FRY] territory'.[131] Consequently, the ECtHR ruled that the impugned act (the bombing, killing and injuring) of the individuals by the NATO states 'does not engage their Convention [ECHR] responsibility'.[132]

The case was thus declared inadmissible on the argument of *ratione loci*, barring the passage to consideration of the merits of the claims raised. The Court thus denied the application of the ECHR to the NATO member states for their actions that produced extraterritorial human rights violations in FRY. In effect, it held that member states of the

[127] Gondek (note 15 above) 385.

[128] See *Bankovic and Others* v. *Belgium and 16 Other Contracting States*, Application No. 52207/99, Admissibility Decision of 12 November 2001 ('the *Bankovic* case').

[129] Although non-European members of NATO such as the United States and Canada took part in the air strikes, the *Bankovic* case was limited to the European members as the ECtHR lacks jurisdiction over non-European states which are not parties to the ECHR.

[130] *Bankovic* case, para. 59. [131] *Ibid.*, para. 71. [132] *Ibid.*, para. 100.

ECHR cannot be obligated to observe the essentially negative duty to respect human rights beyond the European legal space, which was held to be coterminous with their territory.

According to the *Bankovic* decision, 'jurisdiction' implies 'some form of structured relationship, normally existing over an extended period of time, and the swift attack by NATO members in FRY territory would not bring the events in the former's jurisdiction for purposes of establishing human rights responsibilities'.[133]

In the final analysis, the ECtHR precedent in the *Bankovic* case established the system of impunity for the states that jeopardised the human rights of individuals and groups in areas that are beyond their own territorial jurisdiction. Concomitantly, it denied the victims any recourse or access to remedies for the violation of their rights against the culprit states. Nevertheless, the *Bankovic* ruling was partly a culmination of the preceding case law of the European regional jurisprudence but it also became a template, albeit with some corrections and modifications, for subsequent decisions.[134]

Pre-Bankovic jurisprudence According to Gondek, the pattern of cases with extraterritorial elements in the pre-Bankovic period came in three different forms.[135] The first group arose from violations occurring from territories controlled by the implicated foreign state. In the case of *Loizidou* v. *Turkey*,[136] the applicant complained that she was prevented from accessing her own plots of land in northern Cyprus by the occupying Turkish authorities. The ECtHR ruled:

> bearing in mind the object and purpose of the Convention, the responsibility of a Contracting Party may also arise when as a consequence of military action – whether lawful or unlawful – it exercises effective control of an area outside its national territory. The obligation to secure, in such an area, the rights and freedoms set out in the Convention derives from the fact of such control whether it be exercised directly, through its armed forces, or through a subordinate local administration.[137]

[133] See Matthew Happold, 'Bankovic v. Belgium and the Territorial Scope of the European Convention on Human Rights', 3 *Human Rights Law Review* (2003) 77–90, 87.
[134] Gondek (note 15 above) 353. [135] *Ibid.*, 354.
[136] *Loizidou* v. *Turkey* (Preliminary Objections), Application No. 40/1993/435/514, ECtHR, 23 March 1995, Ser. A, Vol. 310.
[137] *Ibid.*, para. 62.

A few years later, the Court had another opportunity to rule on the territorial reach of the 'jurisdiction' clause of the ECHR. In the *Cyprus* v. *Turkey* case,[138] it stated:

> having effective overall control over northern Cyprus, [Turkey's] responsibility cannot be confined to the acts of its own soldiers or officials in northern Cyprus but must also be engaged by virtue of the acts of local administration which survives by virtue of Turkish military and other support. It follows that, in terms of Article 1 of the Convention, Turkey's 'jurisdiction' must be considered to extend to securing the entire range of substantive rights set out in the Convention and those additional Protocols which she has ratified, and that violations of those rights are imputable to Turkey.[139]

Thus, the jurisprudence of the ECtHR shows that territorial control by a state would bring the said territory under its jurisdiction and trigger the application of the ECHR for the purpose of the state's human rights obligations. In essence, control of another state's territory entails the extraterritorial responsibility of the controlling states where their acts or omissions cause human rights violations in those foreign states' territories.

The second group of pre-Bankovic cases involves not control over territory but control over individuals by state agents in third state territories. In *Stocke* v. *Germany*, a German national was lured from France to Germany by German state agents with a view to securing his arrest in his home country. The Court ruled that the jurisdiction of a state party:

> is not limited to the national territory of the High Contracting Party concerned, but extends to all persons under its actual authority and responsibility, whether this authority is exercised on its own territory or abroad. Furthermore . . . authorized agents of a State not only remain under its jurisdiction when abroad, but bring any other person 'within the jurisdiction' of that State to the extent that they exercise authority over such persons. Insofar as the State's acts or omissions affect such persons, the responsibility of the State is engaged.[140]

The (now defunct) European Commission on Human Rights employed the same logic in its earlier decisions in the cases of *Cyprus* v. *Turkey*[141]

[138] *Cyprus* v. *Turkey*, Application No. 25781/94, ECtHR, 10 May 2001.

[139] *Ibid.*, para. 77.

[140] *Stocke* v. *Germany*, Application No. 28/1989/188/248, ECtHR, 12 October 1989, Ser. A, Vol. 199, 24, para. 166.

[141] *Cyprus* v. *Turkey*, Application Nos. 6780/74 and 6950/75, ECommHR, 26 May 1975, 2 DR (1975) 136.

and *W. M.* v. *Denmark*.[142] The basis for jurisdiction in these cases was thus the 'incidental control' exercised over individuals by the implicated states outside their territories.[143]

The third group of pre-Bankovic cases implicated the responsibility of states extraterritorially as a result of a state's violations of obligations of *non-refoulement*, expulsion or extradition of a person to another state where such would result in the person's torture or cruel, inhuman or degrading treatment or punishment or any other infringement of fundamental rights and freedoms.[144] Some argued that complaints arising from violations of a state's duty of *non-refoulement* do not entail the state's extraterritorial obligations as the violations occur while the victims are within the territory of the implicated state, hence territorial. Cerone, for instance, argues that such a violation 'is not an example of extraterritorial application as the individual alleging a violation is actually within the territory of the state'.[145]

This line of argument is erroneous as it ignores the extraterritorial implications of a state's intra-territorial decisions, such as the violation of the duty of *non-refoulement* that is a territorial obligation. But the effects of the violation of the duty of *non-refoulement* may not stop at the border of the relevant state. As the UN Human Rights Committee (HRC) observed, 'if a State party takes a decision relating to a person within its jurisdiction, and the necessary and foreseeable consequence is that that person's rights under the Covenant [on Civil and Political Rights] will be violated in another state's jurisdiction, the state party itself may be in violation of the Covenant'.[146] According to the HRC, this conclusion is a logical follow-up of 'the fact that a State party's duty under article 2 of the Covenant would be negated by the handing over of a person to another State (whether a State party to the Covenant or not) where treatment contrary to the Covenant is certain or is the very purpose of the handing over'.[147] The HRC indeed took an example of an extradition decision by a state as a source of extraterritorial responsibility thereof if the decision

[142] *W. M.* v. *Denmark*, Application No. 17392/90, ECommHR, 14 October 1992.

[143] Gondek (note 15 above) 355.

[144] See *Soering* v. *United Kingdom*, Application No. 1/1989/161/217, ECtHR, 7 July 1989, Ser. A, Vol. 161.

[145] John Cerone, 'Out of Bounds? Considering the Reach of International Human Rights Law' (Center for Human Rights and Global Justice Working Paper, NYU School of Law, 2006) 12.

[146] Communication No. 470/1991, *Kindler* v. *Canada*, UN Human Rights Committee (CCPR/C/48/D/470/1991), 30 July 1993, para. 6.2.

[147] *Ibid.*

to hand a person to another state was made 'in circumstances in which it was foreseeable that torture would take place [in the other state's jurisdiction]'.[148] According to the HRC, the foreseeability of the extraterritorial consequence of an extradition decision should be understood to 'mean that there was a present violation by the State party, even though the consequence would not occur until later on'.[149] The HRC thus found Canada to be in violation of the Covenant for extraditing individuals in circumstances wherein it was foreseeable that the extradited person's right to life[150] and freedom from torture[151] would be violated in the receiving state. Therefore, the argument that the third category of the ECHR's decisions is devoid of extraterritorial elements is unfounded. It indeed causes both territorial and extraterritorial violations of the relevant rights of the victim at one and the same time.

Post-Bankovic jurisprudential detour In the post Bankovic period, too, the jurisdiction clause of the ECHR has continued to play a crucial role, albeit slightly relaxed in its scope and application, in the determination of the spatial reach of states' human rights duties in the European jurisprudence. In *Öcalan* v. *Turkey*,[152] the complainant (Abdullah Öcalan) was a leader of the Kurdistan Workers' Party (PKK), the main Kurdish opposition group. Before his arrest at Nairobi Airport in Kenya, Turkey had accused him of terrorism and had issued an international arrest warrant for him. He was seeking refuge in several countries (including Greece, Russia and Kenya) before he was arrested by the joint effort of the Kenyan and Turkish authorities and forcibly transferred to Turkey to face trial which eventually led to a death sentence against him. Although he was arrested outside the European 'legal space', the ECtHR treated this case differently from *Bankovic* and applied the ECHR to circumstances relating to his arrest that happened in Africa.[153] According to the ECtHR, member states of the ECHR will be held liable for violations of ECHR rights when they physically compel individuals situated abroad to return to the ECHR member state, in this case Turkey. The abduction, physical control and transportation by Turkey of the

[148] *Ibid.* [149] *Ibid.* [150] *Ibid.*, para. 8.33–8.38. [151] *Ibid.*, paras. 9.77 *et seq.*

[152] *Öcalan* v. *Turkey* (Merits), Application No. 46221/99, Chamber judgment of 12 March 2003.

[153] See generally Andrew Clapham, 'Symbiosis in International Human Rights Law: The Öcalan Case and the Evolving Law on the Death Sentence', 1 *Journal of International Criminal Justice* (2003) 475–89.

complainant was therefore sufficient to bring the victim under Turkey's jurisdiction. The ECtHR ruled:

> [t]he Court notes that the applicant was arrested by members of the Turkish security forces inside an aircraft registered in Turkey in the international zone of Nairobi Airport ... It is common ground that directly after being handed over to Turkish officials by the Kenyan officials, the applicant was under effective Turkish authority and therefore within the 'jurisdiction' of that state for the purposes of article 1 of the Convention, even though in this instance Turkey exercised its authority outside its territory.[154]

In *Ilascu and Others* v. *Moldova and Russia*,[155] the application was filed by persons who claimed to have been victimised by Moldova and Russia in the Moldovan region of Transnistria. The 'Moldovan Republic of Transdniestria' (MRT) proclaimed its independence but was not recognised as such by any state. The human rights violations complained of had been committed in this region. Arrested by soldiers in Russian army uniforms, Ilascu and others were charged with murder, among other crimes, and were brought before the courts of the self-proclaimed MRT, which subsequently sentenced Ilascu to death and ordered the confiscation of his property. The complaint against Moldova was based on the fact that it failed to prevent or end the violations that were committed in the MRT, which, for all legal purposes, was its territory. Russia was implicated through its active involvement in the MRT through its military presence which exercised *de facto* control of the area.[156] Moldova was the territorial state, while Russia's extraterritorial human rights duties were implicated. The decision of the Grand Chamber of the ECtHR once again hinged on the meaning of the jurisdiction clause of the ECHR. It considered Russia's involvement and control of the MRT, and found the violations complained of to have been committed in Russia's jurisdiction (as well as within the jurisdiction of Moldova).

Similarly, the case of *Issa and Others* v. *Turkey* brought into issue the meaning of jurisdiction before determining the implications of the alleged involvement of Turkey in Iraq.[157] The case concerned the alleged arrest and subsequent killings of six Iraqi shepherds in Iraq by Turkish

[154] *Öcalan* case (note 152 above), para. 91.

[155] *Ilascu and Others* v. *Moldova and Russia* (Merits), Application No. 48787/99, ECtHR, Judgment of 8 July 2004.

[156] *Ibid.*, para. 3.

[157] *Issa and Others* v. *Turkey*, Application No. 31821/96, ECtHR, Judgment of 16 November 2004.

soldiers. As in *Bankovic*, the ECtHR refused to hold that the alleged victims were within Turkish jurisdiction at the material time, but on this occasion apparently on the basis that there was a lack of evidence proving that Turkish soldiers had in fact operated in the area. Neither the ECtHR nor Turkey questioned the applicability of the ECHR to Turkish forces operating in Iraq.[158]

It appears that the ECtHR would have held Turkey responsible for the alleged violations in Iraqi territory had the disputed facts of Turkish presence in Iraq been proven. The case thus represented a situation 'where extraterritoriality reached its Zenith'[159] as it would have entitled nationals of Iraq, a country that was outside the European legal space and not a party to the ECHR, to benefit from the protection of the ECHR due to Turkish extraterritorial human rights obligations. It has been argued that the jurisprudence in the *Ilascu* and *Issa* decisions marked the Court's retreat from the overly restrictive interpretation of the ECHR's jurisdiction clause and its application to extraterritorial violations without entirely abandoning its *Bankovic* stance.[160]

A recent judgment of the ECtHR confirms this trend, extending the duty of a member state of the ECHR (the United Kingdom) extraterritorially to the activities of its armed forces in Iraq, outside the European legal space. *Al-Skeini and Others* v. *UK*[161] concerned a complaint related to the death of six Iraqi nationals in and around Basrah, southern Iraq. Mr Mazin Al-Skeini died of beating by the occupying British army (for which the defendant state admitted responsibility), while the others died in British-controlled areas around Basrah. Control over the individual in the case of Mr Al-Skeini, who died in the custody of the UK's army, and control over territory in the case of the other five victims, provided for the jurisdictional link between the state's duties and the violations. The ECtHR ruled that:

> the United Kingdom, through its soldiers engaged in security operations in Basrah during the period in question, exercised authority and control over individuals killed in the course of such security operations, so as to establish a jurisdictional link between the deceased and the United Kingdom.[162]

[158] Cerna (note 60 above) 147. [159] *Ibid.*

[160] Erik Roxstrom, Mark Gibney and Terje Einarsen, 'The NATO Bombing Case (Bankovic et al. v. Belgium et al.) and the Limits of Western Human Rights Protection', 23 *Boston University International Law Journal* (2005) 55–136, 124.

[161] *Al-Skeini and Others* v. *United Kingdom*, Application No. 55721/07, Judgment of 7 July 2011.

[162] *Ibid.*, para. 149.

The ECtHR also held that control over the territory of another state entails positive obligations of investigating the violations that are committed not only by its own army personnel but by non-state actors.[163] Omission of this duty was held to be a violation of the UK's procedural duty of effectively investigating the violations that are committed within its jurisdiction.[164]

An overview of the jurisprudence of the European system shows that the extraterritorial application of human rights is an exception to the rule, and the jurisdiction clause of the ECHR limits a state's human rights obligations to territories or persons under its control. However, the regional case law has now established discernible trends for the extraterritorial application of the ECHR. Control over a territory, control over a person or violation of the principle of *non-refoulement* or extradition of a person to territories where the rights protected under the ECHR would foreseeably be violated would bring the violations within a state's jurisdiction for the purpose of Article 1 of the ECHR.

As a source of inspiration for the African human rights system, the burgeoning case law of the European human rights system is of close relevance. The African Commission, following the obligations clause of the Charter the application of which is not limited territorially, can adopt the same – or even a more relaxed – approach to complaints of human rights violations. Indeed, in the *DRC Invasion* case, the Commission held the defendant states liable for extraterritorial human rights violations that 'took place while the forces of the Respondent States were occupying and in control of the eastern provinces of the Complainant State [DRC]'.[165] In light of the territorially unbound obligations clause of the Charter, it is very open to the Commission to apply its provisions in such a way that establishes states' extraterritorial duties to respect, protect, promote and fulfil Charter-based guarantees across Africa.

5.4.2.2 Extraterritoriality in the Inter-American human rights system

The core human rights instruments in the Inter-American human rights system are the American Declaration on the Rights and Duties of Man ('American Declaration') and the American Convention on Human Rights ('American Convention').[166] The regional mechanism,

[163] *Ibid.*, paras. 168–77. [164] *Ibid.*, paras. 174–7. [165] *DRC Invasion* case, para. 88.

[166] Adopted at the Inter-American Specialized Conference on Human Rights, San José, Costa Rica, 22 November 1969 (entered into force on 18 July 1978).

the Inter-American Commission on Human Rights ('Inter-American Commission'), unlike the African and European regional bodies which have been established by virtue of treaties, was established in 1959 by a political resolution of the Organization of American States (OAS). It was accorded the power to hear individual complaints only in 1965. But it soon discovered that it could base its case law solely on the American Declaration, as other treaties were yet to be adopted at the time. The only regional human rights instrument available to it was the American Declaration, which was originally created as a non-binding instrument that would only serve as the regional standard of achievement in the area of human rights.[167] While unanimously adopted by the OAS members, the American Declaration could only be given its binding force by the Inter-American Commission 'by dint of pushing the jurisdiction envelope'.[168] It has now come to be taken as a binding instrument for the Americas, and has been the normative basis of the Inter-American Commission's jurisdiction on, *inter alia*, the extraterritorial application of human rights.

The American Declaration, as noted by the ECtHR in the *Bankovic* case,[169] does not provide for the jurisdictional scope or territorial limitation of human rights or state obligations. In this regard, it is completely different to the European system that provides for a jurisdiction clause, and is analogous to the African Charter. However, the American Convention introduced a jurisdiction clause to the Inter-American human rights system when it came into effect in 1978. Article 2(1) of the American Convention, entitled 'General Obligations', reads:

> [t]he States Parties to this Convention undertake to respect the rights and freedoms recognized herein and to ensure to all persons subject to their jurisdiction the free and full exercise of those rights and freedoms, without any discrimination for reasons of race, color, sex, language, religion, political or other opinion, national or social origin, economic status, birth, or any other social condition.

However, the lack of a jurisdiction clause under the American Declaration is still pertinent as a great deal of the Inter-American Commission's jurisprudence on the question of the extraterritorial application of human rights has involved non-party states to the Convention, such as the United States.[170] Cerna categorised the cases in which the Inter-American Commission held states responsible for the

[167] Cerna (note 60 above) 142. [168] *Ibid.* [169] See *Bankovic* case, para. 78.
[170] Cerna (note 60 above) 142.

violation of the American Declaration extraterritorially into three distinct groups.[171] All three categories of decisions have their parallels in the European case law, and some of them in the African human rights jurisprudence.

The first category of cases implicated states' extraterritorial human rights responsibility for extraditing or deporting individuals into foreign territories where their rights were likely to be violated. The often cited example of the *Haitian Interdiction Decision*[172] is the case in point. The case was submitted by a number of NGOs on behalf of Haitians fleeing by sea from their country to the United States, which intercepted the boat carrying them on the high seas, giving rise to the question of whether the US was accountable for violations of human rights outside its own territory. The NGOs argued that the people on the boat had a reasonable fear of persecution if deported back to their home country, and would be denied a forum for the resolution of their asylum claims. It was also argued that the Haitians were discriminated against by the US authorities as compared to similarly fleeing Cubans who were given access to US domestic procedures to present their asylum claims. The US argued that the interdiction was 'consistent with the human rights standards of the American Declaration'.[173] Regarding jurisdiction, the US argued that the issue for consideration was not whether there have been human rights violations in Haiti but was rather about whether the US interdiction of Haitians on the high seas, outside its territorial jurisdiction, violates the provisions of the American Declaration, which the US denied.

The Inter-American Commission found the US in violation of numerous human rights provisions of the American Declaration. It stated that the interdiction and repatriation of the Haitians put them at the 'genuine and foreseeable risk of death' in violation of the right to life under Article 1 of the American Declaration.[174] It relied on the ECtHR decision in the *Soering* case[175] and the UN Human Right Committee's decision of *Ng* v. *Canada*,[176] finding that a state violates human rights when it wilfully

[171] *Ibid.*, 147.

[172] *Haitian Centre for Human Rights* v. *United States* ('*US Interdiction of Haitians on the High Seas*'), IACHR Report No. 51/96, Case No. 10.675, 13 March 1997.

[173] *Ibid.* [174] *Ibid.*

[175] *Soering* v. *United Kingdom*, Application No. 14038/88, Ser. A, No. 161, ECtHR, 7 July 1989, 11 EHRR 439.

[176] *Chitat Ng* v. *Canada*, Communication No. 469/1991, UN Doc. CCPR/C/49/D/469/1991 (1994).

exposes individuals to reasonably foreseeable risk in another state's jurisdiction. Thus, in a marked departure from the ECtHR's *Bankovic* jurisprudence, control by the US of persons sufficed to trigger its human rights obligations beyond its borders.

The second category of cases concerns those in which states were held liable for violations of human rights in territories under their effective control, even if those territories were not part of the implicated state's territory. In *Coard and Others*,[177] the US armed forces toppled the then newly installed military Government of Grenada, of which Coard and others were leaders, arrested and held the complainants incommunicado and mistreated them before handing them over to the judiciary that was alleged to have been bribed by the US. For all practical and legal purposes, the acts alleged to have violated the complainants' human rights were entirely committed within Grenadian territory. While the extraterritorial application of the American Declaration was not raised by the defendant state, the Inter-American Commission sought to address the issue. It ruled:

> [w]hile the extraterritorial application of the American Declaration has not been placed at issue by the parties, the Commission finds it pertinent to note that, under certain circumstances, the exercise of its jurisdiction over acts with an extraterritorial locus will not only be consistent with but required by the norms which pertain. *The fundamental rights of the individual are proclaimed in the Americas on the basis of the principles of equality and non-discrimination – 'without distinction as to race, nationality, creed or sex'. Given that individual rights inhere simply by virtue of a person's humanity, each American State is obliged to uphold the protected rights of any person subject to its jurisdiction. While this most commonly refers to persons within a state's territory, it may, under given circumstances, refer to conduct with an extraterritorial locus where the person concerned is present in the territory of one state, but subject to the control of another state – usually through the acts of the latter's agents abroad. In principle, the inquiry turns not on the presumed victim's nationality or presence within a particular geographic area, but on whether, under the specific circumstances, the State observed the rights of a person subject to its authority and control.*[178]

Similarly, the Inter-American Commission reiterated the same principles in a case in which Cuba's extraterritorial human rights obligations

[177] *Coard and Others* v. *United States*, Inter-American Human Rights Commission, Report No. 109/1999, Case No. 10.951 (29 September 1999).

[178] *Ibid.*, para. 37 (emphasis added; footnotes omitted).

were implicated. In the *Brothers to the Rescue* case,[179] Cuban military aircraft shot down two unarmed civilian aircraft (belonging to 'Brothers to the Rescue', an anti-Fidel Castro organisation) flying in international airspace, killing four people on board the planes. Three of the four victims were US nationals, and one was a Cuban who fled his country and was living in the US. The ruling of the Inter-American Commission repeated the *Coard* case almost *verbatim*.[180]

The third group of cases consists of those in which neither the court nor the implicated state questioned the duty to abide by the American Declaration when a state acts outside its own territory. In one case, the US was involved in the overthrow of the regime of General Manuel Noriega from power in 1989, when it conducted an operation within Panamanian territory.[181] The petitioners, all Panamanian citizens, claimed that the 24,000 US soldiers who ensured the downfall of the Noriega regime acted in an 'indiscriminate manner with reckless disregard for the safety of Panamanian civilians during the US military operations in Panama' and committed numerous violations of the rights guaranteed in the American Declaration. In a stark similarity to the *DRC Invasion* case and the *Burundi Embargo* case of the African Commission, there was no questioning of the legality of the state's extraterritorial human rights duties. The Inter-American Commission thus decided to consider the case,[182] despite the fact that the material facts giving rise to the complaints were committed by the US forces in Panamanian territory.

In sum, the jurisprudence of the Inter-American human rights system employs a broader extraterritorial application of human rights than does the European system. As long as the state has caused human rights violations, the nationality of the victims or territory of the offence are immaterial in the attribution of responsibility. As Cassel has noted, 'the extraterritorial reach of the American Declaration seems almost unbound within the Americas'.[183] Among other things, this is due to the fact that – in contrast to the European and much like the African human right systems – the text of the American Declaration 'contains no defined – and hence-no limiting – jurisdictional clause'.[184] This position

[179] *Armando Alejandre Jr, Carlos Costa, Mario de la Peña and Pablo Morales* v. *Cuba* ('*Brothers to the Rescue* case'), Case Report No. 86/99, Case 11.589, 29 September 1999.
[180] *Brothers to the Rescue* case, para. 23.
[181] *Salas and Others* v. *United States* ('*US Military Intervention in Panama*'), IACHR Report No. 31/93, Case 10.573 (United States), 14 October 1993, para. 6.
[182] *Ibid.* [183] See Cassel (note 5 above) 181. [184] *Ibid.*

has a stark similarity to the obligations clause of the African Charter, providing the potential for inspirational reference for the African Commission that is bound to receive an increasing number of cases involving extraterritorial violators.

The upshot of the analysis is that, in the Inter-American human rights system, the state's duty to respect human rights extraterritorially has clearly been established, which confirms the propriety of the position of the African Commission as explicated in the *DRC Invasion* case and the *Burundi Embargo* case. However, like the European system, the case law of the Inter-American system has yet to develop positive extraterritorial obligations which are more pertinent to the sharing of transboundary fresh water resources. Thus, the case law of the Inter-American Commission, just like that of its European counterpart, leaves much to be desired in terms of explicating positive extraterritorial state obligations. In this sense, the jurisprudence of the Inter-American human rights system offers little guidance or 'inspiration' for the African Commission in terms of elaborating a state's positive extraterritorial obligations (especially the duty to fulfil) of sharing international rivers in a manner sensitive to those beyond a state's borders.

5.5 Towards concretising extraterritorial states' human rights duties

5.5.1 Extraterritoriality through the layers of state obligations

The foregoing analysis of global and regional human rights jurisprudence has demonstrated that the realisation of human rights and freedoms – including the human right to water – entails state obligations of extraterritorial application. Inasmuch as the extraterritorial human rights obligations of states are grounded in the normative corpus of international treaties and regional human rights instruments, they can be explained in terms of the various layers of states' human rights duties to respect, protect, promote and fulfil human rights, just as in the case of a state's domestic human rights obligations.[185] Although the state's duties to respect, protect, promote and fulfil the human rights of

[185] See 'Maastricht Principles on Extraterritorial Obligations of States in the Area of Economic, Social and Cultural Rights', adopted at Maastricht University on 28 September 2011, http://hrbaportal.org/archives/noticeboard/launch-of-maastricht-principles-on-the-extraterritorial-obligations-of-states-in-the-area-of-economic-social-and-cultural-rights (accessed 7 November 2012) ('Maastricht Principles').

individuals and groups have been developed to bind the states when acting domestically, 'there is no reason to conclude that this explanation, specifying the nature of state parties' obligations, is limited to domestic obligations'.[186] For example, the UN Special Rapporteur on the right to food has shown that each of the four layers of state human rights obligations could be applicable extraterritorially. He specifically refers in his reports to the extraterritorial obligation to respect, protect and fulfil.[187] The basic meaning of the layers of state obligations to extraterritorial beneficiaries remains intact, except that the right-holders are (non-)nationals residing in a third state's territory.[188]

As demonstrated above, there is ample normative basis for the extraterritorial duty to *respect* the human rights of individuals and groups in third states' territories. According to Craven, this goes almost without saying. He noted, '[i]n so far as the international community as a whole has an obligation to take cognizance of human rights in its interactions, it is axiomatic that States parties have a similar duty to respect the realisation of the rights of other countries'.[189] As Cahill observed, the extraterritorial state obligations to respect are the least controversial.[190] This layer of states' duty also finds expression in 'all international human rights treaties'.[191] It would be a violation of a state's extraterritorial duty for a state to negatively affect the rights of individuals and groups that are being enjoyed in third states. A contrary interpretation would fall foul of the object and purpose of human rights treaties in general. As the HRC ruled:

> [I]t would be unconscionable to so interpret the responsibility under article 2 of the Covenant as to permit a State party to perpetrate violations of the Covenant on the territory of another State, which violations it could not perpetrate on its own territory.[192]

[186] Salomon (note 7 above) 190.

[187] CESCR, 'The Right to Food: Report of the Special Rapporteur on the Right to Food, Jean Ziegler' (Commission on Human Rights, United Nations Economic and Social Council (E/CN.4/2005/47, 24 January 2005)), paras. 35–8.

[188] See Skogly (note 40 above) 419–20; Salomon (note 7 above) 189–95.

[189] Craven (note 89 above) 148.

[190] Amanda Cahill, 'Protecting Rights in the Face of Scarcity: The Right to Water' in Mark Gibney and Sigrun Skogly (eds.), *Universal Human Rights and Extraterritorial Obligations* (University of Pennsylvania Press, 2010) 194, 197.

[191] Skogly (note 17 above) 66–7.

[192] *Sergio Euben Lopez Burgos* v. *Uruguay*, Communication No. R.12/52 (UN Human Rights Committee), UN Doc. Supplement No. 40 (A/36/40) (1981), para. 12.3.

The CESCR's General Comment No. 15 states that 'States parties have to *respect* the enjoyment of the right in other countries'.[193] According to the CESCR, the extraterritorial duty to respect requires 'States parties to refrain from actions that interfere, directly or indirectly, with the enjoyment of the right to water in other countries'.[194] The 'respect layer' of a state's obligation pertains not only to the human rights (of individuals and groups) *per se* but also to rights and duties of a state *vis-à-vis* another state. The CESCR emphasised that a state is responsible for ensuring that any activities – omissions or commissions – it undertakes within its territorial jurisdiction do not deprive another state of the ability to realise the right to water for persons in its jurisdiction.[195] In consonance with its General Comment No. 8,[196] the CESCR enjoined states from the use of water as a political and economic weapon against another state, and particularly from the imposition of embargoes or other measures that prevent the supply of water, as well as goods and services essential for securing the right to water.[197]

At a higher and more positive level, the state's extraterritorial duty to protect requires positive action by way of ensuring that state agents and non-state actors (including multinational companies and individuals within the state's jurisdiction) do not infringe upon the rights and freedoms being enjoyed in third states.[198] At this level, states incur international responsibility for the violation of international human rights law for the culpable conduct of non-state actors who, from within the jurisdiction of a state, engage in conduct that produces extraterritorially prejudicial activities.[199] Among other things, it also requires states to ensure protection of human rights when adopting bilateral and multilateral agreements.[200] A state can thus be held liable for human rights violations in third states for its failure to take into consideration the enjoyment of the rights while taking decisions, imposing sanctions, establishing programmes and making policies as a member of international organisations.[201] Arguably, this aspect of states' extraterritorial

[193] General Comment No. 15 (note 109 above), para. 31 (emphasis added). [194] *Ibid.*

[195] *Ibid.*

[196] See CESCR, 'General Comment No. 8: The Relationship between Economic Sanctions and Respect for Economic, Social and Cultural Rights' (UN Committee on Economic, Social and Cultural Rights, 1997).

[197] *Ibid.*, para. 32. [198] Vandenhole (note 22 above) 103.

[199] For the CESCR's analysis of the state's duty to protect human rights in relation to the human right to water, see CESCR, General Comment No. 15 (note 109 above), para. 23–4.

[200] Sepúlveda Carmona (note 85 above) 91. [201] Coomans (note 16 above) 187–90.

duty is also an expression of the obligation not to discriminate against those beyond its borders.[202]

According to General Comment No. 15, states have the extraterritorial duty to protect the human right to water in other states. States have the duty 'to prevent their own citizens and companies from violating the right to water of individuals and communities in other countries'.[203] The CESCR also declared that states owe an extraterritorial positive obligation of fulfilling the human right to water in other states. According to the CESCR:

> [d]epending on the availability of resources, States should facilitate realization of the right to water in other countries, for example through provision of water resources, financial and technical assistance, and provide the necessary aid when required.[204]

The extraterritorial state duty to promote human rights implies that a state must take positive measures aimed at enabling the enjoyment of relevant human rights and freedoms in other states.[205] This includes, for instance, provision of information and transparency regarding impending projects that have repercussions on the realisation of the human right to water in other states.

The most controversial of all extraterritorial obligations is one that requires a state to *fulfil* human rights in third states.[206] In comparative terms, there is little controversy that both the domestic state and foreign states must respect and protect the human rights of individuals.[207] However, whether states' extraterritorial obligations, such as the duty of international assistance and cooperation, entail the state's duty to 'fulfil' human rights in third states' jurisdictions is politically and legally controversial.[208] This layer of obligation requires the state to provide material resources, free of charge, to those who cannot afford to pay for those life-sustaining resources. In its extraterritorial sense, the same meaning is retained, except that the beneficiaries are based outside the

202 John H. Knox, 'The Myth and Reality of Transboundary Environmental Impact Assessment', 96 *American Journal of International Law* (2002) 291–319, 300.

203 *Ibid.*, para. 33. See also Coomans (note 104 above) 29.

204 General Comment No. 15 (note 109 above), para. 34.

205 Sepúlveda Carmona (note 85 above) 92.

206 Craven (note 89 above) 149; Skogly (note 17 above) 71; Cahill (note 190 above) 198.

207 Margot E. Salomon, 'Legal Cosmopolitanism and the Normative Contribution of the Right to Development' (LSE Law, Society and Economy Working Papers 16/2008, London School of Economics and Political Science, 2008) 6.

208 *Ibid.*

duty-bearer state's territory. In other words, the duty to fulfil is triggered when the donee state is not in a position to provide the bare necessities of life – in this case, water for drinking and sanitation purposes – for individuals and groups within its territory. As a result, the type of extraterritorial act required at the level of the duty to fulfil falls within the realm of international assistance, which lies outside the framework of reciprocity among the states concerned. As the donee would not be expected to perform any obligation in return, the concept of international cooperation *per se* which requires reciprocity is less relevant in relation to a state's obligation to fulfil. Thus a state's extraterritorial duty to fulfil the human right to water is more closely associated with the more unilateral duty of international assistance under Article 2(1) of the ICESCR and Article 21 of the African Charter.

In line with the complementary and supplementary nature of states' extraterritorial human rights duties to 'fulfil', the CESCR stressed that the extraterritorial duty to fulfil is aimed at enabling third states to realise the minimum core of the right to water within their territories. In relation to the duty to fulfil, international assistance and cooperation among states must be of such a nature as to enable water-deficient states 'to fulfill their core obligations'.[209] In other words, the duty does not go any further than the provision of adequate quantities and quality of water for personal and domestic uses by the inhabitants of third states.

5.5.2 *Problems specific to the extraterritorial duty to fulfil*

Numerous questions need clarification and explication in relation to a state's extraterritorial duty to fulfil. First, as has been elaborated in Chapter 4, the domestic state bears the primary responsibility for the realisation of the human right in relation to which the extraterritorial duty to fulfil is required. Thus the existence of an extraterritorial obligation which would require foreign states to come to a deprived state's aid does not affect the normal human rights duties of the latter's domestic responsibility. In this sense, extraterritorial obligations do not lower or obliterate the responsibility of domestic states.[210] The extraterritorial duties to fulfil 'are always *complementary* to domestic state obligations'.[211] Unlike the state's extraterritorial duties to respect, protect and promote, which are constantly and concurrently applicable

[209] *Ibid.*, para. 38. [210] Vandenhole (note 22 above) 87.
[211] *Ibid.* (emphasis in original).

alongside every state's domestic duties regarding those duties,[212] the duty to fulfil imposes primary responsibility on the domestic state while its extraterritorial aspect comes into play at the 'secondary or subsidiary'[213] or 'supplementary'[214] and 'complementary'[215] level when a domestic state becomes unable, for reasons beyond its control, to fulfil the rights in question. This is because no one state can be held responsible, notwithstanding states' extraterritorial human rights duties, to guarantee complete implementation of human rights in another state's territory. Jean Ziegler, the UN Special Rapporteur on food, saw fit to reframe the duty to fulfil as the duty to 'support to fulfil' in contrast to the duty to fulfil *per se*:

> another Government cannot be obliged to guarantee complete implementation of the right to food in other countries, but only to assist, so a better formulation would be 'the obligation to support to fulfil' the right to food in other countries. This clarification is important. It underlines that the principal obligation to guarantee the right to food is incumbent on the national Government, but other States, if they have available resources, have a complementary obligation to help the national State, when it does not have the resources to realize the right to food of its population.[216]

Another question that is a subject of debate in connection with the extraterritorial duty to fulfil human rights is the amount of resources the foreign state needs to commit as a matter of duty. According to Salomon, '[j]urisprudentially, few advances have been made in determining specifically that which constitutes a state's maximum available resources for the purpose of meeting its obligation of international assistance and cooperation'.[217] It appears that the exact amount and form of assistance is dependent upon the extent of need in the recipient state,[218] and, more importantly, the capacity of the 'donor' state as measured in terms of the amount of the relevant resources at its disposal.[219] Put differently, while states' duties to extraterritorially respect, protect and promote human rights are constant and double-layered, applying to both home states and foreign states at once and permanently, the extraterritorial duty to fulfil is transitory and conditional, depending

212 Salomon rightly argued that negative obligations are 'simultaneous' for the domestic state and the foreign state. See Salomon (note 7 above) 190.
213 *Ibid.* 214 Coomans (note 16 above) 196.
215 Ziegler's 2005 report (note 117 above), para. 47. 216 *Ibid.*
217 Salomon (note 7 above) 101. 218 Coomans (note 16 above) 196.
219 See CESCR, General Comment No. 15 (note 109 above), para. 34.

upon the donee state's needs and the donor state's capacity to help. When the 'donee' state's resource capacity improves, the extraterritorial duty to fulfil may wither away.

The donor state bears primary responsibility for the fulfilment of the same rights towards its own population. However, its extraterritorial duty to fulfil does not seem to require too much beyond ensuring the fulfilment of the core minimum of the right in question in third states. As the CESCR stated:

> [f]or the avoidance of any doubt, the Committee wishes to emphasize that it is particularly incumbent on States parties and other actors in a position to assist, to provide 'international assistance and cooperation, especially economic and technical' which enable developing countries to fulfil their core and other obligations.[220]

Sepúlveda Carmona rightly argued that this statement is 'closely linked to the obligation to comply with the "core obligations"', and is meant to 'refer to obligations to ensure the minimum essential level of each right'.[221] As a member of the CESCR commented, the minimum core obligations and the obligations relating to international assistance and cooperation 'should be seen as two halves of a package.'[222] The full realisation can be a subject of a duty of international cooperation on some reciprocal basis. But the need to ensure that everyone's survival is guaranteed through the provision of the minimum core levels of rights realisation comes within the ambit of the duty of international assistance, and is seen as a non-reciprocal and objective obligation of the states involved.[223]

5.6 Extraterritoriality: its implications for the human right to water

As outlined at the outset, the state's duty to respect the human right to water may woefully fail to guarantee the realisation of the human right to water. If international assistance and cooperation is to play a meaningful

[220] CESCR, 'General Comment No. 14: Substantive Issues Arising in the Implementation of the International Covenant on Economic, Social and Cultural Rights – The Right to the Highest Attainable Standard of Health' (E/C.12/2000/4), (Committee on Economic, Social and Cultural Rights, 11 August 2000), para. 45.

[221] Sepúlveda Carmona (note 85 above) 88–9.

[222] Hunt, quoted in *ibid.*, 104, footnote 18.

[223] For the same point in relation to the human right to water, see CESCR, General Comment No. 15 (note 109 above).

role in the realisation of the human right to water, it needs to be taken to imply the state's duty to protect, promote and fulfil the right in third states through the provision of water and financial and technical resources. In the face of the impending resource constraints that have started to threaten millions of lives the world over, 'to limit the discourse to the human rights obligations of states at the domestic level, or to narrowly framed external obligations of states, is far too insignificant a gesture to confront the task at hand'.[224] The duty of international assistance and cooperation should be taken to imply concurrent responsibilities of home states and foreign (especially riparian) states to fulfil the human right to water through the implementation of their duties to respect, protect, promote and fulfil the right.[225]

According to the CESCR:

> [d]epending on the availability of resources, States should facilitate realization of the right to water in other countries, for example through provision of water resources, financial and technical assistance, and provide the necessary aid when required.[226]

Thus General Comment No. 15 of the CESCR has construed the state's international duty of assistance and cooperation to entail not only the duty to respect and protect, but also the duty to fulfil ('facilitate' and 'provide') the human right to water in third states' territories. General Comment No. 15 stated that 'States parties have to *respect* the enjoyment of the right in other countries'.[227] According to the CESCR, the extraterritorial duty to respect requires 'States parties to refrain from actions that interfere, directly or indirectly, with the enjoyment of the right to water in other countries'.[228]

The 'respect layer' of a state's obligation pertains not only to the human rights (of individuals and groups) *per se* but also to rights and duties of a state *vis-à-vis* another state. The CESCR emphasised that a state is responsible for ensuring that any activity, omissions or commissions it undertakes within its territorial jurisdiction do not deprive another state of the ability to realise the right to water for persons in its jurisdiction.[229] In consonance with its General Comment No. 8,[230] the CESCR enjoined states from the use of water as a political and economic

[224] Salomon (note 7 above) 204.
[225] See Maastricht Principles (note 185 above), para. 33.
[226] CESCR, General Comment No. 15 (note 109 above), para. 34.
[227] *Ibid.*, para. 31 (emphasis added). [228] *Ibid.* [229] *Ibid.*
[230] See CESCR, General Comment No. 8 (note 196 above).

weapon against another state, and particularly from the imposition of embargoes or other measures that prevent the supply of water, as well as goods and services essential for securing the right to water.[231]

According to General Comment No. 15, states also owe the extraterritorial duty to protect the human right to water in other states. Accordingly, states have the duty 'to prevent their own citizens and companies from violating the right to water of individuals and communities in other countries'.[232] The CESCR also declared that states owe an extraterritorial positive obligation of fulfilling the human right to water in other states. The CESCR stated that this duty requires states to facilitate the realisation of the right to water, not least through provision of water resources, financial and technical assistance, and provide the necessary aid when required.[233]

In line with the complementary and supplementary nature of states' extraterritorial human rights duties to 'fulfil', the CESCR stressed that the extraterritorial duty to fulfil aims at enabling third states to realise the minimum core of the right to water within their territories. Accordingly, in relation to the duty to fulfil, the international assistance and cooperation among states must be of such a nature which enables water-deficient states 'to fulfill their core obligations'.[234] It would not go any further than the provision of an adequate quantity and quality of water for personal and domestic uses of the inhabitants of third states. Arguably, therefore, a state's extraterritorial duty to fulfil constitutes a minimum threshold requirement and, as such, imposes obligations that are immediate in application.

5.7 Conclusion

This chapter stressed that the realisation of the right to water in one state in Africa is extremely dependent on the conduct of third states. Unless states' use of Africa's international rivers is regulated in such a way that is sensitive to all those who share the water resources of those rivers, the declaration of the human right to water by the African Commission or by the CESCR is illusory. Unless a state's human rights obligations are applied in a way that holds the state to account for the consequences

[231] *Ibid.*, para. 32. [232] *Ibid.*, para. 33.
[233] CESCR, General Comment No. 15 (note 109 above), para. 34. [234] *Ibid.*, para. 38.

its (in)activities cause abroad, the human right to water in Africa can be violated in circumstances in which the duty-bearer is allowed to evade responsibility.

In the African Charter and the ICESCR, there is no textual basis to limit the spatial reach of socio-economic rights such as the right to water or correlative state obligations to a state's territorial jurisdiction. In terms of its 'inspirational' value to the African Charter and African Commission, Article 2(1) of the ICESCR and General Comment No. 15 of the CESCR could provide a template for positive as well as negative states' duties. The lack of a 'territoriality' or 'jurisdiction' clause in both Article 2(1) of the ICESCR and Article 1 of the Charter may permit the African Commission, following the example of the CESCR, to interpret the Charter's provisions in a way that entails their extraterritorial application.

The African Commission has established its regional jurisprudence for holding states responsible for their extraterritorial conduct which violates human rights abroad. Its approach has already been accepted and applied in the case law of the other regional systems, to which the Commission may turn for the purpose of 'drawing inspiration' in interpreting and applying the African Charter. For its part, the Inter-American Commission has been willing to expand states' human rights responsibilities for violating human rights abroad. The European human rights system has also gradually relaxed the meaning of the 'jurisdiction clause' of the ECHR, and states have now come to be held responsible for some violations of human rights that they commit beyond borders. However, the case law of the tripartite regional systems has yet to look beyond the establishment of a state's extraterritorial negative duties to respect human rights abroad.

This means that, as regards the human right to water, all co-riparians states are accountable for their omissions or commissions that violate the human right to water in all the territories of the co-riparian states (duty to respect). This is because they would exercise *de jure* or *de facto* control over the water in relation to which their (in)actions cause harm in other co-riparian states' territories. Put differently, individuals and groups in all co-riparian states would have direct recourse against the particular co-riparian state that violates their rights in their home state, or jeopardises or slows down the realisation of their human right to water.

In terms of discrete state obligations, the extraterritorial duties to respect and protect human rights have their bases in the jurisprudence of the regional and international human rights instruments. The more contentious layer is the duty to fulfil, according to which a state may be called upon to provide water to help realise the human right to water in third states. Inasmuch as the normative basis and scope of the state's duty to fulfil remains vague, the protection afforded the human right to water in shared river basins leaves much to be desired. However, the duty to fulfil, albeit differently worded, has long been elaborated in treaties outside the human rights regime and affirmed in decisions of various international tribunals over water-related inter-state disputes. This is the subject of the next chapter.

6

Extraterritoriality of the human right to water in international water law

> Neither Syria nor Iraq can lay claim to Turkey's rivers any more than Ankara could claim their oil. This is a matter of sovereignty. We have a right to do anything we like. The water resources are Turkey's, the oil resources are theirs. We don't say we share their oil resources, and they can't say they share our water resources.[1]

6.1 Introduction

The preceding chapter illustrated that international and regional human rights regimes provide rules and principles supporting individuals' and groups' extraterritorial human right to water and the corresponding state obligations. These rules and principles could thus be used by foreign-based right-holders against foreign states in cases where the human right to water is violated by acts or omissions that are attributable to such states. So, too, the overarching states' duty of international assistance and cooperation has been shown to oblige states to help others in their efforts to realise the human rights of the latter's residents. However, as demonstrated in Chapter 5, the jurisprudence on the extraterritorial states' obligations pertaining to the human right to water is still evolving and tends to show a degree of vagueness, especially in the areas of a state's duty to *promote* and *fulfil* the human rights of a third state's residents.

In an attempt to search for better normative clarity of the same, the present chapter analyses the utility of the rules and principles of international water law in the establishment of an extraterritorial human right to water and the correlative obligations of states that are co-riparians to shared

[1] Statement of Turkey's former President, Suleyman Demirel, at the opening of the Ataturk Dam on 25 July 1992, quoted in Knut Bourquain, *Freshwater Access from a Human Rights Perspective: A Challenge to International Water Law and Human Rights Law* (Martinus Nijhoff Publishers, 2008).

water resources.[2] It argues that, beyond or besides the corpus of international human rights law, international water law provides for the extraterritorial human right to water and enshrines some more developed, discrete and elaborate positive as well as negative state obligations of an extraterritorial character specific to the human right to water. It is argued that, properly understood and used by human rights complainants before human rights tribunals such as the African Commission, international water law provides foreign-based holders of the human right to water with enforceable rights against foreign riparian states for the states' roles in the non-realisation of the human right to water. Universal as they are, the rules and principles of international water law apply to African states and can be used by the African Commission in the interpretation and application of, *inter alia*, the human right to water and related rights.

The analysis seeks to illustrate that some rules and principles of international water law have the character of human rights treaties, namely, that they 'are not a web of inter-State exchange of mutual obligations . . . [but] concern the endowment of individuals with rights'.[3] In this sense, some of the major rules and principles of international water law closely resemble those of typical human rights treaties which normally enshrine objective standards wherein '[t]he principle of inter-State reciprocity has no place'.[4] State obligations envisaged by these rules and principles are directly owed to non-national, non-resident right-holders independently of (and in addition to) those owed as between

[2] The concepts expressed by the terms 'shared', 'transboundary' or 'international' waters are synonymous. They all refer without distinction to atmospheric, surface or underground waters shared between/among two or more states. See Dante A. Caponera, 'Shared Waters and International Law' in Gerald H. Blake, William Hilldesley, Martin Pratt, Rebecca Ridley and Clive Schofield (eds.), *The Peaceful Management of Transboundary Resources* (Graham & Trotman, 1995) 121, 121. An international river is either a successive river, traversing the territories of two or more states, or a boundary river (also called a contiguous river) if it is one that separates the territories of two or more states. Thus, an international river can be both successive, in its segments that traverse, for instance, the territories of riparian States A and B, and a boundary river, separating for instance riparian States B and C. See Jerome Lipper, 'Equitable Utilization' in A. H. Garretson, R. D. Hayton and C. J. Olmstead (eds.), *The Law of International Drainage Basins* (Oceana Publications Inc., 1967) 1, 16.

[3] UN Human Rights Committee, 'General Comment No. 24: Issues Relating to Reservations Made upon Ratification or Accession to the Covenant or the Optional Protocols Thereto, or in Relation to Declarations under Article 41 of the Covenant' (CCPR/C/21/Rev.1/Add.6), adopted at the 52nd Session, 1994 (UN Human Rights Committee, 4 November 1994), para. 17.

[4] *Ibid.* See also Mark Osiel, *The End of Reciprocity: Terror, Torture, and the Law of War* (Cambridge University Press, 2009) 112.

states (state *qua* state). In Craven's words, non-reciprocity in relation to human rights means that the rights are 'rights of individuals, and not of other states, and the framework within which they are protected was one of a "regime" or "legal order", and not simply a relation in the nature of a bilateral [or multilateral] agreement'.[5]

The analysis draws attention to the oft-neglected rules and principles of international water law that are primarily designed to benefit human beings directly as opposed to states. Chapter 2 demonstrated that international water law, used in coordination with the rules of international human rights law, provides a firm legal basis for establishing an independent human right to water. The endeavour in the present chapter is to demonstrate that the rules and principles of international water law provide a firm legal basis of the right and of the right's extraterritorial application. As Cahill argued, the extraterritorial aspect of states' obligations concerning the realisation of the human right to water is already established in international water law.[6] Given such, foreign residents could avail themselves of the rules and principles of international water law to ensure that their human right to water is not violated by a foreign state's (in)actions or hold the same to help realise their water rights extraterritorially. In the event that such co-riparian states fail in their duties, foreign right-holders are able to lodge complaints in human rights tribunals such as the African Commission against the co-riparian state to seek and obtain remedies. In the end, non-national, non-resident rights-holders are given the leeway to influence third states' domestic water-related (in)actions and decision-making processes in a way that boosts the human right to water for the benefit of all populations that inhabit the co-riparian states of a river basin.

6.2 International water law: from states' rights to human rights

6.2.1 *International water law: its relevance to the human right to water*

A proper analysis of the human rights and states' obligations entailed by the rules and principles of international water law – an area which has

[5] Matthew Craven, 'Legal Differentiation and the Concept of the Human Rights Treaty in International Law', 11(3) *European Journal of International Law* (2000) 489–519, 508.

[6] Amanda Cahill, 'Protecting Rights in the Face of Scarcity: The Right to Water' in Mark Gibney and Sigrun Skogly (eds.), *Universal Human Rights and Extraterritorial Obligations* (University of Pennsylvania Press, 2010) 194, 194.

been very rarely seen, if at all, to be of any relevance to human rights – necessitates a brief sketch of the development of the relevant norms and their interaction with the human rights framework. The regime of international water law is a special area of international law – named after the resource that it regulates – primarily concerned with the delineation of the rights and duties of states,[7] and (as is argued below) the protection of human right-holders in the regulation of their access to international water resources. It regulates the interactions between right-holders and duty-bearers in relation to the navigational (non-consumptive) and non-navigational (consumptive) uses of international rivers.[8] Non-consumptive uses of water include such uses of rivers as navigation and floating of timber. Their impact on the quantum of a river's water in contrast to the consumptive uses (which include the use of water for drinking and sanitation, agricultural and other similar uses) is minimal.[9]

Early developments of international water law focused on the resolution of inter-riparian relationships over the non-consumptive utilisation of international rivers.[10] The rules and principles regulating non-navigational (consumptive) uses of international rivers are late comers, as they emerged in tandem with the ever growing population numbers and the consequent rapidly increasing use of shared water resources.[11] Much ink has been spilt in an attempt to codify, develop and clarify the rules of international water law applicable to the consumptive utilisation of transboundary waters.

The rules and principles regulating the consumptive uses of transboundary water resources have now been compiled in the 1997 Convention on the Law of the Non-Navigational Uses of International

[7] Stephen R. Tully, 'The Contribution of Human Rights to Freshwater Resource Management', 14 *Yearbook of International Environmental Law* (2003) 101–37, 102.

[8] B. R. Chauhan, *Settlement of International Water Law Disputes in International Drainage Basins*, Wasserrecht und Wassserwirtschaft (Erich Schmidt Verlag, 1981) 106. As the concern of the present project is with the consumptive uses of transboundary waters (for personal and domestic uses), the analysis will be limited to a discussion of the Watercourses Convention, which embodies rules and principles relating only to non-navigational uses of water.

[9] Chauhan (note 8 above) 106.

[10] Stephen C. McCaffrey, *The Law of International Watercourses* (Oxford University Press, 2nd edn, 2007).

[11] See generally Stephen C. McCaffrey, 'The Evolution of the Law of International Watercourses', 45 *Austrian Journal of Public International Law* (1993) 87–111; Salman M. A. Salman, 'The Helsinki Rules, the UN Watercourses Convention and the Berlin Rules: Perspectives on International Water Law', 23(4) *Water Resources Development* (2007) 625–40. See also McCaffrey (note 10 above) 57.

Watercourses ('Watercourses Convention' or 'Convention').[12] The Convention is an embodiment of customary rules of international water law as well as rules representing progressive development of the law.[13] It was drafted, elaborated and adopted by the International Law Commission (ILC)[14] in a process that took almost two and a half decades.[15] The ILC eventually handed the draft treaty over to the 'Working Group of the Whole', i.e. the Sixth (Legal) Committee of the UN General Assembly, in 1994.[16] The process of formal and informal negotiations and deliberations at the Sixth Committee was open to all member states of the UN,[17] and it took three more years (1994–7) before the draft Convention was presented to the UN General Assembly for final adoption.[18] The Working Group was generally satisfied with the ILC's efforts at codification and progressive development of the rules of non-navigational uses of transboundary water resources and thus did not introduce significant changes into the ILC's draft.[19] The process

[12] Adopted by the UN General Assembly on 21 May 1997. The adoption of the Convention saw 103 states voting in favour, 3 against (Burundi, China and Turkey) and 27 abstaining. See GA Res. 51/229, Annex, Official Records of the General Assembly, Fifty-First Session, Supplement No. 49 (A/51/49), available at http://untreaty.un.org/ilc/texts/instruments/english/conventions/8_3_1997.pdf (accessed 22 February 2011).

[13] The Convention explicitly states that it is an embodiment not only of the progressive development of international water law but also of the codification of an existing custom. See the Preamble to the Convention, para. 4.

[14] The ILC is a UN body that comprises thirty-four experts who are nominated by states and elected by the UN General Assembly, for the specific task of 'the promotion of the progressive development of international law and its codification'. See Articles 1 and 2 of the Statute of the International Law Commission, adopted by the General Assembly in Resolution 174 (II) of 21 November 1947, as amended by Resolutions 485 (V) of 12 December 1950, 984 (X) of 3 December 1955, 985 (X) of 3 December 1955 and 36/39 of 18 November 1981.

[15] The ILC was mandated by the UN General Assembly, by virtue of Resolution 2669 XXV of 8 December 1970, to take up a study of the law of the non-navigational uses of international watercourses with a view to its progressive development and codification. It started working on the draft Convention in 1971 and completed and adopted the same in 1994. See Salman (note 11 above) 631. For a broader discussion of the Convention's drafting process, see Stephen C. McCaffrey, 'Background and Overview of the International Law Commission's Study of the Non-Navigational Uses of International Watercourses', 3 *Colorado Journal of International Environmental Law and Policy* (1992) 17–29.

[16] The Sixth (Legal) Committee of the UN General Assembly was responsible for finalising the draft Convention that was prepared and submitted by the ILC to it. The Sixth Committee deliberated on the draft and it opened the process to states who argued their positions at the negotiation stage. See McCaffrey (note 10 above) 359–60.

[17] McCaffrey (note 10 above) 59. [18] Salman (note 11 above) 631.

[19] McCaffrey (note 10 above) 376.

enhanced states' participation, and gave them a wide latitude to argue their positions and in some instances cast votes for the adoption or otherwise of a provision of the then draft Convention at the negotiation stage, long before the draft Convention was presented to the UN General Assembly for its final adoption as a treaty. Effectively, the states who took part in the negotiations at the Sixth Committee's deliberations thus had their concerns heard both at the Committee's deliberations and at the final adoption of the draft by the UN General Assembly, and voted at each stage.[20]

It is widely acknowledged that the draft prepared by the ILC, even as adopted by the UN General Assembly, was based on the prior works of two international non-governmental organisations composed of experts renowned for their expertise in international water law: the Institute of International Law (IIL) and the International Law Association (ILA).[21] The IIL and the ILA as precursors had compiled and elaborated non-binding rules of international water law,[22] which later provided the basis upon which the ILC's draft was built.[23] In its commentary, the ILC acknowledged the utility of some of the 'most notable'[24] works of the

[20] *Ibid.*, 359–60. [21] *Ibid.*, 377–81.

[22] Between 1911 and 1979, the IIL developed at least three major documents on consumptive uses of transboundary water resources: the 1911 Madrid Resolution on International Regulations Regarding the Use of International Watercourses, the 1961 Salzburg Resolution on the Use of International Non-Maritime Waters and the 1979 Athens Resolution on the Pollution of Rivers and Lakes and International Law. Similarly, the ILA developed the 1966 'Helsinki Rules on the Uses of the Waters of International Rivers' ('Helsinki Rules'), and, in response to developments entailed by the Convention, revised and adopted the 'Berlin (Revised Helsinki) Rules' at the Berlin Conference of the International Law Association in 2004.

[23] For an analysis of the roles of the IIL and ILA, see Charles B. Bourne, 'The International Law Association's Contribution to International Water Resources Law' in Patricia Wouters (ed.), *International Water Law: Selected Writings of Professor Charles B. Bourne* (Kluwer Law International, 1997) 233; McCaffrey (note 10 above) 377–81; Eyal Benvenisti, 'Collective Action in the Utilization of Shared Freshwater: The Challenges of International Water Resource Law', 90 *American Journal of International Law* (1996) 384–415, 384; Peter Beaumont, 'The 1997 UN Convention on the Law of Non-Navigational Uses of International Watercourses: Its Strengths and Weaknesses from a Water Management Perspective and the Need for New Workable Guidelines', 16(4) *Water Resources Development* (2000) 475–95, 475–6.

[24] ILC, 'Draft Articles on the Law of the Non-Navigational Uses of International Watercourses and Commentaries Thereto and Resolution on Transboundary Confined Ground Water', 2(2) *Yearbook of the International Law Commission* (1994) 89, 100 ('ILC Draft Articles').

ILA and used them as evidence of the acceptance of the rules and principles that it included in the (then draft) Convention.[25]

The Convention, from its inception, was not meant to be an instrument that primarily seeks to regulate the human rights of individuals and groups living in member states' territories. The approach to the development of international water law for consumptive uses has generally been state-centric, restricting its focus to the issues of inter-state rights and duties,[26] as opposed to individuals' and groups' rights and freedoms relative to international water resources.[27] Indeed, during the drafting of the Convention, a discussion on the human right to water took place and caused much disagreement among the negotiating states and experts.[28] Thus, some of the drafters of the Convention argued that the Convention should be limited to its traditional role of addressing inter-state relations in the regulation of shared rivers' utilisation.[29] The Convention as adopted was thus primarily said to be intended to 'address obligations of governments rather than being cast in terms of individual rights'.[30] It is claimed that such state-centrism entailed deadlocks such that 'no provision regarding the right could be agreed upon' in the Convention.[31] Hey asserts that '[t]he Watercourses Convention is not about ensuring that individuals and groups, both of present and future generations, have access to sufficient clean water'.[32]

25 *Ibid.*

26 The situation was apparent during the drafting processes of the Convention, where some members of the ILC found it unacceptable for the Convention to refer to persons other than states. They perceived the impending treaty 'to deal with relations between states and should not extend into the field of actions by natural or legal persons under domestic law'. See ILC Draft Articles (note 24 above) 133.

27 Neil A. F. Popović, 'In Pursuit of Environmental Human Rights: Commentary on the Draft Declaration of Principles on Human Rights and the Environment', 27 *Columbia Human Rights Law Review* (1996) 487–603, 494.

28 See Amanda Cahill, '"The Human Right to Water – A Right of Unique Status": The Legal Status and Normative Content of the Right to Water', 9(3) *International Journal of Human Rights* (2005) 389–410, 389.

29 See ILC Draft Articles (note 24 above) 133.

30 Stephen C. McCaffrey, 'The Human Right to Water' in Edith Brown Weiss, Laurence Boisson de Chazournes and Nathale Bernasconi-Osterwalder (eds.), *Fresh Water and International Economic Law* (Oxford University Press, 2005) 93, 100.

31 Cahill (note 28 above) 389.

32 Ellen Hey, 'The Watercourses Convention: To What Extent Does It Provide a Basis for Regulating Uses of International Watercourses?', 7(3) *Review of European Community and International Environmental Law* (1998) 291–300, 292.

The approach of the ILC in the codification and progressive development of the law was invariably state-centred,[33] as it saw the Convention as a 'self-contained regime',[34] a set of rules designed to define states' rights and duties as well as remedies for violations of the same. The resultant rules, principles and theoretical and doctrinal debates[35] have generally neglected individuals' and peoples' right to access water of adequate quality and quantity.[36]

This sharply contrasts with the parallel and concomitant developments that have taken place in recent decades in the field of international human rights law wherein efforts have been geared towards the development of norms providing for the human right to water and a state's duty to ensure individuals' and peoples' access to a sufficient quantity and quality of water needed for them to lead a decent life. As illustrated in Chapter 2, the development of the human right to water, beginning in the early 1970s around the same time as the Convention's drafting process, has focused on guaranteeing access by humans to water and is concerned with states only through imposing on the latter the duties to respect, protect and fulfil a human right to water. The trends associated with the development of the human right to water have sought, among others, to impose limitations on states' freedom of action regarding the manner of utilisation and prescribed the order of priority of uses to which the waters of shared rivers can be put.

Accordingly, the efforts to codify and develop a normative framework of a right to water have taken two divergent and unrelated approaches

[33] *Ibid.*

[34] Günther Handl, 'The International Law Commission's Draft Articles on the Law of International Watercourses (General Principles and Planned Measures): Progressive or Retrogressive Development of International Law?', 3 *Colorado Journal of International Environmental Law and Policy* (1992) 123–34, 125.

[35] Four prominent theories have been vying for recognition in the international watercourses debate: absolute territorial sovereignty, absolute territorial integrity; limited territorial sovereignty; and the community of interests. These four theories on international watercourses law operate from the perspective of state sovereignty, and, whether one or more of these is accepted, do not aim at ensuring the human right to water of individuals and peoples. See Caponera (note 2 above) 123–4; McCaffrey (note 10 above) 111–70.

[36] Ellen Hey, 'Sustainable Use of Shared Water Resources: The Need for a Paradigm Shift in International Watercourses Law' in Gerald H. Blake, William Hilldesley, Martin Pratt, Rebecca Ridley and Clive Schofield (eds.), *The Peaceful Management of Transboundary Resources* (Graham & Trotman, 1995) 127, 130–3; Stephen C. McCaffrey, 'A Human Right to Water: Domestic and International Implications', 5(1) *Georgetown International Environmental Law Review* (1992) 1–24, 1–2.

that have left a grey area between them. The parallel developments of the Convention and international human rights law with reference to the 'right to water' now beg the question of whose right is being considered. Valid answers to this inquiry turn on whether one approaches the issue from the perspective of international water law or, alternatively, from an international human rights law standpoint.[37] In the former, the right to water conventionally designates states' rights,[38] while in the latter the right to water is a human right, distinct from a state's right to the use of the shared resources.

The divergence in approaches between the development of the Convention and the international human rights regime is prejudicial to the implementation of the human right to water in at least four major ways. First, the prevailing view that the Convention places an almost exclusive emphasis on the regulation of inter-state interactions fails to give adequate attention to the rights of the constituent individuals and groups who are the ultimate beneficiaries. Secondly, and as a result, it appears that individuals and groups would not be able to avail themselves of the rules and principles of the Convention in their complaints about the violation of their human right to water by third states. This is because international law generally lacks rules providing for compulsory adjudication,[39] and this would apply to the norms of international water law. Unless individuals and groups are allowed to use international water law norms before international or national tribunals competent to adjudicate human rights complaints, the regime as a whole would be of distant relevance to the realisation of the human right to water. Thirdly, the view entails that complaints based on violations of the Convention and those focusing on the human right to water need to be lodged before differing fora. Violation of the Convention would be a subject of inter-riparian litigation or arbitration in which individual and group complaints would have no standing, while complaints based on violations of the human right to water need to be lodged before human rights tribunals. Accordingly, individuals and groups in one state have lacked the standing or legal interest or both against a foreign state whose actions or omissions (or those of actors under its control) caused a violation of their human right to water. This leaves wide room for impunity,

[37] Desheng Hu, *Water Rights: An International and Comparative Study* (IWA Publishing, 2006) 19–45.

[38] Hey (note 32 above) 292.

[39] R. Y. Jennings, 'Treaties' in Mohammed Bedjaoui (ed.), *International Law: Achievements and Prospects* (UNESCO, 1991) 135, 162.

as private parties could not seek remedies for a violation for which a foreign state would otherwise be held liable. Finally, and consequently, individuals' and groups' right to remedies would be curtailed or weakened.

Thus, there is a need for a paradigmatic shift towards a regime wherein individuals and groups take centre stage as compared to the state. International water law possesses the potential to be 'humanised'. There is indeed room for possible regime complementarity between international water law and international human rights law. Thus the understanding that the two bodies of law aim at achieving different ends for different subjects should not be overstated. There is a need for 'humanization of international [water] law',[40] because it is 'the recognition of [the] human being as being the ultimate addressee of that [international] law which matters'.[41] Authors have argued that the human right to water must be seen in relation to and be informed by international water law.[42]

Even if it is admitted that the Convention's primary focus is the regulation of inter-state water governance, there are numerous provisions in the text of the Convention which specifically provide not only for the human right to water[43] but also for its extraterritorial application, of which the right-holders may avail themselves in international human rights tribunals. This holds true in relation to the right-holders in Africa who could approach the African Commission to enforce or remedy their water rights issues. Before the chapter shifts its focus to an analysis of the Convention's rules and principles that could be used to guarantee the protection, promotion and fulfilment of the human right to water of riparian populations who are dependent upon transboundary waters, a brief overview of the status of the rules and principles of the Convention is in order.

6.2.2 *The Convention as an embodiment of customary rules of international water law*

The Convention is the only instrument with a promise of universal applicability to the non-navigational (consumptive) uses of

40 Shiv R. S. Bedi, *The Development of Human Rights Law by the Judges of the International Court of Justice* (Hart Publishing, 2007) 268.

41 *Ibid.*

42 McCaffrey (note 10 above) 371; Beaumont (note 23 above) 483; Cahill (note 6 above) 194.

43 See Chapter 2.

transboundary waters. But it has yet to enter into force as it is awaiting the necessary trigger ratification.[44] As is discussed below in more detail, the fact that the Convention has not entered into force does not mean that it is of no current relevance. Its adoption is a significant milestone in the codification and development of rules of international water law for consumptive purposes. This remains the case irrespective of whether or not the Convention enters into force.[45] First, more weight is attached to its provisions than is the case with many other treaties of similar status due to the fact that it was prepared by the ILC, a UN body responsible for the codification and progressive development of international law.[46] This view also gains some support from judicial practice. Judge Ad Hoc Sorensen stated in the *North Sea Continental Shelf* cases:[47]

> a convention adopted as part of the combined process of codification and progressive development of international law may well constitute, or come to constitute the decisive evidence of generally accepted new rules of international law . . . The Convention may serve as an authoritative guide for the practice of states faced with the relevant new legal problems, and its provisions thus become the nucleus around which a set of generally recognised legal rules may crystallise.

Secondly, although the ILC did not draw a line between the Convention's principles that codify existing rules and those that are a progressive development of the law, the rules and principles of the Convention that are most pertinent to the human right to water[48] are clearly rules of customary international law.[49] This is discussed further below. Thirdly, the negotiation of the Convention involved all interested member states of the UN, and the resultant Convention, in large measure,

[44] Thirty-five states need to ratify the Convention for it to come into operation. See Watercourses Convention, Article 36(1) and (2). As of 22 February 2013, there were thirty parties to the Convention, and an additional four states that had signed but not yet ratified the Convention. See International Water Law Project, 'Status of the Watercourses Convention', at www.internationalwaterlaw.org/documents/intldocs/watercourse_status.html (accessed 17 June 2013).

[45] McCaffrey (note 10 above) 375. [46] *Ibid.*, 375.

[47] *Federal Republic of Germany* v. *Denmark; Federal Republic of Germany* v. *the Netherlands, ICJ Reports* 1969, 241, para. 244 (dissenting opinion).

[48] As is discussed below, these refer to the principles of equitable and reasonable utilisation and the no-significant-harm rule enshrined in Articles 5 and 7 of the Convention, respectively. These rules are part of customary rules of international water law. See McCaffrey (note 10 above) 376.

[49] See sections 6.3.2 and 6.4.1 below; see also McCaffrey (note 10 above) 376.

may be considered to be reflective of the views of the international community on the subject.[50]

Fourthly, the adoption of the Convention has already begun to influence the development of rules and judicial decisions pertaining to the consumptive uses of shared rivers, indicating an affirmative reception by states of the rules and principles contained in the Convention.[51] For instance, the provisions of the Revised Helsinki Rules[52] are modelled on, and closely resemble, the rules and principles of the Convention.[53] The International Court of Justice (ICJ) also made repeated references to the equitable and reasonable utilisation principle of the Convention in the determination of the *Gabčíkovo-Nagymaros* case.[54] These references to the principle were made not only due to its role as a customary rule of international law,[55] but also with specific reference to its wording under Article 5 of the Convention.[56] The ICJ referred to the Convention despite the fact that the Convention has yet to enter into force, and, more importantly, against the fact that the parties to the dispute had yet to ratify the Convention.

Finally, the Convention has also begun to influence regional (basin-specific) treaties.[57] Regional water-related treaties, especially in African river basins, are based on or have incorporated the principles enshrined in the Convention. This is especially the case in transboundary water-sharing treaties in southern Africa and the Nile and Senegal river basins. In the Southern African Development Community (SADC), a sub-regional arrangement comprising fifteen African states,[58] the Convention inspired[59] the revision of the 1995 'Protocol on Shared Watercourse System in the Southern African Development Community

[50] McCaffrey (note 10 above) 376. [51] See Bourquain (note 1 above) 30.

[52] This is also referred to as the 'Berlin Rules on Water Resources'. The Rules were adopted by the International Law Association at its conference in Berlin in August 2004.

[53] See Bourquain (note 1 above) 30.

[54] See *Case Concerning the Gabčíkovo-Nagymaros Project* (*Hungary* v. *Slovakia*), Judgment of 25 September 1997, *ICJ Reports* 1997 ('*Gabčíkovo-Nagymaros* case (note 54 above)'), paras. 78, 85 and 147.

[55] See Berlin Rules (note 52 above) 3.

[56] See *Gabčíkovo-Nagymaros* case (note 54 above), para. 147.

[57] See also McCaffrey (note 10 above) 376–7.

[58] See the Southern African Development Community (SADC) website at www.sadc.int (accessed 23 February 2011).

[59] As Salman noted, the need to revise the 1995 SADC Watercourses Protocol was necessitated by the need 'to take into account the development in the field of international water law as reflected in the UN [Watercourses] Convention'. See Salman M. A. Salman, 'Introductory Note: Revised Protocol on Shared Watercourses in the

(SADC) Region' ('SADC Protocol').[60] The SADC Protocol incorporates the principle of equitable utilisation,[61] which was already enshrined in the Convention, as a guiding principle of transboundary water-sharing arrangements, as well as factors[62] similar to those provided for in the Convention's Article 6 that are used in the determination of the equitability and reasonableness of utilisation of shared water resources, including the 'population dependent on the shared watercourse in each watercourse state'.[63] The state parties to the SADC Protocol also recognised the existence of customary rules of international water law, of which the principle of equitable and reasonable utilisation is a part. They undertook 'to respect the existing rules of customary international law relating to the utilisation and management of the resources of shared watercourses'.[64] As this provision comes as part of the same provision that provides for equitable utilisation, arguably the Protocol's reference to customary international water law refers to, *inter alia*, the principle of equitable and reasonable utilisation.

Thus, instead of directly applying the provisions of the Convention *per se* in their regional water-sharing arrangements, the SADC states have resorted to the incorporation of the principles contained therein in their respective regional (or basin-wide) treaty arrangements. This is indeed an expected outcome of the Convention, which was designed from the outset to serve as a framework upon which basin-specific arrangements can be moulded.[65]

Southern African Development Community', 40 ILM 317 (2001), 318. See also Owen McIntyre, 'The Role of Customary Rules and Principles of International Environmental Law in the Protection of Shared international Freshwater Resources', 46 *Natural Resources Journal* (2006) 157–210, 206.

60 Adopted on 23 August 1995, and entered into force on 29 September 1998.

61 SADC Protocol, Article 3. See also Salman (note 59 above) 318.

62 SADC Protocol, Article 3(8). See also Salman (note 59 above) 318.

63 SADC Protocol, Article 3(8)(a)(iii). 64 *Ibid.*, Article 3(3).

65 Under its Article 3(2), the Convention stipulates that state parties 'may, where necessary, consider harmonizing such [basin-specific] agreements with the basic principles of the present Convention'. See also Hey (note 32 above) 292–4. See also Stephen C. McCaffrey and Mpazi Sinjela, 'The 1997 United Nations Convention on International Watercourses', 92(1) *American Journal of International Law* (1998) 97–107, 98; Takele Soboka Bulto, 'Between Ambivalence and Necessity: Occlusions on the Path Towards a Basin-Wide Treaty in the Nile Basin', 20(1) *Colorado Journal of International Environmental Law and Policy* (2009) 291–320, 291–2: Keith Hayward, 'Supplying Basin-Wide Reforms with an Independent Assessment Applying International Water Law: Case Study of the Dnieper River', 18(3) *Colorado Journal of International Environmental Law and Policy* (2007) 633–64, 633.

This is no less true of the Nile basin states. The Nile Basin Initiative (NBI) Act,[66] adopted by the NBI countries, explicitly incorporated the principle of equitable and reasonable utilisation of the waters of the Nile among the ten riparian states. Under the Act, the riparian states undertook 'to achieve sustainable socio-economic development through *equitable utilization of, and benefit from, the common Nile Basin water resources*'.[67] However, the Act, as a transitional document, does not entail an immediate obligation for the states. It is a 'terms of reference' instrument which forms the framework within which the impending final basin-wide treaty is to be formulated. Although an agreement to further agreement, the NBI Act, incorporating the principle of equitable and reasonable utilisation of the Nile waters, can be expected to guide the modality of apportionment of the Nile waters in the final framework agreement. Indeed, the emerging trends in the Nile basin negotiations indicate that 'even those who are most dependent on the Nile recognise the need for equitable use by all those who drink its water'.[68] Similarly, the basin-wide agreement covering the Senegal River also incorporates the principle of 'equitable and reasonable use of the River's water' among the riparian states.[69]

However, even if issues associated with the normative status of the Convention are addressed, the analysis of their utility in the realisation of the human right to water is not yet at an end. There is another major problem in the use of the rules and principles of the Convention for human rights purposes, and that has to do with the determination of the subjects protected by the treaty: are human beings meant to be the beneficiaries of the Convention's guarantees?[70] The following sections explore the possibilities for individuals and groups to use the rules and principles of international water law before human rights tribunals for the purpose of promoting the realisation of the human right to water.

6.3 The principle of equitable and reasonable utilisation as an extraterritorial duty to fulfil

The principle of equitable and reasonable utilisation could contribute to the realisation of the human right to water at two levels. At one level, the

[66] Adopted 11 October 2002, entered into force 1 November 2002.
[67] The NBI Act, 2002, Preamble, para. 3 (emphasis added).
[68] Robert O. Collins, *The Nile* (Yale University Press, 2002) 233.
[69] See Water Charter of the Senegal River, 18 May 2002, quoted in McCaffrey (note 10 above) 274.
[70] See Hey (note 32 above) 292.

Convention enshrines positive extraterritorial obligations which are aimed at enhancing the capacities of riparian states to fulfil their domestic duties that are entailed by the recognition of the human right to water. It does so by allowing states to access and share water resources originating in other riparian states, on the one hand, and by imposing obligations on co-riparian states to give priority to the vital human needs of basin populations before allocating shared waters for other uses, on the other. On the other hand, the principle of equitable and reasonable utilisation enshrines individuals' and groups' right to the extraterritorial human right to water and access to transboundary remedies.

6.3.1 *Introducing the concept*

The principle of equitable and reasonable utilisation of common water resources is the pillar of inter-state interactions over consumptive uses of international waters.[71] It is variously referred to as a 'fundamental norm',[72] 'canon',[73] 'backbone'[74] and 'pre-eminent rule'[75] of international water law. It has been enshrined in Article 5(1) of the Convention, which states:

> [w]atercourse States shall in their respective territories utilize an international watercourse in an equitable and reasonable manner. In particular, an international watercourse shall be used and developed by watercourse States with a view to attaining optimal and sustainable utilization thereof and benefits therefrom, taking into account the interests of the watercourse States concerned, consistent with adequate protection of the watercourse.

Predicated on the sovereign equality of states,[76] this principle dictates not only that all basin states have access to a reasonable and equitable amount of the shared waters, but also imposes duties upon all riparian

[71] See Hayward (note 65 above) 642. See also Salman M. A. Salman and Kishor Uprety, *Conflict and Cooperation on South Asia's International Rivers: A Legal Perspective* (World Bank, 2002) 15.

[72] McCaffrey (note 10 above) 384.

[73] Dissenting Opinion of Judge Ad Hoc Skubiszewski in the *Gabčíkovo-Nagymaros* case (note 54 above), para. 8.

[74] A. Nollkaemper, 'The Contribution of the International Law Commission to International Water Law: Does It Reverse the Flight from Substance?', 27 *Netherlands Yearbook of International Law* (1996) 39–73, 44.

[75] McIntyre (note 59 above) 158.

[76] McCaffrey (note 10 above) 390–1.

states to use the resource in an equitable and reasonable manner.[77] At the heart of the principle of equitable utilisation is the 'equality of rights' as between co-riparian states,[78] which means that co-riparian states enjoy an equal right to the use of a common water resource for equally pressing needs.[79] In the *Gabčíkovo-Nagymaros* case between Hungary and Slovakia over the waters of the Danube River, the ICJ, concurring with its predecessor's decision in the *River Oder* case,[80] stated:

> [the] community of interest in a navigable river becomes the basis of a common legal right, the essential features of which are the perfect equality of all riparian States in the use of the whole course of the river and the exclusion of any preferential privilege of any one riparian State in relation to the others.[81]

However, the equality of rights among riparian states may not necessarily imply volumetric equality of shares.[82] As the US Supreme Court explained,[83] the principle of equitable and reasonable utilisation does not imply an equal division of the waters of a shared river among its riparian states.[84] The equality of rights among states implies that similar interests of riparian states should be treated the same.[85] This means that the principle of equitable and reasonable utilisation confers as much reciprocal inter-state rights as it imposes similarly reciprocal inter-state duties. According to the ILC:

77 Bonaya Adhi Godana, *Africa's Shared Water Resources: Legal and Institutional Aspects of the Nile, Niger, and Senegal River Systems* (Lynne Rienner Publications Inc., 1985) 50.

78 Lipper (note 2 above) 44. 79 *Ibid.*, 63.

80 *Territorial Jurisdiction of the International Commission of the River Oder*, Judgment No. 16, 1929, PCIJ, Ser. A, No. 23, p. 27 ('River Oder case').

81 *Gabčíkovo-Nagymaros* case (note 54 above), para. 85.

82 David Goldberg, 'World Bank Policy on Projects on International Waterways in the Context of Emerging International Law and the Work of the International Law Commission' in Gerald H. Blake, William Hilldesley, Martin Pratt, Rebecca Ridley and Clive Schofield (eds.), *The Peaceful Management of Transboundary Resources* (Graham & Trotman, 1995) 153, 155.

83 The principle of equitable and reasonable utilisation was born out of early-twentieth-century decisions of the US Supreme Court, who bequeathed it to international water law. The application and implications of the principle in international water law remained the same. See McCaffrey (note 10 above) 384; William W. Van Alstyne, 'The Justiciability of International River Disputes: A Study in the Case Method', 13 *Duke Law Journal* (1964) 307–40, 307.

84 *Connecticut* v. *Massachusetts*, 282 US 660, 670–1 (1931).

85 It seeks to 'guarantee that no legitimate aspiration of any interested riparian shall be ignored in developing a river basin . . . it is to be deplored only if it is taken to confer an unqualified veto, enabling each riparian to frustrate river development except on its own terms'. Van Alstyne (note 83 above) 334.

> [Article 5(1)] states the basic rule of equitable utilization. Although cast in terms of an obligation, the rule also expresses the correlative entitlement, namely that a watercourse State has the right, within its territory, to a reasonable and equitable share, or portion, of the uses and benefits of an international watercourse. Thus a watercourse State has both the right to utilize an international watercourse in an equitable and reasonable manner and the obligation not to exceed its right to equitable utilization or, in somewhat different terms, not to deprive other watercourse States of their right to equitable utilization.[86]

The exact formula for the equitable and reasonable apportionment of the common water thus depends upon the degree of comparable interests of each state. At the core of the principle of equitable and reasonable utilisation lies the prohibition of an exclusion of any riparian from its equitable and reasonable share of a common water resource.[87] Any arrangement for water allocation that denies one or more of the riparian states access to a shared fresh water resource is inequitable. As the ICJ ruled, even when a riparian state pulls out of a regional or bilateral water-sharing arrangement or treaty, its right to access an equitable and reasonable amount of the shared resource remains intact.[88] Irrespective of the geographic position of a riparian state along the river's flow, unilateral control of a shared fresh water, via diversion or otherwise, is a violation of the principle of equitable and reasonable utilisation.[89]

The precise amount of a state's share *vis-à-vis* those of other riparian states should be 'proportional' to the needs of each riparian state.[90] The actual dividend of a riparian state from the common river thus turns upon multiple objective and subjective factors. The Convention provides for an illustrative (non-exhaustive) list of seven relevant criteria of equitability and reasonableness of a use by a riparian state,[91] including the socio-economic needs of the riparian states and, most importantly, the size of the population dependent upon the shared water resource.[92] The socio-economic needs of riparian states and the size of their populations dependent on shared waters

[86] ILC Draft Articles (note 24 above) 97. [87] Van Alstyne (note 83 above) 334.
[88] *Gabčíkovo-Nagymaros* case (note 54 above), para. 78. [89] *Ibid.*, para. 85. [90] *Ibid.*
[91] See Article 6(1)(a)–(g).
[92] Other factors include: geographic, hydrographic, hydrological, climatic, ecological and other factors of a natural character; the effects of the use or uses of the watercourses in one watercourse state on other watercourse states; existing and potential uses of the watercourse; conservation, protection, development and economy of use of the water resources of the watercourse and the costs of measures taken to that effect; and the

are factors that are very relevant to the direct protection of individuals' and groups' rights in all riparian states in water-sharing arrangements. The size of the population dependent, especially for drinking and domestic uses, upon shared waters and the degree of their dependence could be used by riparian states to justify their claims to equitable and reasonable access to the common fresh water resources shared with other co-riparian states. The principle of equitable and reasonable utilisation has a direct impact on the enhancement of a riparian state's capacity to realise the human right to water for its domestic right-holders.

6.3.2 *The normative status of the principle of equitable and reasonable utilisation*

Apart from its codification in the Convention, the principle of equitable and reasonable utilisation enjoys the overwhelming support of scholarship and state practice such that 'nearly all international accords regarding international rivers are based on this principle'.[93] It is broadly agreed that the principle of equitable and reasonable use is part of customary international law.[94] The 1966 Helsinki Rules[95] and the 1994 ILC Draft Articles[96] had already espoused the principle before its eventual incorporation into the Convention. According to McCaffrey, 'it is clear that the Helsinki Rules are, in every sense, important precursors of the ILC's draft articles and thus of the UN Convention'.[97] Historically, the principles of equitable and reasonable utilisation had been recognised in China and India for many centuries

availability of alternatives, of comparable value, to a particular planned or existing use. See Article 6(1).

93 Haggai Erlich, *The Cross and the River: Ethiopia, Egypt, and the Nile* (Lynne Rienner Publishers, 2002) 7.

94 See McCaffrey (note 10 above) 408; Richard Paisley, 'Adversaries into Partners: International Water Law and the Equitable Sharing of Downstream Benefits', 3 *Melbourne Journal of International Law* (2002) 280–300, 283; Charles B. Bourne, 'The International Law Commission's Draft Articles on the Law of International Watercourses: Principles and Planned Measures', 3 *Colorado Journal of International Environmental Law and Policy* (1992) 65–92, 82.

95 See the 'Helsinki Rules on the Uses of the Waters of International Rivers', adopted by the International Law Association at its 52nd conference, held in Helsinki in August 1966, Article IV.

96 See ILC Draft Articles (note 24 above), Articles 4 and 5.

97 McCaffrey (note 10 above) 381.

and have acquired prominence over the past 500 years with the development of the nation state.[98]

As such, its inclusion in Article 5 of the Convention is a codification of a customary rule of international law[99] rather than a progressive development of the rules of international law regarding non-navigational uses of international watercourses. As the survey of the ILC confirmed:

> all available evidence of the general practice of States, accepted as law, in respect of the non-navigational uses of international watercourses – including treaty provisions, positions taken by States in specific disputes, decisions of international courts and tribunals, statements of law prepared by intergovernmental and non-governmental bodies, the views of learned commentators and decisions of municipal courts in cognate cases – reveals that there is overwhelming support for the doctrine of equitable utilization as a general rule of law for the determination of the rights and obligations of States in this field.[100]

The status of the principle of equitable and reasonable use of transboundary water resources as a customary rule of international law has been implicitly confirmed in the *Gabčíkovo-Nagymaros* case, where the ICJ ruled that the principle applies irrespective of Hungary's withdrawal of its consent.[101] It stated:

> [i]t is true that Hungary, in concluding the 1977 Treaty, had agreed to the damming of the Danube and the diversion of its waters into the bypass canal. But it was only in the context of a joint operation and a sharing of its benefits that Hungary had given its consent. The suspension and withdrawal of that consent constituted a violation of Hungary's legal obligations, demonstrating, as it did, the refusal by Hungary of joint operation; *but that cannot mean that Hungary forfeited its basic right to an equitable and reasonable sharing of the resources of an international watercourse.*[102]

The legal status of the principle of equitable and reasonable utilisation as a rule of customary international law is of crucial relevance in Africa generally and in the Nile basin states specifically. As in many other parts

[98] Erlich (note 93 above) 7. The more recent Berlin Rules also provide for the principle under its Article 12, and the accompanying commentary affirms the pre-eminent weight of the principle in international water law. See Berlin Rules (note 52 above).

[99] *Ibid.* [100] ILC Draft Articles (note 24 above) 98.

[101] According to the ILA, the decision of the ICJ in this case affirms the fact that the principle of equitable and reasonable utilisation is part of customary international law. See Berlin Rules (note 52 above) 3.

[102] *Gabčíkovo-Nagymaros* case (note 54 above), para. 78 (emphasis added).

of the world where disputes over water-sharing arrangements loom large, none of the Nile riparian states has ratified the Convention. Currently, no Nile riparian can be bound by the Convention as a treaty *per se*. But, due to its status as a rule of customary international law, the principle of equitable and reasonable utilisation still applies as a binding norm to regulate the apportionment of the Nile waters among the riparian states and continues to bind them irrespective of their consent.[103]

The Convention has been viewed with suspicion, and even rejected, by the Nile riparian states. Ethiopia complained of the lack of balance between the rights of downstream states and those of upstream states. It retorted at the negotiation stage that the Working Group had 'no serious desire to accommodate' the interests of the upstream states, 'particularly [those of] . . . a developing country such as Ethiopia'.[104] Rwanda pointed out that the Convention lacked regard for sovereignty, which it considered a 'sacrosanct principle' in the treaty-making process.[105] Burundi rejected the Convention outright and voted against it alongside the only two other countries that voted against the Convention altogether, namely, China and Turkey. For their parts, Egypt, Ethiopia, Rwanda and Tanzania abstained in the voting process and have not subsequently signed or ratified the Convention.[106] Democratic Republic of Congo, Eritrea and Uganda were absent altogether at the voting, and have not subsequently signed or acceded to the Convention. The only two Nile basin states that voted in favour of the Convention were Kenya and Sudan, but even these two states have yet to ratify it.

Thus, to the extent that the Convention is a progressive development of international water law,[107] to date none of the ten riparian states of the Nile can be bound by the provisions of the Convention. Had it not been

103 In any case, even if all ten riparian states of the Nile were to ratify the Convention now, they could not bring the Convention into force. While thirty-five ratifications are required to bring the Convention into force, to date, only thirty states have ratified the Convention, and therefore the Convention is not yet in force.

104 Aaron Schwabach, 'The United Nations Convention on the Law of Non-Navigational Uses of International Watercourses, Customary International Law, and the Interests of Developing Upper Riparians', 33 *Texas International Law Journal* (1998) 257–80, 275–6.

105 *Ibid.*, 276–7.

106 See the 'African Water Page', at www.africanwater.org/UNPressWater.htm (accessed 23 February 2011).

107 The Convention states that it is not only a 'successful codification' of international custom but also that it is a 'progressive development of rules of international law regarding non-navigational uses of international watercourses'. See Convention, Preamble, para. 4.

for the customary status of the principle of equitable and reasonable utilisation, the lack of ratification of the Convention by the Nile basin states would have left the Nile basin in a desperate situation where any inter-state regulatory framework is utterly absent as there is no basin-wide treaty regarding the utilisation of the river's waters. Further, by agreeing – albeit in principle – to heed the requirements of the principle of equitable and reasonable utilisation in the NBI Act, the Nile riparian states have obviated the remaining suspicion that some of them could be persistent objectors to the principle. For a state to be a persistent objector to customary international law there must be a clear, consistent and uninterrupted objection to the rule being objected to.[108] The unanimous agreement by the Nile riparian states to the principle has removed the possibility of any claim by the riparian states to be persistent objectors to the application of equitable and reasonable use of the Nile waters. It has been observed, rightly, that:

> [e]ven where there is an applicable [basin-specific] agreement, the Convention may play an important role in the interpretation of that agreement, as in the Gabčíkovo-Nagymaros case. For these reasons, the success of the Convention does not seem to be dependent upon whether it enters into force. Its influence is more likely to derive from its status as the most authoritative statement of general principles and rules governing the non-navigational uses of international watercourses.[109]

6.3.3 *The relevance of the equitable and reasonable utilisation principle for the human right to water*

As has been outlined above, the controlling principle in the sharing of the waters of international rivers is the principle of equitable and

[108] Lynn Loschin, 'The Persistent Objector and Customary Human Rights Law: A Proposed Analytical Framework', 2 *University of California Davis Journal of International Law and Policy* (1996) 147–72, 150–1; David A. Colson, 'How Persistent Must the Persistent Objector Be?', 61 *Washington Law Review* (1986) 957–70, 962. For a detailed discussion of the persistent objector rule, see generally J. Brock McClane, 'How Late in the Emergence of a Norm of Customary International Law May a Persistent Objector Object?', 13 *ILSA Journal of International Law* (1989) 1–26; Ted L. Stein, 'The Approach of the Different Drummer: The Principle of the Persistent Objector in International Law', 26(2) *Harvard International Law Journal* (1985) 457–82; Prosper Weil, 'Towards Relative Normativity in International Law?', 77 *American Journal of International Law* (1983) 413–42.

[109] Stephen McCaffrey, 'The Contribution of the UN Convention on the Law of the Non-Navigational Uses of International Watercourses', 1(3/4) *International Journal of Global Environmental Issues* (2001) 250–63, 261; Jonathan I. Charney, 'Universal International Law', 87 *American Journal of International Law* (1993) 529–51.

reasonable utilisation. According to the Convention, one of the crucial criteria of equitability and reasonableness of access to shared water resources is the size of 'population dependent on the watercourse in each Watercourse State'.[110] This provision is intended to stress the importance of constantly keeping in mind 'both the size of the population dependent on the watercourse and the degree or extent of their dependency' in water-sharing arrangements.[111] The degree of such dependence takes its acute form when the use made of the shared resource is for drinking and domestic purposes. Any formula for apportioning shared water resources among riparian states that ignores the needs of the populations of each state involved therein is thus not equitable or reasonable.[112]

Thus, the Convention, through the incorporation of the provision on equitable and reasonable utilisation, has the potential to protect the human right to water of individuals and groups in at least two ways.[113] First, the principle of equitable and reasonable utilisation requires co-riparian states to treat the population of all co-riparian states equally with respect to drinking and sanitation water.[114] Secondly, the principle imposes shared obligations among riparian states to the effect that in their negotiations or treaties concerning water-sharing arrangements, they must give priority to the 'vital human needs' of the population of each of the states involved.[115] The combined application of the 'equal treatment' duty on the one hand and the priority accorded to the 'vital human needs' on the other produce the effect of guaranteeing the human right to water for the right-holders in the territories of co-riparian states.

6.3.3.1 Equitable and reasonable utilisation as a human rights duty of co-riparian states

It may happen that, in water-related agreements, states make adequate arrangements for the water rights of some of the basin populations and neglect those of others. Such a scenario would lead to a violation of the

[110] Convention, Article 6(1)(c). [111] ILC Draft Articles (note 24 above) 101.

[112] See Charles B. Bourne, 'The Primacy of the Principle of Equitable Utilisation in the 1997 Watercourses Convention', *Canadian Yearbook of International Law* (1997) 215–32, 227.

[113] See Amanda Cahill-Ripley, *The Human Right to Water and Its Application in the Occupied Palestinian Territories* (Routledge, 2011) 9.

[114] This flows from the sovereign equality of riparian states which is the cornerstone of the principle of equitable and reasonable utilisation (discussed above).

[115] Convention, Article 10(2).

principle of equitable and reasonable utilisation.[116] In such instances, not only the home state but also the other riparian states involved incur responsibility towards the basin population for causing harm (albeit only in cases where the harm is significant).[117] The importance of this obligation has rightly been highlighted in General Comment No. 15 of the CESCR on the right to water:

> States parties should ensure that the right to water is given due attention in international agreements and, to that end, should consider the development of further legal instruments. With regard to the conclusion and implementation of other international and regional agreements, States parties should take steps to ensure that these instruments do not adversely impact upon the right to water.[118]

The principle of equitable and reasonable utilisation is a right that a riparian state may exercise as against all other co-riparian states in its efforts to realise the human right to water for its own residents.[119] Adherence to equitable and reasonable utilisation, a principle based on the sovereign equality of states, entails that each and every riparian state has the right to demand that others treat its residents equally in water-sharing arrangements. As Beaumont notes, 'it would seem reasonable for a state to claim this minimum [amount of water] . . . per inhabitant per annum, for its subjects who are dependent on the waters of the particular transboundary river for their survival'.[120]

In effect, each co-riparian state bears a duty to ensure that the needs of its residents be taken into account while entering into any water-sharing arrangement. This also follows from the fact that a state is the primary duty-bearer for the realisation of the human rights of its residents, including the human right to water.[121] Even in instances where a state is not a party to a regional water-sharing treaty, the Convention provides that all states that would be affected by a planned water-sharing arrangement or negotiations pertaining thereto among other riparian states are 'entitled to participate in consultations on such an agreement . . . to the

[116] Such violations bring into play individuals' and groups' right to extraterritorial remedies. See section 5.5 below.

[117] See section 5.4.2 below.

[118] CESCR, 'General Comment No. 15: Substantive Issues Arising in the Implementation of the International Covenant on Economic, Social and Cultural Rights (Adopted 11–29 November 2002)' (UN Committee on Economic, Social and Cultural Rights, 11–29 November 2002), para. 35.

[119] See generally van Alstyne (note 83 above).

[120] Beaumont (note 23 above) 483–4.

[121] See Chapter 3.

extent that its use is thereby affected'.[122] According to the ILC, this provision is designed to guard against the prejudicial arrangements for the use of shared watercourses which could put the rights of non-negotiating co-riparian states in jeopardy:

> [I]f a watercourse agreement is concerned with only part of the watercourse or only a particular project, programme or use relating thereto, it must be subject to the proviso that the use, by one or more other watercourse States not parties to the agreement, of the waters of the watercourse is not, to a significant extent, adversely affected by the agreement. Otherwise, a few States of a multi-State international watercourse could appropriate a disproportionate amount of its benefits for themselves or unduly prejudice the use of its waters by watercourse States not parties to the agreement in question. Such results would run counter to fundamental principles which will be shown to govern the non-navigational uses of international watercourses, such as the right of all watercourse States to use an international watercourse in an equitable and reasonable manner and the obligation not to use a watercourse in such a way as to injure other watercourse States.[123]

The principle of equitable and reasonable utilisation is thus of direct relevance for the implementation of the human right to water. It compels states to cater for the needs of their respective populations in their water-sharing arrangements. It also imposes a duty upon all riparian states to ensure that all the populations of a shared basin that are dependent on common waters are treated equally. Or, put otherwise, it entails riparian states' obligations to ensure that all basin populations are treated equally in their access to an equitable and reasonable use of shared water for equally pressing needs.[124] The riparian states' common responsibility to ensure equal treatment of a basin population means that each state owes to all and all states owe to each the duty to help – or allow – co-riparian states to fulfil the human right to water of the basin population. Riparian states' failure to live up to these duties could be a cause of action in the inter-state complaints procedures of the African Charter,[125] in which a state may complain about the violation of its residents' human right to water as a result of another riparian state's actions or omissions.

[122] Convention, Article 4(2). [123] ILC Draft Articles (note 24 above) 93.
[124] Nollkaemper (note 74 above) 54. [125] See Articles 47–54 of the African Charter.

6.3.3.2 The 'vital human needs' exception as a source of states' extraterritorial obligations to human beings

The provision of the Convention on 'vital human needs' is designed for the regulation of water scarcity in shared river basins. Where the total available water is not sufficient for all types of uses in all the states sharing the water resource under consideration, Article 10(2) of the Convention, under the title 'Relationship between Different Kinds of Uses', provides that:

> [i]n the event of a conflict between uses of an international watercourse, it shall be resolved with reference to the principles and factors set out in articles 5 to 7, with special regard being given to the requirements of vital human needs.

Article 10(2) is a reversal of, or an exception to, the provisions of Article 6 of the Convention which normally prohibits the preferential treatment of any of the criteria listed under its Article 6(1). Article 6(3) of the Convention provides:

> [t]he weight to be given to each factor is to be determined by its importance in comparison with that of other relevant factors. In determining what is a reasonable and equitable use, all relevant factors are to be considered together and a conclusion reached on the basis of the whole.

Accordingly, one criterion can be the most important consideration in one context while other criteria may take precedence in other circumstances. The factor (criterion) must indeed be relevant as an aid in the determination or satisfaction of the social and economic needs of the co-riparian states of the basin. Once this threshold is met, it is generally not permissible to attach a fixed weight or inherent priority to a single criterion in all cases. The relative weight of a given relevant factor turns upon its merits relative to all the other factors at a given point in time.[126] As Lipper observed, 'a mechanical order of preference may lead to injustice'.[127] In the final analysis, 'no other factor occupies a position of pre-eminence *per se* with respect to any other factor'.[128] Some factors

[126] Dinah Shelton, 'Equity' in Daniel Bodansky, Jutta Brunneé and Ellen Hey (eds.), *The Oxford Handbook of International Environmental Law* (Oxford University Press, 2007) 639, 649; van Alstyne (note 83 above) 335.

[127] Lipper (note 2 above) 63.

[128] C. J. Olmstead *et al.*, 'Helsinki Rules on the Uses of the Waters of International Rivers' in A. H. Garretson, R. D. Hayton and C. J. Olmstead (eds.), *The Law of International Drainage Basins* (Oceana Publications Inc., 1967) 779, 785.

may even be irrelevant in a given scenario at a given time for the determination of a case at hand.[129] Under Article 6(3) of the Convention, the determination of what is a reasonable and equitable use in a particular case turns upon a weighted consideration of 'all relevant factors ... together and a conclusion [should be] reached on the basis of the whole'.

The Convention in principle guards against temptations to attach a special weight to a given type of use.[130] The 'vital human needs' clause is therefore a solitary exception, and it applies in cases where conflict of uses occurs among the riparian states.[131] The application of this exception could prove crucial for the realisation of the human right to water for the populations of shared river basins[132] where the overall amount of water available may be inadequate to cater for all the beneficial uses of the riparian states, as is the case in the Nile basin.

The *raison d'être* underpinning this exception is that human life takes priority over economic development or environmental or similar concerns.[133] This approach is in line with pre-existing domestic and international – albeit regional – state practice long before (but also after) the crystallisation of the rule in the Convention.[134] The US Supreme Court, whose jurisprudence lent to and influenced rules of international water law,[135] on numerous occasions and consistently has long held that 'drinking and other domestic uses are the highest uses of water' in water-sharing arrangements among American states.[136] Similarly, the Rau Commission of India, in its decision over the dispute between the Indian states of Sind and Punjab, attached priority to drinking water in a case concerning the utilisation of the Indus River.[137] This was once again confirmed by the Krishna Water Disputes Tribunal (India), in a case between Maharashtra and Myrose states, on the one hand, and the state of Andhra Pradesh on the other. It stated that the 'use of water for drinking, house-hold purposes and watering of cattle is regarded as the

[129] *Ibid.* [130] Article 10(1). [131] ILC Draft Articles (note 24 above) 110.
[132] See section 6.4.2 below. [133] McCaffrey (note 36 above) 22.
[134] See Lipper (note 2 above) 61.
[135] A. Dan Tarlock, 'Four Challenges of International Water Law', 23 *Tulane Environmental Law Journal* (2010) 369–408, 375; McCaffrey (note 10 above) 384–5.
[136] *Connecticut* v. *Massachusetts*, 282 US 660, 673 (1931); *Nebraska* v. *Wyoming*, 325 US 589, 656 (1954); *New Jersey* v. *New York*, 283 US 336 (1931); *Wisconsin* v. *Illinois*, 281 US 179, 200 (1930).
[137] See Government of India, Report of the Indus (Rau) Commission (Simla, 1942) 11.

primary use to which all other uses are subordinate'.[138] At the international level, the 1909 Treaty between the United States and Great Britain relating to boundary waters and the 1944 Treaty between the United States and Mexico relating to the utilisation of the Rio Grande established the order of preference among the various uses, and municipal uses are given precedence over other uses.[139]

More recently, the Berlin Rules, which are the revised and updated version of the Helsinki Rules that had informed the content of the Convention, have explicitly stated under Article 14(1) that '[i]n determining an equitable and reasonable use, States shall first allocate waters to satisfy vital human needs'.[140] The ILA commentary states that this provision 'tracks' the language of Article 10 of the Convention, and that its Article 14(1) is a clearer version of the same.[141] While it is not clear whether the 'vital human needs' provision is a rule of customary international law as is its parent principle of equitable and reasonable utilisation, it nevertheless commands longstanding and wide acceptance of domestic courts as well as international state practice in cases where questions of competing uses are at issue.

In fact, the special treatment of water for personal and domestic uses had already been recognised by states and courts even before the rule was crystallised in the form of a treaty provision under Article 10(2) of the Convention. Writing a few years before the Convention's drafting process was begun by the ILC in the early 1970s, Lipper found authorities for such a preferential treatment of water for vital human needs.[142] He thus argued, '[w]here the need for water for domestic purposes is genuine, it is inconceivable that it would not prevail on the merits'.[143]

Although Article 6 of the Convention is broadly worded in terms of the types of uses for which the population concerned could claim access to the shared water, Article 10(2) is specific to the vital human needs of populations dependent on shared waters, which refers to personal and domestic uses (in other words, the minimum core of the human right to water) that are essential for sustaining human life.[144] By elevating 'vital human needs' in cases of conflict above any other beneficial uses – be it navigational, agricultural, hydroelectric, irrigation, etc. – the Convention

[138] See Government of India, Report of the Krishna Water Disputes Tribunal (New Delhi, 1973), Vol. 2, 138.

[139] See Ximena Fuentes, 'The Criteria for the Equitable Utilization of International Rivers', 67 *British Year Book of International Law* (1996) 337–412, 352.

[140] See Berlin Rules (note 52 above) 22. [141] *Ibid.* [142] Lipper (note 2 above) 61.

[143] *Ibid.* [144] McCaffrey (note 10 above) 369; ILC Draft Articles (note 24 above) 110.

has sought to curtail the consideration of other competing uses of water before first ensuring individuals' and groups' access to water for personal and domestic uses.[145] Vital human needs enjoy primacy of consideration and must be catered for before any other uses in the determination of equitability and reasonableness of a water-sharing arrangement.[146] According to the ILC, the 'vital human needs' provision would in any event be taken into account as part of the 'socio-economic needs' of the riparian states under Article 6(1)(b) of the Convention.[147] However, the special provision under Article 10(2) represents 'an accentuated form of the factor contained in article 6, paragraph 1 (b)'.[148] Therefore, Article 10 (2) has the effect of insulating the vital human needs from the balancing act against other uses in water-sharing processes.[149] As Shelton observed, 'a strictly legal approach grounded in human rights may alter the weighing of factors by designating one use as inherently more important than all others'.[150]

Admittedly, in cases where there is sufficient water to cater equitably and reasonably for all types of uses by the basin populations, the question of priority of uses of shared waters is of less relevance. The process boils down to a relatively simple matter of states taking into consideration all the major needs of all riparian populations while apportioning shared waters amongst themselves. However, in regions where water resources are scarce, states may tend to prioritise their own residents above those of the co-riparian states. Given that states are primarily responsible to their domestic beneficiaries rather than to non-national non-residents, they would tend to treat those in their own respective territories as a matter of priority.[151] This would jeopardise the human rights of those in the co-riparian states' territories, who would thus have to access the shared waters when and if there is surplus water after satisfying at least the basic needs (personal and domestic uses) of the upstream populations. This is among the major problems that have been circumscribed by Article 10(2) of the Convention through its introduction of a

[145] Tully (note 7 above) 130; Patricia W. Birnie, Alan E. Boyle and Catherine Redgwell, *International Law and the Environment* (Oxford University Press, 3rd edn, 2009) 564.

[146] A resolution of a conflict among different types of uses that results in vital human needs being unmet is not equitable. See Birnie, Boyle and Redgwell (note 145 above) 565.

[147] ILC Draft Articles (note 24 above) 110. [148] *Ibid.*

[149] Nollkaemper (note 74 above) 62. [150] Shelton (note 126 above) 149.

[151] Mark Gibney, Katarina Tomaseviski and Jens Vedsted-Hansen, 'Transnational State Responsibility for Violations of Human Rights', 12 *Harvard Human Rights Journal* (1999) 267–95, 267.

hierarchical priority that it attached to vital human needs. This provision in effect precludes the allocation of shared waters to other uses before basic human survival is ensured. Thus, '[a]ny other use, including using water for commercial irrigation, in mining, in manufacturing, to generate power, or for recreation, is not included within the concept of "vital human needs"'.[152]

Worded as a provision of residual application,[153] Article 10(2) therefore offers a promising potential for the protection and fulfilment of at least the core minimum of the riparian population's right to water as a whole in water-scarce basins such as the Nile. After all, 'the principal barriers to ensuring universal water coverage are not absolute water scarcity but rather the challenges of improving global water governance'.[154] Similarly, it has been observed that the problem affecting inter-state relations over the apportionment of international watercourses is not so much wasteful or exhaustive use of the common resources as it is prioritising among the competing uses of the available water.[155] This has been shown to be the case particularly in Africa.[156] A re-ordering or prioritising of the beneficial uses of shared water resources is thus essential when the common water resources are fully used, as in the Nile basin,[157] and forces some uses to be sacrificed in favour of other more vital ones.[158] In the event of denial of priority to vital human needs, the injury to individuals' and groups' right to water will almost inevitably be felt across boundaries in water-scarce regions such as the

[152] Berlin Rules (note 52 above) 12.

[153] Under normal circumstances, saving customary or treaty rules to the contrary, 'no use of an international watercourse enjoys inherent priority over other uses'. See Article 10 (1) of the Convention.

[154] Tully (note 7 above) 124. See also Stephen McCaffrey, 'The Coming Fresh Water Crisis: International Legal and Institutional Responses', 21 *Vermont Law Review* (1997) 803–21, 821.

[155] Birnie, Boyle and Redgwell (note 145 above) 564.

[156] Elli Louka, *Water Law and Policy: Governance without Frontiers* (Oxford University Press, 2008) 14.

[157] Ashok Swain, 'Managing the Nile River: The Role of Sub-Basin Co-operation' in Manas Chatterji, Saul Arlosoroff and Gauri Guha (eds.), *Conflict Management of Water Resources* (Ashgate, 2002) 145, 152.

[158] However, this does not take away a significant proportion of shared waters as the total water needed for basic human needs is less than ten per cent of global water consumption. Agriculture is the biggest consumer of global fresh waters (65 per cent), followed by industrial uses (25 per cent). See Sandra Postel, *The Last Oasis: Facing Water Scarcity* (Earthscan Publications Ltd, 1st edn, 1992) 21–2; Tully (note 7 above) 130.

Nile basin. As discussed below, the victims thereof will then have the right to challenge the omissions or commissions resulting in the violations of their right to water and may avail themselves of their right to seek extraterritorial remedies as guaranteed under the Convention.

Professor McCaffrey, who had been Special Rapporteur of the ILC and one of the drafters of the Convention, noted:

> [i]f an individual would otherwise have access to reliable supplies of such quantities but uses by another state reduce the quantities below the minimum requirement just indicated [under Article 10(2) of the Convention], a case could be made for treating this as a *prima facie* violation of the obligation of equitable and reasonable utilisation by the other states.[159]

According to McCaffrey, using the violation of the principle of equitable and reasonable utilisation through neglect by states of 'vital human needs' of non-residents as a violation of their human right to water is prevented by the nature of human rights, which he assumed to be entirely territorial.[160] He argues that Article 10(2) of the Convention should be understood to enjoin riparian State A from using shared waters 'in such a way as to deprive individuals in State B of sufficient water to satisfy their vital needs'.[161]

However, as shown in Chapter 5, the territoriality of human rights and related treaties cannot be assumed. The human rights regime has witnessed a steady trend of increasing extraterritorial application of human rights and related state duties in recent decades in the African, European and Inter-American systems of human rights as well as in the UN human rights bodies. Given the possibility of extraterritorial application of international human rights, the obstacle is removed and individuals and groups in State B could have recourse against State A for violation of their human right to water in the event that the latter's use brought water available to them to a level that is below the minimum required levels.

The provision regarding 'vital human needs', owed by all riparian states jointly and severally to all riparian populations, thus provides extraterritorial obligations owed to individuals and groups residing in all the co-riparian states. In the final analysis, the provisions of the Convention on the equitable and reasonable use of shared waters, and the 'vital human rights' provision in particular, offer a promising

[159] McCaffrey (note 10 above) 371. [160] *Ibid.* [161] McCaffrey (note 36 above) 113.

potential to support extraterritorial human rights and state obligations relating to individuals' and groups' human right to water.

6.4 The 'no-significant-harm' rule as extraterritorial duties to respect and protect

The no-significant-harm rule of international water law – itself a yardstick for equitable and reasonable utilisation – imposes both negative and positive extraterritorial obligations upon co-riparian states. It prescribes that activities undertaken by states in their territories should not be allowed to cause significant harm in other co-riparian states' territories. This covers prohibitions of such activities by state agents (duty to respect) or non-state actors in the co-riparian state's territory (duty to protect). As discussed below, the rule implies that a co-riparian state is prohibited from doing anything that can weaken other co-riparian states' capacity to realise the human right to water in their respective territories. Additionally, the damage that such significant harms might cause could also be a cause of action for individual and group victims (holders of the human right to water residing in co-riparian states) to mount a complaint against the culprit state extraterritorially. As shown below, an implicated state must allow foreign complainants to access its domestic judicial and administrative bodies, and remedy injuries thereto.

6.4.1 Introducing the principle

The origin of the no-significant-harm rule may be traced to the Roman law maxim: *sic tuo utere ut alienum non laedas* (use your property in such a way as not to harm others).[162] It was originally based on the concept of restrictive enjoyment of one's own property, or limited and regulated proprietary rights subject to the prevention of harm to one's neighbours.[163] Put in the context of interstate relations, it implies that neighbouring states 'are not allowed to use or to tolerate the use of their

[162] Sompong Sucharitkul, 'State Responsibility and International Liability in Transnational Relations' in Jerzy Makarczyk (ed.), *Theory of International Law at the Threshold of the 21st Century: Essays in Honour of Krzysztof Skubiszewski* (Kluwer Law International, 1996) 283, 289.

[163] *Ibid.*

territory for causing damage to their neighbours'.[164] Just like the principle of equitable and reasonable utilisation, the no-significant-harm rule 'appears to have acquired customary force, as is attested by international practice'.[165] The no-significant-harm rule is enshrined in the Convention. According to Article 7(1) of the Convention:

> [w]atercourse States shall, in utilizing an international watercourse in their territories, take all appropriate measures to prevent the causing of significant harm to other watercourse States.

The rule has already been relied upon by numerous international tribunals in the determination of transboundary disputes among states. A 'classic case'[166] is the *Trail Smelter* arbitration[167] which arose from a United States' complaint about the transboundary air and water pollution produced in its territory from the Trail Smelter based in British Columbia, Canada. In its much quoted paragraph, the arbitral tribunal ruled that:

> under the principles of international law . . . no State has the right to use or permit the use of its territory in such a manner as to cause injury by fumes in or *to the territory of another or the properties or persons therein*, when the case is of serious consequence and the injury is established by clear and convincing evidence.[168]

The *Trail Smelter* ruling was consistent with, and was indeed confirmed by, later ICJ decisions in cases involving transboundary harm. A good example is the *Corfu Channel* case, where the ICJ ruled that there exist:

> certain general and well-recognised principles, namely . . . every State's obligation not to allow knowingly its territory to be used for acts contrary to the rights of other States.[169]

The no-significant-harm rule has also been applied in some of the ICJ's more recent cases. In the *Pulp Mills* case between Argentina and Uruguay, the ICJ reaffirmed its own previous decision in the *Corfu*

164 Lucius Caflisch, 'Regulation of Uses of International Watercourses' in Salman M. A. Salman and Laurence Boisson de Chazournes (eds.), *International Watercourses: Enhancing Cooperation and Managing Conflict: Proceedings of a World Bank Seminar* (World Bank, 1998) 3, 12.

165 See *Case Concerning Pulp Mills on the River Uruguay* (*Argentina* v. *Uruguay*), Judgment of 20 April 2010 ('*Pulp Mills* case'), para. 101. See also Lucius Caflisch, quoted in McCaffrey (note 10 above) 417.

166 Bourne (note 94 above) 85.

167 *Trail Smelter* Case (*US* v. *Canada*), 3 RIAA (1941) ('*Trail Smelter* case').

168 *Ibid.*, para. 49 (emphasis added).

169 *Corfu Channel* Case (*United Kingdom* v. *Albania*), *ICJ Reports* 1949, 22.

Channel case,[170] and ruled that 'the principle of prevention [of significant harm], as a customary rule, has its origins in the due diligence that is required of a State in its territory'.[171] The Court ruled that the obligation entailed by this principle implies that:

> [a] State is thus obliged to use all the means at its disposal in order to avoid activities which take place in its territory, or in any area under its jurisdiction, causing significant damage to the environment of another State.[172]

Similarly, the ICJ has emphasised a state's duty to prevent the causation of significant transboundary harm. In its Advisory Opinion in the *Legality of the Use of Nuclear Weapons* case, it stated that:

> [t]he existence of the general obligation of States to ensure that activities within their jurisdiction and control respect the environment of other States or of areas beyond national control is now part of the corpus of international law relating to the environment.[173]

States' duties to refrain from and prevent the causation of significant harm across international boundaries have also been recognised in various soft laws. Under its Principle 21, the Stockholm Declaration states that 'States have … the responsibility to ensure that activities within their jurisdiction or control do not cause damage to the environment of other States or of areas beyond the limits of national jurisdiction'.[174] Two decades later, this principle was reaffirmed, almost *verbatim*, in the Rio Declaration.[175]

Historically, the no-significant-harm rule has strived to play two related roles pertaining to the law of international rivers.[176] First, it has sought to provide guidelines for the allocation of the rights of shared water basins, and, secondly, it is also of crucial relevance in the area of environmental protection. While it has continued to hold sway in relation to environmental considerations, particularly in the prevention and remedying of transboundary environmental harm and pollution, its

[170] *Pulp Mills* case, para. 101. [171] *Ibid.* [172] *Ibid.*

[173] *Legality of the Threat or Use of Nuclear Weapons*, Advisory Opinion, *ICJ Reports* 1996, para. 29. See also *Gabčíkovo-Nagymaros* case (note 54 above), para. 80.

[174] Declaration of the United Nations Conference on the Human Environment, adopted at Stockholm, 5–16 June 1972, Principle 21.

[175] See Rio Declaration on Environment and Development, adopted at the United Nations Conference on Environment and Development, Rio de Janeiro, 3–14 June 1992, Principle 2.

[176] Caflisch (note 164 above) 12.

water allocation utility has waned in recent decades.[177] This is because most international water basins are fully used or overused today and an attempt at a new use by a riparian state would result in harm to the existing uses. The effective result of an unmitigated application of the no-significant-harm rule is to maintain the *status quo*. Considered in the context of the Nile basin, where the water is already fully utilised and upper riparian states are attempting to put the waters to new uses,[178] the strict application of the no-significant-harm rule would deny the upper riparian states any possibility of developing or expanding their uses of the Nile waters.[179]

The question that poses itself is as to which one of the two – the principle of equitable and reasonable utilisation or the no-significant-harm rule – takes precedence in the event that the two contradict each other. In situations where an upstream state commences a new project that would otherwise be a reasonable and equitable use of a common international river, the new use upstream would almost inevitably result in the reduction of either the quantity or the quality – or both – of the downstream water. Such a reduction would inevitably cause harm to the pre-existing uses of the downstream states by diminishing the quantity or quality of the water owing to the new upstream use.

Under the doctrine of equitable and reasonable utilisation, the fact that there had been prior uses made of the common waters by some of the riparian states would be only one of the considerations in arriving at the equitable and reasonable allocation of the common waters.[180] A use by a riparian state may cause harm to the pre-existing uses in other riparian states. A choice must be made between the application of the two competing principles.

Historically, the need for clarification of the interplay of the two principles arose much earlier in the context of the 1966 Helsinki Rules. The ILA considered that 'the principle of equitable and reasonable utilization should be the guiding principle . . . [wherein the no significant harm] rule was one among the series of elements to be considered for determining whether a given use was "equitable and reasonable"'.[181]

It has been observed that there exists unanimity of opinion among scholars that, in the event of conflicts between the principles, 'the most fundamental principle of international water law is that of equitable

[177] *Ibid.* [178] Swain (note 157 above) 146–52. [179] Caflisch (note 164 above) 13.
[180] See Convention, Article 6(1)(e) and (3). [181] Caflisch (note 164 above) 13.

utilisation'.[182] In short, the principle of equitable and reasonable utilisation takes precedence over the no-significant-harm rule. If it were otherwise, the resultant rule would freeze the development of many upper riparian states of international basins, and this would certainly be the case in the Nile basin. An immediate result of the precedence of equitable and reasonable utilisation over the no-significant-harm rule would be to lay to rest the 'prior appropriation' doctrine that has been overly emphasised by the lower riparian states of the Nile basin.[183] According to the prior appropriation doctrine, also variously called 'acquired', 'natural' or 'historic' rights, 'the first user of the water acquires a definitive right to it, "first in time, first in right"'.[184]

Thus, downstream states are not allowed to block new upstream uses by demonstrating that the later development would cause them harm.[185] New upstream uses could be necessitated due to the ever increasing population whose 'vital human needs' pose pressures on riparians to revisit the current share of water resources amongst themselves. A continual revision of the equitability and reasonableness of an existing share of each riparian state is needed in shared river basins in keeping with increasing populations. This is certainly inevitable in the Nile basin where just Egypt and Ethiopia – two of the basin's most populous nations – each add a million people every eight months to the existing population figures.[186]

The principle of equitable and reasonable utilisation takes into account both the current and future water needs of the populations of riparian states and is sufficiently elastic to accommodate a changing set of circumstances. As McCaffrey noted, the principle of equitable and reasonable utilisation:

> is more than a rule . . . It is a dynamic process, which depends heavily on active cooperation between states sharing fresh water resources. A state's regime of utilization that is equitable *vis-à-vis* its co-riparians today may

[182] Stephen C. McCaffrey, 'The Law of International Watercourses: Some Recent Developments and Unanswered Questions', 17(3) *Denver Journal of International Law and Policy* (1989) 505–26, 509. See generally Bourne (note 112 above).

[183] See, for instance, Erlich (note 93 above) 5–6.

[184] Amare Girma, 'Nile Issue: The Imperative Need for Negotiation on the Utilization of Nile Waters', in *Occasional Papers*, Vol. 2, No. 6 (Ethiopian International Institute for Peace and Development, 1997); Erlich (note 93 above) 5–6.

[185] *Ibid.*

[186] Okbazghi Yohannes, *Water Resources and Inter-Riparian Relations in the Nile Basin* (State University of New York Press, 2008) 5.

> not be so next year. A new use in one state may change the equitable calculus as among all riparians and therefore should be the subject of prior notification, consultation, and if necessary, negotiation. And this is true whether the new use is made by an upstream or downstream state: new upstream uses may have physical impacts upon those downstream; and new downstream uses may have legal impacts upon those upstream, because they may alter the equitable balance of uses in such a way as to make subsequent new uses in an upstream state inequitable[187]

During the preparation of the draft Convention, the ILC commented that:

> [*prima facie*], utilisation of an international water course is not equitable if it causes other watercourse states appreciable harm ... The Commission recognizes, however, that in some instances the achievement of equitable and reasonable utilisation will depend upon the toleration by one or more watercourse states of a measure of harm.[188]

Applied alongside the principle of equitable and reasonable utilisation, thus, the no-significant-harm rule implies the *duty of due diligence*[189] on the riparian states that begin to put the common waters to a new or more use than had been the case. The due diligence duty goes beyond requiring a state to abstain from causing harm to the other co-riparian states and includes a positive duty to 'take all appropriate measures to prevent the causing of significant harm to other watercourse States'.[190]

The co-riparian states' duty to prevent harm would be violated if activities in their territories caused or threatened to cause 'significant' harm. Thus, Article 7 of the Convention cannot be relied upon in every mundane case where the harm caused or the threat thereof is minimal.[191] Although the term 'significant harm' is not defined in the Convention, and its threshold is somewhat vague,[192] it is clear that only a harm that is

187 McCaffrey (note 10 above) 404–5.

188 See Report of the International Law Commission on the Work of its Fortieth Session, 43 UN GAOR Supplement No. 10, UN Doc. A/43/10 (1988), para. 84.

189 See ILC Draft Articles (note 24 above) 103.

190 Article 7(1) of the Convention. See also Sucharitkul (note 162 above) 289.

191 Handl noted that the degree of due diligence duty required by the no-significant-harm rule does not entail a state's obligation to ensure 'zero transboundary impact' of activities in its territory. See Günther Handl, 'Transboundary Impacts' in Daniel Bodansky, Jutta Brunneé and Ellen Hey (eds.), *The Oxford Handbook of International Environmental Law* (Oxford University Press, 2007) 531, 535.

192 It has been commented that 'the definition of harm lies in the eye of the beholder'. See Fasil Amdetsion, 'Scrutinizing the Scorpion Problematique: Arguments in Favor of the Continued Relevance of International Law and a Multidisciplinary Approach to Resolving the Nile Dispute', 44(1) *Texas International Law Journal* (2009) 1, 30.

not negligible or trivial is prohibited and a certain degree of toleration of harm is expected. In the *Trail Smelter* arbitration, the tribunal stated that a case of transboundary harm implicates a state's international responsibility when 'the case is of a serious consequence'.[193] A study of relevant state practice and case law also reveals that a significant harm is one that is sufficiently serious.[194] The SADC Protocol defines the term 'significant harm' as a 'non-trivial harm capable of being established by objective evidence' but it may not necessarily be substantial.[195] The obligation not to cause a significant harm merely requires the 'avoidance of harm in a way and to the extent that is reasonable under the circumstances'.[196] The causation of some harm is considered reasonable, and what is proscribed is one of legal injury as opposed to factual injury.[197] As Handl noted, significant harm is understood to mean:

> 'a legally significant injury' rather than a mere factual finding of a not insubstantial transboundary impact. As a term of art, the concept had been taken to suggest injurious transboundary effects due to what, in the circumstances of the case concerned, was unreasonable conduct on the part of the source state.[198]

Distinctions are made between transboundary harm pertaining to water quality (pollution) and those related to water quantity. It appears that a stricter threshold of harm would implicate a state's responsibility for causing pollution than would be the case for the causation of harm through the reduction of the quantity of the common waters.[199]

Thus, the no-significant-harm rule has been tied to a 'reasonable' standard of state conduct for its application. It is taken as a factor to be considered in gauging the equitability and reasonableness of the utilisation of the shared waters in a state's territory and its violation depends upon whether the injurious activity complained of, seen against the state's duty of diligence, is reasonable under the specific circumstances of the case.[200] According to Handl, '[t]he reasonableness of the source State's conduct, in turn, was determined by way of an analysis in which

193 *Trail Smelter* case, 1965.

194 Owen McIntyre, *Environmental Protection of International Watercourses under International Law* (Ashgate, 2007) 93.

195 SADC Protocol, Article 1.

196 McCaffrey (note 10 above) 407. See also ILC Draft Articles (note 24 above) 105.

197 McCaffrey (note 10 above) 431; Bourne (note 94 above) 85. See Handl (note 34 above) 129–30.

198 Handl (note 34 above) 129–30.

199 Bourne (note 94 above) 83.

200 Nollkaemper (note 74 above) 58.

the injurious transboundary impact of the incriminated conduct was one among a number of factors to be taken into account'.[201] This would in effect reintroduce the principle of equitable and reasonable utilisation.[202] Indeed, Article 7(2) is explicit in providing that the measures it requires of states for the mitigation or prevention of harm need to be adopted 'with due regard for the provisions of Articles 5 and 6 [of the Convention]' (relating to equitable utilisation).[203]

6.4.2 *The 'no-significant-harm' rule as states' extraterritorial human rights duty*

As has been discussed above, the principle of equitable and reasonable utilisation accords priority to 'vital human needs' and enjoins states to allocate water for immediate consumption, i.e. for personal and domestic uses. It has been observed that '[a] use which causes significant harm to human health and safety is understood to be inherently inequitable and unreasonable'.[204] Harm to vital human needs gives rise to the rebuttable presumption that a state's use of shared waters or conduct associated therewith is not equitable or reasonable.[205] The injury to this basic human need would be immediate and life-threatening, such that almost any act or omission that jeopardises the provision of water for basic human needs seems to violate a state's duty of diligence and causes significant harm. It threatens the right-holders' access to the minimum core of the human right to water, the fulfilment of which is part of the immediate obligations of states as opposed to progressive realisation.

Under Article 32 of the Convention, riparian states owe the duty to prevent the causation of significant harm, as well as to remedy it when one occurs. Article 32 of the Convention provides:

> [u]nless the watercourse States concerned have agreed otherwise for the protection of the interests of persons, natural or juridical, who have suffered or are under a serious threat of suffering significant transboundary harm as a result of activities related to an international watercourse, a watercourse State shall not discriminate on the basis of nationality or

201 Handl (note 34 above) 230.
202 *Ibid.*, 130 (quoting McCaffrey); Bourne (note 112 above) 227.
203 See also Attila Tanzi, 'The UN Convention on International Watercourses as a Framework for the Avoidance and Settlement of Water Law Disputes', 11 *Leiden Journal of International Law* (1998) 441–72, 464.
204 Report of the ILC, quoted in Bourne (note 112 above) 227.
205 Bourne (note 112 above) 227.

> residence or place where the injury occurred, in granting to such persons, in accordance with its legal system, access to judicial or other procedures, or a right to claim compensation or other relief in respect of significant harm caused by such activities carried on in its territory.

Accordingly, any persons 'who have suffered or are under a serious threat of suffering significant transboundary harm as a result of activities related to an international watercourse' can have recourse against the state which is the author of the harm in order to claim compensation or other relief. In granting compensation and other relief sought, the implicated state is enjoined from discriminating among victims on the basis of nationality or residence or place where the injury occurred. Thus, a transboundary right-holder who has suffered a violation of his or her human right to water or a threat thereto has the right to the protection of his or her right to equality in the search for extraterritorial remedies and access to the implicated state's judicial and administrative bodies.

The provisions of Article 32 apply not only in cases where actual harm is caused but also to threats thereof.[206] The fact that it applies to harm of a prospective nature would entitle individuals and groups who have been threatened by extraterritorial harms to complain of the threats even before the harm materialises. If threats of transboundary harm are properly remedied, i.e. if the potential harm is averted, or the violation of the right is adequately redressed, the human right to water generally, or at least the 'vital human needs' of the right-holders, could be effectively protected. In other words, the right to preventive remedies can thus be used to enforce the state's substantive duty to respect and protect foreign residents' human right to water extraterritorially.

Arguably, therefore, the existence of the right to an extraterritorial remedy presupposes a primary (extraterritorial substantive) human right to water, enforceable against a foreign riparian state. While there is no right without a remedy,[207] the converse is also true: 'where there is no right, there is no obligation [to provide a remedy] and *vice versa*'.[208] The incorporation of the right to an extraterritorial domestic remedy in Article 32 of the Convention therefore implies the understanding that the Convention's provisions entail an extraterritorial human right to

[206] ILC Draft Articles (note 24 above) 132. [207] See Chapter 6.

[208] Matthew Craven, 'The Violence of Dispossession: Extra-Territoriality and Economic, Social and Cultural Rights' in A. Mashood and Robert McCorquodale Baderin (eds.), *Economic, Social and Cultural Rights in Action* (Oxford University Press, 2007) 71, 82.

water. Thus where there is no primary right (and state duty), the inclusion of the right to a remedy cannot be perceived.

From its inception, Article 32 was adopted with a view to protecting, *inter alia*, the human right to water extraterritorially. Its adoption was achieved against the opposition of some and the reluctance of other members of the ILC who found it inappropriate to accept the protection of human rights in a treaty that was supposedly intended to deal with relations between states.[209] One member of the ILC considered it wrong to include Article 32 in the Convention, a provision that has direct human rights relevance in an instrument that was initially designed to 'deal with the relations between States'.[210] Two other ILC members considered its inclusion undesirable due to the provision's extraterritorial effects. It was stated:

> [t]wo members of the Commission held the view that the article was undesirable within the broad scope of the present articles because it may be interpreted as establishing an obligation of States to grant to foreign nationals based on their respective territories rights which not only procedurally but also in all other respects would be equal to the rights of their own nationals. In the view of those members, such a broadening of the principle of the exhaustion of local remedies would not correspond to the present content of this principle.[211]

Nonetheless, such concerns were espoused by a minority of ILC members, and had no influence subsequently on the content of the provision at the negotiations that took place at the Sixth Legal Committee or at the Convention's eventual adoption by the UN General Assembly. Thus, there seems to be broad agreement on the implications of the provision in the realisation of the human right to water and related state obligations, including its extraterritorial reach. The opposition to, or ambivalence towards, the inclusion of the provision that guarantees the human right to water against transboundary harm was based on the argument that the Convention, as a state-centred instrument, 'should not extend into the field of actions by natural and legal persons under domestic law'.[212] There was no objection *per se*, however, to a state's direct accountability to human beneficiaries in the apportionment of shared resources among them; only that the propriety of enshrining a human rights provision in a Convention of predominantly inter-state focus was at issue.[213]

[209] ILC Draft Articles (note 24 above) 133. [210] *Ibid.*, 133. [211] *Ibid.* [212] *Ibid.*
[213] *Ibid.*

Unlike the other provisions of the Convention that are couched in terms of co-riparian states' rights and duties *per se*, the protection accorded under Article 32 is explicit in its objectives of directly protecting individuals' and groups' right to water extraterritorially. This is clear from its explicit reference to 'natural persons'. This is the only provision in the Convention that refers directly and explicitly to individuals and groups.[214] The fact that the provisions of Article 32 have been designed to protect individuals and groups as opposed to states has been an agreed premise from the drafting stage of Article 32.

Article 32 has both substantive and procedural implications[215] for guaranteeing the human right to water, and both aspects have far-reaching implications for right-holders to bring actions against a third state for the violation of the human right to water. In its substantive sense, the fact that the case can be brought by human beings against a foreign state whose omission or commission caused or threatens to cause a significant harm to individuals' and groups' human right to water means that individuals and groups are given the leeway to ensure that their right to water is not violated by a foreign state. In other words, residents of all riparian states are empowered to access procedures that can enjoin foreign riparian states to *respect* the human right to water extraterritorially. In cases of a transboundary threat to their human right to water, foreign right-holders can seek preventive remedies.

In addition, where the injured individuals and groups bring a case against a state that has caused harm to their human right to water, the culpable state has the duty to repair the damage caused.[216] Thus, the state causing extraterritorial harm to foreign residents does so at the risk of paying compensation or providing other appropriate relief – which might include an injunction against the causing of further and/or future harm – to non-residents (non-nationals) for the injurious acts carried out in its territory. The remedies must be available, adequate and effective.[217]

The duty to provide extraterritorial remedies gives a strong incentive for the riparian states to ensure that activities carried out in their territories are conducted in a manner conforming to the state's duty to respect the human rights of residents of other riparian populations. As the state is responsible, under Article 32, for 'activities carried on in its

[214] Hey (note 36 above) 133.
[215] For the procedural aspect of Article 32 of the Convention, see section 6.5 below.
[216] See section 6.5 below. [217] See Chapter 7.

territory' irrespective of the identity of the specific author (public or private), riparian states owe the duty to prevent state and non-state actors alike from causing harm to extraterritorial beneficiaries of the shared water, thereby discharging the duties to *respect* and *protect* the human right to water extraterritorially. If all basin states have discharged the duty to respect and protect the human right to water of all basin populations with which they share water, they have gone a long way towards enhancing each other's capacities to *fulfil* the human right to water domestically.

6.5 The prohibition of extraterritorial discrimination and the right to extraterritorial remedy

The requirement of special treatment of personal and domestic uses is bolstered by the non-discrimination provision (Article 32) of the Convention, which seeks to ensure the equal treatment of all basin populations in this regard. Procedurally, each riparian state has the duty to ensure foreign nationals' and/or residents' access to its own judicial or other appropriate domestic procedures for submitting complaints and seeking remedies to redress the state's or non-state actor's violations of the extraterritorial water rights of injured right-holders. Such access brings into play the riparian state's duty to accord national treatment to non-national non-residents as it cannot discriminate among national and foreign plaintiffs.[218] According to the ILC, Article 32 of the Convention:

> obliges States to ensure that any person, whatever his nationality or place of residence, who has suffered significant transboundary harm as a result of activities related to an international watercourse should, regardless of where the harm occurred or might occur, receive the same treatment as that afforded by the country of origin to its nationals in case of domestic harm.[219]

Similarly, Professor McCaffrey's 'Sixth Report' to the ILC showed that the inclusion of Article 32 in the Convention was necessitated by the need to treat foreign complainants in domestic jurisdictions of co-riparian states on an equal footing to their own nationals and/or

[218] The practice and problems associated with extraterritorial access to domestic remedies and procedures in Africa and elsewhere is discussed in Chapter 7.

[219] See ILC Draft Articles (note 24 above) 132.

residents in relation to complaints about harm or the threat of harm to their water rights. His draft was worded thus:

> [i]n considering the permissibility of proposed, planned or existing activities, the adverse effects that such activities entail or may entail in another State shall be equated with adverse effects in the watercourse State where the activities are or may be situated.[220]

The procedural aspect of riparian states' duties to respect and protect the human right to water is intertwined with the substantive right to the protection against discrimination: in allowing such access to its local courts and procedures, the transboundary plaintiff's right to equality is protected. The accused state cannot impose more onerous terms or costs as a precondition for foreign complainants to access its local procedures and courts.[221] Otherwise, this would be a violation of the complainant's right to equality which has been guaranteed under the Convention.

According to McCaffrey, from the perspective of states' obligations, the provision on non-discrimination in its extraterritorial sense was designed to serve dual roles.[222] On the one hand, it enjoins the authorities of all riparian states to treat any adverse effects that activities which took place or are planned in their respective territories may have in other states in the same way as they would treat the domestic effects of those activities.[223] Accordingly, if the licensing authorities of a riparian state are required by law when considering whether to issue a licence for the commencement of planned projects to consider the harmful effects of the project as a precondition for the grant of such licence, the non-discrimination clause of the Convention requires that a project's harmful effects in a co-riparian state must also be given equal weight before issuing the licence.[224]

On the other hand, it provides a legal basis for the consideration by co-riparian states' judicial and administrative authorities of complaints of foreign plaintiffs.[225] A right of foreign plaintiffs to participate in judicial and administrative proceedings would lose its essence if such authorities do not have the jurisdiction to hear them. Thus, the riparian states would be obliged to provide a legal basis for their judicial and

[220] Stephen C. McCaffrey, 'Sixth Report of the Law of the Non-Navigational Uses of International Watercourses, By Mr Stephen C. McCaffrey, Special Rapporteur' (A/CN.4/427 and Add. 1), in *Yearbook of the International Law Commission* (1990), Vol. II (2), 41–82, 59.

[221] See ILC Draft Articles (note 24 above) 132. [222] McCaffrey (note 220 above) 59.

[223] *Ibid.* [224] *Ibid.* [225] *Ibid.*

administrative tribunals to hear cases of foreign plaintiffs arising from injuries or threats of activities pertaining to transboundary water uses or misuses.[226] The non-discrimination clause of Article 32 of the Convention covers all 'activities' as opposed to 'planned measures', which implies that the former is 'considered broad enough to cover the full panoply of uses that should be covered'.[227]

This presupposes the availability of domestic remedies to which residents of a co-riparian state can have recourse. Article 32 of the Convention merely requires a riparian state to provide remedies to extraterritorial victims in the same way (equally) and to the same degree that its legal system has afforded the same to those within its territory. It does not entail a state's obligation to provide a remedy when none inheres in its domestic laws, however. Neither does it enjoin the state to provide better domestic remedies to foreign-based complainants. Clearly, the state's duty of equal treatment of residents and non-resident complainants thus applies only when a relevant remedy exists. Thus Article 32 of the Convention merely prohibits states from discriminating against individuals and groups on the basis of their nationality in accessing domestic remedies, but only where the remedies are already available under national laws.[228] Its role is therefore limited to obliging states to treat residents and non-residents alike, in granting them the right to access local remedies. It does not prescribe the nature and content of the remedies that a state's legal system should provide. In particular, Article 32 of the Convention, in providing for equal access to domestic remedies for resident and foreign litigants alike, is 'concerned only with the elimination of any substantive or procedural obstacles to obtaining relief for extraterritorial harm'.[229] Article 32 of the Convention allows a victim of transboundary violation of the human right to water to have direct recourse to local remedies in the state where the source of the harm is located.[230] As shown in Chapter 7, where there are no domestic remedies for threats to or violations of the human right to water in the domestic legal system for residents of a state, none can be availed by non-resident non-nationals in the domestic procedures of such states. The viable alternative would therefore be to resort to the

[226] *Ibid.* [227] *Ibid.*

[228] Alistair Rieu-Clarke, *International Law and Sustainable Development: Lessons from the Law of International Watercourses* (IWA Publishing, 2005) 150.

[229] McCaffrey (note 15 above) 27.

[230] See also Birnie, Boyle and Redgwell (note 145 above) 306.

regional or global mechanisms for the protection and promotion of human rights.

In conclusion, under Article 32 of the Convention, the right to a remedy is available to the whole population of a basin and applies both to cases involving actual harm and to those in which the harm is prospective in nature.[231] The availability or type of a remedy cannot be made conditional on the nationality or residence of the complainant or on the place where the harm is committed or the injury is suffered. It is sufficient that the injury is imputable to a riparian state or to those for whom the riparian state is answerable for the purpose of triggering a foreign plaintiff's right to a domestic remedy in the state's judicial or administrative fora.

6.6 Conclusion

The fact that the relevant rules and principles of international water law have achieved customary status means that they invariably bind African states and can be used for the benefit of right-holders in Africa. Three main interrelated concerns permeate the chapter's analysis. First, the potential utility of the rules and principles of international water law as a source of an extraterritorial human right to water is gauged. It has been argued that individual and group right-holders can use the rules and principles of international water law to bring complaints against foreign riparian states (diagonally) on the ground of the state's role in the non-realisation of the human right to water through the manner of its use (or abuse) of the shared fresh water resource on which riparian populations depend for drinking and personal uses. Secondly, the inter-riparian states' horizontal extraterritorial human rights obligations are explored. From this viewpoint, international water law provides for a two-tiered system of state obligations. On the one hand, there is a diagonal obligation between a riparian state and residents of other co-riparian states. On the other hand, there are inter-riparian horizontal obligations according to which states are obliged to use shared waters in such a way that enhances or at least prevents activities that undermine the capacity of other co-riparian states to realise the human right to water in their respective territories. The third main concern of the chapter is related to the remedial aspects of an extraterritorial human right to water. Here, the analysis is focused on the ramifications of foreign residents' right of

[231] ILC Draft Articles (note 24 above) 132.

equal access to extraterritorial domestic remedies that are available in third (co-riparian) states to seek redress for any transboundary harm they suffered at home as a result of omissions or commissions emanating from within a co-riparian state's territory.

The analysis has illustrated that there are textual bases in the Convention for the extraterritorial application of the human right to water and related state obligations as well as remedies for their violations. The chapter depicted the potential utility of rules of international water law that could be employed by right-holders themselves in human rights tribunals such as the African Commission, without the assistance of their own states, to oblige foreign states to respect, protect, promote and fulfil the human right to water in third states and to provide accessible, adequate and effective remedies in cases where these extraterritorial human rights and states' obligations are breached.

True, the hitherto prevailing state-centric approach to international water law has tended to assign to the legal regime the role merely of regulating inter-riparian relations exclusive of individuals and groups residing in those states. However, the dearth of established jurisprudence which applies the rules and principles of international water law for the purpose of enhancing individuals' and groups' rights does not mean that the regime cannot be used in the realisation of the human right to water. Undeniably, there has not been a significant attempt in the Nile basin, or elsewhere, to use the Convention's provisions (as rules of customary international water law), but it is a viable option that right-holders can avail themselves of in the future. As shown above, individual and group beneficiaries of the human right to water could still resort to the provisions of the Convention as such to enforce their human right to water in human rights tribunals. The fact that most of its provisions are stated in terms of states' rights and duties *vis-à-vis* each other is therefore not an insurmountable obstacle for the human beneficiaries to use them for the protection of their rights.

The principle of equitable utilisation as a rule of customary international law obliges states to share transboundary fresh water resources originating in or traversing their territories with co-riparian states in a way that attaches utmost importance to the vital human needs of all riparian populations. Granting primacy to the vital human needs of basin populations insulates the human right to water from competing considerations in water-sharing arrangements. Failure to share such resources in a manner that grants primacy to such uses entails the causation of significant harms to basin populations, which triggers their right to appropriate remedies. In the determination of an equitable and reasonable amount of a country's share of common waters, the basin populations should be treated the same. A failure to do so entails a violation of the prohibition of non-discrimination on the grounds of nationality or residence of the basin population. The use of the human rights perspective in the apportionment of shared water resources thus gives rise to the extraterritorial human right to water and imposes important extraterritorial positive and negative obligations on riparian states.

Given the extraterritorial nature of the states' duties and of the human right to water, the human rights regime could benefit from use of the substantive and procedural aspects of the Convention for enforcing the vital human needs of basin populations. The Convention has laid down firm legal bases for a transboundary human right to water, and correlative state obligations, as well as the right to extraterritorial remedies in foreign states' judicial and administrative tribunals. Once the extraterritorial human right to water, the correlative duties of states, and the related remedies, are established, the complainants may use relevant rules and principles of international water law not only in domestic adjudicatory bodies but also in the regional human rights tribunals of Africa and the relevant UN human rights treaty bodies. However, the legal possibility, procedural factors (such as jurisdiction, *locus standi* and cost), the adequacy of relevant remedies and the expediency for individuals and groups to follow such local remedies are determinative of the choice of forum in which to complain about the violation of the human right to water by non-resident non-nationals. The analysis of operationalising the extraterritorial human right to water and attendant state obligations is taken up in the next chapter.

7

The human right to water and extraterritorial remedies

A strange justice that is bound by a river! Truth on this side of the Pyrenees, error on the other.[1]

7.1 Introduction

A substantive guarantee of the right to water is incomplete unless right-holders are provided with adequate avenues of reparation in the event that the right is infringed. Indeed, a right is not fully protected unless its violation is accompanied by remedies which the culpable duty-bearer should provide. As Chief Justice Holt proclaimed, '[i]f a plaintiff has a right, he must of necessity have a means to vindicate and maintain it, and a remedy if he is injured in the exercise or enjoyment of it; and indeed it is a vain thing to imagine a right without a remedy; for . . . want of a right and want of a remedy are reciprocal.'[2] Accordingly, the right to a remedy, itself a self-standing entitlement, is a cross-cutting guarantee that ensures that violations of other rights are prevented or redressed. Thus, '[t]he right to a remedy is the implementing agent for other human rights'.[3]

The violation of a legal right calls into play the victim's right to reparation and the duty of the state responsible for the breach to redress the injury. Indeed, 'it is a general and indisputable rule, that where there is a legal right, there is also a legal remedy by suit or action at law,

[1] Blaise Pascal, quoted in Anonymous, 'Constructing the State Extraterritorially: Jurisdictional Discourse, the National Interest, and Transnational Norms', 103 *Harvard Law Review* (1990) 1273–1305, 1273.

[2] *Ashby* v. *White*, 92 Eng Rep 126 (King's Bench, 1703).

[3] Neil A. F. Popović, 'In Pursuit of Environmental Human Rights: Commentary on the Draft Declaration of Principles on Human Rights and the Environment', 27 *Columbia Human Rights Law Review* (1996) 487–603, 561.

whenever that right is invaded'.[4] However, the inclusion of individual remedies for violations of individuals' and groups' rights in the regulation of transboundary water resources has hitherto been seldom used in shared river basins.[5] Alternatively, victims have resorted to their home state to have recourse on their behalf against the foreign state to obtain redress for the latter's violation of their rights extraterritorially. But, it is not always feasible for the home state to espouse each and every single incident of the water rights violations of its inhabitants caused by co-riparian states. Indeed, states do not owe a duty to seek redress on behalf of their residents in all incidents of human rights violations caused by third states.[6]

It is therefore essential that individual and group right-holders have a direct recourse against a foreign co-riparian violator if they are to be able to ensure that transboundary actors do not jeopardise the realisation of their human rights. However, whether they have the right to such recourse against the foreign state causing water pollution or scarcity has yet to be sufficiently analysed, let alone answered. It is observed:

> non-resident non-citizens can only claim and enforce rights against other states through their own state and under strictly defined conditions – if they can claim them at all . . . International law is designed to make each state responsible for the human rights protection of its own population; this includes litigation for violations targeting another state.[7]

Chapters 5 and 6 demonstrated the existence of substantive legal bases for the extraterritorial application of the human right to water and correlative states' duties. The current chapter analyses the extraterritorial application of the right to a remedy where individuals' and groups' human right to water in one state is infringed by a commission or omission imputable to a foreign (co-riparian) state. It seeks to show

[4] *Marbury* v. *Madison*, 5 US (1 Cranch) 137, 163 (1803) (quoting 3 Blackstone, *Commentaries on the Laws of England* 109 (1783)).

[5] Stephen C. McCaffrey, 'Trans-Boundary Pollution Injuries: Jurisdictional Considerations in Private Litigation between Canada and the United States', 3 *California Western International Law Journal* (1973) 191–259, 192; Joel A. Gallob, 'Birth of the North American Plaintiff: Transboundary Pollution and the 1979 Draft Treaty for Equal Access and Remedy', 15 *Harvard Environmental Law Review* (1991) 85–148, 86.

[6] See *Victor Saldano* v. *Argentina*, Petition, Report No. 38/99, Inter-American Court of Human Rights, OEA/Ser.L/V/II.95 Doc. 7 rev. at 289 (1998), para. 30.

[7] Mark Gibney, Katarina Tomaseviski and Jens Vedsted-Hansen, 'Transnational State Responsibility for Violations of Human Rights', 12 *Harvard Human Rights Journal* (1999) 267–95, 267.

the relevance of the African human rights regime for enforcing access to transboundary remedies for extraterritorial violations of the human right to water. It emphasises the potential of the regional system to obligate states to enshrine the right to adequate and effective remedies in their domestic legal systems for the benefit of transboundary litigants. The chapter therefore analyses the role and content of local remedies that a riparian state should make available to transboundary complainants in relation to violations of their human right to water. It also discusses possible domestic procedural deterrence – substantive, jurisdictional and/or others – that might be established by states in order to make access to transboundary remedies more difficult or onerous for foreign complainants and the role of supranational human rights mechanisms in overcoming these hurdles.

7.2 The right to a remedy

Just as the four layers of states' obligations may be considered to be part of every human right,[8] so too are remedies. Habitually invoked by international courts and scholars as the principle of *ubi jus ubi remedium* (where there is a right, there is a remedy),[9] the right to a remedy has a long-standing application in international law generally and international human rights law specifically. A state must provide, within its legal system, a remedy that prevents an impending violation and/or redresses the actual violation of human and peoples' rights.

7.2.1 The right to a remedy in international law

The right to a remedy had been an integral part of general international law before its eventual incorporation into the human rights regime that emerged as a full-fledged regime after 1945.[10] The right has both substantive and procedural dimensions to it. The substantive dimension of the right to a remedy guarantees the right to receive relief when a

8 See Chapter 4.

9 Sonja B. Starr, 'Rethinking "Effective" Remedies: Remedial Deterrence in International Courts', 83 *New York University Law Review* (2008) 693–768, 698.

10 See generally Manfred Nowak, 'The New Trend towards Re-politicising Human Rights' in Monique Castermans-Holleman, Fried van Hoof and Jaqueline Smith (eds.), *The Role of the Nation-State in the 21st Century: Human Rights, International Organisations and Foreign Policy – Essays in Honour of Peter Baehr* (Kluwer Law International, 1998) 151.

substantive right is infringed or threatened by an infringement.[11] The types, propriety and extent of such relief turn upon the facts of a case but they include declaratory judgments (finding of a violation), restitution, compensation and guarantee of non-repetition.[12] The procedural aspect of the right to a remedy implies the right to be heard by an impartial and competent tribunal.[13] Denial by the state of, or a failure to provide for, substantive, procedural or both dimensions of remedies is a violation of its duties to repair the injury its commissions or omissions threatened to cause or actually caused to right-holders.[14]

The right to a remedy is one of the 'pillars'[15] or a 'bedrock'[16] principle of international human rights law. Its existence and application pre-date the establishment of the contemporary human rights regime, as it had already been accepted as part of a state's duties in instances where its responsibility is implicated. In the oft-cited *Chorzow Factory* case, the Permanent Court of International Justice (PCIJ) held that '[i]t is a principle of international law, and even a general conception of law, that any breach of an engagement involves an obligation to make a reparation'.[17] This ruling has been described as the 'leading international formulation of the "no right without a remedy" principle'.[18]

In the *Chorzow Factory* case, the Court not only established the right to a remedy (and the state's duty to provide the same), it also specified the applicable remedial principle. In establishing what is referred to as the 'full remedy rule',[19] the court ruled that the right to a remedy entitles

[11] *Ibid.*, 701; J. E. S. Fawcett, 'The Exhaustion of Local Remedies: Substance or Procedure?', 31 *British Year Book of International Law* (1954) 452–8, 452; Dinah Shelton, *Remedies in International Human Rights Law* (Oxford University Press, 2nd edn, 2005) 7.

[12] Shelton (note 11 above) 255–367; Gino J. Naldi, 'Reparation in the Practice of the African Commission on Human and Peoples' Rights', 14 *Leiden Journal of International Law* (2001) 681–93, 685–9.

[13] Starr (note 9 above) 701; Fawcett (note 11 above) 452; Shelton (note 11 above) 7.

[14] As the African Commission ruled, albeit in relation to the right to development, 'the right to development is a two-pronged test, that it is both constitutive and instrumental, or useful as both a means and an end. A violation of either the procedural or substantive element constitutes a violation of the right to development.' Communication 276/2003, *Centre for Minority Rights Development (Kenya) and Minority Rights Group International on behalf of Endorois Welfare Council* v. *Kenya*, 27th Annual Activity Report (2009), para. 277.

[15] Lisa J. Laplante, 'The Law of Remedies and the Clean Hands Doctrine: Exclusionary Reparation Policies in Peru's Political Transition', 23 *American University International Law Review* (2008) 51–90, 54.

[16] Starr (note 9 above) 694.

[17] *Chorzow Factory* (*Germany* v. *Poland*), 1928 PCIJ, Ser. A, No. 17, para. 29.

[18] Starr (note 9 above) 699. [19] *Ibid.*

the victim of a violation to the restoration of the *status quo ante*, thereby disallowing a remedial shortfall. In '[o]ne of the most oft-quoted passages in international law',[20] the PCIJ ruled that:

> [t]he essential principle contained in the actual notion of an illegal act . . . is that reparations must, as far as possible, wipe out all consequences of the illegal act and re-establish the situation which would, in all probability, have existed if that act had not been committed.[21]

The *Chorzow Factory* judgment 'remains the cornerstone of international claims for reparations, whether presented by states or other litigants'.[22] It linked the two closely related principles that are central to the right to a remedy, namely, that a violation of an international obligation engenders the duty of reparation, and that such a remedy must be of the type and extent that can wipe out the effects of the violations.

The right to a remedy and the implicated state's duty to provide one have therefore existed in international law for many centuries.[23] Thus, the core of the remedy-related provisions of the International Law Commission's (ILC's) Draft Articles on State Responsibility[24] 'clearly represent existing law: every breach of an international obligation carries with it a duty to repair harm caused.'[25] Indeed, Article 1 of the Draft Articles on State Responsibility,[26] setting forth the overarching principle of state responsibility, is 'a restatement of the *Chorzow Factory* declaration' of the PCIJ.[27] The UN Guidelines on the Right to a Remedy ('Guidelines'),[28] containing the same principles requiring culpable states to repair injuries they caused through omission or

[20] Dinah Shelton, 'Righting Wrongs: Reparations in the Articles on State Responsibility', 96 *American Journal of International Law* (2002) 833–56, 835.

[21] *Chorzow Factory* case (note 17 above), para. 47. [22] Shelton (note 20 above) 836.

[23] Laplante (note 15 above) 56.

[24] See International Law Commission's (ILC) Draft Articles on Responsibility of States for Internationally Wrongful Acts (2001), Articles 31 *et seq.*

[25] Shelton (note 20 above) 835.

[26] The provision is entitled 'Responsibility of a State for its Internationally Wrongful Acts', and states that: 'Every internationally wrongful act of a State entails the international responsibility of that State.'

[27] Shelton (note 20 above) 835, note 10.

[28] See, Basic Principles and Guidelines on the Right to a Remedy and Reparation for Victims of Gross Violations of International Human Rights Law and Serious Violations of International Humanitarian Law, adopted 26 March 2006 by a UN General Assembly resolution (A/RES/60/147), 60th session.

commission, are similarly a codification of existing law.[29] Indeed, the Guidelines specifically state that the principles enshrined therein 'do not entail new international or domestic legal obligations but identify mechanisms, modalities, procedures and methods for the implementation of existing legal obligations under international human rights law and international humanitarian law which are complementary though different as to their norms'.[30]

While international and regional human rights tribunals have significantly contributed to the further development and application of the right to a remedy, the rule of *no right without a remedy* is certainly not of their creation.[31] If anything, upon its full-fledged appearance as a regime in the post-1945 period, international human rights law borrowed and applied the principle of *ubi just ubi remedium* into its evolving jurisprudence,[32] as has related scholarship.[33] As Starr observed, 'the remedial principles governing human rights law, a younger field, are heavily influenced by the *Chorzow Factory* line'.[34] Indeed, given the virtual absence or marginal role of inter-state cases in the areas of international law and environmental law, the greatest impact and relevance of the provisions of the ILC's Draft Articles could lie outside the field of state responsibility proper and in other areas such as human rights law.[35]

7.2.2 Right to a remedy: whose right is it?

Historically, under the international law of injury to aliens, a state's duty to ensure the protection of an alien's right, or the duty to provide a remedy to violations of the same, was owed to the national state of the victim and not to the victimised individual or group *per se*.[36] So, too, the direct victim did not have direct recourse against the foreign state, and only through his or her national state could the victim seek remedies for the violations suffered at the hands of the foreign state. The individual, at least not until after 1945, was not the subject of rights or duties under

[29] Laplante (note 15 above) 55–6. For a more elaborate discussion of the drafting history and content of the Guidelines, see generally Dinah Shelton, 'The United Nations Principles and Guidelines on Reparations: Context and Contents' in K. de Feyter *et al.* (eds.), *Out of the Ashes: Reparation for Victims of Gross and Systematic Human Rights Violations* (Intersentia, 2005) 11.

[30] Guidelines, Preamble, para. 7. [31] Laplante (note 15 above) 57. [32] *Ibid.*, 56.

[33] Starr (note 9 above) 706. [34] *Ibid.*, 700. [35] Shelton (note 20 above) 834.

[36] Jo M. Pasqualucci, 'Victim Reparations in the Inter-American Human Rights System: A Critical Assessment of Current Practice and Procedure', 18 *Michigan Journal of International Law* (1997) 1–58, 3.

international law.[37] Only the national state, to the exclusion of the direct human victim, had the right to sue the foreign state in the search for redress for the violations. The PCIJ stated:

> [t]he rules of law governing reparation are the rules of international law in force between the two States concerned, and not the law governing relations between the State which has committed a wrongful act and the individual who suffered damage.[38]

Once the national state has espoused a victim's case, the state – not the individual victim – becomes the sole party to the case, and can decide which violations to complain about and the nature and scope of remedies to be sought. As the PCIJ ruled, '[o]nce a State has taken up a case on behalf of one of its subjects before an international tribunal, in the eyes of the latter, the State is the sole claimant'.[39] Even so, a state that has claimed and acquired reparation on behalf of its national did not have the duty to transfer the compensation thus received to its victimised national. As Sohn observed, '[o]nce a state received compensation from another state for the injury to its citizen, it had no duty under international law to transfer that compensation to the citizen'.[40]

State obligations are thus deemed to be owed between states *qua* states, and the violation of a national's rights is akin to a breach of the national state's rights. Individuals could only indirectly benefit from recourse against a foreign state if a national state took up the victimised national's case.[41] Therefore, stateless persons had no recourse against a foreign state that violated their rights.[42] As established by the PCIJ:

> [b]y taking up the case of one of its subjects and by resorting to diplomatic action or international judicial proceedings on his behalf, a State is in reality asserting its own rights – its right to ensure in the person of its subjects, respect for the rules of international law.[43]

[37] Louis B. Sohn, 'The New International Law: Protection of the Right of Individuals Rather Than States', 32 *American University Law Review* (1983) 1–64, 9; Fried van Hoof, 'International Human Rights Obligations for Companies and Domestic Courts: An Unlikely Combination?' in Monique Castermans-Holleman, Fried van Hoof and Jaqueline Smith (eds.), *The Role of the Nation-State in the 21st Century: Human Rights, International Organisations and Foreign Policy – Essays in Honour of Peter Baehr* (Kluwer Law International, 1998) 47, 52–4.

[38] *Chorzow Factory* case (Merits), 1928 PCIJ, para. 28.

[39] *Mavrommatis Palestine Concessions* (Jurisdiction), 1924 PCIJ, Ser. A, No. 2, para. 12.

[40] Sohn (note 37 above) 9. [41] *Ibid.* [42] *Ibid.*

[43] *Mavrommatis Palestine Concessions* (note 39 above), para. 13.

The right of individual and group right-holders to have direct recourse against a foreign state for violations by the same of the former's rights came into being only in the last half-century through the emergence of the human rights regime.[44] The human rights treaties, with an increasing number of ratification by states, thus created obligations for states to answer to and repair individuals' and groups' rights breaches, including those that they commit extraterritorially.[45]

7.2.3 The role of individual remedies in redressing transboundary violations of the human right to water

There are numerous reasons for putting the individual and group victims of transboundary violations of the human right to water in control of the ensuing litigation and the resultant remedies. First, enabling foreign victims to bring suits against a transboundary violator of their human right to water would be a means of preventing the culture of impunity within a given river basin. It is not always feasible for a home state to espouse each and every single incident of violations of its inhabitants' human right to water by extraterritorial actors. There are indeed very few inter-state cases, as states – due to comity and political, economic or other considerations – are not always inclined to espouse the complaints of their nationals.[46] The state's right to espouse its residents' claims against a foreign state is discretionary, and it may decide at will whether to take it up in an international tribunal. As the Inter-American Commission ruled:

> [t]he Commission must also point out that even if the United States were a Party to the [American] Convention and had accepted the competence of the Commission to receive interstate communications, the exercise by Argentina of the prerogative to lodge such a complaint, under the circumstances analyzed, does not constitute an obligation required by the Convention. It is simply a question left to the discretion of the States Parties ... The Convention does not establish any positive obligation whatsoever to present communications against other States Parties nor does it stipulate the right of persons protected by the Convention to demand that States Parties exercise said prerogative.[47]

Thus, a state may decide not to espouse a case on behalf of its residents against a co-riparian state that causes the violation of the human right to

[44] Pasqualucci (note 36 above) 4. [45] *Ibid.* [46] Shelton (note 20 above) 834.
[47] *Victor Saldano* case (note 6 above), para. 30.

water across borders. In such instances, the victims would suffer the injury to their rights with no possibility of redress for the same unless they are empowered to take up the case against the foreign perpetrator, who would otherwise benefit from the legal gap. It leads to human rights violations with impunity. Indeed, one of the direct implications and benefits of defining access to water as a human right is to arm individual and group right-holders with the right to claim remedies when the right is threatened by a violation or is actually violated.

Secondly, the inclusion of individual remedies for violations of individuals' and groups' rights in the regulation of transboundary water resources has the potential of empowering individuals to influence foreign riparian states' use of shared water resources. More often than not, individuals and groups have sought relevant remedies – judicial or otherwise – through their national states for transboundary harms they suffered as a consequence of other states' omissions or commissions.[48] In earlier times, as seen in the *Trail Smelter* case, residents of a state have sought to address their transboundary grievances through governmental channels.[49] The private party's direct access to foreign judicial and other institutional avenues to bring the acts or omissions of riparian states under proper scrutiny means that states would now be forced to take people's views into consideration before or in the course of the allocation and use of shared water resources. It is considered as a means of ensuring public participation in the management of shared water resources.[50] Such has proved to be effective in some countries, including Canada where litigation had 'had a revolutionary impact on Canadian environmental laws'.[51]

Thirdly, the policy of encouraging resort to transboundary local litigation and remedies ensures that states implement their extraterritorial *duty to protect* foreign residents by holding domestic non-state actors accountable for breaches of the human right to water they cause

48 Constance D. Hunt, 'Implementation: Joint Institutional Management and Remedies in Domestic Tribunals (Articles 26–28 and 30–32)', 3 *Colorado Journal of International Environmental Law and Policy* (1992) 281–94, 288; McCaffrey (note 5 above) 192.

49 In the *Trail Smelter* case, individual claims were converted to a claim by the United States against Canada. See John E. Read, 'The Trail Smelter Dispute', 1 *Canadian Yearbook of International Law* (1963) 213–29, 222–3.

50 Ellen Hey, 'Sustainable Use of Shared Water Resources: The Need for a Paradigm Shift in International Watercourses Law' in Gerald H. Blake, William Hilldesley, Martin Pratt, Rebecca Ridley and Clive Schofield (eds.), *The Peaceful Management of Transboundary Resources* (Graham & Trotman, 1995) 127, 134.

51 Hunt (note 48 above) 289.

abroad by their actions or omissions.[52] It thus helps reallocate the costs of injurious activities that have extraterritorial effects to the actual perpetrator, hence reinforcing the 'polluter pays principle'.[53] This indeed coincides with the realisation that many transboundary environmental and water-related problems are committed by and against private parties, and not necessarily by or against the state as such.[54] Thus, transboundary litigation and access to extraterritorial domestic remedies not only enable the victim to have the injuries remedied, but also offers the possibility of securing redress from multinational companies and other private actors whose operations may not cause harm in the host country or the effects of which are extraterritorial and hence difficult for the domestic actors to complain against.[55]

Fourthly, access by the private – parties to domestic individual remedies has proved to present a greater likelihood of delivering more expeditious justice to remedy transboundary harm than inter-state litigation or negotiations.[56]

52 On the subject of states' human rights responsibility for acts of non-state actors, see Marko Milanovic, 'State Responsibility for Acts of Non-State Actors: A Comment on Griebel and Plucken', 22 *Leiden Journal of International Law* (2009) 307–24; Aoife Nolan, 'Addressing Economic and Social Rights Violations by Non-State Actors through the Role of the State: A Comparison of Regional Approaches to the "Obligation to Protect"', 9(2) *Human Rights Law Review* (2009) 225–55.

53 *Ibid.*, 270 and 303. It has been argued that state responsibility does not arise out of a purely private act of private entities, unless the state is guilty of not showing due diligence to control, prevent or remedy the injurious activities of private actors. According to Lawson, states incur international responsibility for private conduct more often through omission, when its own organs are 'guilty of not having done everything within its power to prevent the injurious act of the private individual or to punish it suitably if it has occurred despite everything'. See Rick Lawson, 'Out of Control – State Responsibility and Human Rights: Will the ILC's Definition of the "Act of State" Meet the Challenges of the 21st Century?' in Monique Castermans-Holleman, Fried van Hoof and Jaqueline Smith (eds.), *The Role of the Nation-State in the 21st Century: Human Rights, International Organisations and Foreign Policy – Essays in Honour of Peter Baehr* (Kluwer Law International, 1998) 91, 96.

54 Patricia W. Birnie, Alan E. Boyle and Catherine Redgwell, *International Law and the Environment* (Oxford University Press, 3rd edn, 2009) 303; David Weissbrodt, 'Non-State Entities and Human Rights within the Context of the Nation-State in the 21st Century' in Monique Castermans-Holleman, Fried van Hoof and Jaqueline Smith (eds.), *The Role of the Nation-State in the 21st Century: Human Rights, International Organisations and Foreign Policy – Essays in Honour of Peter Baehr* (Kluwer Law International, 1998) 175, 187.

55 *Ibid.*

56 Sergei V. Vinogradov, 'Observations on the International Law Commission's Draft Rules on the Non-Navigational Uses of International Watercourses: "Management

Fifthly, private transboundary access to domestic justice also has the potential to reduce extraterritorial tensions – which are more likely to accompany inter-state water-resource-sharing complaints – by avoiding their being unnecessarily and overly politicised.[57] As McCaffrey noted, in situations where a home state espouses the water-related complaints of its populations against a co-riparian state, the home state 'may become embroiled in controversies over invasion of his [the injured citizen's] country's sovereignty and responsibility of the polluter's country in international law'.[58] Inter-state fresh water disputes are usually politically charged.[59] The possibility of transboundary private litigation thus helps to de-escalate disputes 'to their ordinary neighbourhood level' where they can be resolved using national law remedies for transboundary violations.[60]

Finally, this approach disentangles the right to water from states' rights and clearly bestows the human right on human beneficiaries. It thus entails an objective and non-reciprocal extraterritorial human rights and state duties separately from the inter-riparian obligations that exist among the states. It creates a direct diagonal relationship between transboundary right-holders and riparian duty-bearers. In effect, the fact that extraterritorial human rights are defined in terms of individuals' and groups' rights has the advantage that individuals could enforce their rights against a foreign state without such foreign state being allowed to raise as a defence failures by the complainant's home state to discharge its duties to such foreign riparian state relative to the shared water resource. It is therefore essential that individual and group right-holders have a direct recourse for remedies against the foreign co-riparian violator if the human right to water is to be meaningful.

7.3 The right to a remedy under the African Charter

Nearly every human rights treaty – regional or global – unequivocally establishes an individual right to an effective remedy for the violation of rights and freedoms that they enshrine.[61] The Universal Declaration of

and Domestic Remedies"', 3 *Colorado Journal of International Environmental Law and Policy* (1992) 235–59, 249.

57 *Ibid.* 58 McCaffrey (note 5 above) 193.

59 Arun P. Elhance, 'Hydropolitics: Grounds for Despair, Reasons for Hope', 5 *International Negotiation* (2000) 201–22, 201.

60 Birnie, Boyle and Redgwell (note 54 above) 303.

61 Starr (note 9 above) 700; Laplante (note 15 above) 54–5; Naldi (note 12 above) 681.

Human Rights (Article 8),[62] the International Covenant on Civil and Political Rights (Article 2(3)), the European Convention on Human Rights (Article 13)[63] and the Inter-American Convention on Human Rights (Articles 15 and 51(2)) are just a few of those instruments that provide for the right to an effective and adequate remedy for violations of the rights they enshrine.[64] In this regard, the African Charter is an exception. It has no explicit 'remedies clause' in its provisions or in the Communications Rules of Procedure, an absence that attracted severe criticism.[65]

Viljoen argues that the lack of an explicit provision on remedies has led to inconsistent treatment by the Commission of violations of the African Charter.[66] Accordingly, the inconsistency in the provision of remedies by the Commission in its decisions 'leaves uncertain what is required of states, thus impeding follow-up or implementation [of the Commission's decisions]'.[67]

While the absence of a remedies clause may have had negative impacts on the African Commission's awards of remedies to the victims of violations of Charter-based rights and the efficacy of the Commission's recommendations, the significance and effect of the lack of an explicit 'remedies clause' in the African Charter should not be overstated. First, there is nothing to suggest that the right to remedies was deliberately excluded from the corpus of the Charter. The Charter's *travaux préparatoires* does not contain anything about the right to remedies, hence obviating the possibility that it was intentionally excluded.[68] Indeed, it

[62] Adopted on 10 December 1948 by the UN General Assembly.

[63] Adopted 4 November 1950, entered into force 3 September 1953.

[64] Adopted 22 November 1969, entered into force 18 July 1978.

[65] See, for instance, Christof Heyns, 'The African Regional Human Rights System: In Need of Reform?', 2 *African Human Rights Law Journal* (2002) 155–74, 164.

[66] According to Viljoen, the absence of a clear provision on remedies in the African Charter has meant that the Commission's findings of violations of the Charter by a state party led to three types of consequences: no remedies at all, unspecified remedies and specific and detailed remedies. See Frans Viljoen, 'A Human Rights Court for Africa, and Africans', 30 *Brooklyn Journal of International Law* (2004) 1–66, 14. Odinkalu similarly argued that the African Commission's remedial measures have not 'always been as explicit or clear as it could be'. See also Chidi Anselm Odinkalu, 'The Role of Case and Complaints Procedures in the Reform of the African Regional Human Rights System', 1 *African Human Rights Law Journal* (2001) 225–46, 242.

[67] Viljoen (note 66 above) 14–15.

[68] See generally Keba Mbaye, '[Mbaye] Draft African Charter on Human and Peoples' Rights', reprinted in Christof Heyns (ed.), *Human Rights Law in Africa*, Vol. 4, 65–77

was argued that its omission can be explained by a drafting oversight,[69] which has been the case in relation to other substantive human rights as well.[70]

Secondly, there is a more plausible line of thought that explains the lack of an explicit provision on remedies by the fact that it is an implied right in all other rights and freedoms guaranteed in the Charter. Indeed, the right to a remedy is implicit in all other rights and freedoms provided for in a given treaty regime and its absence would not have significant effects on a victim's right to claim a remedy. Accordingly, in any human rights treaty such as the African Charter, the right to a remedy is a 'constituent of the general obligation requiring state parties to give effect to the norms contained therein'.[71] As Musila argued, 'the right to a remedy is so self-evident that it need not be specifically enshrined [in the African Charter]'.[72] As Shelton has shown, the lack of express remedies behind protected rights has led to judicial bodies inferring a remedy for violations of protected rights.[73] This position has found clear support from the jurisprudence of the PCIJ, which ruled that '[r]eparation therefore is the indispensable component of a failure to apply a convention and there is no necessity for this to be stated in the convention itself'.[74]

Additionally, the African Charter contains some specific guarantees that would enable victims of human rights violations to have access to local remedies which state parties should thus provide. Under Article 7 of the Charter, everyone 'has the right to have his cause heard', which is part of the right to accessing a remedy (the procedural aspect of the right to a remedy). Moreover, the inclusion in the Charter of the communications procedure[75] whereby states can be brought before the

(Brill, 2002). See also, generally, James Spigelman, *Statutory Interpretation and Human Rights* (University of Queensland Press, 2008).

[69] Godfrey M. Musila, 'The Right to an Effective Remedy under the African Charter on Human and Peoples' Rights', 6 *African Human Rights Law Journal* (2006) 442–64, 447.

[70] For some of the omissions of the Charter, see Takele Soboka Bulto, 'The Indirect Approach to Promote Justiciability of Socio-Economic Rights of the African Charter on Human and Peoples' Rights' in Rachel H. Murray (ed.), *Human Rights Litigation and the Domestication of International Human Rights in Sub-Saharan Africa* (International Commission of Jurists, 2009) 135, 136.

[71] Musila (note 69 above) 447.

[72] *Ibid.* See also Naomi Roht-Arriaza, 'Punishment, Redress, and Pardon: Theoretical and Psychological Approaches' in Naomi Roht-Arriaza (ed.), *Impunity and Human Rights in International Law and Practice* (Oxford University Press, 1995) 13, 17.

[73] Shelton (note 11 above) 29. [74] *Chorzow Factory* case (note 17 above), para. 29.

[75] See African Charter, Articles 47–59.

Commission for violating human rights presupposes the duty of the defendant state to redress the violations, if any, its actions or omissions caused.[76] Furthermore, the Commission has played a proactive role in clarifying the status of the right to a remedy under the African Charter. In the *Free Legal Assistance Group* v. *Zaire* case, the Commission ruled that the main goal of the communications procedure is to initiate a process 'which remedies the prejudice complained of'.[77] It in fact has almost invariably ordered states to provide specific remedies to redress injuries caused to right-holders through the states' violations of the rights concerned.[78]

Thus, while there is no clear basis in the Charter that authorises the Commission to order remedies in cases where it finds for the complainant, the Commission seems to have assumed, rightly, that this right is inherent in the substantive rights whose violations are complained of. It has deemed itself to have the mandate to order remedies it finds necessary and adequate to redress the injury caused to individuals and groups.[79] This is in line with the jurisprudence of the International Court of Justice, which ruled that:

> where jurisdiction exists over a dispute on a particular matter, no separate basis for jurisdiction is required by the court to consider the remedies a party has requested for the breach of the obligation.[80]

Finally, recent normative developments in the African human rights system have helped shed more light on the normative basis of the right to a remedy. Under the Protocol establishing the African Court on Human and Peoples' Rights,[81] the Court is empowered, where it 'finds that there has been a violation of a human or peoples' right, [to] make appropriate orders to remedy the violation, including the payment of fair

[76] Chidi Anselm Odinkalu, 'The Individual Complaints Procedures of the African Commission on Human and Peoples' Rights: A Preliminary Assessment', 8 *Transnational Law and Contemporary Problems* (1998) 359–405, 374.

[77] (Joined) Communications 25/89, 47/90, 56/91, 100/93, *Free Legal Assistance Group and Others* v. *Zaire*, 9th Annual Activity Report (1995), para. 39.

[78] See Viljoen (note 66 above) 14–15; Naldi (note 61 above) 685–9.

[79] See Naldi (note 12 above) 685–9.

[80] *Lagrand Case* (*Germany* v. *United States of America*), ICJ, Judgment of 27 June 200, para. 48 (citing the *Chorzow Factory* precedent, para. 22).

[81] Protocol to the African Charter on Human and Peoples' Rights on the Establishment of an African Court on Human and Peoples' Rights, adopted in Ouagadougou, Burkina Faso, 10 June 1998, entered into force 25 January 2004.

compensation or reparation'.[82] Similarly, in the African Women's Protocol,[83] states have the duty not only to 'provide for appropriate remedies to any woman whose rights or freedoms . . . have been violated' but also to provide the right-holders with the opportunity to have the appropriate remedies that are to be 'determined by competent judicial, administrative or legislative authorities, or by any other competent authority provided for by law'.[84]

Therefore, the absence of an explicit right to remedies is not as serious as some authors have claimed it to be for the purpose of redressing violations of the Charter's substantive guarantees. It is not only an implicit right in the African human rights system, but it has now also found its way into the more recent regional instruments upon which the Commission's and the Court's decisions on remedies may be based. This is merely a 'postscript' to the already established regional human rights jurisprudence, in which the Commission took for granted its power to order appropriate remedies for violations of the Charter. There can be little doubt therefore that a violation of the human right to water under the African Charter should be followed by appropriate, effective and adequate remedies.

A state is thus duty-bound not only to provide for the substantive rights guaranteed in treaties it has ratified but also to provide appropriate legal avenues for complainants to seek and obtain remedies in cases of their infringement. This duty also includes one of enshrining in its laws adequate and effective remedies and empowering impartial and competent tribunals to hear such complaints and award remedies when one is warranted. This may also necessitate amendment of its laws to ensure normative compatibility between domestic norms and the international treaty obligations of the state. Either before or immediately after a state ratifies a treaty, it is expected to review its domestic laws and practices to ensure that it is in compliance with the obligations contained in the treaty. As far back as 1925, the PCIJ asserted that a ratifying state's obligation to make the changes to its legislation that are necessary for the fulfilment of the duties undertaken in the treaties is simply 'a principle that is self-evident'.[85]

[82] *Ibid.*, Article 27(1).

[83] Protocol to the African Charter on Human and Peoples' Rights on the Rights of Women in Africa, adopted by the 2nd Ordinary Session of the Assembly of the African Union, Maputo, Mozambique, 11 July 2003, entered into force 25 November 2005.

[84] *Ibid.*, Article 25.

[85] *Exchange of Greek and Turkish Populations*, Permanent Court of International Justice, Advisory Opinion, PCIJ Reports 1925, Ser. B, No. 10, 20.

However, the relationship between international human rights law and domestic law is such that individuals and group complainants of human rights violations must access and exhaust domestic remedies available within the state that is alleged to have violated the human right to water before having recourse to the remedies available in international tribunals. As shown in Chapter 5 and revisited below, international water law and the human rights treaties speak in unison in giving priority to local remedies before international tribunals are approached and international law remedies are sought for human rights violations.

7.4 Primacy of national remedies over international remedies

International law complements, supplements and overrides contrary domestic law in matters involving the protection of human and peoples' rights. As Henkin observed, '[t]he international law of human rights parallels and supplements national law, superseding and supplying the deficiencies of national constitutions and laws, but it does not replace and indeed depends on national institutions'.[86] As the African Commission ruled, '[i]nternational mechanisms are not substitutes for domestic implementation of human rights, but should be seen as tools to assist the domestic authorities to develop a sufficient protection of human rights in their territories'.[87] This entails the need to bring domestic legislation, administrative rules and practices into conformity[88] with the international treaties which are 'high-minded legal formulations'.[89] Accordingly, therefore, there is a *structural* (as opposed to substantive) dependence of international human rights law on the domestic laws and procedures for its domestic implementation.[90] Thus, remedies available in international law, especially in the human rights regime, are merely subsidiary to national remedies and not meant to replace, but rather to

[86] Louis Henkin, *The Rights of Man Today* (Stevens, 1979) 79.

[87] Communication 268/2003, *Ilesanmi* v. *Nigeria*, 18th Annual Activity Report (2005), para. 44.

[88] This is part of the domestic implementation of ratified treaties, which specifically require the state parties to take, *inter alia*, legislative measures to ensure their domestic applicability. Article 2(2) of the International Covenant on Civil and Political Rights and Article 1 of the African Charter are just two examples.

[89] Philip Alston, 'The Purposes of Reporting' in *Manual on Human Rights Reporting under Six Major International Human Rights Instruments* (United Nations, 1997) 24.

[90] Carlos Manuel Vazquez, 'Treaties as Law of the Land: The Supremacy Clause and Presumption of Self-Execution', 121(1) *Harvard Law Review* (2008) 1–76, 14.

supplement, domestic remedies.[91] Primacy is therefore accorded to national legal remedies as opposed to those available through international procedures.[92] Thus, victims of human rights violations must exhaust locally available remedies before having recourse to international remedies.

The rule of exhaustion of local remedies has long been used in international law and international human rights disputes to reinforce the primacy of national remedies over international remedies. Just like the right to a remedy, the rule of exhaustion of local remedies is part of customary international law.[93] Originally, it was imposed upon aliens seeking the diplomatic protection of their state of nationality where their rights were violated in and/or by a foreign state.[94] It is one of the most frequently used objections or defences to admissibility of international claims.[95] It reinforces the primacy of national remedies over international remedies. The rule dictates that a state cannot espouse a complaint of its nationals against another state before the individuals or groups exhaust remedies available in the implicated state, without obtaining reparation for the harm suffered.[96] It has thus been a means of preventing *horizontal* extraterritorial cases and consequent extraterritorial remedies (between states).[97] Unless and until the direct victim (individual or group) exhausts local remedies that are available in the state that is the author of the injury or violation, the national state of the complainants cannot espouse a case on their behalf or the claim is inadmissible in

[91] Frans Viljoen, 'Communications under the African Charter: Procedure and Admissibility' in Malcolm Evans and Rachel Murray (eds.), *The African Charter on Human and Peoples' Rights: The System in Practice, 1986–2006* (Cambridge University Press, 2nd edn, 2008) 76, 111.

[92] W. Gary Vause, 'The Subsidiarity Principle in European Union Law – American Federalism Compared', 27 *Case Western Reserve Journal of International Law* (1995) 61–82, 65–6.

[93] Riccardo Pisillo Mazzeschi, 'Exhaustion of Domestic Remedies and State Responsibility for Violation of Human Rights', 10 *Italian Yearbook of International Law* (2000) 17–41, 17; Fawcett (note 11 above) 452.

[94] See Mazzeschi (note 93 above) 17; Francisco Forrest Martin *et al.*, *International Human Rights and Humanitarian Law: Treaties, Cases and Analysis* (Cambridge University Press, 1st edn, 2006) 290.

[95] Fawcett (note 11 above) 452; Ian Brownlie, *Principles of Public International Law* (Oxford University Press, 7th edn, 2008) 492.

[96] Sohn (note 37 above) 4; Mazzeschi (note 93 above) 17.

[97] See generally Dinah L. Shelton, 'Case Concerning Avena and Other Mexican Nationals (Mexico v. United States)', 98 *American Journal of International Law* (2004) 559–66.

international tribunals.[98] Thus, the field of application of the local remedies rule has been extraterritorial, but horizontal as between states. It has applied to cases of diplomatic protection as opposed to instances of direct injury to the state espousing the case.[99]

With its incorporation into the human rights treaties, not least in the African Charter,[100] the rule came to have additional dimensions and application not only *vertically* (as between residents and their state of residence) but also *diagonally* (as between an individual in one state and a foreign state whose responsibility for an extraterritorial human right violation is implicated). As the discussion below on the application of the rule in the African human rights system shows, the rule of exhaustion of local remedies is a double-edged sword. While imposing the duty on complainants to exhaust local remedies, it concomitantly entails a state's duty to maintain the legal basis for the domestic protection of treaty-based rights as well as to provide adequate and effective remedies in cases of their violation.

7.5 Beyond national jurisdictions: accessing regional tribunals and remedies

A precondition itself, the rule of exhaustion of domestic remedies applies only if certain cumulative criteria are satisfied. In other words, the primacy of national remedies over international ones and the requirement of exhaustion of local remedies are not absolute. International remedies may be resorted to immediately and local remedies may be disregarded in exceptional circumstances where national laws and state conduct fails to meet certain criteria. The African Commission ruled that it 'has never held the requirement of local remedies to apply literally in cases where it is impractical or undesirable for the complainant to seize the domestic courts in the case of each violation'.[101] It is clear from the case law of the African Commission that a remedy must meet all prongs

[98] Sohn (note 37 above) 4; Brownlie (note 95 above) 492.

[99] Martin *et al.* (note 94 above) 290.

[100] The African Charter explicitly provided for the rule as an essential precondition of the admissibility of non-state communications. Article 56 of the Charter states that: 'Communications relating to human and peoples' rights referred to in Article 55 [communications other than those of state parties] received by the Commission, shall be considered if they . . . are submitted within a reasonable period from the time local remedies are exhausted or from the date the Commission is seized with the matter.'

[101] *Free Legal Assistance Group* case (note 77 above), para. 36.

of a three-prong test: '[t]hree major criteria could be deduced from the practice of the [African] Commission in determining this rule, namely: the remedy must be available, effective and sufficient.'[102] Failing any one of the availability, effectiveness and/or sufficiency tests, the duty of the complainant to exhaust domestic remedies is excused and direct resort to international remedies is allowed.

7.5.1 *Problems of remedial deterrence*

An individual or group claimant's duty to exhaust local remedies before seizing an international jurisdiction may be exempt when a state's legal system or practice presents certain barriers to a private party's efforts to obtain transboundary relief before a riparian state's domestic courts. In river basins such as the Nile, where there is no basin-wide binding legal framework to force states to accord equal access to justice to each other's nationals/residents, such remedial deterrents could prove domestically insurmountable, thereby giving rise to the situation where regional human rights bodies become forums of first instance.

In the Nile basin states, transboundary litigation arising out of harms caused to foreign nationals by a riparian state or entities situated therein has yet to be seen. Indeed, attempts at transboundary individual litigation arising from the mode of use of international rivers would be a novel approach in Africa. But there exists experience in other regions of the world – particularly between the United States and Canada and in Europe – where individuals have litigated to obtain redress for transboundary harms they suffer.[103] The experiences of the American and European regions have shown that domestic courts and tribunals may deliberately seek to avoid adjudication of transboundary complaints[104] by resorting to procedural avoidance mechanisms.[105] The litigants have faced a series of serious procedural and substantive remedial deterrents, a situation that has allowed complainants to access the regional human rights system directly. Such judicial strategies include claims of lack of material jurisdiction, or denial of standing (*locus standi*) to one or both parties involved.[106] In the *Trail Smelter* case, for instance, residents of

[102] (Joined) Communications 147/95 and 149/96, *Sir Dawada K. Jawara* v. *The Gambia*, 13th Annual Activity Report (2000), para. 31.

[103] Birnie, Boyle and Redgwell (note 54 above) 303. [104] Starr (note 9 above) 743.

[105] *Ibid.*, 724–6.

[106] *Ibid.*; Gallob (note 5 above) 97–100. See also Stephen C. McCaffrey, 'Background and Overview of the International Law Commission's Study of the Non-Navigational Uses

the US state of Washington were denied standing in Canadian courts due to the common law doctrine of the 'local action rule' which required that suits to recover for injury to land be brought before a jurisdiction where the land is located.[107] Conversely, jurisdiction could not be obtained over the smelter in the US as the defendant was situated in Canada.[108] The plaintiffs had to request the US government to take up the case on their behalf, and the government decided to espouse the case only after this was requested by the victims of the transboundary pollution.

In what is at times referred to as 'judicial subterfuge',[109] judges may also resort to a narrow interpretation of a given substantive right, in this case the human right to water, in such a way that enables them to avoid adjudication of the rights of a foreign claimant. The courts achieve this through remedial equilibrium, a method which calculates the appropriate remedy likely to be awarded before establishing the scope of the substantive right alleged to be breached – hence an equilibration between the right and the remedy.[110] Thus, the normal order of enquiry would be reversed: in the ordinary run of things, the scope of the relief is derived more or less logically from the substantive violation and the plaintiff will get a remedy that is measured by and commensurate with the harm caused by the defendant's breach of duty.[111] However, instead of first answering the question of whether there is a substantive right that is allegedly violated, courts may calculate (or anticipate) the ensuing remedy first, and only then decide the existence and ambit of the right in issue. They often do not admit that they are changing a rights interpretation (or an admissibility or prejudice rule) in order to avoid a particular remedial consequence.[112] If the remedy to the violation complained of is too intrusive, the courts tend to refuse to hold that the right exists at all.[113] Courts may thus avoid adjudication of extraterritorial claims by

of International Watercourses', 3 *Colorado Journal of International Environmental Law and Policy* (1992) 17–29, 27; Blake R. Bertagna, '"Standing" up for the Environment: The Ability of Plaintiffs to Establish Legal Standing to Redress Injuries Caused by Global Warming', *Brigham Young University Law Review* (2006) 415–71, 421–4.

107 For a detailed analysis of the *Trail Smelter* case and the jurisdictional issues involved therein, see McCaffrey (note 106 above) 27–8.

108 *Ibid.* 109 Starr (note 9 above) 743.

110 Daryl J. Levinson, 'Rights Essentialism and Remedial Equilibrium', 99(4) *Columbia Law Review* (1999) 857–940, 889–99; Starr (note 9 above) 720–4.

111 Abram Chayes, 'The Role of the Judge in Public Law Litigation', 89(7) *Harvard Law Review* (1976) 1281–1316, 1282.

112 Starr (note 9 above) 743.

113 Richard H. Fallon, Jr, 'The Linkage between Justiciability and Remedies – And Their Connections to Substantive Rights', 92 *Virginia Law Review* (2006) 633–706, 635.

denying the very existence of a substantive right, narrowing down its scope, or heightening the standard of proof of the violation of the right in respect of which access to a remedy is sought.[114] Such judicial manoeuvring of the rights–remedies relationship will eventually 'lead the courts to engage in *ad hoc* manipulations of justiciability doctrines, especially standing'.[115]

In addition to procedural avoidance mechanisms, the cost of travel or of litigation may be so prohibitive for transboundary litigants as to prevent access to domestic remedies in a foreign state. Or the complainants could be indigents who may not be able to afford the cost of accessing transboundary tribunals and remedies. If the law of the relevant riparian state does not allow *actio popularis*, the possibility of accessing extraterritorial domestic remedies could be closed to a claimant with limited resources. As is the case in Ethiopia, the right to counsel may be available only in criminal cases and may be unavailable in civil matters. The cost implications of accessing extraterritorial remedies can be aggravated by the cost of translation of evidentiary documents from the language of the complainant into the local language of the forum state. States may refuse to issue entry visas for complainants to access their domestic tribunals. In a case against Sudan, the Commission noted that 'the refugees' [complainants] legal representative was repeatedly denied entry into the country by the Respondent State's authorities', and decided that, 'even if certain domestic remedies were available, it was not reasonable to expect refugees to seize the Sudanese Courts of their complaints'.[116]

Therefore, the legal and practical availability, effectiveness and adequacy of transboundary remedies are assessed before forcing transboundary claimants to exhaust transboundary local remedies in a riparian state. If practical access is extremely difficult or the human right to water is not protected and/or remedies for its violations are not available, effective or adequate to someone in the position of the transboundary litigant, the complainants may be relieved from exhausting such remedies and access regional mechanisms to have their injuries redressed.

114 Thus, problems of standing and justiciability could be overly politicised by the courts. See generally Richard J. Pierce, Jr, 'Is Standing Law or Politics?', 77 *North Carolina Law Review* (1999) 1742–90.

115 Fallon (note 113 above) 637.

116 Communication 235/2000, *Dr Curtis Francis Doebbler* v. *Sudan*, 27th Annual Activity Report (2009), para. 116.

The African Charter provides for grounds of exemptions from exhausting local remedies in selected cases. In those instances, the complainant may directly approach the African Commission and/or Court in search of legal remedies that would redress the impending or current injury complained of. It is indeed the application of the exemptions to, rather than the rule of, exhaustion of domestic remedies that seems to have immediate relevance to the enforcement of the human right to water in Africa.

7.5.2 Exceptions to the local remedies rule and the human right to water

In instances where there are no domestic remedies, or where the available remedies are less than effective or adequate, international monitoring and adjudicatory bodies would be the fora of first instance to hear cases of and mete out appropriate remedies to redress the violations of treaty-based rights by local authorities.[117] Individuals and groups who are victims of violations of (treaty-based) human rights would thus be given treaty-based remedies irrespective of any domestic laws that deny or restrict access to such by the right-holders.

In those cases, the complainant would be allowed to directly and immediately access regional mechanisms and access remedies available under the regional human rights system. The Commission has long ruled that a remedy 'the availability of which is not evident, cannot be invoked by the state to the detriment of the complainant'.[118] The case law of the African Commission thus shows some discernible trends in relation to exemptions from the exhaustion of the local remedies rule.

7.5.2.1 Lack of protection for the human right to water in domestic law

As outlined above, the requirement of exhausting local remedies before submitting a case for adjudication of international bodies presupposes the existence of a right which is the subject of the complaint and corresponding remedies in the event of its violation. Thus, not only the remedy but also the substantive right must have a legal basis and be

[117] See Bulto (note 70 above) 160. See also Communication 155/96, *Social and Economic Rights Action Centre and the Centre for Economic and Social Rights* v. *Nigeria*, 15th Annual Activity Report (2001–2), para. 44 ('the *SERAC* case'), paras. 36–41.

[118] Jawara (note 102 above), para. 34.

actionable in the domestic law. It could be enshrined in the national constitution, or other legislation. Or it could result from the ratification and domestication by the relevant state of a regional or international treaty such as the African Charter and/or the ICESCR respectively. In the latter case, the treaty that is the basis of the right in question must have a direct domestic application and be granted judicial notice for individual and group complainants to invoke it in the domestic administrative and judicial proceedings of the state.

Where the substantive right that is violated is a breach of international human rights law but not of domestic law (which fails to provide for the right), 'the local remedies rule does not *ex hypothesi* come into play at all; for since there has been nothing done contrary to the local law, there can be no local remedies to exhaust.'[119] The substantive protection of the human right to water may not be available in the country's legal system. But, 'if the right is not well provided for, there cannot be effective remedies or any remedies at all'.[120] Complainants alleging a violation of (treaty-based) rights can approach the regional mechanism directly and immediately.

7.5.2.2 Problems of domestic non-justiciability of socio-economic rights

A crucial aspect of the right to access a tribunal that is competent to investigate and judicially appraise arbitrary violations of human rights lies in the fact that it leads to the award of an adequate and effective remedy. The remedy could take the form of an injunction, compensation, restoration of confiscated property, reinstatement in a job, guarantee against repetition, or a combination of these or other types of relief.[121] Where the right to a remedy is lacking in a state's domestic legal system, or the remedies available therein are ineffective or inadequate, the regional bodies would be the principal and primary port of call for holding the state accountable for human rights violations.

The practice of many African states poses particularly serious challenges to the domestic justiciability of socio-economic rights treaties. One of the most fundamental problems that stands in the path towards

[119] Fawcett (note 11 above) 455. [120] *Ibid.*

[121] See generally Kent Roach, 'Crafting Remedies for Violations of Economic, Social and Cultural Rights' in John Squires, Malcolm Langford and Bret Thiele (eds.), *The Road to a Remedy: Current Issues in the Litigation of Economic, Social and Cultural Rights* (Australian Human Rights Centre, 2005) 111; Naldi (note 12 above) 685–9.

accessing domestic remedies on the African continent is the lack of the justiciability of socio-economic rights (hence the human right to water). Having ratified treaties with justiciable socio-economic rights such as the African Charter, some states promulgate or maintain national legislation that is in conflict with ratified treaties. This scenario leads to a violation of the obligation of ensuring justiciability of the rights enshrined in the ratified treaties and the duty to ensure the availability of domestic remedies for the rights contained therein, giving rise to a clear incompatibility between the national and the international norms relative to a given human right. In many of the national jurisdictions, socio-economic rights are consigned to the status of Directive Principles of State Policy (DPSP),[122] and hence are non-justiciable *per se*. The DPSP are meant to guide the executive and legislative branches of the state to the exclusion of the judicial branch.[123] The inclusion of a right under the DPSP excludes the possibility of complaining about its violation in the regular courts or quasi-judicial bodies.[124] In Namibia, for instance, the Supreme Court decided that the DPSP 'are not enforceable in any court of law, and, therefore, should they be ignored or infringed the aggrieved have no legal remedy to compel positive action'.[125] Consequently, the ratification of the Charter alone without domestic justiciability may be of little assistance in the search for domestic remedies and the enjoyment of the rights at the local level may still be illusory.

Where the violated socio-economic right is part of the DPSP of a country's constitution, the African Commission has excused complainants from exhausting local remedies and took it upon itself to serve the purpose of a court of first instance. This was the prevailing situation in Nigeria in which the Commission decided to be seized of the *SERAC* case which it later declared admissible.[126] In the *SERAC* case, the

[122] See generally John Cantius Mubangizi, 'The Constitutional Protection of Socio-economic Rights in Selected African Countries: A Comparative Evaluation', 2 *African Journal of Legal Studies* (2006) 1; Viljoen (note 91 above) 568–85.

[123] Viljoen (note 91 above) 576.

[124] See Frans Viljoen, *International Human Rights Law in Africa* (Oxford University Press, 2007) 576. See also generally Mubangizi (note 122 above); Justice N. Nwobike, 'The African Commission on Human and Peoples' Rights and the Demystification of Second and Third Generation Rights under the African Charter: Social and Economic Rights Action Centre (SERAC) and the Centre for Economic and Social Rights (CESCR) v. Nigeria', 1 *African Journal of Legal Studies* (2005) 129–46, 140–1.

[125] See *Government of the Republic of Namibia and Others* v. *Mwilima and Others*, 2002 NR 235 (SC), para. 53.

[126] *SERAC* case (note 117 above), para. 44.

Commission commented that one of the underlying justifications behind the admissibility requirement of exhaustion of domestic remedies is the need to avoid the rendering of contradictory judgments from international and national forums.[127] Accordingly, '[w]here a right is not well provided for in domestic law such that no case is likely to be heard, potential conflict does not arise'.[128]

The problem in such cases is not so much about the lack of the substantive right itself as it is about the legal hurdle that puts the adjudication of complaints about violations of such rights beyond judicial reach. Effectively, the DPSP present an ouster of judicial jurisdiction in matters relating to the socio-economic rights in general and the human right to water in particular.

In the Nile basin, for instance, the Ugandan Constitution provides for the Ugandan state to ensure that 'all Ugandans enjoy rights and opportunities and access to . . . clean and safe water',[129] but it placed the right under the DPSP clause and thus prevented its justiciability.[130] The Ethiopian Constitution, on the other hand, seems to have provided for the human right to water but has done so, not in the Bill of Rights section (Chapter Three) but in Chapter Ten (National Policy Principles and Objectives). The relevant provision states that:

> [t]o the extent the country's resources permit, policies shall aim to provide all Ethiopians access to public health and education, clean water, housing, food and social security.[131]

The inclusion of socio-economic rights generally under the National Policy Principles and Objectives chapter of the Constitution has been taken to imply that the justiciability of such rights is removed from the purview of judicial review.[132] The human right to water, unlike the other socio-economic rights, finds no mention under the Bill of Rights chapter of the Constitution and only appears under the National Policy Principles and Objectives chapter.

[127] *Ibid.*, para. 37. [128] *Ibid.*

[129] Constitution of the Republic of Uganda (1995), DPSP XIV.

[130] See Viljoen (note 91 above) 580.

[131] Proclamation No. 1/1995, Proclamation of the Constitution of the Federal Democratic Republic of Ethiopia, *Federal Negarit Gazeta* Year 1, No. 1 (21 August 1995), Article 90(1).

[132] Viljoen (note 91 above) 580–1; Sisay Alemahu, 'The Constitutional Protection of Economic and Social Rights in the Federal Democratic Republic of Ethiopia', 22(2) *Journal of Ethiopian Law* (2008) 135–54, 141.

Thus, where domestic laws curtail judicial scrutiny of socio-economic rights provisions (and the human right to water) through a DPSP clause, the duty of exhausting local remedies is dispensed with and complainants could approach the regional mechanisms for redress. In cases where judicial power to scrutinise a human rights complaint is ousted, local remedies are said to be 'non-existent' or 'ineffective',[133] and the ensuing situation illustrates 'the futility of seeking a remedy' in the domestic courts.[134]

Other states ratify instruments such as the African Charter (and other treaties) with justiciable rights and freedoms but fail to incorporate them into the domestic legal system. Such 'incomplete internalisation' of international human rights treaties has posed a thorny problem of domestic implementation of human rights. It represents 'the prevalence of seemingly disingenuous acceptance of human rights instruments by states with poor human rights records'.[135] It has been shown that many states in Africa sign and ratify international human rights treaties without necessarily having the underlying commitment to implement the rights and freedoms domestically.[136] Heyns and Viljoen have found significant evidence in Africa – and elsewhere – of states wanting to '"jump on the bandwagon," or respond to international pressure to ratify'.[137] Domestic courts could thus find it difficult to take judicial notice of the treaties that are ratified but are not domesticated.

In other cases, the jurisdiction of the ordinary courts over the subject-matter of a complaint is ousted by domestic laws and procedures, or such jurisdiction may be given to special tribunals that are not impartial and/or competent. In such situations, local remedies are said to be unavailable.[138] Thus, while constituting domestic obstacles to the judicial and/or quasi-judicial enforcement of the human right to water, the DPSP provisions and normative incompatibility between national and international standards do not affect the applicability and justiciability of the human right to water at the regional level. It rather absolves the

[133] (Joined) Communications 105/93, 128/94, 130/94 and 152/96, *Media Rights Agenda and Others* v. *Nigeria*, 12th Annual Activity Report (1999), para. 50.

[134] *Ibid.*, para. 51.

[135] See Ryan Goodman and Derek Jinks, 'Incomplete Internalization and Compliance with Human Rights Law', 19(4) *European Journal of International Law* (2008) 725–48, 725.

[136] See generally Jean Allain and Andrea O'Shea, 'African Disunity: Comparing Human Rights Law and Practice of North and South African States', 24 *Human Rights Quarterly* (2002) 86–125.

[137] Christof Heyns and Frans Viljoen, 'The Impact of the United Nations Human Rights Treaties on the Domestic Level', 23 *Human Rights Quarterly* (2001) 483–535, 492.

[138] Jawara (note 102 above), paras. 33–4.

complainants from exhausting local remedies and allows them to access international tribunals and remedies.[139] The complainants would thus have direct access to the procedures and mechanisms of the regional human rights system.[140]

7.5.2.3 'Serious' or 'massive' violations and the human right to water

There is an established case law of the African Commission according to which victims of serious or massive violations are not required to exhaust local remedies available within the legal system of the perpetrating state. Whether the violations complained of are 'serious or massive' turns upon whether the alleged violations are of such a nature that is of 'vast and varied scope and [reflective of] the general situation' in the relevant state.[141] In the case of *Free Legal Assistance Group and Others* v. *Zaire*, the Commission ruled that the widespread arrests, detentions, extrajudicial executions, unfair trials, restrictions of press freedom, deprivation of property and access to education constituted serious and massive violations that were the order of the day in Zaire. According to the Commission, in such instances 'it is impractical or undesirable for the complainant to seize the domestic courts in the case of each violation'.[142] The Commission reiterated its position in a recent decision against Sudan, and stated that, 'where the violations involve many victims, it becomes neither practical nor desirable for the complainants or the victims to pursue such internal remedies'.[143]

Serious and massive human rights violations engender a *prima facie* presumption that domestic remedies are not available or effective.[144] In addition, as outlined above, the requirement of exhaustion of local remedies loses its *raison d'être* in cases of serious and massive violations. One of the principal justifications behind the local remedies rule is the consideration that a state must be given prior adequate notice of the complaint so that it may be able to remedy the violations. In the cases of

[139] See A. A. Oba, 'The African Charter on Human and Peoples' Rights and Ouster Clauses under the Military Regimes in Nigeria: Before and After September 11', 4 *African Human Rights Law Journal* (2004) 275–302, 301.

[140] Lilian Chenwi, 'Correcting the Historical Asymmetry between Rights: The Optional Protocol to the International Covenant on Economic, Social and Cultural Rights', 9 *African Human Rights Law Journal* (2009) 23–51, 36.

[141] *Free Legal Assistance Group* case (note 77 above), para. 37.

[142] *Ibid.*

[143] Communication 235/2000, *Dr Curtis Francis Doebbler* v. *Sudan*, 27th Annual Activity Report (2009), para. 117.

[144] Viljoen (note 124 above) 119.

serious and massive violations, the situation is too big to elude the attention of the state authorities, and its non-reparation triggers the presumption that the state condones or is unwilling to prevent, abate or remedy the violations. In the *Free Legal Assistance Group* case, the Commission stated: 'the government has had ample notice of the violation' and complainants do not need to be required to exhaust the state's local remedies.[145]

The emerging jurisprudence is of close relevance to violations of the human right to water. Where, for instance, the human right to water is violated through pollution, or construction of dams to divert such an amount of water that would cause significant harm to those who have had access to the water resources, the problem would affect thousands of victims. It would be serious in degree and massive in terms of the number of victims (to be) affected. In this age of information technology and free flow of information, it would be unlikely that states would be unaware of the situation. Indeed, more often than not, projects and activities related to the use of international rivers are the subject of a state's prior approval or are planned and undertaken by state agencies or with their permission and blessing. Inaction to remedy the situation could thus point to *prima facie* evidence of a state's complicity in the violation or unwillingness to remedy it at all.

Thus, under the 'serious and massive violations' jurisprudence of the Commission, victims of violations of the human right to water would more likely be exempt from exhausting local remedies. Violations of such scale and scope would hardly escape the attention of the media, which would bring the problems to the attention of the state authorities. In the *SERAC* case, where the Nigerian government was accused of complicity in the despoliation and destruction of water and food sources of the Ogoni people of its Niger Delta region, the Commission bypassed the local remedies rule and declared the communication admissible. It stated that the government must have been aware of the violations due to the sustained international attention given to the Ogoniland situation.[146]

It is thus relatively easier to prove that the state was duly aware of the situation and that the violations caused to the beneficiaries of the human right to water are serious and massive. Complainants of the violation of the human right to water would, in such and similar situations, be able to

[145] *Free Legal Assistance Group* case (note 77 above), para. 36.
[146] *SERAC* case (note 117 above), para. 38.

submit their cases directly to the African Commission without the need to resort to domestic remedies and procedures of the implicated state.

In conclusion, the duty to exhaust local remedies for violations of the human right to water (among other socio-economic rights) may not always be applicable. It can be excused due to the lack of the substantive right in the national legal system or remedies in cases of its violation may be unavailable, inadequate or ineffective. Or the judicial bodies may be prevented from hearing complaints based on violations of the right due to DPSP clauses.

7.6 Conclusion

This chapter completed the discussion of the third element in the tripartite jigsaw of extraterritorial application of the human right to water. Building upon the discussion in Chapters 2 and 3 that established that there is an independent human right to water (rights aspect) and against the backdrop of the analysis in Chapters 5 and 6 that established the legal bases for extraterritorial states' duties (duties aspect), the present chapter focused on individuals' and groups' access to extraterritorial remedies (remedial dimension) in cases where co-riparian states are responsible for violations of the human right to water.

The chapter has shown that the right to an extraterritorial remedy has long been in use in the field of diplomatic protection. Its extension into the field of international and regional human rights law has meant that the plaintiffs are individual claimants as opposed to states espousing their nationals' cases in the field of diplomatic protection. The defendant is still a foreign state, and the complainant-victim is still a foreigner, be it individual or group, and the types and modalities of remedies are still the same. Just as in the field of diplomatic protection, the African Charter provides for the complainant's duty to exhaust local remedies before approaching the regional mechanisms for transboundary remedies.

However, the rule admits numerous exceptions, and the domestic legal systems of African states pose numerous remedial deterrence mechanisms such that many of the transboundary complaints about the violation of the human right to water may be admissible before the regional bodies. In short, the rule may turn out to be the exception, and the exception may become the rule until states guarantee adequate and effective remedies and remove domestic obstacles to enable foreign litigants to access their domestic remedies on the same footing as their own residents. Indeed, they are obligated to bring their domestic norms into line with their Charter-based obligations. Until and unless states ensure normative compatibility between their domestic laws on the human right to water and their Charter-based undertakings, complainants seeking remedies for violations of their human right to water, just as is the case with its substantive normative basis, would base their claims on the regional human rights treaties. For the foreseeable future, the fate of the human right to water in Africa is therefore closely tied to the effectiveness of the African Charter and the work of the African Commission and Court. While this would clearly defy the principles of complementarity and subsidiarity, problems relating to the lack of a domestic substantive basis for the human right to water, possible judicial manoeuvres such as remedial equilibration, the disabling effects of DPSP provisions, foreign residents' possible lack of standing and their economic incapacity would tend to make the regional mechanism the primary forum of redress for transboundary violations of the human right to water.

8

Conclusion

> [I]t would be unconscionable to so interpret the responsibility under article 2 of the Covenant [on Civil and Political Rights] as to permit a State party to perpetrate violations of the Covenant on the territory of another State, which violations it could not perpetrate on its own territory.[1]

8.1 Introduction

Since 85 per cent of African fresh water comes from international rivers, the realisation of the human right to water depends on the volume and quality of shared water resources. Each continental African state shares a river with at least one other state. Thus a state has the capacity to hamper the realisation of the right in third states by reducing the volume or polluting the shared river unless they are legally prevented from jeopardising the right abroad. The realisation of the right to water in one state in Africa is thus extremely dependent on the conduct of third states. In other words, the right would prove an empty promise for millions of right-holders unless they are given legal avenues to hold third states accountable for their (in)actions that produce extraterritorial consequences. Unless states' use of Africa's international rivers is regulated in such a way that is sensitive to all those who share the bounty of the common river, the declaration of the human right to water by the African Commission can only flatter to deceive. Put differently, the human right to water in Africa can be violated in circumstances in which the duty-bearer is allowed to evade responsibility unless a state's human rights obligations are applied in a way that holds the state to account for the consequences its (in)activities cause abroad.

The present study examined the extraterritorial reach of the human right to water and correlative human rights duties of states in the African

[1] *Sergio Euben Lopez Burgos* v. *Uruguay*, Communication No. R.12/52 (UN Human Rights Committee), UN Doc. Supplement No. 40 (A/36/40) (1981), para. 12.3.

human rights system in light of the regional case law and comparative jurisprudence. The study of the extraterritorial application of human rights in general and the human right to water in particular has been a 'Cinderella' of international human rights law and related scholarship. The regime of international human rights law has focused thus far almost exclusively on the development of the *vertical* relationship between a state and its residents.[2] However, the exclusive emphasis placed on designing the means for a domestic state's accountability for human rights' (non-)realisations has led to a scenario in which the human rights discourse has 'totally ignored'[3] the web of states' actions and omissions that have positive or negative impacts on the fate of human rights in spaces beyond their own territory.

This book has examined the role and adequacy of the human rights framework in general and that of the African human rights system in particular for holding co-riparian states to account when their actions and omissions jeopardise the human right to water in third states. It also critically appraised states' positive duties to non-resident non-nationals. The book contended that co-riparian states have the duty not to use or allow the use of their territories in a manner that jeopardises the human right to water in co-riparian states (duty to respect). Furthermore, it argued that co-riparian states owe positive extraterritorial obligations to protect, promote and fulfil the realisation of the human right to water through their (in)actions, policies, laws and practices.

The book also highlighted that the legal basis and scope of the right to water has been extremely contentious and unsettled. Unless the debate about the legal basis and status of the human right to water is established, the analysis of related domestic states' duties would not make a logical sense and the discussion of the right's extraterritorial application will be an anomaly. As demonstrated in Chapters 2 and 3, the human right to water currently stands on a contentious legal ground and has been vying for a status and recognition similar to that accorded to the other explicitly recognised socio-economic rights. The normative terrain underlying the human right to water is thus still muddied.

Debates about the legal bases and content of the right to water have taken three divergent approaches. To some, the right lacks an explicit

[2] Sigrun Skogly and Mark Gibney, 'Introduction' in Mark Gibney and Sigrun Skogly (eds.), *Universal Human Rights and Extraterritorial Obligations* (University of Pennsylvania Press, 2010) 1, 1.

[3] *Ibid.*, 2.

and comprehensive recognition in international human rights law such that it does not exist as such. To others, it can be derived from the more explicitly guaranteed rights, including the right to health and the right to life, but its scope is limited such that it cannot be claimed except when the rights of which it is a component are threatened due to lack of an adequate quantity and quality of water. In this sense, the right to water is an auxiliary entitlement that is subservient to other explicitly protected rights, and it is dependent on the main right in the interest of which access to water is recognised. It thus lacks an independent or free-standing status, and its realisation *per se* cannot be demanded. Access to drinking and sanitation water should therefore be enveloped with other rights and claimed as such. A third approach, which is endorsed by the CESCR and the African Commission, is that which unequivocally affirms the existence of the right *per se*. This approach considers the right to water as an implied and latent component of other rights such as the right to the highest standards of physical and mental health and the right to life and personal integrity, but as a free-standing entitlement. This approach, supported in this book, relies on teleological treaty interpretation, interdependence, interrelatedness and indivisibility of human rights and is in tune with emerging state practice and the majority of related scholarship. The book argued that a close analysis of the ICESCR, the African Charter, international environmental law and international water law provides firm legal bases to found a free-standing human right to water in Africa.

As the search for and debate over the legal basis and scope of the human right to water continues to pervade academic literature, its implementation also throws up intractable, perhaps more obstinate, normative problems. The imperatives for the study of problems associated with the implementation of the human right to water and its extraterritorial application arise mainly from the scarcity of water resources, the shared nature of international rivers (which are the sources of 80 per cent of the world's fresh water) and the pattern of their geographic distribution that causes relative scarcity in many states across the world. In the African continent, due to relative water scarcity and consequent state incapacity, it would be extremely difficult for millions of people inhabiting various river basins to enjoy their right to water unless co-riparian states come to each other's aid as a matter of legal duty. Put differently, unless the right is extraterritorially applied, millions of lives would be in peril due to the lack of an adequate quantity and quality of drinking and sanitation water within the territory or under the control of their home states.

8.2 Extraterritoriality: a human rights response to water scarcity and state incapacity

Domestically, all states bear the same layers of obligations to realise the right to water. As outlined in Chapter 4, every state bears the duty to respect, protect, promote and fulfil the human right to water in its own territory. It is axiomatic that the domestic state bears the primary brunt of responsibility for realising the human rights of those in its territory and jurisdiction (vertically). After all, the home state is in principle in effective control of its territory and situations therein, and should be held responsible for human rights situations occurring in territories under its control. As a national state is normally the primary actor within its jurisdiction, domestic right-holders would turn to it for the fulfilment of their human rights guarantees or seek to hold it accountable for redressing violations.

Yet, no state can fully prevent the possible violations of human rights in its own territory that can be caused by actions or omissions of other states. A state's dependence on predominantly shared waters means that its willingness to meet its domestic human rights duties may be undermined by actions or omissions that take place in other states' territories, thereby impacting upon its capacity to meet the standards required by the four duties. This is perhaps nowhere more true than in the context of implementing the human right to water, which provides a textbook example of a right whose realisation or violation in one state can be directly and immediately enhanced or hampered by actions or omissions of other states. A co-riparian state may over-utilise, pollute or otherwise cause water shortages across borders, thereby undermining the foreign state's capacity to meet its human rights duties for domestic right-holders. In the end, the right-holders' access to drinking and sanitation water will be jeopardised.

Concerns over the implementation of individuals' and peoples' access to adequate, safe and accessible water supplies for drinking and sanitation uses therefore engender normative issues that are in many ways more complex than those that need to be tackled in the course of realising other socio-economic rights. Unlike other rights such as the right to health or housing which depend respectively upon hospitals or houses that are available within a state's territory (although the state may need foreign resources to build them), the human right to water may heavily and primarily depend upon a state's access to resources that originate outside its boundaries. The fate of the human right to water in some states could be completely dependent perennially on the (in)actions of the other co-riparian states. This is the case in numerous non-island African states that receive more than 90 per cent of their national waters from other neighbouring states. To varying degrees, each African state depends on an international river in order to realise the human right to water in its territory. The implementation of the right to water in each state would impact on or be impacted upon by (in)actions of other co-riparian states as each will control and utilise a segment of the shared water resources in their respective territories.

The two most relevant legal regimes – international water law and international (including regional) human rights law – adopt divergent regulatory approaches to alleviating the problem. As demonstrated in Chapter 6, international water law requires states to use shared waters equitably and reasonably, with a special emphasis on water needed to fulfil vital human needs (drinking and sanitation water). It also requires states to prevent the use of their territories in such a way that causes significant harm across borders. The right-holders and duty-bearers have traditionally been states themselves, while individuals and groups inhabiting these states have not been able to use international water law to claim their right to water. This statist approach does not take the analysis of the human right to water beyond the predominant *status quo*, in which states *qua* states have been the right-holders and duty-bearers in international water law.

However, now that the human right to water has made its way into the human rights vocabulary, individuals and group right-holders need to be able to claim their rights and remedies for its violation. In cases where the violations are attributable to a foreign state, the human right to water would be violated with impunity unless right-holders are given the leeway to hold the foreign state accountable for the breaches it caused across borders. This inevitably entails an extraterritorial application of the human right to water, and related state obligations. Without such, the right to water cannot be fully realised or violations thereof fully remedied as home states may not have the duty or at times the desire to take up a case on behalf of their domestic human rights victims.

A complete analysis of the extent of extraterritorial application of the human right to water – or any other right, for that matter – cannot be presented as a singular question. It is rather a bundle of triple questions involving rights, duties and remedies. Once the extraterritorial reach of the human right to water is affirmed, the issue of the spatial reach of states' duties correlative to the right makes its appearance. The violation of the human right to water (and the related duties) necessitates states' obligations to repair the transboundary injury caused by a foreign co-riparian state, calling for extraterritorial remedies. This book has therefore examined the normative bases of the extraterritorial application of the human right to water at triple but interrelated layers: the right, the duties and remedies.

8.3 The right to water and the tripartite dimensions of extraterritoriality

8.3.1 Extraterritoriality from the right's perspective

The book has demonstrated that the human right to water and its extraterritorial application find firm normative bases in international human rights law, as supplemented by international water law, international environmental law and state practice. The former has primarily provided for states' extraterritorial duties to respect, protect, promote and fulfil human rights. Similarly, individuals' and groups' positive extraterritorial human right to water, or 'vital human needs', has been explicitly guaranteed in the Watercourses Convention. The right-holders are thus allowed to enforce their rights against and seek remedies from foreign co-riparian states in relevant situations.

The 'vital human needs' proviso under Article 10(2) of the Watercourses Convention, a criterion of equitable and reasonable utilisation, prescribes that co-riparian states must give priority to allocating shared waters for drinking and sanitation purposes in each co-riparian state before any other use. This provision has thus attached an utmost importance and accorded priority to the requirement of allocating water for the realisation of the human right to water. It insulates water needed for drinking and sanitation purposes against other competing claims to water for other uses before and until the requirements of the human right to water are met. This provision is primarily applicable in water-sharing arrangements among co-riparian states for the benefit of those right-holders in their respective territories. Article 10(2) is therefore primarily extraterritorially focused, and has been designed to resolve priorities of competing uses in the territories of co-riparian states. Its scope of application is therefore transboundary.

Read in conjunction with the provisions of Article 32 of the Watercourses Convention which enjoins co-riparian states to treat all riparian populations equally in ensuring access to transboundary remedies for violations of the right to water, the 'vital human needs' provision implies that the use of shared rivers in one co-riparian state should take into consideration the realisation of the right to water in other co-riparian states. Failure on the part of co-riparian states to ensure that vital human needs are catered for in all the co-riparian states would lead to the causation of a significant harm extraterritorially. While the meaning and scope of the rule of 'no significant harm' provision of Article 7 of the Watercourses Convention is contentious, states' (in)actions that threaten the quality or quantity of water needed for drinking and sanitation in a co-riparian state would immediately threaten life and health, and almost invariably tend to cause a significant harm. Upon proof of breach of the duty of no significant harm, a state is held extraterritorially accountable for the violations its actions or commissions would cause. In such events, the relevant state would be required to remedy the extraterritorial violations attributed to its actions or commissions.

Obviously, the primary subjects of the Watercourses Convention are not individuals and groups but states. Yet, the inclusion of rights inherent in human persons with an extraterritorial reach offers a promising potential for use by human rights litigants before human rights tribunals in Africa and beyond. For its part, the African Charter has enjoined the African Commission to heed rules of international law that enhance the protection of human and peoples' rights.[4]

8.3.2 *Extraterritoriality from the states' duties perspective*

8.3.2.1 The duty of international assistance and cooperation

As illustrated in Chapter 4, the duty of international assistance and cooperation enshrined in regional and international human rights treaties imposes extraterritorial states' human rights obligations. This holds true in relation to the human right to water. As is the case with all socio-economic rights, the realisation of the human right to water is predicated on the fulfilment of states' duty of international assistance and cooperation for the purposes of resource redistribution.

Nevertheless, the implementation of the human right to water in Africa defies two related assumptions underlying economic, social and cultural rights guarantees of international and regional human rights

[4] See Articles 60 and 61 of the African Charter.

normative frameworks: first, that each state has sufficient resources at its disposal from within its own territorial space to fulfil the rights; and, secondly, each state *primarily* depends on these internal resources for the realisation of its inhabitants. As shown in Chapters 4 and 5, a state's treaty-based duty to seek international assistance and cooperation has been designed to respond to exceptional shortfalls, perhaps of a temporary nature, to top up the internally available resources. Otherwise, international human rights law is premised on the rebuttable presumption that the domestic state is able and willing to realise its human rights duties from domestic resources. The foreign state's extraterritorial duties are ones of complementary and supplementary nature. They come into play as subsidiary duties to those of the national state.

However, since there are numerous states in Africa, notably in the Nile basin, where life would be in peril without a state's access to water resources originating in other states' territories, the order of inquiry must be reversed. International cooperation and assistance are bound to provide the *primary and permanent* source of the scarce water resources to respond to domestic water rights problems.

As discussed in Chapter 4, the duty of international assistance and cooperation has been said to inhere in an unidentified international community, obscuring the identity of the duty-bearers (implementing agents). This is not the case amongst co-riparian states. Having been joined by a river, the duty-bearers are a few identifiable co-riparian states who continually depend on each other in order to realise the human right to water in their respective territories. The obligation is one that operates amongst them, and there is no problem of identifying the duty-bearers. The duty among the co-riparian states is therefore to work together continually to achieve an equitable and reasonable formulae for apportioning the shared river, and to help prevent the causation of a significant harm to right-holders in co-riparian states' territories or provide remedies if caused. In this sense, the duty of international assistance and cooperation entails each co-riparian state's duties to respect, protect, promote and fulfil the human right to water in all co-riparian states.

8.3.2.2 The Watercourses Convention and states' extraterritorial duties

As regards the human right to water, the Watercourses Convention provides for discrete extraterritorial obligations. The controlling principle of the Convention – or international water law generally – is one that requires states to use shared waters in an equitable and reasonable manner. Whether the use is equitable and reasonable is determined on the basis of the needs of the population dependent on the shared waters in each co-riparian state. Another consideration is the duty of due diligence which enjoins each co-riparian state not to cause a significant harm in co-riparian states' territories. The twin principles of international water law, i.e. the duty of equitable and reasonable utilisation and the no-significant-harm duty, are international water law's analogy of the duty of international assistance and cooperation that permeates international human rights treaties.

As demonstrated in Chapter 5, the principle of equitable utilisation imposes a duty on each co-riparian state to prioritise the vital human needs of the population in other co-riparian states' territories. Vital human needs, which correspond to the minimum core of the human right to water, must be guaranteed at all times and be fulfilled before shared waters are put to other uses. This is therefore another way of requiring foreign states to provide water for drinking and sanitation for residents of other co-riparian states. This clearly implies that a state is to be held accountable for the realisation of the human right to water in other co-riparian states, hence the duty to fulfil extraterritorially.

Stated negatively, the obligation entails the requirement that states must guarantee that their laws, policies or practices do not jeopardise access to drinking and sanitation water in other countries. Failure to do so violates another aspect of the principle of equitable and reasonable utilisation, namely, the co-riparian states' duty not to cause a significant harm to residents of other states. The 'no-significant-harm' rule is a rule of customary international law, as is the principle of equitable and reasonable utilisation, and is binding on all states. The obligations it entails or those engendered by the duty of sharing water equitably and reasonably do not depend on the state's ratification of or accession to the Watercourses Convention. As customary rules of international law, they apply irrespective of consent, denying any African state – or any other non-state party – the possibility to evade responsibility on the ground that it is not a party to the Watercourses Convention. These duties thus entail extraterritorial duties to respect, protect and fulfil the human right to water. They lead to extraterritorial remedies, primarily in the implicated state's local or administrative tribunals, but also, once such remedies are exhausted or prove unavoidable, ineffective or inadequate, in international tribunals such as the African regional bodies.

8.3.3 *Remedial extraterritoriality*

The extraterritorial human right to water and attendant state obligations are incomplete unless the breaches of the right and of related duties entail the right-holders' access to remedies and the foreign violator's duty to repair the injury caused by the violation. However, the fact that the extraterritorial application of human rights has been generally ignored thus far means that the right to extraterritorial remedies has not often been sought by the victims of rights violations. The attendant duties and associated procedures have been ignored.

As this book demonstrated in Chapter 6, the human rights regime and international water law provide for extraterritorial remedies for violations of the human right to water. Under Article 32 of the Watercourses Convention, transboundary victims of violations of the human right to water are allowed to access the domestic judicial and administrative bodies of a co-riparian state whose omissions or commissions posed a threat to the right to water or caused actual breaches across borders. A co-riparian state is therefore bound to provide adequate and effective remedies for extraterritorial victims of its actions or omissions.

Under the Watercourses Convention, the implicated state's duty is to treat extraterritorial complainants on an equal footing with national complainants of violations of the human right to water. Article 32 therefore is effectively a procedural norm, intending to prohibit co-riparian states from discriminating against complainants of human rights violations on the grounds of nationality, place of residence or of injury. To this extent, it is an extraterritorial duty on the part of a state to allow foreign complainants to access its domestic judicial, quasi-judicial or administrative bodies and procedures capable of remedying the effect of extraterritorial violations attributable to the particular state.

The procedural nature of a co-riparian state's duty of equal treatment of residents and non-residents can only go halfway in resolving access by transboundary complaints to extraterritorial remedies. It does not provide for the nature and scope of remedies that a state must make available to the foreign complainants, or to its own residents for that matter. Indeed, it is silent about a state's duty to provide remedies for violations of the human right to water at all. It does not go beyond the requirement of according national treatment to foreign victims in relation to access to its domestic remedies, if and when available. A state is not required, therefore, to ensure that its legal system provides for the right to remedies for violations of the human right to water.

However, so long as the substantive right, such as the human right to water, is provided for in the legal system, the principle of *ubi jus ubi remedium* implies that the state's duty to provide remedies for a violation of the right is self-evident. Given a right, a remedy for its breach is merely a corollary. Nevertheless, the fact that the human right to water is emerging from obscurity has entailed that some states do not provide for the right in their domestic legal system, and, consequently, their domestic system may be devoid of remedies for violations thereof. Individuals' and groups' right to water in those jurisdictions may spring from the state's ratification of the African Charter or of the ICESCR. In those cases, national laws may not be of direct relevance for the domestic right-holders; much less so for the foreign complainants. There is thus an inherent limit to the right to a remedy under the Watercourses Convention.

This remedial gap has been alleviated by the provisions of the African Charter which allow transboundary complainants (and domestic right-holders alike) to seek domestic remedies in the implicated state's judicial and administrative systems. As in the Watercourses Convention, Article 56(5) of the Charter requires complaints to exhaust locally available remedies before resorting to the regional human rights tribunals and associated remedies. Unlike Article 32 of the Watercourses Convention, however, the Charter and the jurisprudence of the African Commission require a state to enshrine in its laws remedies that are effective and adequate. Where such remedies are unavailable or prove ineffective or inadequate to remedy the violations complained of, the victims would be excused from the duty to exhaust local remedies in the implicated state and may bring their case before the African Commission in search of international remedies.

The upshot of the analysis is that the right to extraterritorial remedies for transboundary violations of the human right to water can be found in the combined use of the rules of the Watercourses Convention and the norms of the African human rights system. Effective access to transboundary remedies in the context of the human right to water requires, therefore, that a transboundary complainant or litigant would have to coordinate the rules of the Watercourses Convention and the regional human rights treaties that are capable of complementing each other.

8.4 Extraterritoriality and questions of attribution

One of the biggest hurdles in the extraterritorial application of human rights in general and the human right to water in particular is the 'jurisdiction' clauses of some human rights treaties. At first sight, these clauses give the impression that a complainant alleging human rights violations should show that they were in an implicated state's jurisdiction at the time of the violation. Conversely, states have used 'jurisdiction clauses' as a means of limiting their human rights obligations to their own territories. As seen in the *Bankovic* case before the European Court of Human Rights, seventeen European states have relied on the jurisdiction clause in Article 1 of the European Convention on Human Rights in order to evade liability for killing and injuring persons via a NATO air raid which took place outside the European legal space. The American Convention on Human Rights contains a similar provision on jurisdiction.

The African Charter is diametrically opposed in this regard. It does not provide for a jurisdiction clause, and arguably its application is not limited to the territory of a state whose actions or omissions are said to have caused violations of human rights extraterritorially. Indeed, the African Commission has never required complainants to show that a victim was in an implicated state's territory or jurisdiction for the purpose of holding states extraterritorially responsible. As demonstrated in Chapter 5, no state that has been called before the Commission has heretofore objected to its extraterritorial duties as long as the link between its actions or omissions and the violations are proven. The *DRC Invasion* case and the *Burundi Embargo* case provide stark examples.

In this regard, the spatial reach of the African Charter guarantees is analogous to those of the ICESCR and the American Declaration on the Rights and Duties of Man, which are devoid of a 'jurisdiction' clause. As discussed in Chapter 5, both the ICESCR and the American Declaration have been interpreted to imply extraterritorial duties of states by their respective monitoring bodies. Interestingly, therefore, neither the African Charter nor the ICESCR (which is the main inspirational source of the human right to water and its implementation in Africa) provide for territorially bound states' duties, opening the leeway for a principled argument that they apply extraterritorially. A territorial approach to most of the socio-economic rights, especially the human right to water, would have given states a free hand to violate human rights through their commissions or omissions in other co-riparian states.

Even in the other regional human rights systems where the main treaties provide for 'jurisdiction' as a causal link between states' duties and their extraterritorial obligations, the term has not been applied strictly. The jurisprudence emerging from the European and Inter-American bodies demonstrates that the jurisdiction clause of these regional treaties is not taken at face value. The term 'jurisdiction' has been given a purposive interpretation. In both the European and the Inter-American human rights systems, the emerging jurisprudence has shown similar traits in their approach to the understanding of the term 'jurisdiction'. In both regional systems, control over the territory of another state, over an individual therein, or states' acquiescence to extraterritorial responsibility have been taken as sufficient juridical links to bring the victims within a state's jurisdiction for the purpose of holding the relevant state accountable for its role in human rights violations. Similarly, violations of the principle of *non-refoulement* and extraditing persons to territories in which their rights would foreseeably be violated has been held to entail a state's extraterritorial responsibility for the violations that would ensue outside its territory. While a violation of the *non-refoulement* principle is a territorial violation of a person's right, the violation of the person's rights in the receiving state, to the extent it was foreseeable before his or her extradition, entails the extra-territorial liability of the extraditing state for facilitating such violations in spaces beyond its own.

The European and Inter-American regional case law and principles are among the sources of inspiration for the African human rights system under Articles 60 and 61 of the African Charter. As shown in Chapters 2 and 5, the African Commission has explicitly and repeatedly relied on the case law of the other regional systems. Regarding the subject of extraterritoriality, as outlined in Chapter 5, the African Commission has accordingly followed the approach of the European and Inter-American case law in attributing state responsibility for violating human rights in a territory controlled by a state's army (the *DRC Invasion* case) or when states have failed to raise objections to being held extraterritorially responsible (the *Burundi Embargo* case). Thus, the term 'jurisdiction', whenever applicable, is not interpreted literally. To the extent that states violate the human right to water in territories under their control, or in relation to persons under their control, the violations are deemed to have been committed within their jurisdiction. Individuals could therefore enforce their rights against the foreign state whose actions or omissions caused the violations of their right to water.

Be that as it may, possible extraterritorial violations of the human right to water could, more often than not, result from the actions or omissions of a state that take place in the culprit state's own territory.

A state may utilise international rivers inequitably and unreasonably, or pollute them within its own territory. The resultant violations would thus be felt elsewhere in the co-riparian states. Indeed, within the existing case law, those cases relating to *non-refoulement* seem to provide a close analogy to violations of the human right to water. A state's inequitable or unreasonable use of an international river fairly foreseeably causes violations of the human right to water abroad. The actions or omissions are territorial, while the effects would be transboundary. Just as in cases where a state is held extraterritorially responsible for extraditing an individual where his or her human rights would predictably be violated, the use of international water resources in a state's territory in a manner or to an extent that jeopardises the human rights of those dependent on the river along its continuum is a clearly foreseeable result. This would trigger a state's extraterritorial responsibility for the violation of the human right to water in other co-riparian states. Thus defences based on the site of an injury, or individuals' or groups' nationality, cannot be maintained against a claim of extraterritorial violations of the human right to water as long as the causal relationship between a state's commission or omission and the violation of the right abroad is established.

8.5 Conclusion

The core concern of this book is that, in Africa, the mere recognition of access to water for drinking and sanitation purposes may prove an inadequate guarantee for the realisation of the right for the right-holders. The human right to water in Africa cannot be realised for millions of people inhabiting various river basins unless the human rights regime acknowledges the constraints of some domestic states' capacities and extends the duties of other states to help realise the right for those beyond its borders. The search for legal avenues for ensuring the extraterritorial application of the human right to water is thus an issue that is extremely pressing and urgent. In this vein, this book has evaluated the role of the human rights framework in the distribution of shared resources in the realisation of the human right to water with a particular focus on the situation in Africa.

This study demonstrated that there is an adequate legal basis for the human right to water, and the extraterritorial application of the correlative state duties and related remedies. Unlike the treaties on civil and political rights, the socio-economic rights treaties, including the African

Charter, do not limit a state's human rights duties to its territory or jurisdiction. There is therefore an inadequately explored and underutilised potential in the regimes of international human rights law and international water law for the extraterritorial application of the human right to water, attendant state duties and relevant remedies.

However, the scope of the study leaves space for further research. This book has been confined to the analysis of the extraterritorial application of the human right to water in relation to water resources of the international rivers (primarily) of the African continent. The study of waters of shared rivers leaves aside problems of transboundary violations of the human right to water caused by a state's use of transboundary aquifers or its contribution to climate change, among others, which have yet to be analysed. The book analysed the duties of co-riparian states, leaving room for the study of the duties of non-riparian states and non-state actors such as intergovernmental organisations, multinational companies and NGOs in the realisation of the human right to water. Moreover, the present study has focused exclusively on the sharing of wet water, but the extraterritorial impacts of virtual water transfers on the realisation of the human right to water deserve a study in their own right. In effect, the book has merely uncovered the tip of the iceberg of the much broader problem of extraterritorial application of the human right to water. In the face of the worsening reality wherein millions of lives are lost every year due to preventable water quality and quantity problems caused by transboundary actors, the need for further analysis of the wider problem of extraterritorial harms to water rights and means of curbing their effects cannot be over-emphasised. Time is running out, as is water.

BIBLIOGRAPHY

Books and articles

Abi-Saab, Georges, 'The Legal Formulation of the Right to Development' in Rene-Jean Dupuy (ed.), *The Right to Development at the International Level, Workshop of the Hague Academy of International Law 1979* (Sijthoff and Noordhoff, 1980) 159

Achebe, Chinua, *Arrow of God* (Heinemann Ltd, 1989)

Agbakwa, Shadrack, 'A Line in the Sand: International (Dis)order and the Impunity of Non-State Corporate Actors in the Developing World' in Antony Anghie *et al.* (eds.), *The Third World and International Disorder: Law, Politics and Globalization* (Martinus Nijhoff Publishers, 2003) 1

Albuquerque, Catarina de, 'Climate Change and the Human Rights to Water and Sanitation' (Position Paper of the Independent Expert on the Issue of Human Rights Obligations Related to Access to Safe Drinking Water and Sanitation, 2010)

Alemahu, Sisay, 'The Constitutional Protection of Economic and Social Rights in the Federal Democratic Republic of Ethiopia', 22(2) *Journal of Ethiopian Law* (2008) 135

Allain, Jean, and Andrea O'Shea, 'African Disunity: Comparing Human Rights Law and Practice of North and South African States', 24 *Human Rights Quarterly* (2002) 86

Alston, Philip, 'The Purposes of Reporting' in *Manual on Human Rights Reporting under Six Major International Human Rights Instruments* (United Nations, 1997)

Alston, Philip, and Gerard Quinn, 'The Nature and Scope of States Parties' Obligations under the International Covenant on Economic, Social and Cultural Rights', 9 *Human Rights Quarterly* (1987) 156

Amdetsion, Fasil, 'Scrutinizing the Scorpion Problematique: Arguments in Favor of the Continued Relevance of International Law and a Multidisciplinary Approach to Resolving the Nile Dispute', 44(1) *Texas International Law Journal* (2009) 1

Anonymous, 'Constructing the State Extraterritorially: Jurisdictional Discourse, the National Interest, and Transnational Norms', 103 *Harvard Law Review* (1990) 1273

Anyangwe, Carlson, 'Obligations of State Parties to the African Charter on Human and Peoples' Rights', 10(4) *African Journal of International and Comparative Law* (1998) 625

Arsano, Yacob, *Ethiopia and the Nile: Dilemmas of National and Regional Hydropolitics* (Center for Security Studies, Swiss Federal Institute of Technology, 2007)

'Towards Conflict Prevention in the Nile Basin' (Paper presented at the 5th Nile 2002 Conference, 1997)

Arsano, Yacob, and Imeru Tamrat, 'Ethiopia and the Eastern Nile Basin', 67 *Aquatic Sciences* (2005) 15

Ashton, Peter J., 'Avoiding Conflicts over Africa's Water Resources', 31(3) *Ambio* (2002) 236

Ayeb, Habib, 'Hydraulic Politics: The Nile and Egypt's Water Use: A Crisis for the Twenty-First Century?' in *Counter-Revolutions in Egypt's Countryside: Land Reform in the Era of Economic Reform* (Zed Books, 2002)

Bakker, Karen, 'The "Commons" Versus the "Commodity": Alter-Globalization, Anti-Privatization and the Human Right to Water in the Global South', 39 (3) *Antipode* (2007) 430

Barak-Erez, Daphne, and Aeyal M. Gross, 'Introduction: Do We Need Social Rights? Questions in the Era of Globalisation, Privatisation, and the Diminished Welfare State' in Daphne Barak-Erez and Aeyal M. Gross (eds.), *Exploring Social Rights: Between Theory and Practice* (Hart Publishing, 2007) 3

Barlow, Maude, and Tony Clarke, *Blue Gold: The Battle against Corporate Theft of the World's Water* (The New Press, 2002)

Baxi, Upendra, *Human Rights in a Posthuman World: Critical Essays* (Oxford University Press, 2007)

Beaumont, Peter, 'The 1997 UN Convention on the Law of Non-Navigational Uses of International Watercourses: Its Strengths and Weaknesses from a Water Management Perspective and the Need for New Workable Guidelines', 16(4) *International Journal of Water Resources Development* (2000) 475

Bedi, Shiv R. S., *The Development of Human Rights Law by the Judges of the International Court of Justice* (Hart Publishing, 2007)

Benvenisti, Eyal, 'Collective Action in the Utilization of Shared Freshwater: The Challenges of International Water Resource Law', 90 *American Journal of International Law* (1996) 384

Bertagna, Blake R., '"Standing" up for the Environment: The Ability of Plaintiffs to Establish Legal Standing to Redress Injuries Caused by Global Warming', *Brigham Young University Law Review* (2006) 415

Birnie, Patricia W., Alan E. Boyle and Catherine Redgwell, *International Law and the Environment* (Oxford University Press, 3rd edn, 2009)

Bourne, Charles B., 'The International Law Association's Contribution to International Water Resources Law' in Patricia Wouters (ed.), *International Water Law: Selected Writings of Professor Charles B. Bourne* (Kluwer Law International, 1997) 233

'The International Law Commission's Draft Articles on the Law of International Watercourses: Principles and Planned Measures', 3 *Colorado Journal of International Environmental Law and Policy* (1992) 65

'The Primacy of the Principle of Equitable Utilisation in the 1997 Watercourses Convention', *Canadian Yearbook of International Law* (1997) 215

Bourquain, Knut, *Freshwater Access from a Human Rights Perspective: A Challenge to International Water Law and Human Rights Law* (Martinus Nijhoff Publishers, 2008)

Boyle, Kevin, 'Stock-taking on Human Rights: The World Conference on Human Rights, Vienna 1993', 43(1) *Political Studies* (1995) 79

Brownlie, Ian, *Principles of Public International Law* (Oxford University Press, 7th edn, 2008)

Bulto, Takele Soboka, 'Between Ambivalence and Necessity: Occlusions on the Path Towards a Basin-Wide Treaty in the Nile Basin', 20(1) *Colorado Journal of International Environmental Law and Policy* (2009) 291

'The Emergence of the Human Right to Water in International Human Rights Law: Invention or Discovery?', 12(2) *Melbourne Journal of International Law* (2011) 290–314

'The Indirect Approach to Promote Justiciability of Socio-Economic Rights of the African Charter on Human and Peoples' Rights' in Rachel H. Murray (ed.), *Human Rights Litigation and the Domestication of International Human Rights in Sub-Saharan Africa* (International Commission of Jurists, 2009) 135

'The Utility of Cross-Cutting Rights in Enhancing Justiciability of Socio-Economic Rights in the African Charter on Human and Peoples' Rights', 29(2) *University of Tasmania Law Review* (2010) 142

Caflisch, Lucius, 'Regulation of Uses of International Watercourses' in Salman M. A. Salman and Laurence Boisson de Chazournes (ed.), *International Watercourses: Enhancing Cooperation and Managing Conflict: Proceedings of a World Bank Seminar* (World Bank, 1998) 3

Cahill, Amanda, 'Protecting Rights in the Face of Scarcity: The Right to Water' in Mark Gibney and Sigrun Skogly (eds.), *Universal Human Rights and Extraterritorial Obligations* (University of Pennsylvania Press, 2010) 194

'"The Human Right to Water – A Right of Unique Status": The Legal Status and Normative Content of the Right to Water', 9(3) *International Journal of Human Rights* (2005) 389

Cahill-Ripley, Amanda, *The Human Right to Water and Its Application in the Occupied Palestinian Territories* (Routledge, 2011)

Caponera, Dante A., 'Shared Waters and International Law' in Gerald H. Blake *et al.* (eds.), *The Peaceful Management of Transboundary Resources* (Graham & Trotman, 1995) 121

Carmona Sepúlveda, Magdalena, 'The Obligation of "International Assistance and Cooperation" under the International Covenant on Economic, Social and Cultural Rights: A Possible Entry Point to a Human Rights Based Approach to Millennium Development Goal 8', 13(1) *International Journal of Human Rights* (2009) 86

Carozza, Paolo G., 'Subsidiarity as a Structural Principle of International Human Rights Law', 97 *American Journal of International Law* (2003) 38

Cassel, Douglass, 'Extraterritorial Application of Inter-American Human Rights Instruments' in Fons Coomans and Menno T. Kamminga (eds.), *Extraterritorial Application of Human Rights Treaties* (Intersentia, 2004) 175

Cerna, Christina M., 'Extraterritorial Application of the Human Rights Instruments of the Inter-American System' in Fons Coomans, and Menno T. Kamminga (eds.), *Extraterritorial Application of Human Rights Treaties* (Intersentia, 2004) 141

Cerone, John, 'Out of Bounds? Considering the Reach of International Human Rights Law' (Center for Human Rights and Global Justice Working Paper, New York University School of Law, 2006)

Chapagaina, Ashok K., and Arjen Y. Hoekstrab, 'The Global Component of Freshwater Demand and Supply: An Assessment of Virtual Water Flows between Nations as a Result of Trade in Agricultural and Industrial Products', 33(1) *Water International* (2008) 19

Chapman, Audrey R., and Sage Russell, 'Introduction' in Sage Russell and Audrey R. Chapman (eds.), *Core Obligations: Building a Framework for Economic, Social and Cultural Rights* (Intersentia, 2002) 3

Charney, Jonathan I., 'Universal International Law', 87 *American Journal of International Law* (1993) 529

Chauhan, B. R., *Settlement of International Water Law Disputes in International Drainage Basins*, Wasserrecht und Wassserwirtschaft (Erich Schmidt Verlag, 1981)

Chayes, Abram, 'The Role of the Judge in Public Law Litigation', 89(7) *Harvard Law Review* (1976) 1281

Chenwi, Lilian, 'Correcting the Historical Asymmetry between Rights: The Optional Protocol to the International Covenant on Economic, Social and Cultural Rights', 9 *African Human Rights Law Journal* (2009) 23

Chirwa, Danwood Mzikenge, 'The Doctrine of State Responsibility as a Potential Means of Holding Private Actors Accountable for Human Rights', 5 *Melbourne Journal of International Law* (2004) 1

Clapham, Andrew, *Human Rights Obligations of Non-State Actors* (Oxford University Press, 2006)

'Symbiosis in International Human Rights Law: The Öcalan Case and the Evolving Law on the Death Sentence', 1 *Journal of International Criminal Justice* (2003) 475

Collins, Robert O., *The Nile* (Yale University Press, 2002)

Colson, David A., 'How Persistent Must the Persistent Objector Be?', 61 *Washington Law Review* (1986) 957

Coomans, Fons, 'Some Remarks on the Extraterritorial Application of the International Covenant on Economic, Social and Cultural Rights' in Fons Coomans and Menno T. Kamminga (eds.), *Extraterritorial Application of Human Rights Treaties* (Intersentia, 2004) 183

'The Extraterritorial Scope of the International Covenant on Economic, Social and Cultural Rights in the Work of the United Nations Committee on Economic, Social and Cultural Rights', 11(1) *Human Rights Law Review* (2011) 1

Coomans, Fons, and Menno T. Kamminga, 'Comparative Introductory Comments on the Extraterritorial Application of Human Rights Treaties' in Fons Coomans and Menno T. Kamminga (eds.), *Extraterritorial Application of Human Rights Treaties* (Intersentia 2004) 1

Craven, Matthew, 'Legal Differentiation and the Concept of the Human Rights Treaty in International Law', 11(3) *European Journal of International Law* (2000) 489

'Some Thoughts on the Emergent Right to Water' in Eibe Riedel and Peter Rothen (eds.), *The Human Right to Water* (Berliner Wissenschafts-Verlag GmbH, 2006) 37

'The International Covenant on Economic, Social and Cultural Rights' in Raija Hanski and Markku Suksi (eds.), *An Introduction to the International Protection of Human Rights: A Textbook* (Institute for Human Rights, Abo Akademi University, 2nd reprinted edn, 2002) 101

The International Covenant on Economic, Social, and Cultural Rights: A Perspective on Its Development (Clarendon Press, 1995)

'The Violence of Dispossession: Extra-Territoriality and Economic, Social and Cultural Rights' in A. Mashood and Robert McCorquodale Baderin (eds.), *Economic, Social and Cultural Rights in Action* (Oxford University Press, 2007) 71

Dankwa, Victor, Cees Flinterman and Scott Leckie, 'Commentary to the Maastricht Guidelines on Violations of Economic, Social and Cultural Rights', 20 *Human Rights Quarterly* (1998) 705

Deva, Surya, 'Acting Extraterritorially to Tame Multinational Corporations for Human Rights Violations: Who Should "Bell the Cat"?', 5 *Melbourne Journal of International Law* (2004) 37

Douzinas, Costas, *The End of Human Rights: Critical Legal Thought at the Turn of the Century* (Hart Publishing, 2007)

Dupuy, Pierre-Marie, 'Reviewing the Difficulties of Codification: On Ago's Classification of Obligations of Means and Obligations of Result in Relation to State Responsibility', 10(2) *European Journal of International Law* (1999) 371

Eide, Asbjørn, 'Realization of Social and Economic Rights and the Minimum Threshold Approach', 10(1–2) *Human Rights Law Journal* (1989) 35

'The International Human Rights System' in Asbjørn Eide *et al.* (eds.), *Food As a Human Right* (United Nations University, 1984) 152

El-Jazairi, Lara, 'Policies of Denial: Lack of Access to Water in the West Bank' (Centre on Housing Rights and Evictions (COHRE), 2008)

Elhance, Arun P., 'Hydropolities: Grounds for Despair, Reasons for Hope', 5 *International Negotiation* (2000) 201

Hydropolitics in the Third World: Conflict and Cooperation in International River Basins (United States Institute of Peace Press, 1999)

Erlich, Haggai, *The Cross and the River: Ethiopia, Egypt, and the Nile* (Lynne Rienner Publishers, 2002)

Evans, Malcolm D., 'State Responsibility and the European Convention on Human Rights: Role and Realm' in Malgosia Fitzmaurice and Dan Sarooshi (eds.), *Issues of State Responsibility before International Judicial Institutions* (Hart Publishing, 2004) 139

Fallon, Richard H., Jr, 'The Linkage between Justiciability and Remedies – And Their Connections to Substantive Rights', 92 *Virginia Law Review* (2006) 633

Farer, Tom, '"Bombing for Peace: Collateral Damage and Human Rights": Remarks by Tom Farer', 96 *American Society of International Law Proceedings* (2002) 104

Fawcett, J. E. S., 'The Exhaustion of Local Remedies: Substance or Procedure?', 31 *British Year Book of International Law* (1954) 452

Foster, Michelle, *International Refugee Law and Socio-Economic Rights: Refuge from Deprivation* (Cambridge University Press, 2007)

Francioni, Francesco, 'Alternative Perspectives on International Responsibility for Human Rights Violations by Multinational Corporations' in Wolfgang Benedek, Koen de Feyter and Fabrizio Marrella (eds.), *Economic Globalisation and Human Rights* (Cambridge University Press, 2007) 245

Fredman, Sandra, *Human Rights Transformed: Positive Rights and Positive Duties* (Oxford University Press, 2008)

French, Duncan, 'Treaty Interpretation and the Incorporation of Extraneous Rules', 55 *International and Comparative Law Quarterly* (2006) 281

Fuentes, Ximena, 'The Criteria for the Equitable Utilization of International Rivers', 67 *British Year Book of International Law* (1996) 337

Gallob, Joel A., 'Birth of the North American Plaintiff: Transboundary Pollution and the 1979 Draft Treaty for Equal Access and Remedy', 15 *Harvard Environmental Law Review* (1991) 85

Getches, David H., *Water Law* (West Publishing Co., 1997)

Gewirth, Alan, 'Are There Any Absolute Rights?' in Jeremy Waldron (ed.), *Theories of Rights* (Oxford University Press, 1984) 91

Gibney, Mark, 'Book Review: Extraterritorial Application of Human Rights Treaties, Edited by Coomans and Kamminga', 100 *American Journal of International Law* (2006) 282

Gibney, Mark, Katarina Tomaseviski and Jens Vedsted-Hansen, 'Transnational State Responsibility for Violations of Human Rights', 12 *Harvard Human Rights Journal* (1999) 267

Girma, Amare, 'Nile Issue: The Imperative Need for Negotiation on the Utilization of Nile Waters' in *Occasional Papers*, Vol. 2, No. 6 (Ethiopian International Institute for Peace and Development (EIIPD)), 1997)

Gleick, Peter H., 'The Human Right to Water', 1(5) *Water Policy* (1998) 487

Godana, Bonaya Adhi, *Africa's Shared Water Resources: Legal and Institutional Aspects of the Nile, Niger, and Senegal River Systems* (Lynne Rienner Publications Inc., 1985)

Goldberg, David, 'World Bank Policy on Projects on International Waterways in the Context of Emerging International Law and the Work of the International Law Commission' in Gerald H. Blake *et al.* (eds.), *The Peaceful Management of Transboundary Resources* (Graham & Trotman, 1995) 153

Gondek, Michal, 'Extraterritorial Application of the European Convention on Human Rights: Territorial Focus in the Age of Globalisation?', 52(3) *Netherlands International Law Review* (2005) 349

The Reach of Human Rights in a Globalising World: Extraterritorial Application of Human Rights Treaties (Intersentia, 2009)

Goodman, Ryan, and Derek Jinks, 'Incomplete Internalization and Compliance with Human Rights Law', 19(4) *European Journal of International Law* (2008) 725

Goodwin-Gill, Guy S., 'Obligations of Conduct and Result' in P. Alston and K. Tomaseviski (eds.), *The Right to Food* (Martinus Nijhoff Publishers, 1984) 111

Gorsboth, Maike, 'Identifying and Addressing Violations of the Human Right to Water: Applying the Human Rights Approach' (Brot fur die Welt (Bread for the World), 2006)

Gross, Aeyal M., 'The Right to Health in an Era of Privatisation and Globalisation: National and International Perspectives' in Daphne Barak-Erez and Aeyal M. Gross (eds.), *Exploring Social Rights: Between Theory and Practice* (Hart Publishing, 2007) 289

Halpin, A. K. W., 'Hohfeld's Conceptions: From Eight to Two', 44(3) *Cambridge Law Journal* (1985) 435

Handl, Günther, 'The International Law Commission's Draft Articles on the Law of International Watercourses (General Principles and Planned Measures): Progressive or Retrogressive Development of International Law?', 3 *Colorado Journal of International Environmental Law and Policy* (1992) 123

'Transboundary Impacts' in Daniel Bodansky, Jutta Brunnee and Ellen Hey (eds.), *The Oxford Handbook of International Environmental Law* (Oxford University Press, 2007) 531

Happold, Matthew, 'Bankovic v. Belgium and the Territorial Scope of the European Convention on Human Rights', 3 *Human Rights Law Review* (2003) 77

Hardberger, Amy, 'Whose Job Is It Anyway? Governmental Obligations Created by the Human Rights to Water', 41 *Texas International Law Journal* (2006) 533

Hayward, Keith, 'Supplying Basin-Wide Reforms with an Independent Assessment Applying International Water Law: Case Study of the Dnieper River', 18(3) *Colorado Journal of International Environmental Law and Policy* (2007) 633

Hazelzet, Hadewych *et al.*, 'Conclusions – New Human Rights Duty-Bearers: A Conversation on Policy Implications' in Margot E. Salomon, Arne Tostensen and Wouter Vandenhole (eds.), *Casting the Net Wider: Human Rights, Development and New Duty-Bearers* (Intersentia, 2007) 395

Henkin, Louis, *The Rights of Man Today* (Stevens, 1979)

Hey, Ellen, 'Sustainable Use of Shared Water Resources: The Need for a Paradigm Shift in International Watercourses Law' in Gerald H. Blake *et al.* (eds.), *The Peaceful Management of Transboundary Resources* (Graham & Trotman, 1995) 127

'The Watercourses Convention: To What Extent Does It Provide a Basis for Regulating Uses of International Watercourses?', 7(3) *Review of European Community and International Environmental Law* (1998) 291

Heyns, Christof, 'Civil and Political Rights in the African Charter' in Malcolm Evans and Rachel Murray (eds.), *The African Charter on Human and Peoples' Rights: The System in Practice, 1986–2000* (Cambridge University Press, 2002) 137

'The African Regional Human Rights System: In Need of Reform?', 2 *African Human Rights Law Journal* (2001) 155

'The African Regional Human Rights System: The African Charter', 108 *Penn State Law Review* (2004) 679

Heyns, Christof, and Waruguru Kaguongo, 'Constitutional Human Rights Law in Africa', 22(4) *South African Journal on Human Rights* (2006) 673

Heyns, Christof, and Frans Viljoen, 'The Impact of the United Nations Human Rights Treaties on the Domestic Level', 23 *Human Rights Quarterly* (2001) 483

The Impact of the United Nations Human Rights Treaties on the Domestic Level (Kluwer Law International, 2002)

Higgins, Rosalyn, 'A Babel of Judicial Voices? Ruminations from the Bench', 55 *International and Comparative Law Quarterly* (2006) 791

Problems and Processes: International Law and How We Use It (Oxford University Press, 1995)

Hirji, Rafik, and David Grey, 'Managing International Waters in Africa: Process and Progress' in Salman M. A. Salman and Laurence Boisson de Chazournes (eds.), *International Watercourses: Enhancing Cooperation and Managing Conflict: Proceedings of a World Bank Seminar* (World Bank, 1998) 77

Hohfeld, Wesley Newcomb, *Fundamental Legal Conceptions As Applied in Judicial Reasoning and Other Legal Essays* (Yale University Press, 1923)

Hoof, Fried van, 'International Human Rights Obligations for Companies and Domestic Courts: An Unlikely Combination?' in Monique Castermans-Holleman, Fried van Hoof and Jaqueline Smith (eds.), *The Role of the Nation-State in the 21st Century: Human Rights, International Organisations and Foreign Policy – Essays in Honour of Peter Baehr* (Kluwer Law International, 1998) 47

Hu, Desheng, *Water Rights: An International and Comparative Study* (IWA Publishing, 2006)

Huang, Ling-Yee, 'Not Just Another Drop in the Human Rights Bucket: The Legal Significance of a Codified Human Right to Water', 20 *Florida Journal of International Law* (2008) 353

Humphreys, Stephen, 'Competing Claims: Human Rights and Climate Changes' in Stephen Humphreys and Mary Robinson (eds.), *Human Rights and Climate Change* (Cambridge University Press, 2010) 37

Hunt, Constance D., 'Implementation: Joint Institutional Management and Remedies in Domestic Tribunals (Articles 26–28 and 30–32)', 3 *Colorado Journal of International Environmental Law and Policy* (1992) 281

Hunt, Paul, and Rajat Khosla, 'Climate Change and the Right to the Highest Attainable Standard of Health' in Stephen Humphreys and Mary Robinson (eds.), *Human Rights and Climate Change* (Cambridge University Press, 2010) 238

Jennings, R. Y., 'Treaties' in Mohammed Bedjaoui (ed.), *International Law: Achievements and Prospects* (UNESCO, 1991) 135

Kalin, Walter, and Jorg Kunzli, *The Law of International Human Rights Protection* (Oxford University Press, 2009)

Kamchibekova, Damira, 'State Responsibility for Extraterritorial Human Rights Violations', 13 *Buffalo Human Rights Law Review* (2007) 87

Kaye, Stuart, 'Threats from the Global Commons: Problems of Jurisdiction and Enforcement', 8(1) *Melbourne Journal of International Law* (2007) 185

Knauth, Arnold W., 'Uses of the Waters of International Rivers Report', 48 *International Law Association Reports of Conferences* (1959) 19

Knox, John H., 'Climate Change and Human Rights', 50(1) *Virginia Journal of International Law* (2009) 164

'Diagonal Environmental Rights' in Mark Gibney and Sigrun Skogly (ed.), *Universal Human Rights and Extraterritorial Obligations* (University of Pennsylvania Press, 2010) 82

'The Myth and Reality of Transboundary Environmental Impact Assessment', 96 *American Journal of International Law* (2002) 291

Kok, Anton, and Malcolm Langford, 'The Right to Water' in Danie Brand and Christof Heyns (eds.), *Socio-Economic Rights in South Africa* (Pretoria University Law Press, 2005) 191

Korsah-Brown, Douglas, 'Environment, Human Rights and Mining Conflicts in Ghana' in Lyuba Zarsky (ed.), *Human Rights and the Environment: Conflicts and Norms in a Globalizing World* (Earthscan Publications Ltd, 2002) 79

Kraemer, John D., Dhrubajyoti Bhattacharya and Lawrence O. Gostin, 'Blocking Humanitarian Assistance: A Crime against Humanity?', 372(4) *The Lancet* (2008) 1203

Kumm, Mattias, 'The Legitimacy of International Law: A Constitutionalist Framework of Analysis', 15(5) *European Journal of International Law* (2004) 907

Kunnemann, Rolf, 'Extraterritorial Application of the International Covenant on Economic, Social and Cultural Rights' in Fons Coomans and Menno T. Kamminga (eds.), *Extraterritorial Application of Human Rights Treaties* (Intersentia, 2004) 201

Kunnemann, Rolf, and Sandra Ratjen, 'Extraterritorial Obligations: A Response to Globalization' in George Kent (ed.), *Global Obligations for the Right to Food* (Rowman and Littlefield Publishers Inc., 2008) 33

Kuper, Andrew, 'Introduction: The Responsibilities Approach to Human Rights' in Andrew Kuper (ed.), *Global Responsibilities: Who Must Deliver Human Rights?* (Routledge, 2005) ix

Langford, Malcolm, 'A Sort of Homecoming: The Right to Housing' in Mark Gibney and Sigrun Skogly (eds.), *Universal Human Rights and Extraterritorial Obligations* (University of Pennsylvania Press, 2010) 166

Laplante, Lisa J., 'The Law of Remedies and the Clean Hands Doctrine: Exclusionary Reparation Policies in Peru's Political Transition', 23 *American University International Law Review* (2008) 51

Lauterpacht, H., *International Law and Human Rights* (Archon Books, 1968)

Lawson, Rick, 'Out of Control – State Responsibility and Human Rights: Will the ILC's Definition of the "Act of State" Meet the Challenges of the 21st

Century?' in Monique Castermans-Holleman, Fried van Hoof and Jaqueline Smith (eds.), *The Role of the Nation-State in the 21st Century: Human Rights, International Organisations and Foreign Policy – Essays in Honour of Peter Baehr* (Kluwer Law International, 1998) 91

'Life after Bankovic: On the Extraterritorial Application of the European Convention on Human Rights' in Fons Coomans and Menno T. Kamminga (eds.), *Extraterritorial Application of Human Rights Treaties* (Intersentia, 2004) 83

Leckie, Scott, 'Another Step towards Indivisibility: Identifying the Key Features of Violations of Economic, Social and Cultural Rights', 20 *Human Rights Quarterly* (1998) 81

Leckie, Scott, and Anne Gallagher, 'Introduction: Why a Legal Resource Guide for Economic, Social and Cultural Rights?' in Scott Leckie and Anne Gallagher (eds.), *Economic, Social, and Cultural Rights: A Legal Resource Guide* (University of Pennsylvania Press, 2006) xiii

Levinson, Daryl J., 'Rights Essentialism and Remedial Equilibrium', 99(4) *Columbia Law Review* (1999) 857

Liebenberg, Sandra, 'Adjudicating the Positive Duties Imposed by Economic, Social and Cultural Rights', 15(3) *Interights Bulletin* (2006) 109

Linde, Morne van der, 'A Review of the African Convention on Nature and Natural Resources', 2 *African Human Rights Law Journal* (2002) 33

Lipper, Jerome, 'Equitable Utilization' in A. H. Garretson, R. D. Hayton and C. J. Olmstead (eds.), *The Law of International Drainage Basins* (Oceana Publications Inc., 1967) 15

Loschin, Lynn, 'The Persistent Objector and Customary Human Rights Law: A Proposed Analytical Framework', 2 *University of California Davis Journal of International Law and Policy* (1996) 147

Louka, Elli, *Water Law and Policy: Governance without Frontiers* (Oxford University Press, 2008)

Lyster, Simon, *International Wildlife Law: An Analysis of International Treaties Concerned with the Conservation of Wildlife* (Grotius Publications Ltd, 1985)

Majzoub, Tarek *et al.*, '"Cloud Busters": Reflections on the Right to Water in Clouds and a Search for International Law Rules', 20(3) *Colorado Journal of International Environmental Law and Policy* (2009) 321

Marie, Jean-Bernard, 'National System for the Protection of Human Rights' in Janusz Symonides (ed.), *Human Rights: International Protection, Monitoring and Enforcement* (Ashgate, 2003) 257

Martin, Francisco Forrest *et al.*, *International Human Rights and Humanitarian Law: Treaties, Cases and Analysis* (Cambridge University Press, 1st edn, 2006)

Mason, Simon A., *From Conflict to Cooperation in the Nile Basin: Interaction Between Water Availability, Water Management in Egypt and Sudan, and International Relations in the Eastern Nile Basin* (ETH Zurich, 2004)

Mazzeschi, Riccardo Pisillo, 'Exhaustion of Domestic Remedies and State Responsibility for Violation of Human Rights', 10 *Italian Yearbook of International Law* (2000) 17

Mbaye, Keba, '[Mbaye] Draft African Charter on Human and Peoples' Rights', reprinted in Christof Heyns (ed.), *Human Rights Law in Africa* (Brill, 2002) Vol. 4, 65–77

McCaffrey, Stephen, 'A Human Right to Water: Domestic and International Implications', 5(1) *Georgetown International Environmental Law Review* (1992) 1

'Background and Overview of the International Law Commission's Study of the Non-Navigational Uses of International Watercourses', 3 *Colorado Journal of International Environmental Law and Policy* (1992) 17

'Sixth Report of the Law of the Non-Navigational Uses of International Watercourses, By Mr Stephen C. McCaffrey, Special Rapporteur' (A/CN.4/427 and Add. 1), in *Yearbook of the International Law Commission* (1990), Vol. II(2), 41–82

'Taking Stock of Sustainable Development at 20: A Principle at Odds with Itself?', 21 *Pacific McGeorge Global Business and Development Law Journal* (2008) 165

'The 1997 UN Watercourses Convention: Retrospect and Prospect', 21 *Pacific McGeorge Global Business and Development Law Journal* (2008) 165

'The Coming Fresh Water Crisis: International Legal and Institutional Responses', 21 *Vermont Law Review* (1997) 803

'The Contribution of the UN Convention on the Law of the Non-Navigational Uses of International Watercourses', 1(3/4) *International Journal of Global Environmental Issues* (2001) 250

'The Evolution of the Law of International Watercourses', 45 *Austrian Journal of Public International Law* (1993) 87

'The Human Right to Water' in Edith Brown Weiss, Laurence Boisson de Chazournes and Nathale Bernasconi-Osterwalder (eds.), *Fresh Water and International Economic Law* (Oxford University Press, 2005) 93

The Law of International Watercourses (Oxford University Press, 2nd edn, 2007)

'The Law of International Watercourses: Some Recent Developments and Unanswered Questions', 17(3) *Denver Journal of International Law and Policy* (1989) 505

'Trans-Boundary Pollution Injuries: Jurisdictional Considerations in Private Litigation between Canada and the United States', 3 *California Western International Law Journal* (1973) 191

McCaffrey, Stephen C., and Mpazi Sinjela, 'The 1997 United Nations Convention on International Watercourses', 92(1) *American Journal of International Law* (1998) 97

McClane, J. Brock, 'How Late in the Emergence of a Norm of Customary International Law May a Persistent Objector Object?', 13 *ILSA Journal of International Law* (1989) 1

McGoldrick, Dominic, 'Extraterritorial Application of the International Covenant on Civil and Political Rights' in Fons Coomans and Menno T. Kamminga (eds.), *Extraterritorial Application of Human Rights Treaties* (Intersentia, 2004) 41

McIntyre, Owen, *Environmental Protection of International Watercourses under International Law* (Ashgate, 2007)

'The Role of Customary Rules and Principles of International Environmental Law in the Protection of Shared International Freshwater Resources', 46 *Natural Resources Journal* (2006) 157

Mechlem, Kerstin, 'Treaty Bodies and the Interpretation of Human Rights', 42 *Vanderbilt Journal of Transnational Law* (2009) 905

Meron, Theodor, 'Extraterritoriality of Human Rights Treaties', 89 *American Journal of International Law* (1995) 78

Mesquita, Judith Bueno de, Paul Hunt and Rajat Khosla, 'The Human Rights Responsibility of International Assistance and Cooperation in Health' in Mark Gibney and Sigrun Skogly (eds.), *Universal Human Rights and Extraterritorial Obligations* (University of Pennsylvania Press, 2010) 104

Milanovic, Marko, 'State Responsibility for Acts of Non-State Actors: A Comment on Griebel and Plucken', 22 *Leiden Journal of International Law* (2009) 307

Mubangizi, John Cantius, 'The Constitutional Protection of Socio-economic Rights in Selected African Countries: A Comparative Evaluation', 2 *African Journal of Legal Studies* (2006) 1

Mugwanya, George William, *Human Rights in Africa: Enhancing Human Rights through the African Regional Human Rights System* (Transnational Publishers, 2003)

Musila, Godfrey M., 'The Right to an Effective Remedy under the African Charter on Human and Peoples' Rights', 6 *African Human Rights Law Journal* (2006) 442

Mustaniemi-Laasko, Maija, 'The Right to Education: Instrumental Right Par Excellence' in Margot E. Salomon, Arne Tostensen and Wouter Vandenhole (eds.), *Casting the Net Wider: Human Rights, Development and New Duty-Bearers* (Intersentia, 2007) 331

Naldi, Gino J., 'Limitation of Rights under the African Charter on Human and Peoples' Rights: The Contribution of the African Commission on Human and Peoples' Rights', 17 *South African Journal on Human Rights* (2001) 109

'Reparation in the Practice of the African Commission on Human and Peoples' Rights', 14 *Leiden Journal of International Law* (2001) 681

Narula, Smita, 'The Right to Food: Holding Global Actors Accountable under International Law' (Centre for Human Rights and Global Justice Working Paper, New York University School of Law, 2006)

Nickel, James W., 'How Human Rights Generate Duties to Protect and Provide', 15 *Human Rights Quarterly* (1993) 77

Nolan, Aoife, 'Addressing Economic and Social Rights Violations by Non-State Actors through the Role of the State: A Comparison of Regional Approaches to the "Obligation to Protect"', 9(2) *Human Rights Law Review* (2009) 225

Nollkaemper, A., 'The Contribution of the International Law Commission to International Water Law: Does it Reverse the Flight from Substance?', 27 *Netherlands Yearbook of International Law* (1996) 39

Nowak, Manfred, 'The New Trend towards Re-politicising Human Rights' in Monique Castermans-Holleman, Fried van Hoof and Jaqueline Smith (eds.), *The Role of the Nation-State in the 21st Century: Human Rights, International Organisations and Foreign Policy – Essays in Honour of Peter Baehr* (Kluwer Law International, 1998) 151

Nwobike, Justice N., 'The African Commission on Human and Peoples' Rights and the Demystification of Second and Third Generation Rights under the African Charter: Social and Economic Rights Action Centre (SERAC) and the Centre for Economic and Social Rights (CESCR) v. Nigeria', 1 *African Journal of Legal Studies* (2005) 129

O'Boyle, Michael, 'The European Convention on Human Rights and Extraterritorial Jurisdiction: A Comment on "Life after Bankovic"' in Fons Coomans and Menno T. Kamminga (eds.), *Extraterritorial Application of Human Rights Treaties* (Intersentia, 2004) 125

Oba, A. A., 'The African Charter on Human and Peoples' Rights and Ouster Clauses under the Military Regimes in Nigeria: Before and After September 11', 4 *African Human Rights Law Journal* (2004) 275

Odinkalu, Chidi Anselm, 'Analysis of Paralysis or Paralysis by Analysis? Implementing Economic, Social, and Cultural Rights under the African Charter on Human and Peoples' Rights', 23 *Human Rights Quarterly* (2001) 327

'Implementing Economic, Social and Cultural Rights under the African Charter on Human and Peoples' Rights' in Malcolm Evans and Rachel Murray (eds.), *The African Charter on Human and Peoples' Rights: The System in Practice, 1986–2000* (Cambridge University Press, 2002) 178

'The Individual Complaints Procedures of the African Commission on Human and Peoples' Rights: A Preliminary Assessment', 8 *Transnational Law and Contemporary Problems* (1998) 359

'The Role of Case and Complaints Procedures in the Reform of the African Regional Human Rights System', 1 *African Human Rights Law Journal* (2001) 225

Olinga, Alain Didier, 'The Embargo Against Burundi before the African Commission on Human and Peoples' Rights (Note on Communication 157/96)', 5 *African Human Rights Law Journal* (2005) 424

Olmstead, C. J. *et al.*, 'Helsinki Rules on the Uses of the Waters of International Rivers' in A. H. Garretson, R. D. Hayton and C. J. Olmstead (eds.), *The Law of International Drainage Basins* (Oceana Publications Inc., 1967) 779

Orakhelashvili, Alexander, 'Restrictive Interpretation of Human Rights Treaties in the Recent Jurisprudence of the European Court of Human Rights', 14(3) *European Journal of International Law* (2003) 529

Osiel, Mark, *The End of Reciprocity: Terror, Torture, and the Law of War* (Cambridge University Press, 2009)

Otto, Dianne, and David Wiseman, 'In Search of "Effective Remedies": Applying the International Covenant on Economic, Social and Cultural Rights to Australia', 7 *Australian Journal of Human Rights* (2001) 5

Ouguergouz, Fatsah, *The African Charter on Human and Peoples' Rights: A Comprehensive Agenda for Human Dignity and Sustainable Democracy in Africa* (Kluwer Law International, 2003)

Paisley, Richard, 'Adversaries into Partners: International Water Law and the Equitable Sharing of Downstream Benefits', 3 *Melbourne Journal of International Law* (2002) 280

Parenteau, Patrick, 'Come Hell and the High Water: Coping with the Unavoidable Consequences of Climate Disruption', 34 *Vermont Law Review* (2010) 957

Pasqualucci, Jo M., 'Victim Reparations in the Inter-American Human Rights System: A Critical Assessment of Current Practice and Procedure', 18 *Michigan Journal of International Law* (1997) 1

Peel, Jacqueline, 'Climate Change Law: The Emergence of a New Legal Discipline', 32 *Melbourne University Law Review* (2009) 922

Pierce, Richard J., Jr, 'Is Standing Law or Politics?', 77 *North Carolina Law Review* (1999) 1742

Popović, Neil A. F., 'In Pursuit of Environmental Human Rights: Commentary on the Draft Declaration of Principles on Human Rights and the Environment', 27 *Columbia Human Rights Law Review* (1996) 487

Postel, Sandra, *The Last Oasis: Facing Water Scarcity* (Earthscan Publications Ltd, 1st edn, 1992)

Prieur, Michel, 'Protection of the Environment' in Mohammed Bedjaoui (ed.), *International Law: Achievements and Prospects* (UNESCO, 1991) 1017

Rainbolt, George, 'Perfect and Imperfect Obligations', 98(3) *Philosophical Studies* (2000) 233

Rajamani, Lavanya, *Differential Treatment in International Environmental Law* (Oxford University Press, 2006)

Read, John E., 'The Trail Smelter Dispute', 1 *Canadian Yearbook of International Law* (1963) 213

Ress, Georg, 'Problems of Extraterritorial Human Rights Violations – The Jurisdiction of the European Court of Human Rights: The Bankovic Case', 12 *Italian Yearbook of International Law* (2005) 51

Rieu-Clarke, Alistair, *International Law and Sustainable Development: Lessons from the Law of International Watercourses* (IWA Publishing, 2005)

Roach, Kent, 'Crafting Remedies for Violations of Economic, Social and Cultural Rights' in John Squires, Malcolm Langford and Bet Thiele (eds.), *The Road to a Remedy: Current Issues in the Litigation of Economic, Social and Cultural Rights* (Australian Human Rights Centre, 2005) 111

Roberts, Anthea, 'Comparative International Law? The Role of National Courts in Creating and Enforcing International Law', 60(1) *International and Comparative Law Quarterly* (2011) 57

Robertson, Robert E., 'Measuring State Compliance with the Obligations to Devote the "Maximum Available Resources" to Realizing Economic, Social, and Cultural Rights', 16 *Human Rights Quarterly* (1994) 693

Roht-Arriaza, Naomi, 'Punishment, Redress, and Pardon: Theoretical and Psychological Approaches' in Naomi Roht-Arriaza (ed.), *Impunity and Human Rights in International Law and Practice* (Oxford University Press, 1995) 13

Roxstrom, Erik, Mark Gibney and Terje Einarsen, 'The NATO Bombing Case (Bankovic et al. v. Belgium et al.) and the Limits of Western Human Rights Protection', 23 *Boston University International Law Journal* (2005) 55

Russell, Sage, 'Minimum State Obligations: International Dimensions' in Danie Brand and Sage Russell (eds.), *Exploring the Core Content of Socio-Economic Rights: South African and International Perspectives* (Protea Book House, 2002) 11

Sadoff, Claudia W., Dale Whittington and David Grey, *Africa's International Rivers: An Economic Perspective* (World Bank, 2002)

Salman, Salman M. A., 'Introductory Note: Revised Protocol on Shared Watercourses in the Southern African Development Community', 40 *International Legal Materials* (2001) 317

'The Helsinki Rules, the UN Watercourses Convention and the Berlin Rules: Perspectives on International Water Law', 23(4) *International Journal of Water Resources Development* (2007) 625

Salman, Salman M. A., and Kishor Uprety, *Conflict and Cooperation on South Asia's International Rivers: A Legal Perspective* (World Bank, 2002)

Salomon, Margot E., *Global Responsibility for Human Rights: World Poverty and the Development of International Law* (Oxford University Press, 2007)

'Legal Cosmopolitanism and the Normative Contribution of the Right to Development' (LSE Law, Society and Economy Working Papers 16/2008, London School of Economics and Political Science, 2008)

Sands, Philippe, 'Watercourses, Environment and the International Court of Justice: The Gabčíkovo-Nagymaros Case' in Salman M. A. Salman and Laurence Boisson de Chazournes (eds.), *International Watercourses:*

Enhancing Cooperation and Managing Conflict: Proceedings of a World Bank Seminar (World Bank, 1998) 103

Schachter, Oscar, 'The Obligation to Implement the Covenant in Domestic Law' in Louis Henkin (ed.), *The International Bill of Rights: The Covenant on Civil and Political Rights* (Columbia University Press, 1981) 311

Scheinin, Martin, 'Direct Applicability of Economic, Social and Cultural Rights: A Critique of the Doctrine of Self-Executing Treaties' in Drzewicki Krzysztof, Catarina Krause and Allan Rosas (eds.), *Social Rights as Human Rights: A European Challenge* (Institute for Human Rights, Abo Akademi University, 1994) 73

'Extraterritorial Effect of the International Covenant on Civil and Political Rights' in Fons Coomans and Menno T. Kamminga (eds.), *Extraterritorial Application of Human Rights Treaties* (Intersentia, 2004) 73

Schwabach, Aaron, 'The United Nations Convention on the Law of Non-Navigational Uses of International Watercourses, Customary International Law, and the Interests of Developing Upper Riparians', 33 *Texas International Law Journal* (1998) 257

Sepúlveda, Magdalena, *The Nature of the Obligations under the International Covenant on Economic, Social, and Cultural Rights* (Intersentia, 2003)

Shany, Yuval, 'How Supreme Is the Supreme Law of the Land? Comparative Analysis of the Influence of International Human Rights Treaties upon the Interpretation of Constitutional Texts by Domestic Courts', 31(2) *Brooklyn Journal of International Law* (2006) 341

Shelton, Dinah, 'Case Concerning Avena and Other Mexican Nationals (Mexico v. United States)', 98 *American Journal of International Law* (2004) 559

'Decision Regarding Communication 155/96 (Social and Economic Rights Action Centre/Centre for Economic and Social Rights v. Nigeria)', 96 *American Journal of International Law* (2002) 937

'Equitable Utilization of the Atmosphere: A Rights-Based Approach to Climate Change' in Stephen Humphreys and Mary Robinson (eds.), *Human Rights and Climate Change* (Cambridge University Press, 2010) 91

'Equity' in Daniel Bodansky, Jutta Brunnee and Ellen Hey (eds.), *The Oxford Handbook of International Environmental Law* (Oxford University Press, 2007) 639

Remedies in International Human Rights Law (Oxford University Press, 2nd edn, 2005)

'Righting Wrongs: Reparations in the Articles on State Responsibility', 96 *American Journal of International Law* (2002) 833

'The United Nations Principles and Guidelines on Reparations: Context and Contents' in K. de Feyter *et al.* (eds.), *Out of the Ashes: Reparation for Victims of Gross and Systematic Human Rights Violations* (Intersentia, 2005) 11

Shue, Henry, *Basic Rights: Subsistence, Affluence, and US Foreign Policy* (Princeton University Press, 2nd edn, 1996)

'The Independence of Duties' in P. Alston and K. Tomaseviski (eds.), *The Right to Food* (Martinus Nijhoff Publishers, 1984) 83

Simpson, Gerry J., *Great Powers and Outlaw States: Unequal Sovereigns in the International Legal Order* (Cambridge University Press, 2003)

Sinden, Amy, 'Climate Change and Human Rights' (Legal Studies Research Paper Series, Research Paper No. 2008-49: Beasley School of Law, Temple University, 2008)

Skogly, Sigrun I., *Beyond National Borders: States' Human Rights Obligations in International Cooperation* (Intersentia, 2006)

'Extraterritoriality: Universal Human Rights without Universal Obligations?' in Sarah Joseph and Adam McBeth (eds.), *Research Handbook on International Human Rights Law* (Edward Elgar, 2010) 71

'The Obligation of International Assistance and Co-operation in the International Covenant on Economic, Social, and Cultural Rights' in Morten Bergsmo (ed.), *Human Rights and Criminal Justice for the Downtrodden: Essays in Honour of Asbjørn Eide* (Martinus Nijhoff Publishers, 2003) 403

'The Requirement of Using the "Maximum of Available Resources" for Human Rights Realisation: A Question of Quality as Well as Quantity?', 13(3) *Human Rights Law Review* (2012) 393

Skogly, Sigrun, and Mark Gibney, 'Introduction' in Mark Gibney and Sigrun Skogly (eds.), *Universal Human Rights and Extraterritorial Obligations* (University of Pennsylvania Press, 2010) 1

Sohn, Louis B., 'The New International Law: Protection of the Right of Individuals Rather Than States', 32 *American University Law Review* (1983) 1

Spigelman, James, *Statutory Interpretation and Human Rights* (University of Queensland Press, 2008)

Ssenyonjo, Manisuli, *Economic, Social and Cultural Rights in International Law* (Hart Publishing, 2009)

'Reflections on State Obligations with Respect to Economic, Social and Cultural Rights in International Human Rights Law', 15(6) *International Journal of Human Rights* (2011) 969

Starr, Sonja B., 'Rethinking "Effective" Remedies: Remedial Deterrence in International Courts', 83 *New York University Law Review* (2008) 693

Stein, Ted L., 'The Approach of the Different Drummer: The Principle of the Persistent Objector in International Law', 26(2) *Harvard International Law Journal* (1985) 457

Sucharitkul, Sompong, 'State Responsibility and International Liability in Transnational Relations' in Jerzy Makarczyk (ed.), *Theory of International Law at the Threshold of the 21st Century: Essays in Honour of Krzysztof Skubiszewski* (Kluwer Law International, 1996) 283

Swain, Ashock, 'Ethiopia, the Sudan and Egypt: The Nile River Dispute', 35(4) *Journal of Modern African Studies* (1997) 675

'Managing the Nile River: The Role of Sub-Basin Co-operation' in Manas Chatterji, Saul Arlosoroff and Gauri Guha (eds.), *Conflict Management of Water Resources* (Ashgate, 2002) 145

Swedish International Water Institute, 'Responding to Global Changes: Accessing Water for Common Good, with Special Focus on Transboundary Waters' *(Swedish International Water Institute,* 2009)

Tafesse, Tesfaye, *The Nile Question: Hydro Politics, Legal Wrangling, Modus Vivendi and Perspectives* (Transaction Publishers, 2001)

Tanzi, Attila, 'The UN Convention on International Watercourses as a Framework for the Avoidance and Settlement of Water Law Disputes', 11 *Leiden Journal of International Law* (1998) 441

Tarlock, A. Dan, 'Four Challenges of International Water Law', 23 *Tulane Environmental Law Journal* (2010) 369

Tinnevelt, Ronald, and Gert Verschraegen, 'Global Justice between Cosmopolitan Ideals and State Sovereignty: An Introduction' in Ronald Tinnevelt and Gert Verschraegen (eds.), *Between Cosmopolitan Ideals and State Sovereignty: Studies in Global Justice* (Palgrave Macmillan, 2006) 1

Tully, Stephen, 'A Human Right to Access Water? A Critique of General Comment No. 15', 23 *Netherlands Quarterly of Human Rights* (2005) 35

'The Contribution of Human Rights to Freshwater Resource Management', 14 *Yearbook of International Environmental Law* (2003) 101

Van Alstyne, William W., 'The Justiciability of International River Disputes: A Study in the Case Method', 13 *Duke Law Journal* (1964) 307

Vandenbogaerde, Arne, and Wouter Vandenhole, 'The Optional Protocol to the International Covenant on Economic, Social and Cultural Rights: An Ex Ante Assessment of Its Effectiveness in Light of the Drafting Process', 10(2) *Human Rights Law Review* (2010) 207

Vandenhole, Wouter, 'EU and Development: Extraterritorial Obligations under the International Covenant on Economic, Social and Cultural Rights' in Margot E. Salomon, Arne Tostensen and Wouter Vandenhole (eds.), *Casting the Net Wider: Human Rights, Development and New Duty-Bearers* (Intersentia, 2007) 85

Vause, W. Gary, 'The Subsidiarity Principle in European Union Law – American Federalism Compared', 27 *Case Western Reserve Journal of International Law* (1995) 61

Vazquez, Carlos Manuel, 'Treaties as Law of the Land: The Supremacy Clause and Presumption of Self-Execution', 121(1) *Harvard Law Review* (2008) 1

Viljoen, Frans, 'A Human Rights Court for Africa, and Africans', 30 *Brooklyn Journal of International Law* (2004) 1

'Admissibility under the African Charter' in Malcolm Evans and Rachel Murray (eds.), *The African Charter on Human and Peoples' Rights: The System in Practice, 1986–2000* (Cambridge University Press, 2002) 61

'Communications under the African Charter: Procedure and Admissibility' in Malcolm Evans and Rachel Murray (eds.), *The African Charter on Human and Peoples' Rights: The System in Practice 1986–2006* (Cambridge University Press, 2nd edn, 2008) 76

International Human Rights Law in Africa (Oxford University Press, 2007)

Vinogradov, Sergei V., 'Observations on the International Law Commission's Draft Rules on the Non-Navigational Uses of International Watercourses: "Management and Domestic Remedies"', 3 *Colorado Journal of International Environmental Law and Policy* (1992) 235

Waterbury, John, *Hydropolitics of the Nile Valley* (Syracuse University Press, 1979)

The Nile Basin: National Determinants of Collective Action (Yale University Press, 2002)

Weil, Prosper, 'Towards Relative Normativity in International Law?', 77 *American Journal of International Law* (1983) 413

Weissbrodt, David, 'Non-State Entities and Human Rights within the Context of the Nation-State in the 21st Century' in Monique Castermans-Holleman, Fried van Hoof and Jaqueline Smith (eds.), *The Role of the Nation-State in the 21st Century: Human Rights, International Organisations and Foreign Policy – Essays in Honour of Peter Baehr* (Kluwer Law International, 1998) 175

Wells, Celia, and Juanita Elias, 'Catching the Conscience of the King: Corporate Players on the International Stage' in Philip Alston (ed.), *Non-State Actors and Human Rights* (Oxford University Press, 2005) 141

White, Gilbert F., 'Introduction: World Trends and Needs', 16(4) *Natural Resources Journal* (1976) 737

Wilde, Ralph, 'Triggering State Obligations Extraterritorially: The Spatial Test in Certain Human Rights Treaties', 40(2) *Israel Law Review* (2007) 503

Williams, Melina, 'Privatisation and the Human Right to Water: Challenges for the New Century', 28 *Michigan Journal of International Law* (2007) 469

Winkler, Inga T., *The Human Right to Water: Significance, Legal Status and Implications for Water Allocation* (Hart Publishing, 2012)

Yarwood, Lisa, 'Willing and Able: The Domestication of International Justice', 14 *African Yearbook of International Law* (2006) 193

Yohannes, Okbazghi, *Water Resources and Inter-Riparian Relations in the Nile Basin* (State University of New York Press, 2008)

Young, Katharine G., 'The Minimum Core of Economic and Social Rights: A Concept in Search of Content', 33 *Yale Journal of International Law* (2008) 113

Zarsky, Lyuba, 'Global Reach: Human Rights and Environment in the Framework of Corporate Accountability' in Lyuba Zarsky (ed.), *Human Rights and the Environment: Conflicts and Norms in a Globalizing World* (Earthscan Publications Ltd, 2002) 31

Treaties

African [Banjul] Charter on Human and Peoples' Rights, adopted 27 June 1981, OAU Doc. CAB/LEG/67/3 Rev.5, 21 ILM 58 (1982) (entered into force 21 October 1986)

African Charter on the Rights and Welfare of the Child, OAU Doc. CAB/LEG/24.9/49 (1990) (entered into force 29 November 1999)

African Convention on the Conservation of Nature and Natural Resources, adopted in Algiers on 15 September 1968 (entered into force 16 June 1969)

African Convention on the Conservation of Nature and Natural Resources, adopted in Maputo, Mozambique, on 11 July 2003

Convention on the Elimination of All Forms of Discrimination against Women, opened for signature 18 December 1979, 1249 UNTS 13 (entered into force 3 September 1981

Convention on the Rights of the Child, opened for signature 20 November 1989, 1577 UNTS 3 (entered into force 2 September 1990)

International Covenant on Economic, Social and Cultural Rights, opened for signature 16 December 1966, 993 UNTS 3 (entered into force 3 November 1976)

Optional Protocol to the International Covenant on Economic, Social and Cultural Rights, opened for signature 10 December 2008, UN Doc. A/RES/63/117 (not yet in force)

Protocol to the African Charter on Human and Peoples' Rights on the Establishment of an African Court on Human and Peoples' Rights, adopted in Ouagadougou, Burkina Faso, 10 June 1998 (entered into force 25 January 2004)

Protocol to the African Charter on Human and Peoples' Rights on the Rights of Women in Africa, adopted by the 2nd Ordinary Session of the Assembly of the African Union, Maputo, Mozambique, 11 July 2003 (entered into force 25 November 2005)

Vienna Convention on the Law of Treaties, opened for signature 23 May 1969, 1115 UNTS 331 (entered into force 27 January 1980)

United Nations documents

Committee on Economic, Social and Cultural Rights, 'General Comment No. 3: The Nature of States Parties' Obligations (Art. 2, Para. 1, of the Covenant)' (UN Committee on Economic, Social and Cultural Rights, 1990)

'General Comment No. 4: The Right to Adequate Housing (Art. 11 (1) of the Covenant)' (UN Committee on Economic, Social and Cultural Rights, 13 December 1991)

'General Comment No. 8: The Relationship between Economic Sanctions and Respect for Economic, Social and Cultural Rights' (UN Committee on Economic, Social and Cultural Rights, 1997)

'General Comment 14: Substantive Issues Arising in the Implementation of the International Covenant on Economic, Social and Cultural Rights – The Right to the Highest Attainable Standard of Health' (E/C.12/2000/4), 11 August 2000' (Committee on Economic, Social and Cultural Rights, 2000)

'General Comment No. 15: Substantive Issues Arising in the Implementation of the International Covenant on Economic, Social and Cultural Rights (Adopted 11–29 November 2002)' (UN Committee on Economic, Social and Cultural Rights, 11–29 November 2002)

'The Right to Food: Report of the Special Rapporteur on the Right to Food, Jean Ziegler' (Commission on Human Rights, United Nations Economic and Social Council (E/CN.4/2005/47), 24 January 2005)

'The Right to Food: Report of the Special Rapporteur on the Right to Food, Jean Ziegler' (UN Economic and Social Council (E/CN.4/2006/44), 16 March 2006)

Concluding Observations of the Committee on Economic, Social and Cultural Rights: Cameroon, UN ESCOR, 21st Session, 54th Meeting, UN Doc. E/C.12/1/Add.40 (8 December 1999)

Concluding Observations of the Committee on Economic Social and Cultural Rights: Israel, UN ESCOR, 19th Session, 53rd Meeting, UN Doc. E/C.12/1/Add.27 (4 Dec 1998)

Concluding Observations of the Committee on Economic, Social and Cultural Rights: Russian Federation, UN ESCOR, 16th Session, 25th Meeting, UN Doc. E/C.12/1/Add.13 (20 May 1997)

'Basic Principles and Guidelines on the Right to a Remedy and Reparation for Victims of Gross Violations of International Human Rights Law and Serious Violations of International Humanitarian Law', adopted 26 March 2006 by GA Res. (A/RES/60/147), Sixtieth Session

'General Assembly Adopts Resolution Recognizing Access to Clean Water, Sanitation' (64th General Assembly Plenary 108th Meeting (AM)), (General Assembly GA/10967), 28 July 2010

'International Drinking Water Supply and Sanitation Decade', GA Res. 40/171, UN GAOR, 40th Session, 119th Plenary Meeting, Agenda Item 12, UN Doc. A/RES/40/171 (17 December 1985)

'The Human Right to Water and Sanitation', GA Res. 64/292, UN GAOR, 64th Session, 108th Plenary Meeting, Agenda Item 48, UN Doc. A/RES/64/292 (3 August 2010)

'Universal Declaration of Human Rights' , GA Res. 217A (III), UN GAOR, 3rd Session, 183rd Plenary Meeting, UN Doc. A/810 (10 December 1948)

'Vienna Declaration and Program of Action, World Conference on Human Rights' (A/CONF.157/23)' (UN General Assembly, 25 June 2003)

'The Right of Access of Everyone to Drinking Water Supply and Sanitation Services' (Working Paper), UN ESCOR, 50th Session, Agenda Item 4, UN Doc. E/CN.4/Sub.2/1998/7 (10 June 1998)

Human Rights Committee, 'General Comment No. 24: Issues Relating to Reservations Made upon Ratification or Accession to the Covenant or the Optional Protocols Thereto, or in Relation to Declarations under Article 41 of the Covenant' (CCPR/C/21/Rev.1/Add.6), adopted at 52nd Session, 1994 (UN Human Rights Committee, 4 November 1994)

International Law Commission, Draft Articles on Responsibility of States for Internationally Wrongful Acts (2001)

'Draft Articles on the Law of the Non-Navigational Uses of International Watercourses and Commentaries Thereto and Resolution on Transboundary Confined Ground Water' (1994) 2(2) Yearbook of the International Law Commission 89

International Law Commission, Working Group, 'Report on the Convention on the Law of the Non-Navigational Uses of International Watercourses', UN GAOR, 51st Session, 6th Comm., Agenda Item 144, UN Doc. A/51/869 (11 April 1997)

Office of the High Commissioner for Human Rights, 'The Right to Water (Fact Sheet No. 35)' (August 2010) 3

Sub-Commission on the Promotion and Protection of Human Rights, 'Sub-Commission Begins Consideration of Economic, Social and Cultural Rights' (Press Release, 7 August 2003), http://www.unhchr.ch/huricane/huricane.nsf/0/9E2A907D8C9AB866C1256D7C0026017B?opendocument

United Nations Conference on Environment and Development, 'Report of the United Nations Conference on Environment and Development', UN Doc. A/CONF.151/26/Rev.1 (Vol. 1) (1 January 1993)

United Nations Conference on the Human Environment, 'Report of the United Nations Conference on the Human Environment', UN Doc. A/CONF.48/

14/Rev.1 (1 January 1973), Chapter I ('Declaration of the United Nations Conference on the Human Environment')

United Nations Development Programme, 'Beyond Scarcity: Power, Poverty and the Global Water Crisis (Human Development Report 2006)' (United Nations Development Programme, 2006)

United Nations Water Conference, 'Report of the United Nations Water Conference, Mar del Plata', UN Doc. E/CONF.70/29 (25 March 1977), Chapter 1 ('Mar del Plata Action Plan'); the United Nations General Assembly adopted the Report of the United Nations Water Conference on 19 December 1977: see GA Res. 32/158, 32nd Session, 107th Plenary Meeting, Agenda Item 12, UN Doc. A/RES/32/158 (19 December 1977)

Other documents

African Commission on Human and Peoples' Rights, '(Draft) Principles and Guidelines on Economic, Social and Cultural Rights in the African Charter on Human and Peoples' Rights' (2011)

'The African Commission on Human and Peoples' Rights, Information Sheet No. 4', http://www.achpr.org/ACHPR_inf._sheet_No.4.doc (accessed 30 August 2011)

First Africa–South America Summit, Abuja Declaration adopted at the First Africa–South America Summit, 26–30 November 2006 (Abuja, Nigeria), www.asasummit-abuja2006.org (accessed 23 June 2011)

First Asia–Pacific Water Summit, 'Message from Beppu' (First Asia–Pacific Water Summit, Beppu, Japan (4 December 2007)

Intergovernmental Panel on Climate Change, Report of the Intergovernmental Panel on Climate Change (IPCC), Assessment Report 4, Working Group II, Summary for Policy Makers (2007)

International Commission of Jurists, 'Maastricht Principles on Extraterritorial Obligations of States in the Area of Economic, Social and Cultural Rights', adopted on 28 September 2011 by the International Commission of Jurists, http://hrbaportal.org/archives/noticeboard/launch-of-maastricht-principles-on-the-extraterritorial-obligations-of-states-in-the-area-of-economic-social-and-cultural-rights (accessed 7 November 2012)

International Law Association, 'Helsinki Rules on the Uses of the Waters of International Rivers', adopted by the International Law Association at its 52nd conference, Helsinki, August 1966

'The Berlin (Revised Helsinki) Rules', adopted at the Berlin Conference of the International Law Association (2004)

Seminar on Social, Economic and Cultural Rights in the African Charter, 'Statement from Seminar on Social, Economic and Cultural Rights in the

African Charter' (adopted in Pretoria, 13–17 September 2004; published in 5 *African Human Rights Law Journal* (2005) 182)

Third South Asian Conference on Sanitation, 'Delhi Declaration' (Third South Asian Conference on Sanitation, Vighan Bawan, Delhi, 21 November 2008)

University of Limburg, 'The Limburg Principles on the Implementation of the International Covenant on Economic Social and Cultural Rights' (Faculty of Law, University of Limburg, 2–6 June 1986)

University of Maastricht, 'The Maastricht Guidelines on Violations of Economic, Social and Cultural Rights' (Faculty of Law, University of Maastricht, 22–26 January 1997)

INDEX

For EU product safety concerns, contact us at Calle de José Abascal, 56–1°,
28003 Madrid, Spain or eugpsr@cambridge.org.

www.ingramcontent.com/pod-product-compliance
Lightning Source LLC
LaVergne TN
LVHW011526200926
848484LV00001B/170
* 9 7 8 1 1 0 7 0 3 1 0 8 1 *